T0305606

Performance Management Systems

Performance management is the process by which organizations set goals, determine standards, assign and evaluate work, and distribute rewards. But when you operate across different countries and continents, performance management strategies cannot be one dimensional. HR managers and line managers need systems that can be applied to a range of cultural values.

This important and timely text offers a truly global perspective on performance management practices. Split into two parts, it illustrates the key themes of rater motivation, rater–ratee relationships and merit pay, and outlines a model for a global appraisal process. This model is then screened through a range of countries, including Germany, Japan, the US, Turkey, China, India and Mexico. Using case studies and discussion questions, and written by local experts, this text outlines the tools needed to understand and 'measure' performance in a range of socio-economic and cultural contexts.

It is essential reading for students and practitioners alike working in human resources, international business, and international management.

Arup Varma is Distinguished University Research Professor and the Frank W. Considine Chair in Applied Ethics at the Quinlan School of Business, Loyola University Chicago. His research interests include performance appraisal, expatriate issues and human resource management issues in India.

Pawan S. Budhwar is the 50th Anniversary Professor of International HRM, Head of Aston Business School, and Associate Pro-Vice Chancellor International (India) at Aston University, UK. He is also Co-Editor-in-Chief of *Human Resource Management Journal*.

Angelo S. DeNisi is the Cohen Chair in Business at Tulane University, US. His primary research interests are performance appraisals, performance management and the interactions between expatriates and host country nationals.

Routledge Global Human Resource Management Series

Edited by David G. Collings, Dublin City University, Ireland,
Elaine Farndale, Penn State University, USA, and Fang Lee Cooke,
Monash University, Australia

The Global HRM Series has for over a decade been leading the way in advancing our understand of Global HRM issues. Edited and authored by the leading and highest-profile researchers in the field of human resource management (HRM), this series of books offers students and reflective practitioners accessible, coordinated and comprehensive textbooks on global HRM. Individually and collectively, these books cover the core areas of the field, including titles on global leadership, global talent management, global careers, and the global HR function, as well as comparative volumes on HR in key global regions.

The series is organized into two distinct strands: the first reflects key issues in managing global HRM; and the second comparative perspectives human resource management.

Taking an expert look at an increasingly important area of global business, this well-established series has become the benchmark for serious textbooks on global HRM.

The Publisher and Editors wish to thank the Founding Editors of the series – Randall Schuler, Susan Jackson, Paul Sparrow and Michael Poole.

Dedication: The late Professor Michael Poole was one of the founding series editors and the series is dedicated to his memory.

https://www.routledge.com/Global-HRM/book-series/SE0692

Global Talent Management (second edition)
Edited by David G. Collings, Hugh Scullion and Paula M. Caligiuri

International Human Resource Management (sixth edition)
Policies and Practices for Multinational Enterprises
Ibraiz Tarique, Dennis R. Briscoe and Randall S. Schuler

Performance Management Systems (second edition)
A Global Perspective
Edited by Arup Varma, Pawan S. Budhwar and Angelo S. DeNisi

Performance Management Systems

A Global Perspective

**Edited by
Arup Varma,
Pawan S. Budhwar
and Angelo S. DeNisi**

Second Edition

Routledge
Taylor & Francis Group

LONDON AND NEW YORK

Designed cover image: Deepak Sethi

Second edition published 2023
by Routledge
4 Park Square, Milton Park, Abingdon, Oxon, OX14 4RN

and by Routledge
605 Third Avenue, New York, NY 10158

Routledge is an imprint of the Taylor & Francis Group, an informa business

First edition published by Routledge 2008

British Library Cataloguing-in-Publication Data
A catalogue record for this book is available from the British Library

ISBN: 978-1-032-30818-0 (hbk)
ISBN: 978-1-032-30817-3 (pbk)
ISBN: 978-1-003-30684-9 (ebk)

DOI: 10.4324/9781003306849

Typeset in Calvert
by SPi Technologies India Pvt Ltd (Straive)

In loving memory of my mother – Leela Wati

Arup Varma

In loving memory of my parents, Daya Kaur and Major Abhe Ram; my sister-in-law, Deepa Budhwar; and my nephew, Joginder Malik.

Pawan S. Budhwar

For Adrienne – a constant companion and supporter.

Angelo S. DeNisi

Contents

List of Illustrations   ix

List of Contributors   x

Performance Management around the Globe:
Looking Back and Ahead   1
*Arup Varma, Pawan S. Budhwar and
Angelo S. DeNisi*

Performance Management in Multinational
Enterprises: Examining Patterns of
Convergence and Divergence   19
Charles M. Vance and Torben Andersen

Motivation and Performance Management   41
Biyun Hu and Liang Meng

Rater–Ratee Relationships and Performance
Management   60
*Amy Risner, Shaun Pichler, Arup Varma and
Ryan Petty*

Merit Pay   83
Barry Gerhart, Charlie Trevor and Dow Scott

A Model of the Appraisal Process   105
Kevin R. Murphy and Angelo S. DeNisi

Performance Management in the United States   123
*Elaine Pulakos, Rose A. Mueller-Hanson and
Ryan S. O'Leary*

Performance Management in Mexico   148
*Jorge A. Gonzalez, Lorena Perez-Floriano and
R. Aristeo Rodriguez*

Performance Management Systems in the UK   169
Maranda Ridgway, Helen Shipton and Paul Sparrow

Performance Management in France and Germany   190
Cordula Barzantny and Marion Festing

Performance Management Systems in Turkey   222
Gaye Özçelik, Zeynep Aycan and Serap Keleş

Performance Management in India   240
*Tanuja Sharma, Pawan S. Budhwar, Arup Varma
and Peter Norlander*

Performance Management Systems in China   260
Fang Lee Cooke

Performance Management Systems in South Korea   284
Hyuckseung Yang and Chris Rowley

Performance Management in Japan   303
*Akihisa Kagami, Tomoki Sekiguchi
and Azusa Ebisuya*

Performance Management in Australia   326
John Shields

Performance Management around the Globe:
Where Are We Now?   360
*Angelo S. DeNisi, Arup Varma and
Pawan S. Budhwar*

Index   *376*

Illustrations

FIGURES

2.1 General Model of PM Process (Adapted from Vance & Paik, 2014) 23
3.1 The Overall Motivation Model 50
4.1 A model of rater-ratee relationships in performance appraisal 63
6.1 A Model of the Performance Appraisal Process 107
6.2 A Model of the Performance Management Process 108
12.1 Bonus pay-out over the years (Aon India, 2022) 246
16.1 Overall PMS effectiveness in Australian organisations (percentage of organisations with 'agree' and 'strongly agree') 344
16.2 Practice Incidence and Planned Introduction, All Respondents 348
16.3 Practice Incidence by Organisational Size 351
16.4 Practice Incidence by Sector 353

TABLES

5.1 Target Salary as a Percentage of Market Salary (Compa-Ratio) by Performance Rating 86
5.2 Merit Increase Grid 88
5.3 Distribution of Performance Ratings 94
7.1 Guidelines for Addressing Legal Requirements in the United States 127
7.2 Practical Challenges with Cascading Goals 130
7.3 Conclusions about PM from Research and Practice 139
7.4 Manager and Employee Behaviors that Yield Effective PM 142
7.5 Where to Start PM Designs 142
13.1 Key characteristics in performance assessment/ appraisal practices in China 268
14.1 GDP Growth Rates, Unions and Strikes 288
14.2 Adoption Rates of Yunbongje around the 1997 Crisis 292

Contributors

Torben Andersen is a teaching professor, (PhD, Copenhagen Business School and University of Warwick) at Penn State University. He has a broad portfolio of economic, structural, strategic, and change management aspects of HRM and International HRM. He has three periods as a visiting professor at San Francisco State University (2000), University of Auckland, New Zealand (2005), and Bamberg University, Germany (2016). He has been teaching in various countries ranging from Iceland, Germany, UK, China, and New Zealand to US and from undergraduate to PhD courses. He has been the head of studies at various Danish universities and the director for the MBA studies at the Technical University of Denmark. He has published textbooks (both in Danish and English) and journal articles in *Human Resource Management and International Human Resource Management*.

Zeynep Aycan holds the Koç Holding Chair of Management and Strategy. She is the founder and academic director of the Leadership Lab at Koc University (https://leadlab.ku.edu.tr/). Aycan received her PhD from Queen's University, Canada, and conducted postdoctoral research at McGill University. Recognition of Aycan's work includes World Economic Forum Outstanding Young Scientist Award, Best Book Award in Management and Leadership (CMI, London), APA Ursula Gielens Book Award, and AOM Caroline Dexter Award. She is the fellow of the Society for Industrial and Organizational Psychology and the Association for Psychological Science.

Cordula Barzantny is a professor of human resource management with a particular focus on international and intercultural management at Toulouse Business School (TBS Education). Cordula's main research interests are in cross-cultural, European, and international management and global leadership. She has work experience in several countries and is married to a

Frenchman and a mother of two. Prior to completing her PhD at Toulouse University I Capitole, she had a professional career in finance, accounting, and management control with Siemens.

Pawan S. Budhwar is the 50th Anniversary Professor of International HRM, the head of Aston Business School, and an associate pro-vice chancellor international (India) at Aston University, UK. He is also the co-editor-in-chief of *Human Resource Management Journal*. Pawan is globally known for his research in the fields of strategic and international human resource management and emerging markets with a specific focus on India.

Fang Lee Cooke is a distinguished professor at Monash Business School, Monash University, Australia. Her research interests are in the area of strategic human resource management, knowledge management and innovation, outsourcing, international human resource management, diversity and inclusion management, employment relations, migrant studies, human resource management in the care sector, digitalization, and implications for employment and human resource management; climate change, energy transition, and the future of work; and the Sustainable Development Goals and the role of multinational firms.

Angelo S. DeNisi (PhD, Purdue University, US) is the Cohen Chair in Business at Tulane University, US. His primary research interests are performance appraisals, performance management, and the interactions between expatriates and host country nationals. His research has been funded by the National Science Foundation and the US Army Research Institute and has been published in journals such as the *Academy of Management Journal*, the *Academy of Management Review*, the *Journal of Applied Psychology*, the *Journal of Personality and Social Psychology*, and *Psychological Bulletin*. He has received lifetime scholarly contribution awards from SIOP and the HR Division of the Academy. He is a fellow of the American Psychological Association, the Society for Industrial and Organizational Psychology, the Academy of Management, and the Indian Academy of Management, and he has served as president for both the Academy of Management and the Society for Industrial and Organizational Psychology.

Azusa Ebisuya is an associate professor of management at Hosei University. She also has teaching and research experiences at Osaka University and Rutgers University. Her research efforts are centered on an interdisciplinary mix of linguistics, management, and culture. She is primarily interested in international human resource development, virtual-team dynamics, and emotional intelligence in knowledge-based environments.

Marion Festing is a professor of human resource management and intercultural leadership at ESCP Business School's Berlin campus. Marion's research interests include international human resource management and talent management in various institutional and cultural contexts as well as a specific focus on diversity and inclusion. Currently, she serves as the chairperson of the Human Resource Management section (Kommission Personal) in the German Academic Association of Business Research (VHB).

Barry Gerhart is the Ellig Distinguished Chair, Wisconsin School of Business, University of Wisconsin–Madison. He received his PhD in industrial relations from the University of Wisconsin–Madison. Professor Gerhart is a fellow of the Academy of Management and of the American Psychological Association. He has served as a department chair and/or area coordinator at Cornell, Vanderbilt, and Wisconsin, as well as senior associate dean and interim dean at Wisconsin.

Jorge A. Gonzalez is a professor of management and the department chair at the University of Texas Rio Grande Valley. He received his PhD in management from Texas A&M University. He conducts research on diversity and inclusion in organizations, work stress, leadership, and cross-cultural organizational behavior with a focus on Mexico and Latin America. His research has been published in journals such as the *Journal of International Business Studies*, the *Journal of Organizational Behavior*, *Organization Studies*, and *Personnel Psychology*, among others.

Biyun Hu is an assistant professor in the School of Business and Management, Shanghai International Studies University, China. She received her PhD in human resource management and organizational behavior from Temple University. Her research primarily focuses on issues related to organizational trust and fairness, leadership, and workplace deviance.

Akihisa Kagami is a human resource management consultant and a PhD student at the Graduate School of Management, Kyoto University, Japan. He has served as a part-time lecturer at the Graduate School of Osaka University of Commerce, as a visiting researcher at Kwansei Gakuin University, and as a Special Advisor to Osaka City. His research interests include strategic human resource management, performance management, and organizational justice perception.

Serap Keleş is an associate professor of psychology in the Faculty of Arts and Education,Knowledge Centre for Education at the University of Stavanger, Norway.

Liang Meng is a professor in the School of Business and Management, Shanghai International Studies University, who serves as the head of the Department of Management and Organizations. He received his PhD in management from Zhejiang University and worked as a postdoctoral researcher at the University of Pennsylvania. His research primarily focuses on issues related to work motivation, work design, and job crafting.

Rose Mueller-Hanson is the associate director/CFO of Community Interface Services, a nonprofit organization serving adults with developmental disabilities. She is the co-author of several recent articles on the topic of improving performance and career management practices, and the book *Transforming Performance Management to Drive Performance*. Prior to joining Community Interface Services, Rose was a director of talent solutions at PDRI, a CEB Company, and served in the U.S. Air Force. She received her doctorate degree in industrial/organizational psychology from Colorado State University.

Kevin R. Murphy is a professor emeritus, formerly Kemmy Chair of Work and Employment Studies, at the University of Limerick. He is the author of more than 200 articles and chapters and the author or editor of 12 books in areas ranging from psychometrics and statistical analysis to performance assessment appraisal and management. He has served as the president of the Society for Industrial and Organizational Psychology and as editor of the *Journal of Applied Psychology* and *Industrial and Organizational Psychology: Perspectives on Science and Practice.*

Peter Norlander is senior associate dean and an associate professor of management at Loyola University Chicago's Quinlan School of Business, where he is also the interim director of the Institute of Human Resources and Employment Relations. His research focuses on global issues of technology, power, and labor mobility in human resource management and labor relations. He received his doctorate in management from the University of California, Los Angeles Anderson School of Management.

Ryan S. O'Leary has spent his career working with organizations to develop and implement talent management systems in the areas of staffing, assessment, and performance management. He holds a doctorate in industrial/organizational psychology from Auburn University and a Bachelor of Science in psychology from Emory University. He is a fellow of the Society for Industrial and Organizational Psychology. Currently, he is the chief commercial officer for PDRI.

Gaye Özçelik is an associate professor at the School of Communication, İstanbul Bilgi University. She holds a PhD and a master's degree in business administration from Işık University, Turkey, and a BA in psychology from Boğaziçi University, Turkey. Dr. Özcelik's research interests include human resource management practices, psychological contract, decent work, and global mobility. Özçelik has published various articles in internationally qualified peer-reviewed journals, including *European Management Review*, *Personnel Review*, and *Human Resource Development Review*, as well as book chapters and proceedings.

Contributors

Özçelik currently serves as the country representative of the European Academy of Management. Gaye Özçelik currently serves as the visiting associate professor at Karlshochschule International University, the European Business School, and Pforzheim University, Germany.

Lorena Perez-Floriano joined the faculty of business and economics at Universidad Diego Portales in Chile, in 2019. Before joining Diego Portales, she was a research professor at El COLEF and a professor at ITAM University in Mexico. She received her doctorate in industrial and organizational psychology from the California School of Professional Psychology, USA. Perez-Floriano is fascinated by social environments, inequality, and their effects on human behavior, trying to understand the deeper cultural codes that drive our behavior across nations as well as within nations.

Ryan Petty is the dean of the Heller College of Business at Roosevelt University, as well as a tenured associate professor of human resource management. Ryan joined the faculty at Roosevelt in 2010 after earning his PhD from Michigan State University in human resources and labor relations. As a faculty at Roosevelt, he has taught graduate- and undergraduate-level courses in both human resources and management. Ryan has also served in multiple administrative roles during his time on the faculty in the Heller College of Business, including serving as the program director, an associate dean, and an interim dean. Ryan's scholarly research focuses on work–life balance, the use of social media in human resources, and management instructional techniques and has been published in various peer-reviewed journals, edited books, and presented at academic conferences.

Shaun Pichler is a professor of management at the College of Business at California State University, Fullerton. Shaun has published in journals such as *Human Resource Management*, the *Journal of Vocational Behavior*, and *Personnel Psychology*; is an editorial board member of such journals as *Group & Organization Management*, the *Journal of Business & Psychology*, and the *Journal of Vocational Behavior*, is an associate editor of *Human Resource Management*, and is a senior editor of the *Journal of Occupational & Organizational Psychology*.

Elaine Pulakos is the CEO of PDRI and an expert in building organizational and team capabilities that translate into business growth. She is well known for her research and writing on agility and resilience and has extensive global experience helping companies build these capabilities to increase their competitive advantage and performance.

Maranda Ridgway is a senior lecturer in human resource management and a deputy director of research impact at Nottingham Business School. Maranda's principal research interests lie in global mobility, intersectionality, and human resources. Committed to having an impact on policy and practice, in her resource, Maranda is informed by years as a senior human resource professional with international experience in a variety of blue-chip multinational organizations.

Amy Risner is a student at the College of Business at California State University, Fullerton and a member of the Business Honors Program. She is also the current president of the Society of Excellence in Human Resources and has worked in Human Resources at Panasonic North America and First American Title.

R. Aristeo Rodriguez is a first-generation Mexican American graduate student at the University of Texas Rio Grande Valley. As a PhD candidate in management from the Robert C. Vackar College of Business and Entrepreneurship, he centers his research on artist musician entrepreneurs in the culture creation industries. As an instructor, Rodriguez has taught hundreds of students the craft of generating innovative business plans.

Chris Rowley is a professor emeritus, Bayes Business School, City, University of London, UK, and a former research fellow at the Korea Foundation. He has more than 30 years' experience in university systems in the UK, Europe, and Asia and has won several international grants. He is the editor of the SCI-rated journal *Asia Pacific Business Review* and has published more than 800 articles, books, chapters, and practitioner pieces. He regularly provides interviews, expert comments, and opinion pieces to the international media, including news services, TV, radio, and practitioner outlets.

Dow Scott is a professor of human resources in the Quinlan School of Business at Loyola University Chicago. Dr. Scott teaches and conducts applied research and consults on a variety of reward issues including base pay, incentive plans (e.g., merit pay, gainsharing, team rewards and recognition programs), global compensation and expatriate pay, aligning business strategies with compensation, pay fairness, pay transparency, socially responsible rewards, and reward program evaluation.

Tomoki Sekiguchi is a professor in the Graduate School of Management, Kyoto University, Japan. His research interests include employee behaviors, person–environment fit, hiring decision-making, cross-cultural organizational behavior, and international human resource management. His work has been published in such journals as *Personnel Psychology*, *Organizational Behavior*, *Human Decision Processes*, *Human Resource Management Review*, *Human Resource Management*, and the *International Journal of Human Resource Management*.

Tanuja Sharma is a faculty member in the human resource management area at the Management Development Institute, Gurgaon, India. She is a lead for the Center of Excellence for Ethics, ESG Initiatives and Responsible Organizations (CERO@MDI Gurgaon). She has contributed to teaching, training, consulting, and research in performance management systems, compensation management, and business ethics. Her research interests include happiness at work, dignity at work, social capital, and sustainable human resource management. Her doctoral work from the Faculty of Management Studies, Delhi University was on the subject of performance management systems and was awarded the

Mercer Award Asia 2005 by Mercer Human Resource Consulting, Singapore for innovative, practical Asian human resource research.

John Shields is a professor of human resource management and organizational studies at the University of Sydney Business School. His research and teaching interests include performance management, reward management, corporate governance, and leadership. In human resource management, he most recently co-authored books, including *Managing Employee Performance and Reward, 3rd edition* (Cambridge University Press, 2020) and *Human Resource Management: Strategy and Practice, 11th edition* (Cengage, 2020).

Helen Shipton is a professor of human resource management and the director of the Centre of People, Work and Organizational Practice, Nottingham Business School, Nottingham Trent University, UK. Helen is interested in human resource management as an enabler of learning, creativity, and innovation at work. Her research has been published in journals such as *Human Resource Management*, the *British Journal of Management*, and the *Human Resource Management Journal*. Helen is an associate editor of the *Human Resource Management Journal* and UK Ambassador for the US Academy of Management.

Paul Sparrow is a professor emeritus of international human resource management at Lancaster University Management School. In 2022, he was awarded the British Academy of Management Richard Whipp Lifetime Achievement Award and, in 2016, the USA Society for HRM's Michael R. Losey Lifetime Achievement in Human Resource Research. He was voted among the most influential human resources thinkers by *Human Resources* magazine 2008–2012 and listed in the Top 10 most influential for 2014–2015.

Charlie Trevor is the Ruth L. Nelson Chair in Business in the Department of Management and Human Resources at the Wisconsin School of Business. He earned his PhD in industrial and labor relations from Cornell University in 1998. His research focuses on employee turnover, the determinants and consequences of employee compensation, job performance, and employee downsizing. He teaches courses on negotiations, compensation, research methods, statistics, and human resource systems.

Charles M. Vance, professor emeritus, Loyola Marymount University, Los Angeles, has authored more than 100 scholarly publications and creative works, as well as three books, including *Managing a Global Workforce*, 4th edition (Routledge), and *Smart Talent Management*, 2nd edition (Edward Elgar). He has twice served as a U.S. Fulbright Scholar and has been active as a guest instructor and consultant in several countries related to training, business curriculum development, and global talent management.

Arup Varma is a distinguished university research professor and the Frank W. Considine Chair in Applied Ethics at the Quinlan School of Business, Loyola University Chicago. He holds a PhD from Rutgers University, New Jersey (US); an MS in personnel management and industrial relations from XLRI, Jamshedpur (India), and a BSc (Hons) from St. Xavier's College, Kolkata (India). Dr. Varma's research interests include performance appraisal, expatriate issues, and human resource management issues in India. He has published more than 100 articles in leading journals and edited six books. He has won multiple awards for teaching, research, and service, including the 2017 Alumnus Award for Academics from his alma mater, XLRI. In 2018, he spent 6 months in India, as a Fulbright Scholar.

Hyuckseung Yang is a leading scholar in human resource management in Korea. He was the director of the Research Centre at Yonsei Business School. His recent academic interest is the changes in the employment and business competition ecosystems that the Fourth Industrial Revolution is evoking. Recently, he published a book titled *People Management in the Era of Great Transformation: The Era of Innovation, Going beyond the Conventions of People Management* (Korean ver.), which focuses on how the company's management paradigm has changed and should be changed.

Performance Management around the Globe

Looking Back and Ahead

Arup Varma, Pawan S. Budhwar and Angelo S. DeNisi

Chapter 1

In 2008, we published the first edition of this book, which received tremendous response from all of you. Thank you. In response, we are pleased to bring this second edition to you. As we noted in the first edition, the increasing and continuing globalization of the world economy has led to the creation of the true multinational enterprise (MNE). While organizations are often able to successfully transfer and implement financial and technical systems to the new location, human resource (HR) systems present unique challenges. Indeed, the literature on international HR issues has seen a steady stream of articles (e.g., DeNisi, Murphy, Varma, & Budhwar, 2021) and books (e.g., De Cieri & Dowling, 2012) addressing the issues faced by MNEs in their people management processes (e.g., expatriate selection, hiring, etc.). However, one topic that has received scant attention is how performance management systems are implemented in different

DOI: 10.4324/9781003306849-1

countries around the globe. Here, it should be noted that performance management (PM) is the key process by which organizations set goals, determine standards, assign and evaluate work, and distribute rewards (Varma & Budhwar, 2020). Furthermore, given that performance management systems (PMSs) are really needed to help organizations ensure a successful implementation of their business strategy (Schuler & Jackson, 1987), we believe that this is a subject that deserves close attention.

There is no doubt that the subject of performance management "across the globe" defies comprehensive coverage in one book. However, given the speed at which organizations are globalizing and becoming MNEs, along with the rapid rise of emerging markets; both researchers and policy makers are interested in finding out about the kind of HR and PMSs relevant to firms operating in different national contexts. In the absence of reliable literature, this book should prove very useful and timely for both the global corporation and the global manager. We believe it fills a critical gap in the literature, for both academics and practitioners, by providing comprehensive coverage of the performance management practices in key countries, with special emphasis on performance appraisal (PA), and some critical themes in performance management. The detailed information on PMSs in these countries, with special emphasis on PA, will allow the reader to become familiar with the unique nature of PM and PA systems in these countries. Furthermore, by presenting individual country information based on a single comprehensive model (presented in Chapter 6), the book will allow readers to compare and contrast the practices and processes in these nations, providing a comprehensive overview of a very critical HR process.

A note about the choice of countries in this, and the first edition. While it is impossible to cover all or even a significant fraction of countries in one book, we have endeavoured to provide a rather comprehensive coverage. To do this, we draw on Ronen and Shenkar's (1985) model clustering countries on attitudinal dimensions and the Goldman Sachs' report on BRIC countries (Brazil, Russia, India, China; Wilson & Purushothaman, 2003). We cover four of the eight clusters from Ronen and Shenkar and two of the four countries (India, China) from the BRIC report. This was indeed a difficult choice, as we would have liked to include all countries proposed by these two papers. However, this would have made the proposed volume extremely unwieldy. Next, for the second edition, we did explore adding new countries or using a completely new set of countries, but these ideas were dismissed early on, as the result would not be a true second edition. We sincerely hope that the remaining countries will be included in a subsequent volume, either by us or other scholars.

Finally, we would like to thank the authors from the first edition who were willing to help us out by revising their chapters from the first edition, as well as the new co-authors for some of the chapters. Furthermore, in some cases, where the original authors were unavailable, we were excited to invite several new collaborators. A special note of thanks and a warm welcome to Charles M. Vance and Torben Andersen (Chapter 2); Biyun Hu and Liang Meng (Chapter 3); Amy Risner (Chapter 4); Dow Scott (Chapter 5); Jorge A. Gonzalez, Lorena Perez-Floriano, and R. Aristeo Rodriguez (Ch. 8); Maranda Ridgway and Helen Shipton (Chapter 9); Gaye Özçelik (Chapter 11); Peter Norlander (Chapter 12); Akihisa Kagami, Tomoki Sekiguchi, and Azusa Ebisuya (Chapter 15); and John Shields (Chapter 16).

PMSS AROUND THE GLOBE

As Denisi and Murphy (2017) noted in their seminal article reviewing a century of research in PA and performance management, the field has come a long way from studying different types of rating scales to emphasizing the context of performance management and evaluation. Next, many MNEs try to take the easy way out by implementing PM systems developed in the home country in host country locations. This is problematic, as most MNEs are based in the US, and performance may be difficult to evaluate appropriately outside the US context by adopting US-based models (Murphy & Cleveland, 1995).

Relatedly, one of the critical issues facing MNEs is the management of their multinational workforce, through developing guidelines on how to staff, evaluate, compensate, and train in the international context. Performance management systems typically have two purposes: (1) administrative decisions, such as promotions, merit raises, and bonuses and (2) developmental goals, such as feedback and training (Murphy & Cleveland, 1995).

It would seem that most organizations, especially MNEs, would be able to achieve these goals with ease by setting up appropriate systems that specify the link between individual performance and organization-level outcomes. However, this seems to be a goal yet too far. The good news, as DeNisi and Murphy concluded, is that raters can be trained.

Furthermore, the very construct of performance is multidimensional (Rao, 2004) and "culture-bound" (Varma & Budhwar, 2020). Indeed, we know now that managers (and employees) view performance differently in different cultures, thus leading to both intercultural and intra-culture differences in the definition and interpretation of performance. So, for example, in an individualistic culture, the emphasis would be on individual effort and outcomes, calling for objective and quantifiable performance criteria (Harris & Moran, 1996). However, collectivist cultures are more likely to reward group loyalty, conformity, and harmonious relationships (Tung, 1984).

Clearly, since performance is viewed differently in different cultures, the mechanisms to evaluate and manage performance must be designed to address the local context. For example, seeking feedback on one's performance may be viewed as appropriate and desirable in individualistic cultures like the US, but such behaviour would be deemed out of place and highly inappropriate in a collectivist culture such as China (Bailey, Chen & Dou, 1997). Thus, an American manager hoping to foster improvements in their Chinese subordinates' performance through feedback is likely to fail in their efforts.

Next, since the goals of performance management systems vary widely between locations of firms, individuals view performance differently in the different locations. For example, in the US, performance appraisals are primarily geared towards determining individual rewards (Cardy & Dobbins, 1994), thus motivating individuals to work harder so they may achieve the desired rewards. However, in a collectivist culture like Japan, performance appraisals emphasize long-term potential (Pucik, 1984), thus encouraging individuals to develop their skills and competencies. Clearly, performance management systems must be context-based to make allowances for the unique circumstances and cultural norms of the location. While the success of all HR initiatives is context-dependent, effective performance management calls for special attention to the national context, as issues of culture and legislation, for example, can have a significant impact on the implementation and practice of PMSs (see, e.g., Chapter 16 in this volume). This is all the more critical as evaluations are the primary tool for the organization to assess performance and thus assess the degree to which the MNE's objectives are being met by individual employees, both host country nationals and expatriates. In addition to managing the performance of host country nationals, MNEs must also concern themselves with the performance management of expatriates (Varma, Wang, & Coleman, 2022), who increasingly form a significant portion of their workforce. Furthermore, there is no clear and/or accepted definition of expatriate performance (Shaffer, Harrison, Gregersen, Black & Ferzandi, 2006), and several different criteria have been used to measure expatriate effectiveness, and even these vary widely between organizations (Shih, Chiang & Kim, 2005). Furthermore, as Yan, Zhu and Hall (2002) argue, the expatriate's own goals should also be incorporated into the evaluation system. Ironically, Shih et al. (2005) report that expatriate evaluations are often treated as a mere extension of domestic evaluation systems and that MNEs often use criteria and measures developed for domestic purposes. Apart from examining the performance management of expatriates, the importance of the impact of such factors is equally strong and worth considering while evaluating the performance of any employees in a given national or local context. Due consideration of such forces will enable researchers to highlight the 'context-specific' nature of PMS and provide a valid picture of the scene. The current volume is thus designed to take a global perspective on PM, by looking at input, mediators and moderators, and outcome variables of the same. More specifically, this edition is designed to update the individual chapters with PMS-related developments in the countries included in this volume.

STRUCTURE OF THE BOOK

This book is divided into two parts. In Part I, apart from this introductory chapter, we have included a chapter on PMS in MNEs and three chapters on critical themes in performance management, namely, rater motivation, rater–ratee relationships, and merit pay. The last chapter in Part I presents a model of the appraisal process that has been incorporated into the country-specific chapters in Part II. Part II includes 10 chapters that present a comprehensive synopsis of PM practices in 11 selected nations (one of the chapters includes two countries). The last chapter is designed to help bring it all together – by highlighting the key findings and emphasizing key similarities and differences among PMSs in the various countries included in this volume and suggesting avenues for future research.

In Chapter 2, Charles M. Vance and Torben Andersen present a discussion of PM practices and policies in MNEs of all nature, from large and small to for-profit and not-for-profit, and every other type in between. They discuss how the increasing globalization has resulted in a proliferation of the MNE and the unique issues associated with managing employees in MNEs. They also present a five-phase model of the PM process, which incorporates job design in Phase 1; mutually agreed-on goals in Phase 2; job monitoring, feedback, and coaching in Phases 3 and 4; and conducting performance appraisal with a view to achieving immediate improvements in performance and addressing future career plans. It is noteworthy that with the authors remind us of the need for training at each of these five phases – for immediate and future needs.

The authors also point out that despite the differences in economic, social, and political contexts between countries around the world, there is a clear trend towards convergence when it comes to PMSs. Specifically, they note the move towards (1) frequent, informal feedback geared towards development; (2) more decentralized, flexible PM processes; (3) the integration of technology and remote work arrangements; and (4) a renewed emphasis on trust and cooperation. Interestingly, they conclude by reminding us that with the increasing global mobility of the workforce, managers should be constantly monitoring the shifting convergence and divergence of PMS practices. Of course, by presenting a comprehensive model of the PMS process in MNEs, the authors have provided a frame of reference for understanding PMS practices in the various countries included in Part II of this book.

Chapter 3 deals with the dynamics of motivation, and the impact of motivation on individual performance. Here, Biyun Hu and Liang Meng discuss why it is important that managers understand what motivates individual employees if they are to draw optimal levels of performance from them. They then go on to briefly discuss various need-based theories of motivation (e.g., Maslow's hierarchy of needs, Herzberg's motivation-hygiene theory, etc.) and process-based theories of motivation (e.g., equity theory, expectancy theory, etc.) and goal-based theory of motivation (i.e., goal setting theory).

This is followed by a comprehensive discussion of their motivation model, which explores the links between the key components of the motivation process, namely, goals, effort, performance, reward, and need fulfillment, as well as how each link can be strengthened through PM.

Finally, the authors discuss the impact of culture (and cross-cultural issues) on motivation levels and remind the reader that while the overall motivational process may cut across cultures, the unique and specific features of various cultures (e.g., diversity levels) make it critical to recognize and understand the impact of culture on individual motivation. The authors conclude by presenting a short case for discussion, which helps with understanding the link between motivation and PM.

In Chapter 4, Amy Risner, Shaun Pichler, Arup Varma, and Ryan Petty explore the impact of rater–ratee relationships on individual performance ratings, and the PM process, as a whole. They start by highlighting the importance of the social context of performance management and go on to discuss how the type of relationship that develops between a rater and their ratees impacts the ratees' outcomes (e.g., performance ratings). Specifically, they discuss two key constructs (interpersonal affect and leader–member exchange [LMX]) that have been studied to understand how rater–ratee relationships interact with, and impact, PA. Here, the authors note that interpersonal affect, as a construct, is critical to understanding the rater–ratee relationship.

Furthermore, the authors note that while the literature on affect is somewhat equivocal on whether affect truly acts as a bias in the performance management process, the LMX literature is overwhelmingly consistent in its findings – that a good relationship (high LMX) with the rater helps the ratee receive higher ratings and other rewards than those with relatively poor relationships (low LMX), controlling for performance. Finally, the authors note that practitioners must be cognizant of how rater–ratee relationships operate in their organization and how these affect performance ratings. They should consider this fact when designing performance appraisal systems and when evaluating the effectiveness of their PMSs.

Chapter 5 deals with merit pay as it relates to PM. Here, Barry Gerhart, Charlie Trevor, and Dow Scott present the reader with a succinct discussion of the relationship between performance and rewards, specifically merit pay. They start by discussing merit pay in the larger context of pay strategy and discuss numerous other pay-for-performance options, such as gain sharing. This is followed by a discussion of the key policy aspects of merit pay systems and the challenges often faced by organizations in implementing merit pay. For example, the authors argue that merit pay is often defined too narrowly and that in order to implement merit pay policies appropriately, both raters and ratees need to understand the impact of performance ratings on individual pay. Using several examples and exhibits, the authors explain the basics of merit pay and the numerous issues that organizations need to consider if they are to attract, motivate, and retain appropriate talent.

Clearly, merit pay is an important outcome of PMSs. Furthermore, as the authors point out, there needs to be substantial variance among performance ratings for merit pay to have a meaningful effect. However, in the global context, this may be easier said than done. For example, while the variance in ratings may be relatively easier to achieve in individualistic countries (e.g., the US), this may be more difficult in collectivist countries, such as China. The authors conclude by presenting a short case, which is designed to help the reader apply the concepts discussed in the chapter and examine the merits of the same.

In Chapter 6, Kevin Murphy and Angelo S. DeNisi present a model to examine and highlight the appraisal process in different contexts. Given that the present volume deals with various perspectives on the performance management process around the world, this chapter provides a set of unifying themes that can be used for the discussions of these perspectives.

The authors propose a two-part model that focuses on the PMS, with Part I focusing on the performance appraisal process while

Part II focuses on the broader performance management issue. In the first part of the model, Murphy and DeNisi cover distal factors such as industry norms and the nation's legislative environment and proximal factors, such as the purpose of the appraisal and how well it is accepted. They propose that distal and proximal factors work through intervening factors, such as rater motivation and rater–ratee relationships to impact PM. Included in the first part of the model are distortion factors, such as reward systems, and the consequences of the appraisal.

The second part of the model deals with feedback given to the ratee and the gap between desired and observed performance levels. Here, PM interventions are introduced with the aim of reducing the gap so as to help meet organizational and individual goals. Adopting the comprehensive framework proposed in this chapter has enabled authors of the country-specific chapters in this volume to comprehensively describe PMSs in different parts of the world, using a common theme.

In Chapter 7, Elaine Pulakos, Rose Mueller-Hanson, and Ryan O'Leary discuss PM practices and policies in the US. They start by discussing the history of the US and the development of its truly individualistic culture, which, in turn, has had a significant impact on the American workplace, in general, and performance management, in particular. Thus, for example, individual performance, accountability, and rewards are key themes of the performance management process in the US.

The authors take the reader through a historical journey tracing the evolution of performance management systems in the US, starting with Taylor's "scientific management", all the way through to competency-based human capital systems that became popular almost 100 years after Taylor's initial efforts at defining and measuring performance.

The authors also discuss the key factors (results-focus automation, legislation) that have shaped the way performance management operates in the US and the key challenges that sometimes inhibit effective PM (e.g., lack of open communication between rater and ratee). While it might seem that the key factors listed here are not unique to the US, it is important to note that given the unique history of the US (emphasis on capitalism, world's leading economy, immigration from all over the world, etc.); these factors take on a special meaning in the context of PM. For example, legislation related to PM issues is very clear and specific, and both rater and ratee are almost always aware of the law and its implications. To underscore the importance of the legislative environment, the authors have provided specific guidelines for addressing legal requirements in the US, especially as these relate to PM. Interestingly, the authors start their chapter by noting that "[w]hile there has never been an 'American style' of PM per se, a decidedly U.S. mindset and set of values have formed the underpinnings of PM since its inception." This is a critical observation, as most PMSs around the world are based on, or draw from, the American PMS design and practices.

Chapter 8 is devoted to discussing PMS in Mexico. Here, Jorge A. Gonzalez, Lorena Perez-Floriano, and R. Aristeo Rodriguez present an overview of PMSs in Mexico. The authors start by noting that despite the challenges faced by HR practitioners in designing and implementing PMSs in Mexico, such systems are fairly common and universally prevalent across all kinds of organizations in the country. The authors next provide a summary of the existing PMS practices (specifically, PA) in Mexican companies, namely, performance evaluation (1) rewards good (proper) behaviour; (2) is rarely related to individual performance; (3) has traditionally been used to make decisions about downsizing, promotions, and salary increases, as well as to increase efficiency; (4) provides a safe space for employees to express their opinions and aspirations, enabling them to engage and communicate with upper management; and (5) is used to evaluate rather than develop employees.

The authors then go on to discuss the role of cultural and socio-economic factors in the conduct of PM and PA in Mexico. For example, the authors discuss the existence of an affiliative orientation among workers in Mexico, which results in high emotional involvement between co-workers, including those at different levels. Not surprisingly, this affiliative orientation has been known to impact PMSs as those are often designed to foster competition rather than collaboration. Next, the authors address three critical factors impacting PMSs in the Mexican workplace – the legal environment, unionization, and profit-sharing. The authors conclude by offering recommendations for developing

Arup Varma et al.

PMSs for companies operating in Mexico, that incorporate a good balance of organizational strategic goals and the Mexican cultural and socio-economic environment.

In Chapter 9, Maranda Ridgway, Helen Shipton, and Paul Sparrow present a discussion of PMS in the UK. The authors start by summarizing the socio-economic and legal contexts of the employment relationship. This is followed by a comprehensive review that traces the development of PMSs in the UK. Next, they identify and discuss key factors that impact PMS practices in the country (e.g., organizational autonomy and supervisor-subordinate relationships). Finally, the authors summarize the challenges facing effective PMS conduct in the UK. To allow for better comparisons with the other chapters in this volume, the authors have linked their discussion to the Murphy and DeNisi model presented in Chapter 6. In the subsequent discussion, the authors address several key issues related to PMS in the UK, including the strategic role played by the HR function. They also go on to discuss the challenges faced by PMS practitioners in the country and discuss possible solutions. Overall, the authors argue that PMSs in the UK are rather mature and able to change and evolve along with changes in socio-economic, political, legal, and strategic focus.

Chapter 10 presents a combined analysis of PMSs in Germany and France, authored by Cordula Barzantny and Marion Festing. It should be noted that the editors requested the authors to combine these two countries into one chapter, based on several factors: (1) the importance of both countries as major economic players in Europe and the world, (2) the convergence and divergence phenomenon of the European Union, and (3) the space limitations of the volume. The authors start by discussing the European context, which, they note, provides for an interesting study of convergent and divergent economies, which are working to be a single unified economic entity while retaining their unique historical, social, and legal environments. They then discuss the European human resource management (HRM) systems, emphasizing the context-specificity of Europe and reiterating that adapting US models may not be the best solution for European companies' needs. The next section discusses PMSs in France, listing the unique characteristics of these systems, such as the legal requirement to invest in employee training and the emphasis on individual accountability. This is followed by a discussion of the impact of the legal and cultural environments on PMSs in France, noting, for example, the high individualism and power distance features of French culture.

Next the authors discuss PMSs in Germany and the impact of the legal and cultural environment on PMSs in Germany. Here, the authors emphasize the strict German legal environment, and the social market economy, and discuss how these affect performance management. For example, the long-standing German practice of long-term employment relationships calls for PMSs to take the long-term view rather than emphasizing a short-term focus. Throughout the chapter, the authors note the similarities and differences between the French and German contexts, enabling the reader to understand the convergence-divergence perspective as it relates to PMSs. For example, while both countries are similar when it comes to emphasizing long-term employment, France is rated high on femininity, while Germany is rated high on masculinity.

In Chapter 11, Gaye Özçelik, Zeynep Aycan, and Serap Yavuz present an analysis of the current state of PMSs in Turkey while also tracing its historical development in the country. Their chapter is developed around four sections, with the first section providing a contextual overview of Turkey's current socio-economic and political background. The next section discusses the cultural and institutional contextual factors that are the driving forces HRM and PMSs in Turkey. The third section discusses the findings of the latest reported Cranfield Survey (2017) for the Turkish data (see Brewster & Hegewisch, 2017). In the final section, the authors address the latest challenges and trends that will shape the future of the PMSs in Turkey.

Next, the authors spend considerable time discussing the cultural and institutional context of PMSs in Turkey. For example, they note the fact that personal relationships are paramount in Turkish culture, leading to efforts to avoid confrontation. Furthermore, the authors point out that the private sector forms the bulk of the Turkish economy and that the majority of the private sector is made up of family-owned small and medium-sized enterprises. Not surprisingly, these organizations are driven by

Arup Varma et al.

informal family norms, making it difficult to implement HRM functions such as PMS.

Chapter 12 is devoted to describing and analyzing the current state of PMSs in India. Here, Tanuja Sharma, Pawan Budhwar, Arup Varma, and Peter Norlander start by noting the current state of the Indian economy – which has been on "overdrive" since the early 1990s when the Government of India changed its economic policies to emphasize an open, capitalistic model. Currently, India is one of the fastest-growing economies in a unique position, differentiating it from the rest of the world, with a gross domestic product growth of almost 9%, promoting the rise of an incredible entrepreneurial atmosphere. Indeed, there has been a noticeable growth in tech start-ups between 2013 and 2018, with roughly 7200 to 7700 start-ups being launched in the period. In addition, India has established itself as a hub for MNE subsidiaries from around the globe.

Next, the Indian workplace is very diverse in terms of customs, languages, and religions and boasts a multigenerational workforce with baby boomers, Gen X, millennials, and Gen Z. The authors note that these complexities make it difficult to generalize or design policies, practices, and systems that would be universally applicable. Thus, HR professionals in India need to carefully design systems that are flexible enough to accommodate the unique context of each company, location, and employee group. Furthermore, in recent times, organizations operating in India, both MNEs and domestic businesses, were impacted by environmental happenings such as COVID-19, the Russia–Ukraine war, and fluctuations in the international markets.

The authors present the history of PMSs in India, noting that while some organizations were using formal and often sophisticated systems decades ago, many others simply had no systems. The authors then discuss some recent changes in the Indian economy, such as the significant increase in the amount of foreign direct investment flowing into India, and the large number of Indian firms going global, by acquiring firms in other nations, as well as establishing operations in different parts of the world. As the authors note, the arrival of MNEs in India has forced domestic Indian companies to revisit their HR systems, in general, and PMSs, in particular, with many admitting a "newfound respect for PMS."

In Chapter 13, Fang Lee Cooke discusses PMSs in China and starts by noting that while performance management is often talked of as a new Western concept introduced to China recently, the truth is that a Chinese version of PA has been practised in China for a very long time. As Cooke notes, one big difference between the Chinese style of PA and that practised in the West is that the Chinese model is much more narrowly focused on evaluation, rewards, and punishments. She argues that many Chinese firms lack strategic orientation, which makes it difficult to adopt Western models of PMSs.

The author has based her chapter on two sets of data – the first being a set of interviews she conducted with government officials in China and the second being studies published in both English-language and Chinese-language journals. Throughout the chapter, Cooke provides excerpts from her interviews.

Cooke starts by providing an overview of HR systems in China, tracing the evolution of HR since the founding of the socialist state in 1949. Next, she discusses the development of PMSs in China. She notes that, from 1949 to the early 1980s, the emphasis in Chinese PM was on factors such as attendance and skills, while the post-1980s market reform era has seen widespread implementation of performance management systems, both in the private and the public sectors. She also notes that China's economic structure has continues to undergo major changes. For example, the emphasis has shifted from agriculture and heavy industry towards the service sector. Furthermore, policy changes have led to a growing diversity of ownership forms, which has critical implications for HR and PMSs in China.

The author also discusses some key factors that impact PMSs, namely, organizational size, structure, and type of business. Next, Cooke discusses how culture influences PMSs, specifically noting unique features of the Chinese culture that have a strong influence on performance appraisal. These include respect for age and seniority and the emphasis on harmony and *face*. The author ends the chapter by discussing the major challenges faced by organizations and managers in implementing PMSs in China, including (1) a lack of strategic goals at the organizational level, (2) PA continuing to be viewed as a mere formality, (3) high levels of subjectivity, and (4) adoption of the collective peer appraisal method.

Chapter 14 is dedicated to discussing PMSs in South Korea. Here, Hyuckseung Yang and Chris Rowley start by emphasizing the impact of Confucian thought on South Korean society, which has impacted the workplace through an emphasis on hierarchical relationships and collectivism. They then discuss two key developments that have transformed HRM systems in South Korea – namely, the establishment of a democratic government in 1987, and the Asian economic crisis of 1997. The authors trace the evolution of Korean society from underdevelopment, poverty, and the impact of Japanese occupation and the Korean War to the post-1960s period when the Korean economy started to transform from an agrarian society to a manufacturing miracle story.

The authors next trace the development of PMSs in Korean firms, which were traditionally known to be paternalistic and collectivistic with seniority and lifetime employment being rewarded. Indeed, changes in PMSs or the adoption of Western systems was resisted as it was believed that performance and pay differentiation would negatively impact teamwork and collaboration. As the authors note, PMSs, and especially PAs, did not carry much weight and were managed by HR departments with limited involvement by line managers. However, as a result of the changes in the environment, such as the Asian financial crisis, Korean companies began to modify their management practices – moving towards being more individualistic, contract-based, and more meritocratic, emphasizing performance and competencies. The authors then discuss some of the specific changes initiated by managers, such as trying to move away from seniority-based pay and promotions to new PMSs that emphasize individual performance. The authors conclude by discussing how the advent of the Fourth Industrial Revolution and the accompanying uncertainty have made Korean corporations realize that they need to revisit their HR systems, including PMSs.

In Chapter 15, Akihisa Kagami, Tomoki Sekiguchi, and Azusa Ebisuya trace the evolution of PMSs in Japan. The authors start by introducing Japanese PMS models and their evolution. They then go on to identify the various factors that have impacted the evolution and transformation of Japanese PMS models, such as changes in employment practices and in the business environment. They then discuss the characterization of Japanese organizations as "learning organizations" and go on to discuss how employee learning and skill development are emphasized throughout an individual's employment.

The authors next explore key features of the Japanese HR systems, including long-term employment and ability-based evaluation and compensation. They explain how these practices contribute to employee retention and loyalty and impact the employee–employer relationship. Of course, these very practices make it difficult to implement individual performance- and merit-based systems. Here, the authors hasten to point out that the introduction of performance-based PMSs with their short-term orientation and a strict results focus has had some unexpected results, such as individuals becoming focused on short-term goals and achievements to the detriment of their acquisition of higher skills. Furthermore, this shift often results in employee dissatisfaction, and collaboration is weakened. Interestingly, a hybrid PMS is emerging which attempts to combine both the traditional ability-based and the recent performance-based systems.

Chapter 16 covers PMSs in Australia. Here, John Shields starts by tracing the evolution of PMSs in Australia, with a special focus on the developments in the Australian economy since the publication of the first edition of this book. Next, the author presents a succinct discussion of the various factors that have shaped the Australian economy and the Australian workplace. Here, he discusses the impact of environmental factors such as the growth of the service sector, internationalization, and the shift in focus from shareholder value to environment, social, and global responsibility. He next discusses how PMSs can play a bigger role in improving business competitiveness and efficiency. Indeed, he notes that there are early signs of a change of approach to PMS purpose, given the rise of factors such as (1) the gig economy, (2) an increasingly multicultural workforce, (3) increasing participation by women in the workforce, (4) an ageing workforce, and (5) declining union participation, among others.

Next, the author tackles an important feature of Australian society and workplace – the legal system. Contrary to the practices in North America, the termination of an employee is very different in Australia and requires adherence to strict legal regulations, which has a significant impact on the design and practice of

PMSs. He concludes by noting a unique feature of the Australian economy – noting that large, for-profit firms may not be the ones leading innovations. Similarly, he suggests that organizational size and resource capability may not always determine HR innovations.

The last chapter (17) by Angelo S. DeNisi, Arup Varma and Pawan Budhwar presents a discussion of the learnings from the different chapters and suggests several critical future research directions. In addition, the authors compare and contrast the PMSs in the different countries, to highlight the convergence and divergence of PMSs across the globe. We are confident that the readers will enjoy this edition as much as they did the first one, if not more. We welcome your comments and feedback and promise to be back with a new edition in due course.

REFERENCES

Bailey, J.R., Chen, C.C., & Dou, S.G. (1997). Conceptions of self and performance-rated feedback in the U.S. Japan, and China. *Journal of International Business Studies*, 3rd quarter, 605–625.

Brewster, C., & Hegewisch, A. (Eds.). (2017). *Policy and practice in European human resource management: The Price Waterhouse Cranfield survey.* Taylor & Francis.

Cardy, R., & Dobbins, G. (1994). *Performance Appraisal: Alternative Perspectives.* Cincinnati, OH: South-Western.

De Cieri, H., & Dowling, P. J. (2012). Strategic human resource management in multinational enterprises: Developments and directions. In *Handbook of Research in International Human Resource Management, Second Edition.* Cheltenham & Camberley, UK; Northhampton, MA: Edward Elgar Publishing.

DeNisi, A.S., & Murphy, K.R. (2017). Performance appraisal and performance management: 100 years of progress? *Journal of Applied Psychology, 102*(3), 421.

DeNisi, A., Murphy, K., Varma, A., & Budhwar, P. (2021). Performance management systems and multinational enterprises: Where we are and where we should go. *Human Resource Management, 60*(5), 707–713.

Harris, P.R., & Moran, R.T. (1996). *Managing Cultural Differences.* Houston, TX: Gulf.

Murphy, K.R., & Cleveland, J.N. (1995). *Understanding Performance Appraisal: Social, Organizational, and Goal-Based Perspectives.* Thousand Oaks, CA: Sage.

Pucik, V. (1984). White collar human resource management: A comparison of the U.S. and Japanese automobile industries. *Columbia Journal of World Business,* 19, 87–94.

Rao, T.V. (2004). *Performance Management and Appraisal Systems: HR Tools for Global Competitiveness.* New Delhi, India: SAGE.

Ronen, S., & Shenkar, O. (1985). Clustering countries on attitudinal dimensions: A review and synthesis. *Academy of Management Review, 10*(3), 435–454.

Schuler, R.S., & Jackson, S. (1987). Linking competitive strategies with human resource management practices. *Academy of Management Executive,* 1, 207–219.

Shaffer, M.A., Harrison, D. A., Gregersen, H., Black, J.S., & Ferzandi, L.A. (2006). You can take it with you: Individual differences and expatriate effectiveness. *Journal of Applied Psychology, 91,* 109–125.

Shih, H.A., Chiang, Y. H., & Kim, I.S. (2005). Expatriate performance management from MNEs of different national origins. *International Journal of Manpower, 26,* 157–176.

Tung, R.L. (1984). Human resource planning in Japanese multinationals: A model for US firms? *Journal of International Business Studies, 15* (2), 139–149.

Varma, A., & Budhwar, P. (Eds.), (2020), *Performance Management: An Experiential Approach.* Sage, ISBN-13: 978-1473975743 ISBN-10: 1473975743.

Varma, A., Wang, C.-H., & Coleman, T. (2022). Performance management of expatriates, In S.M. Toh, & A. DeNisi (Eds.), *Expatriate Management, SIOP Frontier Series.* Routledge.

Wilson, D., & Purushothaman, R. (2003). Dreaming with BRICs: The path to 2050. *Global Economics Paper*, (99), 1.

Yan, A., Zhu, G., & Hall, D.T. (2002). International assignments for career building: A model of agency relationships and psychological contracts. *Academy of Management Review, 27*, 373–391

Performance Management in Multinational Enterprises

Examining Patterns of Convergence and Divergence

Charles M. Vance and Torben Andersen

Chapter 2

INTRODUCTION

The management of an organization's employee performance has long been recognized in practice and extensively studied by researchers as a core responsibility of individual managers and the human resource management (HRM) function (e.g., see Ebina & Joy, 2022; Schrøder-Hansen & Hansen, 2022; Garengo, Sardi, & Nudurupati, 2002; Hansen, 2021; Claus, Baker & Vermeulen, 2020; Claus, 2013; Cascio & Bernardin, 1981). Employee performance management (PM), sometimes referred to as *people* PM systems and processes (Hansen, 2021), is a subset of the broader context of organizational PM and control systems aimed at monitoring progress and achieving organizational performance objectives (Hsu, Hsin & Shiue, 2022; Nickson, 2021). Employee PM (hereafter referred to only as PM) is typically described as the system (including individual processes and practices)

DOI: 10.4324/9781003306849-2

through which organizations focus at the employee level to organize work assignments, determine performance criteria and standards, set work goals, assign work responsibilities, provide performance feedback and secure correction when required, determine training and professional development needs, and distribute rewards to encourage future desired performance (Vance & Paik, 2014).

According to past research in the U.S., organizations with effective PM practices are 51 percent more likely to beat competitors on key financial measures and are 41 percent more likely to lead their competition on nonfinancial yet profitability-linked measures such as employee retention, customer satisfaction, and service or product quality (Bernthal, Rogers & Smith, 2003). More recent research in international contexts corroborates this notion that investments in PM systems and the development of human capital are associated with significant individual, group, and organizational productivity improvement (Van Thielen et al., 2022; Kakkar et al., 2020; Onkelinx, Manolova & Edelman, 2016; Nda & Fard, 2013). But the picture of recognized practices contributing to effective PM has been anything but static. The past two decades have seen large-scale organizational change, including major adaptations in PM practices, such as the adoption of competency-based appraisal systems, 360-degree and crowdsourced performance feedback, performance improvement planning and goal setting, digital platforms/technological tool integration, and regular, ongoing coaching (Ebina & Joy, 2022; Soni, 2022; D'Amato & Banfi, 2021).

Multinational enterprises (MNEs) represent the growing number of profit and nonprofit organizations—large and small, from every sector of the global economy—with headquarters in their home country of origin and one or more operations in other countries. And with increasingly accessible, open borders and the availability of affordable technological innovations, there also is tremendous growth in the number of MNEs based in developing countries (Petricevic & Teece, 2019). Because of the increasing presence of MNEs in our global economy, the effective performance of MNE managers and their employees (including contracted workers) at home and abroad is gaining greater attention (Schrøder-Hansen & Hansen, 2022; Garengo, Sardi, & Sai, 2002).

Charles M. Vance and Torben Andersen

MNEs face a multitude of challenges beyond the domestic home country context, including the often puzzling and frustrating influence of multiple different cultures affecting every aspect of human behavior, differing political and legal environments, different perceptions regarding acceptable performance, and widely diverse working environments (Prajogo et al., 2022; Behery, 2022; DeNisi et al., 2021; Yahiaoui, Nakhle & Farndale, 2021; Paik, Chow & Vance, 2011). For MNE-assigned expatriates, for example, there can be very different perceptions at MNE home headquarters and at host operations about priorities for what should be accomplished and how work should take place.

PM relies on an extensive body of management knowledge derived mainly from Western research based on organizational psychology and management theory. However, we know that often Western-based theory and practice can have limited useful application by MNEs when implemented in other international contexts due to cultural and other institutional differences (Paik, Chow & Vance, 2011; Moran, Harris & Moran, 2010). Nevertheless, due to MNEs' continual efforts, when possible, to achieve economies of scale through standardization (Hussain & Khan, 2013), coupled with their incessant global search for world-class best practices (Chiang, Lemański & Birtch, 2017), there is an inexorable global convergence in MNEs toward common effective management practices, including related to PM (Schrøder-Hansen & Hansen, 2022; Morley et al., 2021; Budhwar, Varma & Patel, 2016). With this quite dynamic picture in mind of trends in MNE PM policies and practices—recently greatly influenced toward acceptance of more remote, flexible working arrangements due to the COVID-19 pandemic (McKinsey & Company, 2021)—we first examine basic and widely recognized PM principles and practices, which is followed by a consideration of important convergent trends affecting their use in a global context. We finally examine important divergence considerations for local PM applications.

THE PM PROCESS

Managers and supervisors hold a central responsibility in working closely with individual employees and teams to help them engage in productive effort and keep them on course to optimize their performance and contribution to organizational goals (Van Thielen et al., 2022). As mentioned earlier, this responsibility for effectively managing individual and team job performance across cultural and national boundaries in our global workplace can present particular challenges, require flexibility, and involve important considerations and critical competencies beyond those typically needed for the domestic workplace. An important fundamental approach for managers and supervisors is to become familiar with best practices in general human resources and PM yet also remain flexible and sensitive to local conditions and cultural differences in the actual application of those practices—that is, "think global, act local" (Morley et al., 2021; Claus & Hand, 2009). PM provides an essential means for aligning individual employee and team working behaviors with organizational performance and productivity goals (Van Thielen et al., 2022). Particularly in an international context, PM can serve as an effective management control mechanism for achieving desired performance and implementing MNE strategy despite significant distance and cultural barriers (Kadak & Laitinen, 2021). In addition, through the use of regular two-way, open communication, PM can be a source of new ideas and innovation promoting organizational learning, effecting performance improvement and organizational capability development throughout the MNE (Beuren, dos Santos & Bernd, 2022).

Figure 2.1 provides a general best-practices PM process model in five phases, comprising important manager–individual employee interactions including two-way communication, coaching and regular performance feedback, performance appraisal, and even correctional activities (Vance & Paik, 2014). It is increasingly acknowledged that a major cause of poor PM is the overemphasis on formal performance appraisals at the exclusion of attention to other important parts of the PM process, such as ongoing feedback and coaching (Mosca, Curtis & Puches, 2022; Kusumah et al., 2021). In addition, and consistent with a clear awareness of the importance of integrating individual HR function activities at home and abroad for optimal coordination and impact on organizational productivity, PM should be closely integrated with other major HR and talent management practices, including work or job design, employee learning and career

Charles M. Vance and Torben Andersen

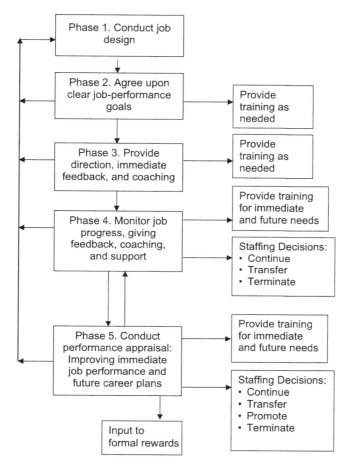

```
┌─────────────────────┐
│ Phase 1. Conduct job │
│      design          │
└─────────────────────┘
         │
         ▼
┌─────────────────────┐        ┌──────────────┐
│ Phase 2. Agree upon │───────▶│ Provide      │
│ clear job-performance│        │ training as  │
│       goals          │        │ needed       │
└─────────────────────┘        └──────────────┘
         │
         ▼
┌─────────────────────┐        ┌──────────────┐
│ Phase 3. Provide    │───────▶│ Provide      │
│ direction, immediate│        │ training as  │
│ feedback, and coaching│      │ needed       │
└─────────────────────┘        └──────────────┘
         │
         ▼
┌─────────────────────┐        ┌──────────────────┐
│ Phase 4. Monitor job│───────▶│ Provide training │
│ progress, giving    │        │ for immediate    │
│ feedback, coaching, │        │ and future needs │
│ and support         │        └──────────────────┘
└─────────────────────┘        ┌──────────────────┐
         │                     │ Staffing Decisions:│
         │                     │ • Continue       │
         │                     │ • Transfer       │
         │                     │ • Terminate      │
         ▼                     └──────────────────┘
┌─────────────────────┐        ┌──────────────────┐
│ Phase 5. Conduct    │───────▶│ Provide training │
│ performance appraisal:│      │ for immediate    │
│ Improving immediate │        │ and future needs │
│ job performance and │        └──────────────────┘
│ future career plans │        ┌──────────────────┐
└─────────────────────┘        │ Staffing Decisions:│
         │                     │ • Continue       │
         ▼                     │ • Transfer       │
┌─────────────────────┐        │ • Promote        │
│ Input to            │        │ • Terminate      │
│ formal rewards      │        └──────────────────┘
└─────────────────────┘
```

Figure 2.1   General Model of PM Process (Adapted from Vance & Paik, 2014)

planning, recruitment and selection, and compensation (Edwards, Tregaskis & McDonnell, 2022; Douthitt & Mondore, 2014).

We now examine each of the five major phases of the general PM process as presented in Figure 2.1, including illustrations of current MNE applications. In addition, we briefly examine important points of integration of this process with other critical HRM activities. Although our primary focus in this chapter is at the individual level, systematic approaches for evaluating and managing group and organizational performance are also needed in an effective, comprehensive PM effort.

Phase 1: Conduct Job Design. In Phase 1, PM is immediatedly integrated with the broader HR function and aligned with MNE strategy, where a specific work assignment is designed or often redesigned—given how frequently jobs become obsolete and need adjustment to meet new demands in our rapidly changing global business environment—to help fulfill current organization objectives. In the first phase, an employee may not yet even be hired or assigned to this job. The focus here is on what the work consists of and how it should be executed to meet performance objectives, and ultimately, MNE productivity goals. The job or work design should determine specific tasks, employee interactions and reporting relationships, performance expectations, and job qualifications appropriate for the specific performance needs. For example, a U.S.-based computer services job that covers South America would likely consider headquarter language fluency in English, as well as Spanish and Portuguese (i.e., Brazil), as essential job qualifications.

Phase 2: Agree On Clear Job Performance Goals. In this second phase of the PM process model, the manager and the employee jointly examine and gain agreement on the specific requirements, tasks, and expectations of the job within a larger picture of the performance goals of the operation and the total organization. As indicated by the arrow to the right at this second phase in Figure 2.1, there often will be a need for immediate or future training for employee skills and knowledge to support the desired work performance (Maja, Serafini & Szamosi, 2022). For example, an otherwise qualified Romanian employee promoted to a management position with a Germany-based MNE in Bucharest, and who in the future will require increasing amounts of interaction with German expatriates, may also begin receiving some forms of instruction to build basic German-language skills and an understanding of the unique MNE corporate culture (Vance & Paik, 2005). As indicated by the arrow recycling back to Phase 1, open and honest two-way communication is essential at this phase to allow for possible employee input related to unanticipated, added job requirements, or employee needs that might require a slight adjustment or significant accommodation from

Charles M. Vance and Torben Andersen

the original job design. The clear, common understanding and mutual agreement on the work performance expectations at this early phase are essential.

Phase 3: Provide Direction, Immediate Feedback, and Coaching. The third phase begins with the initial work performance of the employee and involves close one-on-one direction and immediate performance feedback and possible redirection, whether provided by the employee's direct supervisor or an assigned, experienced work unit peer. In this phase, there is the critical transition from performance expectations to concrete, observable action. Even when the new employee is well qualified for a job, there still should be an arrangement at this work start-up phase for performance observation and immediate feedback to ensure the previously agreed upon expectations are still appropriate. Coaching in this early phase of performance consists of immediate feedback, corrections and additional shaping direction, and encouragement toward optimal performance. In fact, several studies across a variety of cultures and work settings have demonstrated that frequent feedback sharing and goal setting, particularly within the trusting and supportive manager–subordinate coaching relationship and informal context, can be very effective in achieving desired employee performance (Locke & Latham, 2013). No matter how experienced the new employee is, some form of adjustment in the new work assignment is common, whether the employee is working in a familiar home country setting or abroad, and the close one-on-one attention provided at this initial phase of actual work performance can have a very positive influence on work performance correction and subsequent mastery. In addition, it is very important for the employee to begin the job with as positive and productive an experience as possible and with positive expectations for continued performance success. The manager close at hand as a confident coach can facilitate the development of these positive expectations and trust through constructive feedback, encouragement, and ready support as needed (D'Amato & Banfi, 2021).

As in Phase 2, in this work performance start-up phase, there may also appear areas where the need for more formal training is recognized and can be readily provided (on-the-job or off-site) to help fill in skill and knowledge gaps to support optimal performance (Maja, Serafini & Szamosi, 2022). Also, once the actual work has begun, there often appear aspects of the predetermined work design that need fine-tuning and revision. Possible job redesign needs should therefore be carefully considered at this phase, especially with the direct experience-based input of the new employee, which is represented in Figure 2.1 by the arrow pointing back to Phase 1. For example, expatriates arriving at a new international assignment often find that their work expectations and performance objectives, developed beforehand by headquarters executives who may not have an accurate picture of the local host country work environment, need adjustment (Vance & Ensher, 2002). This interactive job crafting and recrafting with employee experience-based input can further improve the ongoing validity of the work design, contributing to continually improved performance, as well as resulting in increased employee engagement and motivation (Berdicchia, Bracci & Masino, 2022).

Phase 4: Monitor Job Progress. As the employee over time becomes more competent and confident in performing the work according to expectations (and making adjustments when work performance needs inevitably shift), the direct supervisor or manager gradually becomes less involved in the close coaching as described in Phase 3. Nevertheless, as part of an important supportive and trusting relationship, the manager remains readily accessible to provide performance feedback, correction, and further coaching when needed to maintain desired performance (D'Amato & Banfi, 2021). Again, further employee learning opportunities may be provided at this phase to reinforce desired work performance and address skill needs that may not have been recognized or mastered previously. In addition, when the achievement and mastery of immediate desired work performance have been sufficiently addressed, important further professional development opportunities may be provided for meeting anticipated job developments or changes. In addition, job design again should be considered, in conjunction with employee input, serving as an

Charles M. Vance and Torben Andersen

ongoing, flexible activity to meet the changing demands of a dynamic global workplace. For example, in an open discussion with the employee at this phase it may be concluded that the original task requirements for a given job have become obsolete and new work demands have arisen requiring additional important tasks, leading to an agreement to redesign the original job and restructure tasks that would involve a new assistant's position providing additional support.

Finally, following several months or more of employee performance, the manager may consider new staffing decisions appropriate for the employee. It might become clear to the manager that, despite previous PM efforts of coaching, training, and correction—including disciplinary measures if needed—the employee is still unable to perform the work in a required fashion.

At this point, as indicated in Figure 2.1 by the second arrow to the right of Phase 4, a staffing decision may result in retaining the employee in the present position, transferring the employee to a new job (e.g., for a new, developmental experience; a promotion to new and greater responsibility; or a demotion), or even employee termination. Where termination is deemed necessary, the manager should be very familiar with the local legal requirements and possible consequences, which in some countries can be substantial in the form of significant termination labor fines and indemnity costs associated with unemployment and severance payments, as well as legal costs associated with worldwide litigation due to claims about unfair and wrongful termination (Shimizu & Wozniak, 2002; Maatman, 2000). Given these potential fines and litigation costs, as well as the significant expense of replacing an employee (often considered as much as three times the employee's annual salary), managers should do all they can to help correct the unacceptable performance of a particular employee, including honestly and carefully considering whether the PM processes themselves need improvement.

Phase 5: Conduct Performance Appraisal. Although still a relatively common practice worldwide, the formal, largely administrative process of performance appraisal (or performance review, evaluation) has been dropped by many organizations

(Schrøder-Hansen & Hansen, 2022). Patty McCord, former chief talent officer at Netflix, has criticized formal annual performance appraisals as pointless since performance feedback doesn't occur in a timely manner and the process appears to be more of a ritual rather than providing relevant content supporting performance improvement (McCord, 2014). Nevertheless, many MNEs continue with the regular performance appraisal process due to its administrative value and overall link to organizational effectiveness (e.g., providing data for decisions related to compensation, promotion, workforce planning; e.g., see Ali, Mahmood & Mehreen, 2019; Brefo-Manuh et al., 2017) yet have shifted their focus to include more aspects of mutual problem-solving, goal setting, and longer term professional development and career planning (Ebina & Joy, 2022, Goler et al., 2016; Buckingham & Goodall, 2015).

At an appointed time (e.g., after 6 months or a year of work—most formal performance appraisals are conducted on an annual basis), a formal performance appraisal is conducted regarding the employee's performance, with the primary purpose of enhancing future job performance. The data for evaluating the quality of the employee's past performance often come from various sources (i.e., direct supervisor, peers, subordinates, customers, employee's self-appraisal), although the most common source is the employee's direct supervisor. As with previous PM process interactions, this official and more formal discussion between supervisor and employee regarding the employee's performance over the past performance period (not just the most recent problematic incidents!) should involve two-way open communication, mutual trust and respect, and especially no blindsiding negative surprises for the employee, since until this point, there should have been regular, constructive feedback regarding the nature of the employee's performance. In addition to this discussion aimed at enhancing future job performance, many MNEs are finding success in terms of increased employee engagement and retention by using this dedicated performance appraisal time as an occasion for also discussing the employee's professional development and future career interests (Davies, Taylor & Savery, 2001; Fey & Bjorkman, 2001). For example, field researchers at a U.S.

Charles M. Vance and Torben Andersen

automotive company subsidiary in India noted the practice, as part of an annual performance appraisal process, of discussing with local Indian employees their future career interests and plans for professional development, including at times plans involving special leadership development expatriate assignments in nearby operations in China and Singapore (Dunnagan et al., 2013). This potentially productive exchange as part of a regular (e.g., annual) performance appraisal process allows the manager to give advice for useful preparation, internal and external networking, and developmental opportunities related to the future career interests identified by the employee.

Specifically related to the first box to the right of Phase 5 in Figure 2.1, at this final phase of the performance management process, results of the formal performance appraisal may indicate specific employee learning needs for improving future performance in the present job, as well as for employee development related to future advancement opportunities. In fact, an emphasis on employee development related to future beneficial career outcomes, rather than judgments about past performance, has been found to contribute to higher levels of employee satisfaction, productivity, and retention in multiple countries (Grant, 2008; Reiche, 2007). And as in Phase 4, this final phase can also lead to staffing decisions about possible employee continuation in the present job, transfer, termination, and promotion (see the second box to the right of Phase 5 in Figure 2.1). In addition, the performance appraisal data are often used as a basis for compensation decisions, increasingly common in MNEs following a general pay-for-performance policy (Bayo-Moriones & de la Torre, 2022). These decisions made, based on the appraisal data, regarding promotions and compensation can have a significant impact on subsequent employee engagement (Dutta, Kunal & Mishra, 2021). Finally, as represented by the arrow in Figure 2.1 pointing back to Phase 4, following the performance appraisal, there should be a continuation in the PM process of ongoing manager monitoring of employee performance and in providing feedback and support as needed in the PM relationship.

MNE CONVERGENCE TRENDS IN PM

Notwithstanding the significant influence of major local host country institutional context forces such as culture, the legal and political environments, and economic conditions, there is evidence that MNEs are in convergence toward hybridized PM systems and practices that differ from otherwise unique local norms (Schrøder-Hansen & Hansen, 2022; Ebina & Joy, 2022; Morley et al., 2021). With the previously discussed general PM process model in mind, we now examine recent converging trends in PM policies and practices by major MNEs related to more frequent and informal developmental performance feedback, more decentralized and flexible PM processes, increased technology integration and remote working arrangements, and PM systems characterized by increased trust and cooperation.

Frequent, Informal Developmental Performance Feedback

Although many MNEs are retaining their annual or semiannual formal employee performance appraisal systems, largely for their administrative value in making compensation and promotion decisions, there is a clear global PM trend toward more frequent, informal developmental feedback on employee performance (Ebina & Joy, 2022; Schrøder-Hansen & Hansen, 2022; Mosca, Curtis & Puches, 2022; Rivera et al., 2021). One recent study found that Indian employees identified frequent, continuous feedback as one of the most positive aspects of their performance management activities (Tripathi et al., 2021). Supporting this growing interest in immediate, frequent feedback are increasingly utilized crowdsourced feedback tools supported by mobile applications (apps) providing multisource, timely employee-solicited feedback for performance improvement and development (Schrøder-Hansen & Hansen, 2022; Cappelli & Travis, 2016).

Driving the increasing PM development emphasis is the growing agreement that MNEs should replace or supplement the traditional backward emphasis (i.e., past performance) involving periodic formal appraisal and regular feedback with a more future-oriented focus on employees' strengths and potential development opportunities (Morris, 2016; Ritchie, 2016). Beyond only a focus on correction in performance improvement, this regular feedback also recognizes the importance of current and longer term employee development, increasingly valued by new generations of workers (Venne & Hannay, 2018). In addition, many MNEs are shifting away from annual performance appraisal

Charles M. Vance and Torben Andersen

ranking approaches, which focus on comparisons among employees, to more frequent absolute rating approaches that provide employee performance feedback that can be more easily linked to development goals (Cappelli & Travis, 2016; Buckingham, & Goodall, 2015).

More Decentralized, Flexible PM Processes

For effective PM in our rapidly changing global work environment characterized by increased volatility, uncertainty, complexity, and ambiguity (VUCA), decentralization and greater flexibility are needed for effective employee work performance goal setting and agility in meeting changing demands (Gofen & Gassner, 2022; Soni, 2022; D'Amato & Banfi, 2021). Rather than following a traditional top-down process of cascading goals, the responsibility for ensuring a link between the employees' individual performance goals and the MNE's strategic plans appears to be becoming more decentralized and more frequently involving the less formal planning and problem-solving efforts between local managers and employees with MNE strategic plans in view (Natukunda, 2022). These open, two-way, more informal communication PM interactions also provide the opportunity for employees to inform their managers of work conditions and local business environment changes that might arise, requiring additional managerial support or a change in work performance expectations (Berdicchia, Bracci & Masino, 2022). Thus, this decentralized approach has the potential to increase adaptability and flexibility in the use of PM goals (Schrøder-Hansen & Hansen, 2022).

Technology Integration and Remote Work Arrangements

Even before the 2020 global onset of the COVID-19 pandemic, there was a major increase in use of remote working arrangements supported by the integration of digitalization and technological advancements in telecommunications (Manyika, 2012), presenting new PM challenges and opportunities. With their experience during the pandemic with greater remote work flexibility, employees worldwide are hesitant to return to the same degree of less flexible, in-person supervised working arrangements, creating new leadership demands in remotely managing employee performance and increasing the focus more on employee performance outcomes and results and less on mere behavior

(Groves & Feyerherm, 2022; Soga et al., 2022; Barabaschi et al., 2022; Adler, 2021; Tziner & Rabenu, 2021). Sarthak Raychaudhuri, vice president of human resources, Asia, Whirlpool Corporation, described a major new PM development with the rise of remote work arrangements: "As goals need to be more sharply defined, focus will shift from measuring effort to measuring results on a regular basis" (Verma, 2020).

Technology advancements also are providing useful tools to support the PM process, such as in the application of gamification to enhance employee motivation and engagement (Silic & Lowry, 2020), the use of crowdsourcing in obtaining timely, multisource performance feedback, and convenient data entry systems for supervisors for entering regular notes on employee perfor- mance to provide a much more balanced picture in evaluating employee performance for the total performance period (Cascio & Montealegre, 2016; Mosley, 2013). With the mentioned growing trend in global PM favoring regular, timely performance feedback for all employees, away from relying primarily on annual formal performance evaluation, employees working remotely are able to benefit from enhanced engagement from visual PM systems providing a relatively rich, regular source of communications sup- porting supervisor–employee virtual interactions (Bititci, Cocca & Ates, 2016).

MNE-assigned expatriates in particular are benefitting from advancements in global telecommunications. Despite their distant separation from back-home supervisors, they are able to readily and conveniently use videoconferencing technologies such as Zoom and Microsoft Teams to support regular management feedback, coaching, and advisement, as well as easily include the same-culture home country supervisor in the formal performance evaluation process, thus not depending only on a local host country supervisor who may appraise expatriate performance through a very different cultural lens (Bader et al., 2021; Kossek, et al., 2017). Despite the remote geographic distance, these improvements in virtual communication technology can allow for regular timely and highly desired performance-enhancing "soft" control mechanisms (i.e., close interpersonal interactions involving regular feedback, coaching, and mentoring) in expatriate and

Charles M. Vance and Torben Andersen

other global employee PM rather than rely only on the traditional "hard" distant PM control components of more abstract goal-setting and annual formal performance appraisal (Fee, McGrath-Champ & Yang, 2011).

Trust and Cooperation

It is increasingly recognized that the effectiveness of performance appraisals and the overall PM system is influenced by employee perceptions of confidence and trust in the appraisal process and in the relationship with the direct supervisor, particularly involving intercultural interactions (Baird, Sophia & Nuhu, 2022; Wang & Varma, 2018; Pichler et al., 2016; Varma, Budhwar & Pichler, 2011). Perceptions of the fairness of their and others' treatment in the various parts of the PM process are critical in achieving employee motivation and work engagement and in their desire to achieve personal development and work improvement goals (Goler, Gale & Grant, 2016). Rather than continuing their use of complex, MNE-wide standardized measures, many organizations are enhancing perceptions of trust and fairness (among supervisors and their employees) by implementing performance appraisals that are simplified and more customized to the local context, with fewer measures and more action-oriented dimensions and feedback sources to enhance transparency and credibility (Murphy, 2020; Bracken, Rose & Church, 2016; Buckingham & Goodall, 2015). One study found that a Western MNE's standardized appraisal system was quite unsuccessful in generating trust and perceptions of fairness when applied in a business subsidiary in China, and concluded that customization to fit distinct cultural values and norms should be carefully considered when applying to foreign operation contexts (Chen & Eldridge, 2010).

Several MNEs are dropping the use of employee performance comparison ranking measures that they believe only encourage self-serving behavior and discourage workplace cooperation, and are adding rating measures that include the assessment of employee cooperation with other employees and work units (Schrøder-Hansen & Hansen, 2022; Buckingham & Goodall, 2015). To illustrate, Accenture now utilizes individual rating measures that emphasize the importance of an employee's contribution to their team and to the company as a whole rather than making employee comparisons and peer rankings (Stone et al., 2019). In a similar manner, in its performance appraisal measures and overall PM processes, Microsoft now emphasizes that employee performance also involves influence and quality of contribution to colleagues' performance and the overall results of Microsoft (Ritchie, 2016). There also is increased effort to build the quality of the working relationship and intercultural understanding between supervisors and employees (e.g., through cross-cultural awareness training) to increase employee trust and confidence in the feedback and coaching and ultimate appraisal in the ongoing PM process (Baird, Sophia & Nuhu, 2022; Varma et al., 2021; Wang & Varma, 2018).

FINAL MNE DIVERGENCE CONSIDERATIONS FOR LOCAL PM APPLICATION

An essential consideration on the potential need for PM system local adaptation is the external context, which consists of the institutional structures (including national culture) of the societies in which MNEs operate (Paik, Chow & Vance, 2011). External cultural factors relate to the predominant norms, values, practices, and beliefs held by the national culture. Cultural elements, including language, impact all areas of management and employee behavior and cognition, including beliefs and perceptions, involved in the PM process (Cheng & Cascio, 2009). Several recent studies have provided evidence of the influence of various dimensions of international culture (e.g., indulgence, masculinity, individualism, collectivism, uncertainty avoidance, power distance) on different PM processes and outcomes (Prajogo et al., 2022; Behery, 2022; Yahiaoui, Nakhle & Farndale, 2021; Harahap, 2021; Lockhart, Nusrat & Bhanugopan, 2020; Abane & Boon-Anan, 2020). Even the basic, common PM process of feedback can differ in preference for delivery and reception in individualistic and collectivistic societies (Cascio, 2006). Furthermore, MNEs in many countries operate in increasingly cosmopolitan environments, with employees from quite diverse within-country cultures (Gerhart & Fang, 2005), and from different countries working together in the same work unit. Within this very diverse work environment, there may be significant cultural differences in willingness and receptivity to the basic PM activity of giving and receiving feedback. Having

Charles M. Vance and Torben Andersen

cultural versatility and sensitivity to these cultural differences in such diverse contexts will be increasingly critical for managers in achieving PM success (Behery, 2022).

Other external structure contextual factors that can have a huge impact on PM policies and practices include local government regulations and legislation, the level of economic development, the dominant industry sectors, and union influence. For example, local unions that prioritize seniority in employee rewards may obstruct MNEs' efforts to implement a pay-for-performance reward policy in their PM system. Notwithstanding the economic advantages of standardization and the general trends toward global convergence discussed here, MNEs should not automatically assume that their effective home country PM policies and practices are readily appropriate for implementation in their foreign operations but should continually consider and review the need to adapt their PM systems to better fit local conditions (Natukunda, 2022; Morley et al., 2021; Chen & Eldridge, 2010).

Nevertheless, this periodic review across the MNE and at local operations should consider standardization and convergence opportunities through host country workforce training toward a unifying corporate mindset and in best practices that are widely embraced by the MNE (van Bakel et al., 2022). In addition, it should be acknowledged that local cultural influences that might have had a significant presence in the past may no longer be in effect, especially for younger generation employees who have had heavy regular exposure to the converging influences of the internet (Klein & Sharma, 2022; Venne & Hannay, 2018). For example, contrary to a widely held Asian stereotype related to saving face, younger generation Chinese workers have expressed dissatisfaction in not receiving preferred timely, direct, and frank feedback supporting performance improvement from their older Chinese managers, who instead mistakenly prefer to use an assumed, much-delayed yet face-saving indirect feedback approach through the nature of resulting employee pay increases and performance bonuses (e.g., see Cheng & Cascio, 2009). Therefore, both at the MNE headquarters and the local operation level, MNE leaders and managers alike should be continually vigilant of the often shifting, dynamic patterns of convergence and divergence and the attending opportunities and challenges they provide to ensure the ongoing effectiveness of their PM practices and policies (DeNisi et al., 2021).

REFERENCES

Abane, J. A., & Boon-Anan, P. (2020). The determinants of performance management outcomes in public organizations in sub-Saharan Africa: The role of national culture and organizational subcultures. *Public Organization Review*, *20*(3), 511–527.

Adler, S. (2021). Performance management in the year of COVID-19: Carpe diem. *Industrial and Organizational Psychology*, *14*(1–2), 168–172.

Ali, Z., Mahmood, B., & Mehreen, A. (2019). Linking succession planning to employee performance: The mediating roles of career development and performance appraisal. *Australian Journal of Career Development*, *28*(2), 112–121.

Bader, A. K., Bader, B., Froese, F. J., & Sekiguchi, T. (2021). One way or another? An international comparison of expatriate performance management in multinational companies. *Human Resource Management*, *60*(5), 737–752.

Baird, K., Sophia, X. S., & Nuhu, N. (2022). The mediating role of fairness on the effectiveness of strategic performance measurement systems. *Personnel Review*, *51*(5), 1491–1517.

Barabaschi, B., Barbieri, L., Cantoni, F., Platoni, S., & Virtuani, R. (2022). Remote working in Italian SMEs during COVID-19: Learning challenges of a new work organization. *Journal of Workplace Learning*, *34*(6), 497–512.

Bayo-Moriones, A., & de la Torre, R. (2022). Analysing the relationship between QM, performance appraisal and pay for performance. *Total Quality Management & Business Excellence*, *33*(9–10), 1056–1083.

Behery, M. (2022). Single-rating, multi-rating 360° performance management and organizational outcomes: Evidence from the UAE. *International Journal of Organizational Analysis*, *30*(1), 47–83.

Berdicchia, D., Bracci, E., & Masino, G. (2022). Performance management systems promote job crafting: The role of employees' motivation. *Personnel Review*, *51*(3), 861–875.

Bernthal, P. R., Rogers, R. W. & Smith, A. B. (2003). *Managing performance: Building accountability for organizational success*. Pittsburgh, PA: Development Dimensions International.

Beuren, I. M., dos Santos, V., & Bernd, D. C. (2022). Effects of using the management control system on individual performance with the intervenience of feedforward and organizational learning. *Journal of Knowledge Management*, *26*(4), 1042–1060.

Bititci, U., Cocca, P., & Ates, A. (2016). Impact of visual performance management systems on the performance management practices of organisations. *International Journal of Production Research*, *54* (6), 1571–1593.

Bracken, D. W., Rose, D. S. & Church, A. H. (2016). The evolution and devolution of 360° degree feedback. *Industrial and Organizational Psychology*, *9*(4), 761–794.

Brefo-Manuh, A. B., Bonsu, C. A., Anlesinya, A., & Odoi, A. A. S. (2017). Evaluating the relationship between performance appraisal and organizational effectiveness in Ghana: A comparative analysis of public and private organizations. *International Journal of Economics, Commerce and Management*, *5*(7), 532–552.

Buckingham, M., & Goodall, A. (2015). Reinventing performance management. *Harvard Business Review*, *93*(4), 40–50.

Budhwar, P. S., Varma, A., & Patel, C. (2016). Convergence-divergence of HRM in the Asia-Pacific: Context-specific analysis and future research agenda. *Human Resource Management Review*, *26*(4), 311–326.

Cappelli, P. & Travis, A. (2016). The performance management revolution. *Harvard Business Review*, *94*(10), 58–67.

Cascio, W. F., & Montealegre, R. (2016). How technology is changing work and organizations. *Annual Review of Organizational Psychology and Organizational Behavior*, *3*(1), 349–375.

Cascio, W. F. (2006). Global performance management systems. In Stahl, G. K. & Bjorkman, I. (eds.), *Handbook of Research in International Human Resource Management* (pp. 176–196). Cheltenham, UK: Edward Elgar Publishing.

Cascio, W. F., & Bernardin, H. J. (1981). Implications of performance appraisal litigation for personnel decisions. *Personnel Psychology*, *34*(2), 211–226.

Chen, J., & Eldridge, D. (2010). Are "standardized performance appraisal practices" really preferred? A case study in China. *Chinese Management Studies*, *4*(3), 244–257.

Cheng, K. H., & Cascio, W. F. (2009). Performance-appraisal beliefs of Chinese employees in Hong Kong and the Pearl River Delta. *International Journal of Selection and Assessment*, *17*(3), 329–333.

Chiang, F. F., Lemański, M. K., & Birtch, T. A. (2017). The transfer and diffusion of HRM practices within MNCs: lessons learned and future research directions. *The International Journal of Human Resource Management*, *28*(1), 234–258.

Claus, L., Baker, S., & Vermeulen, P. (2020). *Be(Come) an Awesome Manager: The Essential Toolkit for Impact Leadership Paperback*, Second Edition, Joseph, OR: Global Immersion Press.

Claus, L. (ed.), (2013). *Global HR Practitioner Handbook*. Silverton, OR: Global Immersion Press. Volume 3.

Claus, L., & Hand, M. L. (2009). Customization decisions regarding performance management systems of multinational companies: An empirical view of Eastern European firms. *International Journal of Cross-Cultural Management*, *9*(2), 237–258

D'Amato, V., & Banfi, A. (2021). Is performance appraisal still performing? *International Journal of Business Performance Management*, *22*(4), 443–460.

Davies, D., Taylor, R., & Savery, L. (2001). The role of appraisal, remuneration and training in improving staff relations in the Western Australian accommodation industry: A comparative study. *Journal of European Industrial Training* *25*(6/7), 366–373.

DeNisi, A., Murphy, K., Varma, A., & Budhwar, P. (2021). Performance management systems and multinational enterprises: Where we are and where we should go. *Human Resource Management*, *60*(5), 707–713.

Douthitt, S., & Mondore, S. (2014). Creating a business-focused HR function with analytics and integrated talent management. *People and Strategy*, *36*(4), 16–21.

Dunnagan, K., Maragakis, M., Schneiderjohn, N., Turner, C., & Vance, C. M. (2013). Meeting the global imperative of local leadership talent development in Hong Kong, Singapore, and India. *Global Business and Organizational Excellence*, *32*(2), 52–60.

Dutta, D., Kunal, K. K., & Mishra, S. K. (2021). Unintended consequences of promotions: Importance of annual incentives for performance management systems. *Human Resource Management*, *60*(5), 787–801.

Ebina, J. M. A., & Joy, M. M. (2022). Managing the most important asset: A twenty-year review on the performance management literature. *Journal of Management History*, *28*(3), 428–451.

Edwards, T., Tregaskis, O., & McDonnell, A. (2022). Towards an understanding of configurational and national influences on international integration in the HR function in MNCs. *The International Journal of Human Resource Management*, *33*(7), 1463–1488.

Fee, A., McGrath-Champ, S., & Yang, X. (2011). Expatriate performance management and firm internationalization: Australian multinationals in China. *Asia Pacific Journal of Human Resources*, *49*(3), 365–384.

Fey, C. F., & Bjorkman, I. (2001). The effect of human resource management practices on MNC subsidiary performance in Russia. *Journal of International Business Studies, 32*(1), 59–75.

Garengo, P., Sardi, A., & Nudurupati, S.S. (2002). Human resource management (HRM) in the performance measurement and management (PMM) domain: A bibliometric review. *International Journal of Productivity and Performance Management, 71*(7), 3056–3077.

Gerhart, B., & Fang, M. (2005). National culture and human resource management: Assumptions and evidence. *International Journal of Human Resource Management, 16*(6), 971–986.

Gofen, A, & Gassner, D. (2022). Delegating power? Performance management from a process perspective. *Governance, 35*(2), 365–384.

Goler, L., Gale, J., & Grant, A. (2016). Let's not kill performance evaluations yet. *Harvard Business Review, 94*(11), 90–94.

Grant, E. A. (2008). How to retain talent in India. *Sloan Management Review 50*(1), 6–7.

Groves, K. S., & Feyerherm, A. E. (2022). Developing a leadership potential model for the new era of work and organizations. *Leadership & Organization Development Journal, 43*(6), 978–998.

Hansen, A. (2021). The purposes of performance management systems and processes: A cross- functional typology. *International Journal of Operations and Production Management, 41*(8), 1249–1271.

Harahap, R. M. (2021). Integrating organisational- and individual-level performance management systems (PMSS): A case study in a large Indonesian public sector organisation. *Qualitative Research in Accounting and Management, 18*(4), 417–454.

Hussain, A., & Khan, S. (2013). International marketing strategy: Standardization versus adaptation. *Management and Administrative Sciences Review, 2*(4), 353–359.

Hsu, M., Hsin, Y., & Shiue, F. (2022). Business analytics for corporate risk management and performance improvement. *Annals of Operations Research, 315*(2), 629–669.

Kadak, T., & Laitinen, E. K. (2021). How different types of performance management systems affect organizational performance? *Measuring Business Excellence, 25*(3), 315–327.

Kakkar, S., Dash, S., Vohra, N., & Saha, S. (2020). Engaging employees through effective performance management: An empirical examination. *Benchmarking, 27*(5), 1843–1860.

Klein, A., & Sharma, V. M. (2022). Cultural perspectives of millennials' decision-making styles in online group buying. *Journal of International Consumer Marketing, 34*(4), 357–379.

Kossek, E. E., Huang, J. L., Piszczek, M. M., Fleenor, J. W., & Ruderman, M. (2017). Rating expatriate leader effectiveness in multisource feedback systems: Cultural distance and hierarchical effects. *Human Resource Management, 56*(1), 151–172.

Locke, E. A. & Latham, G. P. (eds.) (2013). *Developments in Goal Setting and Task Performance*. London: Routledge.

Lockhart, P., Nusrat, K. S., & Bhanugopan, R. (2020). Do organisational culture and national culture mediate the relationship between high-performance human resource management practices and organisational citizenship behaviour? *International Journal of Manpower, 41*(8), 1179–1197.

Maatman, Jr., G. L. (ed.). (2000). *Worldwide Guide to Termination, Employment Discrimination, and Workplace Harassment Laws*. Riverwoods, IL: CCH/Baker and McKenzie.

McCord, P. (2014). How Netflix reinvented HR. *Harvard Business Review*, January–February, 3–8.

McKinsey & Company (May 2021). Grabbing hold of the new future of work, *Organizational Practice*.

Maja, V. K., Serafini, G. O., & Szamosi, L.T. (2022). Integrating training and performance management of civil aviation inspectors: A pilot study of the mediating role of competency-based training. *International Journal of Training & Development, 26*(1), 29–54.

Moran, R. T., Harris, P. R., & Moran, S. (2010). *Managing cultural differences.* London: Routledge.

Morley, M. J., Murphy, K. R., Cleveland, J. N., Heraty, N., & McCarthy, J. (2021). Home and host distal context and performance appraisal in multinational enterprises: A 22 country study. *Human Resource Management, 60*(5), 715–736.

Morris, D. (2016). Death to the performance review: how Adobe reinvented performance management and transformed its business. *World at Work Journal, 25*(2), 25–34.

Mosca, J. B., Curtis, K., & Puches, L. (2022). Annual performance appraisals are replaced with the coaching and leadership of employees. *The Journal of Business Diversity, 22*(1), 1–9.

Mosley, E. (2013). The power of the crowdsourced performance review. *Compensation & Benefits Review, 45*(6), 320–323.

Murphy, K. R. (2020). Performance evaluation will not die, but it should. *Human Resource Management Journal, 30*(1), 13–31.

Natukunda, L. (2022). Communitarian norms and employee performance management in Africa. *Employee Relations, 44*(2), 477–492.

Nda, M. M., & Fard, R. Y. (2013). The impact of employee training and development on employee productivity. *Global Journal of Commerce and Management Perspective, 2*(6), 91–93.

Nickson, H. O. (2021). Performance management perception in Kenya. *Social Responsibility Journal, 17*(6), 795–814.

Onkelinx, J., Manolova, T. S., & Edelman, L. F. (2016). The human factor: Investments in employee human capital, productivity, and SME internationalization. *Journal of International Management, 22*(4), 351–364.

Paik, Y., Chow, I., & Vance, C. M. (2011). Interaction effects of globalization and institutional forces on international HRM practice: Illuminating the convergence-divergence debate. *Thunderbird International Business Review, 53*(5), 647–659.

Petricevic, O., & Teece, D. J. (2019). The structural reshaping of globalization: Implications for strategic sectors, profiting from innovation, and the multinational enterprise. *Journal of International Business Studies, 50*(9), 1487–1512.

Pichler, S., Varma, A., Michel, J. S., Levy, P. E., Budhwar, P. S., & Sharma, A. (2016). Leader-member exchange, group- and individual-level procedural justice and reactions to performance appraisals. *Human Resource Management, 55*(5), 871–883.

Prajogo, D., Mena, C., Cooper, B. and Teh, P. (2022). The Roles of National Culture in Affecting Quality Management Practices and Quality Performance: Multilevel and multi-country analysis. *International Journal of Operations & Production Management, 42*(7), 877–897.

Reiche, B.S. (2007). The effect of international staffing practices on subsidiary staff retention in multinational corporations. *International Journal of Human Resource Management, 18*(4), 523–536.

Ritchie, J. (2016). Transforming a company: How Microsoft's new employee performance system supports its business and cultural transformation. *World at Work Journal, 25*(2), 61–75.

Rivera, M., Qiu, L., Kumar, S., & Petrucci, T. (2021). Are traditional performance reviews outdated? An empirical analysis on continuous, real-time feedback in the workplace. *Information Systems Research, 32*(2), 517–540.

Schrøder-Hansen, K. & Hansen, A. (2022). Performance management trends: Reflections on the redesigns big companies have been doing lately. *International Journal of Productivity and Performance Management*, https://www.emerald.com/insight/1741-0401.htm.

Shimizu, T., & Wozniak, L. (2002). Termination of employment in Asia. *Benefits and Compensation International, 32*(4), 16–22.

Silic, M., & Lowry, P. B. (2020). Using design-science based gamification to improve organizational security training and compliance. *Journal of Management Information Systems, 37*(1), 129–161.

Soga, L., Bolade-Ogunfodun, Y., Islam, N., & Amankwah-Amoah, J. (2022). Relational power is the new currency of hybrid work. *MIT Sloan Management Review, 63*(4), 1–3.

Soni, A. (2022). Trends in performance management system: A study of Indian service provider companies. *Global Business Review, 23*(2), 479–492.

Stone, T. H., Jawahar, I. M., Johnson, G., & Foster, J. (2019). Cutting-edge performance management innovations: What do we know? *World at Work Journal, 28*(2), 26–44.

Tripathi, R., Thite, M., Varma, A., & Mahapatra, G. (2021). Appraising the revamped performance management system in Indian IT multinational enterprises: The employees' perspective. *Human Resource Management, 60*(5), 825–838.

Tziner, A., & Rabenu, E. (2021). The COVID-19 pandemic: A challenge to performance appraisal. *Industrial and Organizational Psychology, 14*(1–2), 173–177.

van Bakel, M. S., Vaiman, V., Vance, C. M., & Haslberger, A. (2022). Broadening international mentoring: Contexts and dynamics of expatriate and HCN intercultural mentoring. *Journal of Global Mobility, 10*(1), 14–35.

Van Thielen, T., Decramer, A., Vanderstraeten, A., & Audenaert, M. (2022). The effects of performance management on relational coordination in policing: The roles of content and process. *International Journal of Human Resource Management, 33*(7), 1377–1402.

Vance, C. M., & Paik, Y. (2014). *Managing a Global Workforce: Challenges and Opportunities in International Human Resource Management* (3rd ed.). London: Routledge.

Vance, C. M., & Paik, Y. (2005). Forms of host country national learning for enhanced MNC absorptive capacity. *Journal of Managerial Psychology, 20*(7), 590–606.

Vance, C. M., & Ensher, E. A. (2002) The voice of the host country workforce: A key source for improving the effectiveness of expatriate training and performance. *International Journal of Intercultural Relations, 26*, 447–461.

Varma, A., Budhwar, P., and Pichler, S. (2011). Chinese host country nationals' willingness to help expatriates: The role of social categorization. *Thunderbird International Business Review 53*(3), 353–364.

Varma, A., Zilic, I., Katou, A., Blajic, B., & Jukic, N. (2021). Supervisor-subordinate relationships and employee performance appraisals: A multi-source investigation in croatia. *Employee Relations, 43*(1), 45–62.

Venne, R. A., & Hannay, M. (2018). Generational change, the modern workplace and performance appraisal: Why changing workplaces need a developmental approach to performance appraisal. *American Journal of Management, 18*(5), 88–102.

Verma, P. (2020, Oct 13). Work Culture in COVID: Pandemic alters the performance appraisal system. *The Economic Times*

Wang, C., & Varma, A. (2018). A process model of how interpersonal interaction leads to effectiveness of the expatriate-host country national relationship. *Cross Cultural & Strategic Management, 25*(4), 670–689.

Yahiaoui, D., Nakhle, S. F., & Farndale, E. (2021). Culture and performance appraisal in multinational enterprises: Implementing French headquarters' practices in Middle East and North Africa subsidiaries. *Human Resource Management, 60*(5), 771–785.

Motivation and Performance Management

Biyun Hu and Liang Meng

Chapter 3

INTRODUCTION

Performance management is the process by which managers engage employees to achieve higher performance and ensure employees' outputs are aligned with the strategic goals of the organization. There are six steps involved in the performance management process, including (1) defining performance outcomes and goals for departments or divisions, (2) developing performance goals and behaviors for individual employees, (3) providing continuous performance-related support and discussions, (4) evaluating employee performance, (5) identifying training and development needs to improve employee performance, and (6) informing consequences for reaching or failing to reach performance goals. Again, the ultimate goal of the six steps is to help organizations achieve their strategic goals and gain competitive advantages.

An essential factor that underpins performance management is employee motivation (Armstrong, 1994). Motivation refers to "a set of energetic forces that originate both within as well as beyond

DOI: 10.4324/9781003306849-3

an individual's being, to initiate work-related behavior, and to determine its form, direction, intensity, and duration" (Pinder, 2008, p. 11). When we refer to a focal employee as being highly motivated, we mean that this employee is trying hard to perform a certain task and is willing to keep up the hard work until the task is accomplished. Not surprisingly, numerous studies have demonstrated that high levels of motivation lead to high job performance (Cerasoli, Nicklin, & Ford, 2014; Van Iddekinge, Aguinis, Mackey, & DeOrtentiis, 2018). Given the importance of employee motivation, it is critical for managers to understand and apply motivation theories so as to implement the performance management system effectively.

In this chapter, we first introduce several relevant theories of work motivation that we then develop the overall motivation model from. We then elaborate on how organizations and managers can use motivation theories to enhance employee motivation and productivity through performance management. We conclude with a case study to help readers apply the knowledge covered in this chapter.

THEORIES OF WORK MOTIVATION
Need-Based Theories of Work Motivation

A need is "a hypothetical concept which stands for a force ... in the brain region, a force which organizes perception, apperception, intellection, conation and action in such a way as to transform in a certain direction an existing unsatisfying situation" (Murray, 1938, pp. 124–125). This definition highlights that a need is a hypothetical entity that drives people's attitudes and behaviors. Indeed, the earliest theories of motivation were developed to understand what employees need, and how to motivate employees to work hard by fulfilling their needs. Maslow's hierarchy of needs, Alderfer's ERG model, Herzberg's motivation-hygiene theory, and McClelland's three needs theory, as well as self-determination theory, are all notably examples of needs-based theories of work motivation.

Maslow's hierarchy of needs is based on the assumption that human needs are ranked hierarchically, from the most basic needs—physiological needs—to safety needs, social needs, esteem needs, and, finally, the highest level of the hierarchy, the need for self-actualization (Maslow, 1943, 1954). Physiological needs include needs for food, drink, shelter, and sleep. Organizations can help fulfill employees' physiological needs by providing a base salary, reasonable work hours, and a comfortable physical workspace (Schermerhorn, 2001). Safety needs include the needs for security and freedom from fear, pain, and danger. Employers may fulfill employees' safety needs by offering fringe benefits and job security, as well as ensuring a safe work environment (Schermerhorn, 2001). Social needs represent one's desire to be accepted and loved by others. Needs for friendship, intimacy, and attachment are examples of social needs. Team activities, pleasant supervisors, and interactions with clients can help satisfy employees' social needs in the workplace (Schermerhorn, 2001). Esteem needs represent one's desire for a positive self-image, as well as respect and recognition from others. Employees' esteem needs can be fulfilled when employers appreciate their efforts, provide promotion opportunities, and/or delegate them more responsibilities and authority (Schermerhorn, 2001). Finally, the need for self-actualization represents one's desire to achieve their full potential and become the best self they can be. Organizations can help fulfill the need for self-actualization by providing work autonomy, optimally challenging work, and opportunities for training, development, and growth. According to Maslow, as a lower level need gets reasonably satisfied, a higher level need will become increasingly important and dominant in motivating one's behaviors.

Alderfer's ERG model is a modification of Maslow's hierarchy of needs (Alderfer, 1969). Instead of five hierarchical needs, Alderfer (1969) grouped basic human needs into three categories, including existence, relatedness, and growth. Existence is similar to Maslow's physiological and safety needs; relatedness is similar to social needs; and growth is similar to the needs for esteem and self-actualization. However, different from Maslow's hierarchy of needs, Alderfer's ERG model does not rank needs into a hierarchical order. Instead, it recognizes that two or more needs can coexist and shape people's behaviors. Moreover, the ERG model has a "frustration-regression" hypothesis, such that when one is frustrated in fulfilling a particular need (e.g., relatedness needs), they may regress to satisfy another need (e.g., existence needs).

Herzberg's motivation-hygiene theory is also known as the two-factor theory. Based on interviews with engineers and accountants, Herzberg et al. (1959) found that job satisfaction is not at the opposite end of job dissatisfaction on a single spectrum, because factors that satisfy employees were very different from factors that dissatisfy them. Herzberg refers to the factors that contribute to employee job satisfaction as motivators, such as achievement, interesting work, responsibility, and growth, all of which are intrinsic to the job. In contrast, Herzberg labels factors causing job dissatisfaction as hygiene factors. Company policy, the relationship with supervisors, working conditions, and salary are representative hygiene factors, and they are extrinsic to the job itself.

McClelland's three needs theory, also known as the acquired-needs theory, is proposed by David McClelland (1961). According to this theory, all individuals acquire three types of needs, including the need for achievement, the need for affiliation, and the need for power, as a result of their past experiences. But due to different backgrounds and life experiences, people may possess one or more dominant needs that vary. Individuals who possess a high need for achievement are motivated by accomplishment and success. As such, they prefer to work on tasks of moderate difficulty and value feedback that can help them better achieve their goals. Those who have a high need for affiliation desire to be accepted and liked by others. Thus, they prefer working in a team and interacting with colleagues. Finally, individuals possessing a high need for power enjoy competition, winning, and being in power and are motivated by influencing other people and controlling their own surrounding environment.

Self-determination theory (SDT) is formulated with an empirical approach and has gained much empirical support from both laboratory experiments and field studies (e.g., Baard, Deci, & Ryan, 2004; Deci, Ryan, Gagné, Leone, Usunov, & Kornazheva, 2001; Gagné, Ryan, & Bargmannm, 2003; Reis, Sheldon, Gable, Roscoe, & Ryan, 2000). SDT differentiates autonomous motivation from controlled motivation. Autonomous motivation represents engaging in a behavior either because it is interesting or because its value has been integrated within one's self. With high autonomous motivation, people tend to put more effort into their jobs, be more persistent, and thus achieve higher task performance (Gagné & Deci, 2005). Controlled motivation, on the contrary, refers to the driving forces of external (e.g., rewards and punishment) or internal (e.g., to feel worthy, not ashamed, guilty, or anxious) pressures (Gagné & Deci, 2005). Unlike autonomous motivation, controlled motivation is barely associated with superior performance, especially performance requiring complexity, flexibility, and creativity (Gagné & Deci, 2005; Koestner, Otis, Powers, Pelletier, & Gagnon, 2008). SDT also suggests that need satisfaction, including satisfaction of the needs for autonomy, competence, and relatedness, provides necessary nutriments for autonomous motivation to function optimally (Gagné & Deci, 2005). In other words, SDT presumes autonomous motivation as an outcome resulting from need satisfaction and environmental factors that can afford need satisfaction (Gagné & Deci, 2005).

To summarize, need-based theories of work motivation propose that individuals are motivated to behave to meet their needs. Guided by these theories, it is important for managers to identify the (dominant) needs of each employee and fulfill those needs by providing proper rewards, adjusting leadership styles, and improving the work environment. However, on one hand, it is usually difficult to provide customized resources to satisfy each employee's needs, and on the other hand, employees may attend to other factors (e.g., equity perceptions) when deciding how to behave at work. In the next section, we discuss process-based theories of work motivation, which focus on explaining the thought processes that underlie one's behaviors.

PROCESS-BASED THEORIES OF WORK MOTIVATION

Process-based theories of work motivation view motivation more as a rational process than some actions aiming to satisfy one's needs. Equity theory and expectancy theory are both notable examples of process-based theories of work motivation.

Equity theory suggests that people's motivation is affected by a sense of fairness. Individuals tend to mentally compare the ratios of their inputs and outcomes to the perceived ratios of others (e.g., colleagues). They would perceive fairness if they believe that the input-to-outcome ratios are proportional (Adams, 1965).

In contrast, if one perceives to be under-rewarded, they might reduce their input (e.g., work effort) to decrease the inequity and restore the balance (Carrell & Dittrich, 1978). In work settings, inputs include all contributions that an employee makes to their organization, such as their education level, skills, experience, and work effort. Outcomes could be any rewards that one receives from their organization, such as pay, benefits, job status, satisfying supervision, and rewards intrinsic to the job (Adams, 1965). Research has shown that the more value an employee places on a particular outcome, the stronger the effects of fairness perceptions involving that outcome will be on the employee's job satisfaction and turnover intentions (Hu & Han, 2021).

Equity theory focuses only on one's perceived fairness of allocation outcomes, or distributive justice (Cook & Hegtvedt, 1983). Employees' fairness perceptions and subsequent behaviors, however, are also affected by the processes that lead to decision/resource allocation (i.e., procedural justice; Leventhal, 1980), as well as whether they are being treated with politeness, respect, and dignity during the processes (i.e., interactional justice; Bies & Moag, 1986). These three dimensions of justice are correlated with each other and are considered as main compositions of organizational justice (Colquitt, 2001; Colquitt, Scott, Rodell, Long, Zapata, Conlon, & Wesson, 2013). Research has shown that both procedural justice and interactional justice significantly affect employees' organizational commitment, task performance, and citizenship behavior (Colquitt et al., 2013). Furthermore, the adverse influence of distributive injustice on employee work behaviors will be weakened if employees believe that the procedures leading to the unfair outcomes are justifiable and/or when they are treated with kindness and respect during the interactions (Skarlicki & Folger, 1997).

Expectancy theory is a well-accepted theory that has gained fairly wide research attention in the past 50 years (e.g., Porter & Woo, 2015; Steers & Mowday, 1977). Expectancy theory states that the level of effort one exerts is determined by their beliefs about (1) the extent to which high levels of effort will lead to good performance (i.e., expectancy), (2) the degree to which good performance will be rewarded (i.e., instrumentality), and (3) the extent to which the rewards are personally attractive and desirable (i.e., valence; Vroom, 1964).

First, one will be more motivated to put forth effort if they believe that they can achieve high performance through hard work. A range of factors may contribute to employees' expectancy perceptions, including employees' abilities, skills, knowledge, the support and resources that they have access to, and personality traits, including self-efficacy and locus of control. For instance, when an employee is assigned a task that is far beyond their ability, their motivation level will suffer because they think they will not be able to complete the task no matter how hard they try. Or, if an employee lacks the necessary resources or equipment tools to achieve high performance, they may simply withhold their effort. Similarly, when an employee has an external locus of control (i.e., a general expectancy that performance is dependent on uncontrollable factors such as luck), or low self-efficacy (i.e., not confident in their ability), expectancy is likely to be low. Thus, organizations wishing to strengthen employees' expectancy perceptions can benefit from a variety of practices, such as delegating tasks with moderate difficulty levels, providing continuous feedback to help employees improve their performance, and offering training opportunities to improve their knowledge and skills. Apart from expectancy, one will be motivated to put more effort when they believe high performance will lead to rewards. As such, it is important for organizations to link rewards to performance and make sure employees are aware of the connections. Finally, employees are more likely to be motivated when the rewards associated with high performance are personally attractive. If a high-performing employee values work–life balance and hopes to get a weeklong paid vacation but the organization rewarded them with more responsibilities and authority instead, this employee might find the reward undesirable (i.e., the valence is negative) and might withhold efforts in the future. Therefore, managers are advised to find out what their employees value via surveying them or talking to them directly. It might also be a good idea if employees have the option to choose the rewards that appeal to them among several equivalent ones.

To summarize, the basic premise of process-based theories of work motivation is that employee motivation is a rational process – employees cognitively process their surrounding environment, and react in certain ways to maximize the expected payoff. It is worth noting that equity theory and expectancy theory are particularly useful to help organizations motivate employees through performance management.

GOAL-BASED THEORIES OF WORK MOTIVATION

A goal represents something that an individual attempts to attain or achieve; it is the aim of an individual's behavior (Locke & Latham, 2002). **Goal-setting theory** (Locke & Latham, 1990, 2002) is one of the most important and influential theories of work motivation, which has received numerous empirical supports across employees from varied industries (Miner, 2003). The fundamental tenet of this theory is that goals guide human behavior. There is strong support that, in the workplace, setting appropriate goals can help enhance employee performance to a large extent (Latham & Locke, 2006; Pritchard, Roth, Jones, Galgay, & Watson, 1988).

The second major tenet of goal-setting theory is that challenging or difficult goals lead to higher levels of performance than easy goals. Meta-analytic evidence shows that when goals are challenging and aggressive, employees tend to work harder or smarter, leading to higher levels of both individual and group performance (Kleingeld, van Mierlo, & Arends, 2011; Steel & Karren, 1987). At first glance, the goal difficulty tenet of goal-setting theory is contradictory to expectancy theory; the latter seems to suggest that easy goals can enhance employees' expectancy perception, resulting in higher levels of motivation. To solve this apparent contradiction, Locke and Latham (2002) explicitly noted that within goal levels (i.e., when goal level is kept constant; the assumption of expectancy theory), higher levels of expectancy perceptions lead to higher performance. However, across goal levels, difficult goals are more likely to result in high performance, even if employees have low-expectancy perceptions.

The next important tenet of goal-setting theory is that specific, measurable, and time-bound goals are more effective in promoting motivation and performance than vague or "do your best" goals. As suggested by empirical evidence, a goal with high specificity, such as the goal of "increase coffee sales by 10% within two months" consistently leads to high performance, compared to a goal without the time or circumstances specified (Locke, Shaw, Saari, & Latham, 1981; Tubbs, 1986).

The last major tenet of goal-setting theory is that incentives, including monetary rewards and feedback, will motivate higher levels of effort and performance but only when the incentives enhance the focal individual's commitment to the goals involved. Here, goal commitment represents the degree to which an individual is attached to the goal, views it as important, and is dedicated to reaching it (Latham & Locke, 1991). Monetary rewards can facilitate goal commitment by making the goal more attractive to an individual; feedback may increase goal commitment since it enhances one's ability or self-efficacy in attaining the goal. Apart from these two incentives, making the goal public, having a positive relationship with managers, or employee participation in goal setting may all lead to high levels of goal commitment (Klein & Kim, 1998; Pritchard et al., 1988).

To summarize, goal-setting theory is highly consistent with process-based theories of work motivation in that they both rely on a cognitive model of human functioning; a person will not develop their goals unless they are aware of the surrounding environment and are fully conscious of the meaning of what constitutes the goals. It is also important to note that none of the aforementioned theories is complete in itself, but each provides unique, valuable insights for organizations to better motivate employees. In Figure 3.1, we integrate these theories into one coherent model of work motivation, which serves a theoretical foundation that explains how employee motivation and productivity can be enhanced through performance management.

MOTIVATING EMPLOYEES THROUGH PERFORMANCE MANAGEMENT

Motivating Employees Through Developing Appropriate Goals

The *goals-to-effort* link presented in Figure 3.1 indicates that specific, difficult, and time-bound goals will motivate employees to put forth more effort, leading to higher job performance, as suggested by goal-setting theory (Locke & Latham, 2002). In addition, factors that help enhance employees' goal commitment, such as proper incentives and employee participation in goal settings, will strengthen the impact of the specific and challenging goals on individual effort (Locke & Latham, 2002).

Biyun Hu and Liang Meng

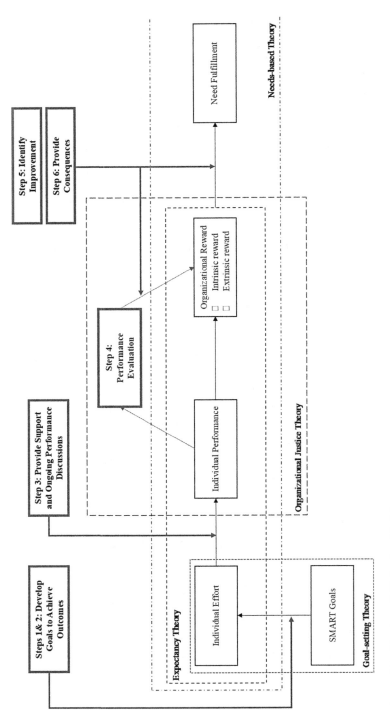

Figure 3.1   The Overall Motivation Model

The first two steps of performance management include identifying the division and individual employee's performance goals that are aligned with corporate strategy. To acquire a motivated workforce, organizations should develop challenging or stretch goals with time constraints, which help "push" employees to make use of the knowledge and skills they possess to work harder or more innovatively. Goal specificity is also important, as specific goals provide employees with clear destinations to strive for. Involving employees in the goal-setting process, such as urging employees to set their own challenging and specific goals, can also be beneficial, since it may largely increase employees' commitment to goal attainment. Indeed, a number of top companies, including Intel, Google, and Amazon, use objective and key results (OKR) as a tool to align employee goals with organizational strategy. These companies encourage employees to set stretch, specific, and time-bound goals that are consistent with the company's strategy, hoping to better motivate employees and maximize company growth.

Motivating Employees Through Continuous Support and Discussions

The *effort-to-performance* link presented in Figure 3.1 suggests that employees will be motivated to put forth more effort if they believe that high levels of work effort will lead to high levels of performance, as noted in expectancy theory (Vroom, 1964). Several factors, including employees' knowledge, skills, ability, and self-efficacy, can facilitate employee motivation by increasing their expectancy perceptions. Some contextual factors, such as equipment tools, managerial support, and performance feedback, can also strengthen the effort-to-performance link by enhancing employees' knowledge, skills, abilities, and/or self-efficacy.

The third step in the performance management process is providing ongoing support and feedback discussions. To form a strong effort-to-performance link, organizations should make all relevant resources, tools, and information readily available, such that employee performance will not be constrained by factors other than their effort and capability. For instance, a considerable number of employees had to work from home during the COVID-19 pandemic. Their expectancy perceptions would have been low if their tasks were dependent on a working laptop but they did not have one at home, regardless of their abilities knowledge, or skills. In addition, it is important for managers to schedule frequent check-ins with each employee to discuss not only their accomplishments and challenges affecting performance but also their feelings and attitudes toward performance. These frequent check-ins will provide opportunities for employees to learn how to perform their tasks more effectively, leading to enhanced knowledge, skills, and/or self-efficacy and, thus, a strong expectancy perception. Today, many organizations are adopting a continuous performance management process, whereby employees have the chance to discuss their performance, work progress, and challenges with their managers and peers on an ongoing basis, aiming to increase employee motivation and performance. Unfortunately, however, some managers are still reluctant to provide ongoing feedback, considering it time-consuming, or even a waste of time. To resolve this issue, organizations can make "conducting frequent check-ins and providing timely, detailed feedback" as one of the managers' job duties that will be evaluated by their supervisors.

Motivating Employees Through Fair Performance Evaluations

The *performance-to-rewards* link presented in Figure 3.1 suggests that employees' motivation level is determined by the extent to which high performance will be rewarded, intrinsically and/or extrinsically (Gagné & Deci, 2005; Vroom, 1964). In work settings, performance evaluation could serve as an important mechanism linking performance and rewards (Pritchard & Payne, 2003). Specifically, the *performance-to-evaluation* link represents the extent to which performance will be fairly evaluated by managers; the *evaluation-to-rewards* link represents the degree to which evaluation is associated with appropriate rewards, with a high evaluation being rewarded and a low evaluation being punished. Therefore, factors that ensure fair evaluation will facilitate employee motivation and work effort, as suggested by equity theory and organizational justice theory (Adams, 1965; Colquitt et al., 2013). (We discuss the *evaluation-to-rewards* link in the next section).

The fourth step of performance management is performance evaluation, or performance appraisal. Different from frequent feedback discussions (which can occur on a daily basis), performance evaluation is a formal, company-wide annual or semi-annual event, in which each employee is evaluated by a rater or raters with regard to whether they have achieved performance goals set in the first two steps. To effectively motivate employees and resolve performance issues, organizations should increase fairness perceptions of the performance evaluations among employees. First, there are several approaches that organizations can adopt to increase perceived outcome fairness (i.e., distributive justice). For instance, organizations could ask the raters to perform performance evaluation based exclusively on the actual performance of the ratee; organizations could reduce organizational politics, which has been shown to hurt distributive justice of performance evaluations (Saad & Elshaer, 2017); organizations should also pay special attention to ranking approaches, which often result in low fairness perceptions of outcomes (Blume, Baldwin, & Ruben, 2005). Continuous, frequent check-ins (as discussed in Step 3 of performance management) may also help, as the check-ins will help ratees better understand the evaluation criterion and process and then consider the evaluation results as fair.

It is often more important for organizations to enhance employees' perceived procedure fairness (i.e., procedural justice) of performance evaluation. Ensuring consistent evaluation standards across different ratees, minimizing rating errors and biases, collaborating with employees to set performance goals (as discussed in Step 2 of performance management), and allowing employees to voice or challenge the evaluation results are all potential practices that organizations could implement to better motivate their employees. For example, organizations can benefit from training the raters to avoid various biases in performance evaluation. These include (1) liking bias (i.e., providing higher evaluations to the ratees who they have a good relationship with), (2) leniency/strictness bias (i.e., providing high/low evaluations to all ratees, despite their actual performance), (3) contrast biases (i.e., providing evaluations based on comparisons between ratees, rather than each employee's objective performance), (4) halo/horns bias (i.e., providing high/low overall evaluations due to one particular positive/negative attribute of the ratees), (5) central tendency bias (i.e., giving middle or average evaluations to all ratees, regardless of their actual performance), and recency bias (i.e., providing evaluations based on the ratees' most recent performance instead of the performance throughout the evaluation period).

Finally, to further motivate employees, organizations should enhance perceived interactional justice among them. Organizations should provide evaluations in an atmosphere of courtesy and respect, remind raters to communicate with ratees in a polite manner, and ensure that the standards of performance evaluation, as well as goals of individuals, teams, and the organization are all transparent.

Motivating Employees Through Identifying Improvement and Providing Appropriate Consequences

The *evaluation-to-rewards* link suggests that employees are likely to put forth more effort if they believe that a high performance evaluation will be rewarded accordingly, with positive evaluations leading to favorable rewards while negative evaluations resulting in unfavorable outcomes. If an employee is rated as above average but is rewarded less than those who receive an average rating, that focal employee will perceive the reward as unfair and be demotivated to work hard further. According to SDT, rewards can be both extrinsic (e.g., promotions, bonuses, and paid vacations), and intrinsic (e.g., recognition, autonomy in decision-making, and training and development opportunities) to the employees (Gagné & Deci, 2005).

The fifth step of performance management involves identifying employee strengths and weaknesses, addressing their weaknesses, and further developing their strengths. Need-based theories of work motivation (e.g., Maslow's hierarchy of needs, Alderfer's ERG model, and SDT) explicitly note that training and development opportunities facilitate employee motivation by satisfying their needs for self-actualization, growth, or competence. Thus, managers are urged to identify individualized training and development needs, as well as discuss activities that can improve employee performance, in a timely manner.

The last step of performance management is providing consequences (i.e., rewards and punishments) based on performance evaluations. To effectively strengthen the evaluation-to-rewards link and motivate employees, it is crucial for organizations to provide fair rewards/punishments, in accordance with each employee's performance ratings. Apart from training and development opportunities, organizations should also reward high performers with promotion opportunities, bonuses, and paid vacation trips, as well as intrinsic rewards, including more responsibilities and autonomy, recognition, and meaningful or interesting work assignments. Furthermore, organizations should clearly communicate the rationales for rewards, apply consistent standards when rewarding or punishing employees, and allow employees to challenge the reward/punishment decisions. Finally, employees should be treated with respect and dignity when being rewarded or punished, and the reward/punishment standards should be transparent to all employees.

Finally, the *rewards-to-need fulfillment* link indicates that employees will not be motivated unless the rewards are able to satisfy one's needs, as highlighted in the need-based theories of work motivation. Thus, when rewarding high performers (Step 6 of performance management), it is crucial for managers to accurately identify each high performer's needs; managers should avoid providing paid vacation trips to employees who desire a promotion or allocating parking spaces to those who do not have a car. Fortunately, it is relatively easy and inexpensive to understand employees' needs; managers can conduct surveys or have a short discussion during frequent check-ins. Organizations may also want to provide multiple rewards with similar monetary values and allow employees to choose the one that best satisfies their needs.

CONCLUSION

Motivation is an essential part of performance management. In this chapter, we integrate multiple theories of work motivation into an overarching model and use it to explain how organizations and managers can motive employees more effectively through each step of performance management. We hope to stimulate research efforts into this important topic, leading to more evidence-based recommendations for performance management.

A CASE STUDY

Marina Osuna is a beginner marketing specialist. She joined the Marketing Department of an FMCG (fast-moving consumer goods) company 3 months ago. She has been working really hard since the first day and seldom found the time for a decent meal. As a marketing specialist, Marina's main job duties include conducting market research to identify customer trends and habits, and building and maintaining relationships with new and existing customers.

She also needs to work closely with her team to brainstorm and develop ideas for creative marketing campaigns. The performance evaluation system at her company is carefully designed to reflect both individual work performance (70%) and team contribution (30%). Employees care about their performance evaluation, as it largely affects their salary, bonus, and promotion.

Recently, Marina got an email from her team leader. The subject line was "Quarterly Team Contribution Evaluation". Marina eagerly opened the email only to find disappointment; she was evaluated as a "Low Performer" in team contribution. Marina considered herself diligent and conscientious and wanted to impress her team by demonstrating excellent work performance. However, it seemed that her endeavors did not pay off; at least her leader did not appreciate her contribution to the team.

Marina was confused and distressed after reading the evaluation results. Although the email was informational, which included clarifications on how team contribution was evaluated and advice on how to improve future performance, Marina was just not in the mood to carefully read through it. Instead, she double-checked the email hoping to find that it was meant to be addressed to someone else, but that did not happen. Then Marina started to feel angry. She believed that her leader must have made a mistake. Perhaps the leader was negligent, failing to properly record each team member's contribution. While Marina admitted that she is more of a "numbers person" by nature, she made adequate preparations before each brainstorming session to ensure that she could speak up and share at least one idea. She thought that only those who never or rarely propose an idea should be evaluated as low performers.

There are a few more workplace newbies in the Marketing Department. Compared with other colleagues who hold high-ranking positions, Marina felt more comfortable socializing with them. Thus, Marina decided to chat with her fellow workplace newbies to find out what was going on. It turned out that Marina was the only one who received a rating much lower than one's own expectations. Marina became even more angry and felt herself to be treated unfairly, even targeted by the leader. She started to wonder whether the leader disliked her personally.

Marina could hardly get back to work. If the leader simply did not like her, there was little she could do to improve her performance evaluation. The overall performance evaluation was yet to be released, but Marina was no longer looking forward to it. The devastating effect of the team contribution evaluation was long-lasting. In the next few brainstorming sessions, Marina still attempted to propose ideas, but everyone could tell that the so-called ideas were far from well developed. Marina just no longer wanted to beat a dead horse. In fact, Marina became more of a listener and observer in these sessions. What's worse, Marina began to self-doubt her ability and suitability for this job. Her inner voice told her to speak to her leader before drawing any conclusion, but she was not brave and candid enough to be confronted with the one who seemed to have brought her the trouble. Marina did not know what to do …

QUESTIONS

1. What is your evaluation of Marina's motivation level, and why?
2. Marina has identified several reasons for her low team contribution evaluation. What are the reasons? Can you identify any other potential reasons for the negative evaluation?
3. Why was Marina's motivation affected by the team contribution evaluation? What motivation theories can be used to explain her reactions?
4. Using the overarching motivation framework, what strategies might Marina adopt to improve her team contribution assessment? Do you see any improvements that Marina's leader can make to improve Marina's motivation?

REFERENCES

Adams, J. S. (1965). Inequity in social exchange. In L. Berkowitz (Ed.), *Advances in experimental social psychology* (Vol. 2, pp. 267–299). New York: Academic Press.

Alderfer, C. P. (1969). An empirical test of a new theory of human needs. *Organizational Behavior and Human Performance, 4*, 142–175.

Armstrong, T. (1994). *Multiple intelligences in the classroom*. Alexandria, VA: Association for Supervision and Curriculum Development.

Baard, P. P., Deci, E. L., & Ryan, R. M. (2004). Intrinsic need satisfaction: A motivational basis of performance and well-being in two work settings. *Journal of Applied Social Psychology, 34*(10), 2045–2068.

Bies, R. J., & Moag, J. F. (1986). Interactional justice: Communication criteria of fairness. In R. J. Lewicki, B. H. Sheppard, & M. H. Bazerman (Eds.), *Research on negotiations in organizations* (Vol. 1, pp. 43–55). Greenwich, CT: JAI Press.

Blume, B. D., Baldwin, T. T., & Ruben, R. S. 2005. Forced ranking: Who is attracted to it? A study of performance management system preferences. Paper presented at *the 65th annual Academy of Management Conference*, Honolulu, HI.

Carrell, M. R., & Dittrich, J. E. (1978). Equity theory: The recent literature, methodological considerations, and new directions. *Academy of Management Review, 3*(2), 202–210.

Cerasoli, C. P., Nicklin, J. M., & Ford, M. T. (2014). Intrinsic motivation and extrinsic incentives jointly predict performance: a 40-year meta-analysis. *Psychological Bulletin, 140*(4), 980–1008.

Colquitt, J. A. (2001). On the dimensionality of organizational justice: A construct validation of a measure. *Journal of Applied Psychology, 86*(3), 386–400.

Colquitt, J. A., Scott, B. A., Rodell, J. B., Long, D. M., Zapata, C. P., Conlon, D. E., & Wesson, M. J. (2013). Justice at the millennium, a decade later: A meta-analytic test of social exchange and affect-based perspectives. *Journal of Applied Psychology, 98*(2), 199–236.

Cook, K. S., & Hegtvedt, K. A. (1983). Distributive justice, equity, and equality. *Annual Review of Sociology, 9*, 217–241.

Deci, E. L., Ryan, R. M., Gagné, M., Leone, D. R., Usunov, J., & Kornazheva, B. P. (2001). Need satisfaction, motivation, and well-being in the work organizations of a former Eastern Bloc country. *Personality and Social Psychology Bulletin, 27*, 930–942.

Gagné, M., & Deci, E. L. (2005). Self-determination theory and work motivation. *Journal of Organizational Behavior, 26*(4), 331–362.

Gagné, M., Ryan, R. M., & Bargmannm, K. (2003). Autonomy support and need satisfaction in the motivation and well-being of gymnasts. *Journal of Applied Sport Psychology, 15*(4), 372–390.

Herzberg, F., Mausner, B., & Snyderman, B. (1959). *The motivation to work*. New York: John Wiley.

Hu, B., & Han, S. (2021). Distributive justice: Investigating the impact of resource focus and resource valence. *Journal of Business and Psychology, 36*(2), 225–252.

Klein, H. J., & Kim, J. S. (1998). A field study of the influence of situational constraints leader-member exchange, and goal commitment on performance. *Academy of Management Journal, 41*(1), 88–95.

Kleingeld, A., van Mierlo, H., & Arends, L. (2011). The effect of goal setting on group performance: A meta-analysis. *Journal of Applied Psychology, 96*(6), 1289–1304.

Koestner, R., Otis, N., Powers, T. A., Pelletier, L., & Gagnon, H. (2008). Autonomous motivation, controlled motivation, and goal progress. *Journal of Personality, 76*(5), 1201–1230.

Latham, G. P., & Locke, E. A. (1991). Self-regulation through goal setting. *Organizational Behavior and Human Decision Processes, 50*(2), 212–247.

Latham, G. P., & Locke, E. A. (2006). Enhancing the benefits and overcoming the pitfalls of goal setting. *Organizational Dynamics, 35*, 332–340.

Leventhal, G. S. (1980). What should be done with equity theory? New approaches to the study of fairness in social relationships. In K. Gergen, M. Greenberg, & R. Willis (Eds.), *Social exchange: Advances in theory and research* (pp. 27–55). New York: Plenum.

Locke, E. A., & Latham, G. P. (1990). *A theory of goal setting & task performance*. Englewood Cliffs, NJ: Prentice Hall.

Locke, E. A., & Latham, G. P. (2002). Building a practically useful theory of goal setting and task motivation: A 35-year odyssey. *American Psychologist, 57*(9), 705–717.

Locke, E. A., Shaw, K. N., Saari, L. M., & Latham, G. P. (1981). Goal setting and task performance: 1969–1980. *Psychological Bulletin, 90*(1), 125–152.

Maslow, A. H. (1943). A theory of human motivation. *Psychological Review, 50*(4), 370–396.

Maslow, A. H. (1954). *Motivation and personality*. New York: Harper.

McClelland, D. C. (1961). *The achieving society*. New York: Van Nostrand.

Miner, J. B. (2003). The rated importance, scientific validity, and practical usefulness of organizational behavior theories. *Academy of Management Learning and Education, 2,* 250–268.

Murray, H. A. (1938). *Explorations in personality: A clinical and experimental study of fifty men of college age.* Oxford University Press.

Pinder, C. C. (2008). *Work motivation in organizational behavior* (2nd ed.). New York: Psychology Press.

Porter, C. M., & Woo, S. E. (2015). Untangling the networking phenomenon: A dynamic psychological perspective on how and why people network. *Journal of Management, 41*(5), 1477–1500.

Pritchard, R. D., Roth, P. L., Jones, S. D., Galgay, P. J., & Watson, M. D. (1988). Designing a goal-setting system to enhance performance: A practical guide. *Organizational Dynamics, 17,* 69–78.

Pritchard, R. D., & Payne, S. C. (2003). Performance management practices and motivation. In D. Holoman, T. D. Wall, C. W. Clegg, P. Sparrow, & A. Howard (Eds.), *The new workplace: A guide to the human impact of modern working practices* (pp. 219–242). Hoboken, NJ: John Wiley and Sons Ltd.

Reis, H. T., Sheldon, K. M., Gable, S. L., Roscoe, J., & Ryan, R. M. (2000). Daily well-being: The role of autonomy, competence, and relatedness. *Personality and Social Psychology Bulletin, 26,* 419–435.

Saad, S. K., & Elshaer, I. A. (2017). Organizational politics and validity of layoff decisions: Mediating role of distributive justice of performance appraisal. *Journal of Hospitality Marketing & Management, 26*(8), 805–828.

Schermerhorn, J. R. (2001). *Management* (6th ed.). New York: John Wiley & Sons.

Skarlicki, D. P., & Folger, R. (1997). Retaliation in the workplace: The roles of distributive, procedural, and interactional justice. *Journal of Applied Psychology, 82*(3), 434–443.

Steel, R. P., & Karren, R. J. (1987). A meta-analytic study of the effects of goal-setting on task performance: 1966–1984. *Organizational Behavior and Human Decision Processes, 39,* 52–83.

Steers, R. M., & Mowday, R. T. (1977). The motivational properties of tasks. *Academy of Management Review, 2*(4), 645–658.

Tubbs, M. E. (1986). Goal setting: A meta-analytic examination of the empirical evidence. *Journal of Applied Psychology, 71*(3), 474–483.

Van Iddekinge, C. H., Aguinis, H., Mackey, J. D., & DeOrtentiis, P. S. (2018). A meta-analysis of the interactive, additive, and relative effects of cognitive ability and motivation on performance. *Journal of Management, 44*(1), 249–279.

Vroom, V. H. (1964). *Work and motivation.* New York: Wiley.

Rater–Ratee Relationships and Performance Management

Amy Risner, Shaun Pichler, Arup Varma and Ryan Petty

Chapter 4

INTRODUCTION

Performance appraisal is one of the most heavily researched topics in the industrial-organizational psychology and human resource management research literature because of its ubiquity in organizations and its importance in administrative decision-making. Performance ratings are typically used to differentiate employee performance and, on this basis, to make decisions about the allocation of training and development activities, compensation, promotions and other organizational rewards. Given its link to the allocation of scarce resources, the performance appraisal process, and the accuracy of resultant ratings, it has received extensive attention in management theory, research and practice.

DOI: 10.4324/9781003306849-4

While researchers have traditionally assumed, based on the psychometric model of performance appraisal, that rating accuracy is a function of rating instrument format, as well as rater cognitive processing abilities, attention has shifted in more recent years to the affective and interpersonal variables that systematically explain variance in performance ratings. As explained later, while mechanisms designed to increase rating accuracy based on the psychometric model have shown some improvement in rating accuracy, interpersonal factors have been found to be particularly important, above and beyond these efforts, in predicting rated performance.

The purpose of this chapter, therefore, is to introduce readers to the primary concepts, theoretical frameworks and research literature that explain how rater–ratee relationships and the quality of those relationships affect the performance appraisal process, performance ratings and appraisal reactions. It is important to note that performance appraisal is but one very important aspect of an organization's overall performance management process. According to the model developed by DeNisi (2000), the purpose of performance appraisal is to accurately diagnose individual and group performance to be able to reward good performance and remedy poor performance such that, in the aggregate, organizational performance will be enhanced. If characteristics of interpersonal relationships between raters and ratees systematically distort performance ratings, this would suggest that performance problems will be under-identified and, perhaps, exacerbated; conversely, good performance may go unrewarded. In the aggregate, this could seriously jeopardize the effective use not only of cash and monetary resources, but also the organization's most valuable resource—its human resources. Rater–ratee relationship quality plays a significant role in how employees react to performance appraisals, and recent research has shed light on its importance. Thus, it is important to examine how rater–ratee relationships affect performance ratings and appraisal reactions, if indeed this systematic variance should be considered as a source of bias or inaccuracy and how this relates to future performance—at both the individual and organizational levels.

THE IMPORTANCE OF SOCIAL CONTEXT

The traditional psychometric model of performance appraisal assumes that ratings that are free from halo, leniency and range restriction are accurate (see, e.g., Saal, Downey, & Lahey, 1980) and that training raters to avoid these biases, or developing rating instruments that prevent these biases, will increase rating accuracy. This is because researchers have assumed that rating biases operate at an unconscious level (Arvey & Murphy, 1998). One prominent inadequacy of this logic is that interpersonal variables explain unique variance in ratings even when ratings are made more accurate through training and instrument development. Researchers have, accordingly, argued that rater motivation, affected in part by interpersonal relations and rater personality, consciously affects performance ratings (c.f. Murphy & Cleveland, 1995; John Bernardin et al., 2015).

In order to understand how to train raters to more accurately observe ratee performance, researchers developed theoretical models based on a cognitive psychology research tradition. In fact, the performance appraisal literature has largely been dominated by cognitive models of the appraisal process (Rynes, Gerhart, & Parks, 2005). These models posit that the way in which raters attend to, encode and retrieve performance-related information in memory affects performance ratings (c.f. DeNisi, Cafferty, & Meglino, 1984; DeNisi & Williams, 1988). While these models have been helpful to our understanding of the appraisal process, they are limited in that they do not fully account for variance in performance ratings, in part because of their limited attention to the social or interpersonal processes that influence the appraisal process. Performance evaluations naturally involve interpersonal processes, and to ignore this broader social context leads to under-specified, incomplete models of the appraisal process. To be sure, subordinates are typically active participants in the appraisal process and make efforts to influence this process through impression and information management (Ilgen & Feldman, 1983; Wayne & Ferris, 1990; Giacalone & Rosenfeld, 2013).

In fact, researchers have, for some time, criticized the performance appraisal literature for failing to consider the social context within which the appraisal occurs (e.g. Guion, 1983; Dipboye,

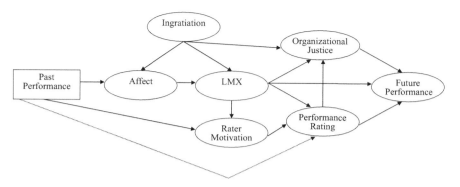

Figure 4.1 A model of rater–ratee relationships in performance appraisal

1985; Wexley & Klimoski, 1984; Rosen, et al., 2016) and have advocated studying how social relationships between supervisors and subordinates affect performance ratings (e.g. Cleveland & Murphy, 1992; Murphy & Cleveland, 1995; Levy & Williams, 2004; Yun et al., 2005). Research on interpersonal affect, based largely on Byrne's (1971) similarity attraction paradigm, and leader–member exchange, based on role theory (Kahn et al., 1964) and social exchange theory (Blau, 1964), have been extremely influential in this respect.

The following section, accordingly, reviews the extant literature on how affect and leader–member exchange are related to performance ratings. Since affect is typically viewed as an antecedent to leader–member exchange, we review this literature first, followed by a section that integrates affect and leader–member exchange. Figure 4.1 represents the relationships discussed in the following sections.

INTERPERSONAL AFFECT AND RATER–RATEE RELATIONSHIPS

In an examination of the effects of job-related and interpersonal factors on performance ratings, Borman, White and Dorsey (1995) found that while ability, knowledge and task proficiency were all related to performance ratings as expected based on previous research, the addition of interpersonal variables to a model of supervisor ratings increased model fit and increased variance explained twofold. Given that the interpersonal variables they studied, for example, dependability and a lack of obnoxiousness, contributed to the social-psychological context of an organization, the authors argued that they should be interpreted as contextual performance as opposed to biasing factors. Of course, subsequent research has confirmed that contextual performance is related to performance ratings (Motowidlo & Van Scotter, 1994; Meinecke, et al., 2017). The key here is in variable operationalization; the interpersonal variables in the study by Borman and colleagues measured personal characteristics of ratees—not characteristics of dyadic rater–ratee relationships per se. While the relationship between ratee dependability and performance ratings may not be viewed as a bias, what about interpersonal attraction between a rater and ratee?

Research on interpersonal affect has been somewhat more contentious. Interpersonal affect is defined as the extent to which a rater likes or dislikes a ratee (Murphy & Cleveland, 1991) and is based on an emotional or affective reaction to and evaluation of that ratee (Zajonc, 1980). Interpersonal affect is paramount to the study of rater-ratee relationships in the context of performance appraisal in that affect is "the major currency in which social intercourse is transacted" (Zajonc, 1980). Tsui and Gutek (1984) defined affect in terms of interpersonal liking, as well as admiration and respect. Thus, their definition of affect, as well as measures and studies based on this definition, emphasize what has been called job-related affect as opposed to purely social likability (Robbins & DeNisi, 1994). Nevertheless, since the affect construct is typically construed and measured largely as interpersonal liking, scholars have traditionally characterized affect as a source of unconscious bias or inaccuracy in performance ratings (Landy & Farr, 1980; Latham & Wexley, 1981; Dipboye, 1985; Varma et al., 2016; Varma, et al., 2020). Consistent with this research, Tsui and Barry (1986) found that affect was systematically related to rating errors, that is, halo, leniency and interrater agreement, in expected ways. Similarly, Jacobs and Kozlowski (1985) found that halo increased as a function of interpersonal familiarity.

In order to explain these relationships, Feldman and others (Feldman, 1981; Wyer & Srull, 1981) have suggested, based on social-cognitive models of the appraisal process, that information about ratees is stored in memory based on ratee categories or prototypes, that is, overall impressions of whether a worker is

Amy Risner et al.

likeable or dislikeable, which lead to systematic under evaluation and over-evaluation in performance ratings. This is because
raters seek performance-related information that reaffirms their
impressions of ratees (Feldman, 1981). In a test of this proposition,
Robbins and DeNisi (1994) found that while raters were more
likely to use affect-inconsistent *and* affect-consistent information
more than affect-neutral information during the encoding and
weighting of performance-related information, partially supporting this hypothesis, it was affect-inconsistent information that
was given more importance when assigning an actual rating, thus
contradicting the hypothesis. Thus, this finding calls into question
whether overall impressions of ratees as likable or dislikable acts
as a source of bias in the appraisal. To answer this, Kacmar's et al.
(2009) study demonstrated how deep-level perceived similarities
affected the relationship quality between the rater and ratee and
rater bias in treating specific employees more favorably. This bias
will become prevalent in performance appraisals, as those subordinates with less deep-level similarities to their supervisor could
be viewed as subpar performers in error.

Robbins and DeNisi (1994) suggested that affect may be difficult to distinguish from past performance in field settings and that
past performance may be a more useful measure in field research
since affect tends to suggest bias, especially when it is a result of
demographic similarity. However, affect inconsistency still predicted performance ratings after controlling for past performance;
moreover, while past performance was more strongly correlated
with job-related affect (.42) than social-related affect (.35), neither
of these correlations would suggest that performance and affect
are indistinguishable. In both a laboratory and field study, Wayne
and Ferris (1990) found that objective performance and affect
explained unique variance in performance ratings, again suggesting that objective performance and affect are separable, mutually important determinants of ratings. Thus, while affect may be
highly correlated, and even determined by, previous performance,
the two constructs seem distinguishable.

As Robbins and DeNisi (1994) highlighted, the ambivalence-
amplification hypothesis proposed by Katz and Glass (1979)
suggests that high performers and low performers will receive
differential ratings based on their level of performance only

when the rater is ambivalent. Positive affect and negative affect, however, are likely to inflate or deflate ratings, respectively, the authors argued. In a test of this theoretical rationale for a biasing mechanism, Varma, Pichler and Srinivas (2005) found differences in the relationship between interpersonal affect and performance ratings across cultures. Performance ratings of low performers in India were systematically inflated when they were liked by their supervisors, whereas this was not the case in their U.S. sample, suggesting that it is important to consider cultural norms in the context of performance appraisal. This is consistent with research by Schaubroek and Lam (2002), who found in a cross-national study of U.S. and Hong Kong bank tellers that personality similarity between supervisors and subordinates was a better predictor of promotions in more collectivist work units. This line of research would suggest that cultural demands, such as group cohesiveness, may increase the likelihood of a relationship between affect and performance ratings. But is this a source of bias per se? We will return to this topic later; until then, let us consider how rater–ratee similarity is related to affect.

Given that demographic similarity is such a strong predictor of interpersonal liking in general (Byrne, 1971; Porter et al., 2016), and since affect predicts performance ratings in work settings, one could hypothesize that liking leads to discriminatory performance ratings as a function of demographic similarity. This general hypothesis has been examined repeatedly. For instance, Varma and Stroh (2001) developed a process model of the relationship between gender and performance ratings that posited that gender similarity influenced likability, which, in turn, influenced leader–member exchange, which ultimately influenced ratings of performance. The authors found support for each component part of their model, indicating that supervisors rate subordinates of the same sex higher than those of the opposite sex as a function of the higher quality relationship that is developed among same-sex dyads through interpersonal attraction. Given that in most occupations, men are more often supervisors compared to women, this could ultimately result in discrimination claims. That said, the mounting research literature tends to suggest, in total, that the demographic similarity ➜ affect ➜ performance rating chain is tenuous (cf. Oppler, Campbell, Pulakos, & Borman, 1992).

In this connection, deep-level similarity may be more important than these surface-level, demographic factors (Harrison,
Price, & Bell, 1998; Kacmar et al., 2009). Indeed, Schaubroek,
and Lam (2002) found that personality similarity predicted promotion decisions; this effect was partially mediated by leader–
member exchange and communication with one's supervisor.
Demographic similarity, however, was of little predictive utility.
Liden, Wayne and Stillwell (1993) found that perceived similarity,
but not demographic similarity, between supervisors and subordinates predicted leader–member exchange.

LEADER–MEMBER EXCHANGE AND PERFORMANCE APPRAISAL

It should be increasingly evident based on the preceding para-
graphs that affect is closely linked to leader–member exchange.
Researchers have consistently suggested that affect determines,
in large part, the relationship quality between supervisors and
subordinates, and empirical evidence is supportive (cf. Liden &
Mitchell, 1988; Wayne & Ferris, 1990; Varma, DeNisi, & Peters,
1996). Early theoretical work posited that mutual liking was
one of three primary components of leader–member exchange
(Dienesch & Liden, 1986). In fact, Liden, Wayne and Stillwell
(1993) found that affect was a more important causal determinant
of exchange quality than were demographic similarity and performance ratings.

It is not surprising, accordingly, that leader–member exchange
theory has been proposed as a primary lens through which to
examine how interpersonal relationships between supervisors
and subordinates are related to performance appraisal processes
and outcomes (cf. Klein, Snell, & Wexley, 1987). It is important to
note that leader–member exchange theory's definition and scope
have not been clearly defined, so there can be ambiguity in its
use (Gottfredson et al., 2020). For this chapter, leader–member
exchange theory is defined by supervisors (leaders) developing
different, that is, in-group and out-group, relationships with subordinates (members), and that the treatment subordinates receive is
based on their relationship quality with supervisors (Dansereau,
Graen, & Haga, 1975; Graen, 1976; Gooty & Yammarino, 2013).
In-group members receive more trust, delegation and rewards as
compared to out-group members. The theory assumes that the

relationship quality that is built from mutual trust, reciprocity and support (Dansereau et al., 1975) can affect a variety of important outcomes for both supervisors and subordinates, including performance ratings, promotions and appraisal satisfaction, that is supported by empirical research (cf. Wayne & Ferris, 1990; Saraih et al., 2018).

One of the reasons supervisors may give lower ratings to out-group subordinates is because they attribute their performance to different factors than in-group members. For instance, Heneman, Greenberger and Anonyuo (1989) found that effective performance was attributed to internal factors, that is, ability and effort, for in-group, but not out-group, members, whereas poor performance was attributed to ability and effort for out-group, but not in-group, members. These results indicate that supervisors make judgments about performance based not only on objective performance but relationship quality as well. This is consistent with theory that argues raters are more likely to recall performance information that is consistent with their overall impressions, i.e. positive or negative, of ratees (e.g. Murphy, Gannett, Herr, & Chen, 1986). Perceptions of leader–member exchange quality affect not only rater–ratee relationship quality but also employees' relationships with each other in a work group (Hooper & Martin, 2008; Gooty & Yammarino, 2013). If an employee perceives that others on their team are being treated more favorably by their supervisor, this creates tension between coworkers and leads to a negative work environment. Hooper and Martin's (2008) study has significant implications for the social context within teams and how this impacts communication, respect and trust among coworkers and their supervisors.

In this connection, Judge and Ferris (1993) offered theoretical rationale for the social-contextual significance of rater–ratee relationships in performance appraisal. They explained that when raters retrieve performance-related information in memory, they typically envisage interpersonal interactions as opposed to specific performance incidents; thus, to the extent that a rater has a high-quality relationship with a ratee, their judgment about that ratee's performance will be influenced by positive affective information. In support of this, Kacmar, Witt, Zivnuska and Gully (2003) found that communication frequency moderated the relationship between leader–member exchange and performance ratings such that frequent communication was related to higher performance ratings for in-group members, whereas frequent communication was related to lower performance ratings for out-group members. The authors offered a rationale for this finding. First, communication reinforces positive or negative interpersonal relations. Second, information recalled in memory when assigning a performance rating is based on these communication patterns and interactions.

In essence, then, communication and leader–member exchange interact to affect the extent to which raters recall positive or negative information about ratees when assigning performance ratings. Since time to observe actual job-related behavior is naturally limited, communication about job performance information to supervisors is obviously important. What is problematic, then, from a performance management perspective is when a high-performing subordinate has difficulty explaining performance-related information to a supervisor simply as a function of their low-quality relationship, thus potentially resulting in an artificially low performance rating. In this connection, if the subordinate feels this rating is unfair because of poor communication, this discrepancy in perceived performance is less likely to lead to increased future performance.

The preceding situation could create a self-fulfilling prophecy such that the subordinate's performance actually decreases after performance feedback. Other negative ramifications such as turnover are also likely. In this connection, Liden, Wayne and Stillwell (1993) found that rater expectations of ratees several days into relationship formation predicted leader–member exchange several weeks and several months later. While performance was not measured at later time periods, these results suggest that rater expectations developed very early in a relationship predict subsequent relationship quality between raters and ratees, as well as subsequent role rewards.

Based on the preceding literature, it seems clear that the ratees' ability to express job-related information to raters is an important determinant of relationship quality and the perceived fairness of performance appraisals—and perhaps future performance. In an investigation of the effects of interpersonal relationships on appraisal content and outcomes, Nathan, Mohrman and Millman

(1991) found that relationship quality between supervisors and subordinates was positively related to three appraisal process variables, namely the extent to which subordinates participated in the process, behavioral criteria were used and career outcomes were discussed. Furthermore, these process variables were related to subsequent changes in job satisfaction and performance, controlling for past performance. Similarly, Elicker, Levy and Hall (2006) developed and tested a comprehensive model of the relationship between supervisor–subordinate relationships and reactions to performance feedback. They found that, when controlling for the discrepancy between self and supervisor ratings of performance as well as subordinate liking of supervisors, leader–member exchange affected the extent to which subordinates felt they were treated fairly during their appraisal, which, in turn, affected appraisal outcomes such as the perceived accuracy and utility of the appraisal, as well as motivation to improve performance.

This research indicates that relationship quality affects ratees' perceptions of the fairness of the appraisal process. Given that results from a survey among Fortune 100 firms indicated that perceived justice is the most important performance appraisal outcome to practitioners (Thomas & Bretz, 1994), it is certainly important to consider the connections between relationship quality and fairness perceptions related to performance appraisal. In fact, Dusterhoff et al. (2013) found that ratees will reciprocate the perceived fairness or lack of fairness of leader treatment by developing high- or low-quality exchanges with raters, which then affects how a ratee reacts to their appraisal. Folger, Konovsky and Cropanzano (1992) argued that perceived justice is a primary criterion by which performance appraisal systems should be judged given inconsistencies between raters in performance judgments. They proposed a due-process model of performance appraisal that allows ratees a voice in the process and opportunities to react to negative feedback. Empirical research indicates reactions to the performance appraisal in terms of perceived fairness and job attitudes are more likely to be positive under a due-process model (Taylor et al., 1995; Pichler, 2019). While a due-process model of the performance appraisal may indeed increase the perceived fairness of the appraisal process, as well as rating accuracy, we are still left with the question of how ratees can influence the rating process when their organization does not follow a due-process model.

One way ratees influence appraisal ratings in such situations is through ingratiation. Ingratiation is a form of supervisor-focus impression management whereby the ratee influences relationship quality through liking (cf. Wayne & Ferris, 1990; Wayne & Liden, 1995). Ingratiation has been found to be positively related to interpersonal affect as well as performance ratings (Wayne & Liden, 1995). Harrell-Cook, Ferris, and Dulebohn (1999) found that supervisor–subordinate relationship quality and supervisor-focused influence tactics were positively related to subordinate perceptions of performance evaluation procedural justice. The authors posited that ingratiation acts as an informal voice mechanism, which was supported by the finding that ingratiation was more strongly related to procedural justice when opportunity for decision control was low and that ingratiation was important regardless of supervisor–subordinate relationship quality. Similarly, Wayne and Liden (1995) found that ingratiation affects supervisor perceptions of interpersonal similarity, which affected performance ratings.

RATER MOTIVATION AND PERFORMANCE RATINGS

Despite the importance of rater motivation in the performance appraisal (PA) process, scholars have lamented the lack of extant empirical research on the topic (Harris, 1994). Although, unfortunately, empirical research on rater motivation is lacking at this point, some scholars have begun to address the topic theoretically (Murphy & Cleveland, 1990; Harris, 1994). Thus, the purpose of this section is to review and integrate the previous theoretical work done on rater motivation so as to inform the reader of the role and effect of rater motivation in the PA process, given the context of rater–ratee relationships.

As explained subsequently, there are both reasons for raters to rate accurately and inaccurately. Following the theoretical work of Murphy and Cleveland (1990), and based in large part on expectancy theory (Vroom, 1964), the degree to which a rater will rate accurately depends on: the existence and valence (or value) associated with the rewards for doing so, the existence and severity of negative consequences for doing so and the expectancy of those rewards/negative consequences. In general, raters will be more motivated to rate accurately, despite the interpersonal character-istics of the rater–ratee dyad, if they are rewarded for doing so, either extrinsically (e.g. raises, promotions, praise by superiors) or intrinsically (e.g. satisfaction), and value these rewards (Park, 2014). Furthermore, raters will be more motivated to rate accu-rately, again despite the interpersonal characteristics of the rater–ratee dyad, if there are punishments for rating inaccurately (e.g., reprisals from superiors). Finally, raters will be more motivated to rate accurately if there is a high probability that rewards or nega-tive consequences will come to fruition following the occurrence of accurate/inaccurate ratings.

Interestingly, examining past empirical research gives us a pes-simistic outlook on the actual motivation for raters to be accurate with their ratings in the real world. With regard to rewards for accurate ratings or punishments for inaccuracy, past empirical work has found that there are typically few if any rewards for accurate ratings or negative consequences for inaccurate ratings (Carroll & Schneier, 1982; Naiper & Latham, 1986). Furthermore, we can reasonably theorize that even if rewards/punishments did exist, it might be unlikely that they would be instituted, given the extra time and effort that would necessarily have to be expended to monitor rating accuracy and distribute rewards/punishments.

While there appear to be few reasons for a rater to make their ratings as accurately as possible, scholars have identified sev-eral reasons why raters may be motivated to provide inaccurate ratings (Murphy & Cleveland, 1990; Harris, 1994; Yun et al., 2005). These reasons can be organized into two categories: relationship-based and self-interest-based.

Relationship-based reasons are motives to provide inaccurate ratings because of their effect on the rater–ratee relationship or the ratee themselves. One such reason for inaccurate (in this case inflated) ratings is that the rater may not wish to damage the positive relationship with the ratee. Negative appraisals may be construed by the ratee as a personal attack by the rater and may have negative effects on the interpersonal affect and leader–member exchange quality of the dyad. A second reason is that the rater wishes to avoid criticism or negative reactions from the ratee (Yun et al., 2005; Rosen et al., 2016). A negative appraisal may result in feelings of injustice by the ratee, who might then publicly criticize the rater within the organization, drawing unwanted attention to the rater's appraisal. One consideration for mitigating negative reactions to a low performance rating in order to maintain high rater–ratee relationship quality is strengths-based appraisals, which focus on developing ratees' strengths instead of exacerbating their weaknesses (Van Woerkom & Kroon, 2020). A third reason is that the rater may wish to avoid demotivating the ratee by giving them a negative appraisal. Some employees respond to performance criticism by becoming demotivated, thus further reducing their performance. A final reason is that the rater may not want to give a negative appraisal because of the possible negative consequences for the ratee. Ratee consequences such as failure to receive a raise, demotion, or termination can all result from a poor appraisal, and many raters will be reluctant to give low appraisal scores, even if they are accurate.

Self-interest-based reasons are motives for raters to provide inaccurate ratings because of the rater's own self-interest. One such reason that a rater may provide inaccurate (inflated) ratings is that it is often the case that those doing the rating are the superiors of the ratees and thus ultimately responsible for their performance. Raters may be reluctant to give negative appraisals, even if accurate, for fear that negative appraisals will act as a signal to higher management that the rater themselves is not an effective manager of human resources (extrinsic consequences). A second reason is that if the rater is responsible for the performance of the ratee, negative appraisals may signal to the manager themselves that they are not an effective manager, which may elicit uncomfortable feelings for the rater such as decreased self-image or self-esteem. A third such reason is that both time and effort are required to give accurate ratings, which impacts the rater's ability to accomplish other activities. As such, it may not be in the rater's self-interest to expend all the time and energy to provide highly accurate ratings, especially in light of the previously discussed empirical evidence that suggests that there are few if any organizational rewards for giving accurate appraisals.

RELATIONSHIP QUALITY AND APPRAISAL REACTIONS

Employee reactions to performance appraisals, which include perceptions of performance appraisal accuracy, fairness, utility, appraisal satisfaction and motivation to improve are directly connected to rater–ratee relationship quality (Keeping & Levy, 2000; Levy & Williams, 2004). Rater–ratee relationship quality has been found to be a key predictor of ratee perceptions of organizational justice as well as appraisal reactions, since it allows the employee a greater sense of control over the process and outcome (Pichler, 2012; Selvarajan et al., 2018; Pichler, 2019). Trust is the foundation of rater–ratee relationship quality; higher levels of trust will lead to better relationship quality and therefore more positive reactions to the performance appraisal process and behaviors afterward (Kim & Holzer, 2014; Varma et al., 2020). For the information exchanged during an appraisal to motivate an employee to improve future performance, the supervisor must create a socially supportive environment pre- and post-performance appraisal (Levy & Williams, 2004; Pichler, 2012). The shared reality perceptions and agreement of a supervisor–subordinate relationship are other important indicators of relationship quality and associated performance of individuals (Cogliser et al., 2009; Markham et al., 2010; Gooty & Yammarino, 2013). This is especially important in work groups, since how individuals on a team view their supervisor, in terms of fairness, can determine the relationship quality of a supervisor and subordinate. If a work group has low differentiation in their views of their supervisor, then leader–member exchange performance ratings associations will be positive since everyone is in agreement about the fairness of their treatment and relationship (Gooty & Yammarino, 2013). By creating shared meaning among the work group, an individual who identifies in that group can be motivated to perform well if the group has positive relations with their leader and desires to produce great outcomes.

Connecting procedural justice climate to the performance appraisal process and leader–member exchange is essential for understanding the social context surrounding an appraisal and an individual's perception of this organizational process (Pichler et al., 2015). There is some question about whether relationship quality precedes perceptions of justice or whether perceptions of justice precede relationship quality. Pichler (2012) found that perceptions of appraisal participation, an aspect of procedural justice, mediate the relationship between relationship quality and appraisal reactions, whereas Selvarajan et al. (2018) found that leader–member exchanges mediate the relationship between perceptions of justice and appraisal reactions. It is likely that there is a reciprocal relationship here such that rater–ratee relationship quality and perceptions of justice in the appraisal context mutually determine each other and thus predict appraisal reactions; this is an important area for future research.

Further research has established a connection between due process performance appraisal and the social context of performance appraisal to appraisal reactions (Pichler et al., 2015). Appraisal reactions are more favorable under conditions of due process and high-quality rater–ratee relationships, even when performance ratings are low (Pichler, 2019). In- and out-groups are another important aspect of appraisal reactions, as ratees will perceive their appraisal differently based on what group they are in and how high the quality of their relationship with the rater is (Pichler et al., 2015). Raters can improve appraisal effectiveness by developing high-quality relationships with ratees and implementing due process characteristics in their performance appraisal systems. In addition, performance appraisals that are perceived by ratees to be morally justified will be perceived as more satisfactory than one that is not (Dusterhoff et al., 2013). Applying this to social exchange, ratees reciprocate the perceived fairness or lack of fairness of leader treatment by developing higher or lower quality exchanges with raters (Dusterhoff et al., 2013). In turn, this will affect how a ratee reacts to and is satisfied with their performance appraisal, since leader–member relationship quality plays a key role in this exchange.

CONCLUSION

Results from existing theory and research clearly indicate that it is important to examine how the social context within which performance appraisal occurs affects performance ratings in terms of their accuracy and perceived fairness. Existing research is still somewhat uncertain as to whether or not interpersonal affect or relationship quality act as biases in the appraisal process per se (cf. Lefkowitz, 2000; Robbins & DeNisi, 1998; Varma et al., 1996; Varma et al., 2005). Regardless, practitioners must be aware of how rater–ratee relationships affect performance ratings when designing performance appraisal systems and evaluating their effectiveness. Researchers should model how these relationships unfold over time, and how they are influenced by other contextual features of organizations (Murphy & Cleveland, 1995).

Kossek et al. (2007) argue that while due-process performance appraisal and other human resource management strategies are important mechanisms to manage increasing organizational diversity, increase justice and enhance organizational effectiveness, it is important to acknowledge the broader culture within which these strategies take place. For instance, if due process is limited to the performance appraisal process, and organizational culture is such that employees have few voice mechanisms, they may be skeptical about exercising their voice in the performance appraisal process for fear of negative repercussions (Meinecke et al., 2017). In fact, Meinecke et al. (2017) found that higher levels of supervisor trust had a direct relationship with increased perceptions of voice. Of course, broader cultural issues at more macro levels of analysis, such as power distance, should also be considered. The idea here is that future researchers should consider and measure the context within which the appraisal is taking place when conducting this research. In this way, we can better understand how context influences appraisal outcomes directly, as well as through its effects on rater–ratee relationship variables.

Since researchers have raised concerns that performance appraisal has little impact on actual performance change (Mohrman, Resnick-West, & Lawler, 1989), another important extension of this research is to, in fact, measure changes in performance as a result of differential motivation due to performance feedback and how relationship quality affects perceptions of feedback. It is also important to investigate the extent to which different types of appraisal reviews, such as strengths-based reviews versus more traditional reviews, affect rater–ratee relationship quality and appraisal outcomes (Van Woerkom & Kroon, 2020).

CASE STUDY

Am I in or out? Confusing Signals at V-Pharmel

April has recently joined the Beijing office of V-Pharmel, a large pharmaceutical conglomerate. She is very excited to learn and make friends with the other management trainees (MTs) who have been hired with her. The MTs quickly bonded and became friends, going to lunch and dinner together as well as attending the various onboarding and other orientation programs. However, April soon began to notice that there was another group of young men, similar to her in age, who were also in the lunchroom but always in a separate group. She soon discovered that they were also MTs but were from a different university in Beijing. She began to notice that their boss, Liu Zhiping, would always sit with the other group and laugh and joke with them. However, whenever Liu met with April's group, she was very reserved and matter-of-fact.

April and the other MTs were rather confused and decided to check with the junior executives who had also started as MTs at V-Pharmel. What they learned was rather shocking to them. The seniors told them that Liu and the other managers tended to create in-groups and out-groups among their subordinates and that those in the in-group almost always received better assignments, more attention and even higher ratings than those who were cast into the out-group. April and the other MTs on her table, so to say, wondered what they had done to achieve the out-group status. They were further shocked when the seniors told them their treatment might have something to do with the fact that the other group went to the same university as Liu and they did not.

CASE QUESTIONS

1. What is the impact of individual managers creating in-groups and out-groups among their subordinates?
2. How does in-group and out-group categorization thus impact both groups of subordinates?
3. What impact does such categorization have on the company's overall performance?
4. What do you think the subordinates in the out-group could do to change their group membership from out-group to in-group?

REFERENCES

Arvey, R.D., & Murphy, K.R. (1998). Performance evaluation in work settings. *Annual Review of Psychology, 49*, 141–168.

Blau, P. (1964). *Exchange and power in social life*. New York: Wiley.

Borman, W.C., White, L.A., & Dorsey, D.W. (1995). Effects of ratee task performance and interpersonal factors on supervisor and peer performance ratings. *Journal of Applied Psychology, 80*(1), 168–177.

Byrne, D. (1971). *The attraction paradigm.* New York: Academic Press.

Carroll, S., & Schneier, C. (1982). *Performance appraisal and review systems: The identification, measurement, and development of performance in organizations.* Glenview, IL: Scott, Foresman.

Cleveland, J.N., & Murphy, K.R. (1992). Analyzing performance appraisal as goal-directed behavior. *Research in Personnel and Human Resources Management, 10,* 121–185.

Cogliser, C.C., Schriesheim, C.A., Scandura, T.A., & Gardner, W.L. (2009). Balance in leader and follower perceptions of leader–member exchange: Relationships with performance and work attitudes. *The Leadership Quarterly, 20*(3), 452–465. https://doi.org/10.1016/j.leaqua.2009.03.010

Dansereau, F.J., Graen, G., & Haga, W.J. (1975). A vertical dyad linkage approach to leadership within formal organizations: a longitudinal investigation of the role making process. *Organizational Behavior and Human Performance, 13*(1), 46–78.

DeNisi, A.S. (2000). Performance appraisal and performance management: a multilevel analysis. In K.J. Klein, & Kozlowski, S.W.J. (Eds), *Multilevel theory, research, and methods in organizations.* San Francisco, CA: Jossey-Bass.

DeNisi, A.S., Cafferty, T.P., & Meglino, B.M. (1984). A cognitive view of the performance appraisal process: A model and research propositions. *Organizational Behavior and Human Performance, 33,* 360–396.

DeNisi, A.S., & Williams, K.J. (1988). Cognitive approaches to performance appraisal. In G.R. Ferris & K.M. Rowland (Eds.), *Research in personnel and human resource management* (vol. 6, pp. 109–155). Greenwich, CT: JAI Press.

Dienesch, R.D., & Liden, R.C. (1986). Leader-member exchange model of leadership: a critique and further development. *Academy of Management Review, 11,* 618–634.

Dipboye, R.L. (1985). Some neglected variables in research on discrimination in appraisals. *Academy of Management Review, 10,* 116–127.

Dusterhoff, C., Cunningham, J.B., & MacGregor, J.N. (2013). The effects of performance rating, leader–member exchange, perceived utility, and organizational justice on performance appraisal satisfaction: Applying a moral 'judgment perspective. *Journal of Business Ethics, 119*(2), 265–273. https://doi.org/10.1007/s10551-013-1634-1

Elicker, J.D., Levy, P.E., & Hall, R.J. (2006). The role of leader-member exchange in the performance appraisal process. *Journal of Management, 32*(4), 531–551.

Feldman, J.M. (1981). Beyond attribution theory: Cognitive processes in performance appraisal. *Journal of Applied Psychology, 66,* 127–148.

Folger, R., Konovsky, M.A., & Cropanzano, R. (1992). A due process metaphor for performance appraisal. In B.M. Staw & L.L. Cummings (Eds.), *Research in organizational behavior.* Greenwich, CT: JAI Press.

Giacalone, R.A., & Rosenfeld, P. (2013). *Impression management in the organization.* Abington, UK: Taylor & Francis Group.

Gooty, J., & Yammarino, F.J. (2013). The leader–member exchange relationship. *Journal of Management, 42*(4), 915–935. https://doi.org/10.1177/0149206313503009

Gottfredson, R.K., Wright, S.L., & Heaphy, E.D. (2020). A critique of the leader-member exchange construct: Back to square one. *The Leadership Quarterly, 31*(6), 101385. https://doi.org/10.1016/j.leaqua.2020.101385.

Graen, G. (1976). Role making processes within complex organizations. In M.D. Dunnette (Ed.), *Handbook of industrial and organizational psychology* (pp. 1201–1245). Chicago, IL: Rand McNally.

Guion, R.M. (1983). Comments on hunter. In F.L. Landy, S. Zedeck, & J. Cleveland (Eds.), *Performance measurement and theory* (pp. 267–275). Hillsdale, NJ: Lawrence Erlbaum & Associates.

Harrell-Cook, G., Ferris, G.R., & Dulebohn, J.H. (1999). Political behaviors as moderators of the perceptions of organizational politics—work outcomes relationships. *Journal of Organizational Behavior, 20*(7), 1093–1105.

Harris, M. (1994). Rater motivation in the performance appraisal context: A theoretical framework. *Journal of Management, 20*, 737–756.

Harrison, D.A., Price, K.H., & Bell, M.P. (1998). Beyond relational demography: time and the effects of surface and deep-level diversity on work group cohesion. *Academy of Management Journal, 41*, 96–107.

Heneman, R.L., Greenberger, D.B., & Anonyuo, C. (1989). Attributions and exchanges: The effects of interpersonal factors on the diagnosis of employee performance. *Academy of Management Journal, 32*(2), 456–476.

Hooper, D.T., & Martin, R. (2008). Beyond personal leader–member exchange (LMX) quality: The effects of perceived LMX variability on employee reactions. *The Leadership Quarterly, 19*(1), 20–30. https://doi.org/10.1016/j.leaqua.2007.12.002

Ilgen, D.R., & Feldman, J.M. (1983). Performance appraisal: A process focus. *Research in Organizational Behavior, 5*, 141–197.

Jacobs, R., & Kozlowski, S.W.J. (1985). A closer look at halo error in performance ratings. *Academy of Management Journal, 28*(1), 201–212.

John Bernardin, H., Thomason, S., Ronald Buckley, M., & Kane, J.S. (2015). Rater rating-level bias and accuracy in performance appraisals: The impact of rater personality, performance management competence, and rater accountability. *Human Resource Management, 55*(2), 321–340. https://doi.org/10.1002/hrm.21678

Judge, T.A., & Ferris, G.R. (1993). Social context of performance evaluation decisions. *Academy of Management Journal, 36*(1), 80–105.

Kacmar, K.M., Harris, K.J., Carlson, D.S., & Zivnuska, S. (2009). Surface-level actual similarity vs. deep-level perceived similarity: Predicting leader-member exchange agreement. *Journal of Behavioral and Applied Management, 10*(3). https://doi.org/10.21818/001c.17263

Kacmar, K.M., Witt, L.A., Zivnuska, S., & Gully, S.M. (2003). The interactive effect of leader-member exchange and communication frequency on performance ratings. *Journal of Applied Psychology, 88*(4), 764–772.

Kahn, R.L., Wolfe, D.M., Quinn, R.P., & Snoek, J.D. (1964). *Organizational stress: Studies in role conflict and ambiguity*. New York: Wiley.

Katz, I., & Glass, D.C. (1979). An ambivalence-amplification theory of behavior toward the stigmatized. In W.G. Austin & S. Worshel (Eds.), *Social psychology of intergroup relations* (pp. 55–70). Monterey, CA: Brooks-Cole.

Keeping, L. M., & Levy, P. E. (2000). Performance appraisal reactions: Measurement, modeling, and method bias. *Journal of Applied Psychology, 85*(5), 708.

Kim, T., & Holzer, M. (2014). Public employees and performance appraisal. *Review of Public Personnel Administration, 36*(1), 31–56. https://doi.org/10.1177/0734371x14549673

Klein, H.C., Snell, S.C., & Wexley, K.N. (1987). Systems model of the performance appraisal interview process. *Industrial Relations, 26*(3), 267–280.

Kossek, E., Pichler, S., Hammer, L., & Bodner, T. (2007). Contextualizing workplace supports for family: An integrative meta-analysis of direct and moderating linkages to work-family conflict. In *National Meetings of the Society of Industrial & Organizational Psychology, New York*.

Landy, F.J., & Farr, J.L. (1980). Performance rating. *Psychological Bulletin, 87*, 72–107.

Latham, G.P., & Wexley, K.N. (1981). *Improving performance through effective performance appraisal*. Reading, MA: Addison-Wesley.

Lefkowitz, J. (2000). The role of interpersonal affective regard in supervisory performance ratings: A literature review and proposed causal model. *Journal of Occupational and Organizational Psychology, 73*, 67–86.

Levy, P.E., & Williams, J.R. (2004). The social context of performance appraisal: A review and framework for the future. *Journal of Management, 30*(6), 881–905. https://doi.org/10.1016/j.jm.2004.06.005

Liden, R.C., & Mitchell, T.R. (1988). Ingratiatory behaviors in organizational settings. *Academy of Management Review, 13*, 572–587.

Liden, R.C., Wayne, S.J., & Stillwell, D. (1993). A longitudinal study on the early development of leader-member exchanges. *Journal of Applied Psychology, 78*(4), 662–674.

Markham, S.E., Yammarino, F.J., Murry, W.D., & Palanski, M.E. (2010). Leader–member exchange, shared values, and performance: Agreement and levels of analysis do matter. *The Leadership Quarterly, 21*(3), 469–480. https://doi.org/10.1016/j.leaqua.2010.03.010

Meinecke, A.L., Klonek, F.E., & Kauffeld, S. (2017). Appraisal participation and perceived voice in annual appraisal interviews. *Journal of Leadership & Organizational Studies, 24*(2), 230–245. https://doi.org/10.1177/1548051816655990

Mohrman, A.M., Resnick-West, S., & Lawler, E.E. (1989). *Designing performance appraisal systems.* San Francisco, CA: Jossey-Bass.

Motowidlo, S.J., & Van Scotter, J.R. (1994). Evidence that task performance should be distinguished from contextual performance. *Journal of Applied Psychology, 79*, 475–480.

Murphy, K., & Cleveland, J. (1990). *Performance appraisal: An organizational perspective.* Boston, MA: Allyn and Bacon.

Murphy, K.R., & Cleveland, J.N. (1991). *Performance appraisal: An organizational perspective.* Boston, MA: Allyn & Bacon.

Murphy, K.R., & Cleveland, J.N. (1995). *Understanding performance appraisal: Social, organizational, and goal-based perspectives.* Thousand Oaks, CA: Sage.

Murphy, K.R., Gannett, B.M., Herr, M.C., & Chen, E. (1986). Effects of subsequent performance on evaluations of previous performance. *Journal of Applied Psychology, 71*, 654–661.

Naiper, N., & Latham, G. (1986). Outcome expectancies of people who conduct performance appraisals. *Personnel Psychology, 39*, 827–837.

Nathan, B.R., Mohrman, A.M., & Millman, J. (1991). Interpersonal relations as a context for the effects of appraisal interviews on performance and satisfaction: A longitudinal study. *Academy of Management Journal, 34*(2), 352–369.

Oppler, S.H., Campbell, J.H., Pulakos, E.D., & Borman, W.C. (1992). Three approaches to the investigation of subgroup bias in performance measurement: Review, results and conclusions. *Journal of Applied Psychology, 77*(2), 201–217.

Park, S. (2014). Motivation of public managers as raters in performance appraisal. *Public Personnel Management, 43*(4), 387–414. https://doi.org/10.1177/0091026014530675

Pichler, S. (2019). Performance appraisal reactions: A review and research agenda. *Feedback at Work,* 75–96. https://doi.org/10.1007/978-3-030-30915-2_5

Pichler, S. (2012). The social context of performance appraisal and appraisal reactions: A meta-analysis. *Human Resource Management, 51*(5), 709–732. https://doi.org/10.1002/hrm.21499.

Pichler, S., Varma, A., Michel, J.S., Levy, P.E., Budhwar, P.S., & Sharma, A. (2015). Leader-member exchange, group- and individual-level procedural justice and reactions to performance appraisals. *Human Resource Management, 55*(5), 871–883. https://doi.org/10.1002/hrm.21724.

Porter, L.W., Angle, H., & Allen, R.W. (2016). *Organizational influence processes.* New York: Taylor & Francis.

Robbins, T.L. & DeNisi, A.S. (1994). A closer look at interpersonal affect as a distinct influence on cognitive processing in performance evaluations. *Journal of Applied Psychology, 79*(3), 341–353.

Robbins, T.L., & DeNisi, A.S. (1998). Mood vs. interpersonal affect: Identifying process and rating distortions in performance appraisal. *Journal of Business and Psychology, 12*, 313–325.

Rosen, C.C., Kacmar, K.M., Harris, K.J., Gavin, M.B., & Hochwarter, W.A. (2016). Workplace politics and performance appraisal. *Journal of Leadership & Organizational Studies, 24*(1), 20–38. https://doi.org/10.1177/1548051816661480

Rynes, S.L., Gerhart, B., & Parks, L. (2005). Personnel psychology: Performance evaluation and pay for performance. *Annual Review of Psychology, 56*, 571–600.

Saal, F.E., Downey, R.G., & Lahey, M.A. (1980). Rating the ratings: Assessing the psychometric quality of rating data. *Psychological Bulletin, 88*, 413–428.

Saraih, U., Karim, M., Hanie Abu Samah, I., Amlus, H., & Nazima Abashah, A. (2018). Relationships between trust, organizational justice and performance appraisal satisfaction: Evidence from public higher educational institution in Malaysia. *International Journal of Engineering & Technology, 7*(2.29), 602. https://doi.org/10.14419/ijet.v7i2.29.13983

Schaubroek, J., & Lam, S.S.K. (2002). How similarity to peers and supervisor influences organizational advancement in different cultures. *Academy of Management Journal, 45*(6), 1120–1136.

Selvarajan, T.T., Singh, B., & Solansky, S. (2018). Performance appraisal fairness, leader member exchange and motivation to improve performance: A study of US and Mexican employees. *Journal of Business Research, 85*, 142–154. https://doi.org/10.1016/j.jbusres.2017.11.043

Taylor, M.S., Tracy, K.B., Renard, M.K. Harrison, J.K., & Carroll, S.J. (1995). Due process in performance appraisal: A quasi-experiment in procedural justice. *Administrative Science Quarterly, 40*, 495–523.

Thomas, S.L., & Bretz, R.D. (1994). Research and practice in performance appraisal: Evaluating employee performance in America's largest companies. *SAM Advanced Management Journal, 4*, 28–34.

Tsui, A.S. & Barry, B. (1986). Interpersonal affect and rating errors. *Academy of Management Journal, 29*(3): 586–599.

Tsui, A.S., & Gutek, B.A. (1984). A role set analysis of gender differences in performance, affective relationships, and career success of industrial middle managers. *Academy of Management Journal, 27*, 619–636.

Van Woerkom, M., & Kroon, B. (2020). The effect of strengths-based performance appraisal on perceived supervisor support and the motivation to improve performance. *Frontiers in Psychology, 11*. https://doi.org/10.3389/fpsyg.2020.01883

Varma, A., Budhwar, P., Katou, A., & Mathew, J. (2016). Interpersonal affect and host country national support of expatriates: An investigation in China. *Journal of Global Mobility, 4*(4), 476–495.

Varma, A., DeNisi, A.S., & Peters, L.H. (1996). Interpersonal affect and performance appraisal: A field study. *Personnel Psychology, 49*, 341–360.

Varma, A., Pichler, S., & Srinivas, E.S. (2005). The role of interpersonal affect in performance appraisal: Evidence from two samples – U.S. and India. *International Journal of Human Resource Management, 16*(11), 2029–2044.

Varma, A., & Stroh, L.K. (2001). The impact of same-sex LMX dyads on performance evaluations. *Human Resource Management, 40*(4), 309–320.

Varma, A., Zilic, I., Katou, A., Blajic, B., & Jukic, N. (2020). Supervisor-subordinate relationships and employee performance appraisals: A multi-source investigation in Croatia. *Employee Relations, 43*(1), 45–62.

Vroom, V. (1964). *Work and motivation*. New York: Wiley.

Wayne, S.J., & Ferris, G.R. (1990). Influence tactics, affect and exchange quality in supervisor-subordinate interactions: A laboratory experiment and field study. *Journal of Applied Psychology, 75*, 487–499.

Wayne, S.J., & Liden, L. (1995). Effects of impression management on performance ratings: A longitudinal study. *Academy of Management Journal, 38*(1), 232–260.

Wexley, K.N., & Klimoski, R. (1984). Performance appraisal: An update. In K.M. Rowland & G.R. Ferris (Eds.), *Research in personnel and human resources management* (vol. 2, pp. 35–79). Greenwich, CT: JAI Press.

Wyer, R.S., & Srull, T.K. (1981). Category accessibility: Some theoretical and empirical issues concerning the processing of social stimulus information. In *Social Cognition* (pp. 161–198). Abington, UK: Routledge.

Yun, G.J., Donahue, L.M., Dudley, N.M., & McFarland, L.A. (2005). Rater personality, rating format, and Social Context: Implications for performance appraisal ratings. *International Journal of Selection and Assessment, 13*(2), 97–107. https://doi.org/10.1111/j.0965-075x.2005.00304.x

Zajonc, R.B. (1980). Feeling and thinking: Preferences need no inferences. *American Psychologist, 35*, 151–175.

Merit Pay

Barry Gerhart, Charlie Trevor and Dow Scott

Chapter 5

Two major purposes of performance management and appraisal programs are recognizing and rewarding performance. Merit pay, typically defined as a policy whereby employees with higher performance (or merit) ratings receive greater base pay or salary increases than employees with lower ratings, is one method of recognizing and rewarding performance. By so doing, management hopes to motivate employees and influence the composition of its future workforce by increasing the probability that high-performing employees will choose to join and stay with the organization. Although considerable evidence indicates that individual incentives, which include merit pay, can increase employee performance, design is a critical element of program success (e.g., Gerhart & Fang, 2013; Nyberg, Peper, & Trevor, 2016; Pham, Nguyen, & Springer, 2021).

In this chapter, we begin by examining merit pay in the broader context of pay strategy. We then describe the fundamental policy aspects of merit pay, as well as the challenges encountered in implementing merit pay policies or programs. We examine the challenges of executing a merit pay program globally and the importance of pay transparency. We make the case that merit pay is often defined and studied too narrowly and that a fuller picture (e.g., one that includes the effect of merit ratings on salary via their influence on promotion) is necessary. We close with a summary of key merit pay decisions and a listing of key decisions that must be considered in developing an effective merit pay program.

MERIT PAY AND PAY STRATEGY

Before addressing merit pay specifically, it is useful to provide context for base pay (salary or wage) compensation and pay

DOI: 10.4324/9781003306849-5

strategies (of which merit pay is a part), in terms of how much organizations pay (pay level) and how they pay (pay basis). Pay level can be defined as an organization's average cash compensation (including wages, salaries, bonuses, and stock-related payouts). More broadly, pay level may also include benefits. In the United States, for example, this adds roughly another 40 cents on top of every dollar paid in base pay. Typically, pay level is established by collecting survey information regarding what competitors pay similar types of employees. An organization must decide whether to pay the same, more, or less, relative to organizations identified as product or labor market competitors. An organization that identifies certain skills as more critical to business strategy execution may have higher pay levels for those jobs than for other jobs that are considered less important.

An organization may also choose different market positions for different components of pay level. For example, an organization may decide to set its base salary at the 40th percentile of competitor companies. With strong company performance, however, profit sharing, stock options, and so forth may, on average over time, result in total cash compensation being higher than average (50th percentile). Benefits levels may also come into play when considering how to position total compensation. In the United States, where benefits are a substantial portion of total compensation, some organizations, especially in the public sector, provide rich benefit packages to overcome base salaries that are lower than the average paid by labor market competitors.

Pay basis refers to the criteria used to decide the amount of pay that individual employees receive. For example, does an organization pay for seniority (e.g., in a unionized setting), does it pay for performance (e.g., using merit pay), or is some combination used? If the focus is on paying for performance, how is performance measured, and how strongly is it rewarded? Are there different target market positions for high performers compared to those performing at lower levels? Do low performers have the option of remaining with the organization, or does consistently low performance result in termination?

Merit pay is typically an increase to base salary (often annually), based on individual performance appraisal ratings. In addition to rewarding merit, this increase is used to adjust pay ranges

Barry Gerhart et al.

up to maintain the organization's pay position in the labor market. Merit bonuses are similar in that they reward performance based on performance appraisal ratings, but they differ in that the payment (bonus) does not become part of the base salary, thus limiting growth in fixed labor costs. A survey of primarily U.S. human resources and compensation professionals found that 89% of wage and salary increases were identified as merit increases (WorldatWork Compensation Programs and Practices Report, 2021). In this chapter, our focus is primarily on merit pay, although much of our discussion is also relevant to merit bonus programs.

An important point is that organizations tend to vary less on the pay-level dimension than on the pay basis (e.g., merit pay) dimension (Gerhart & Milkovich, 1990). One explanation is that constraints on pay level are stronger. Organizations are constrained from paying too little by labor market pressures (the need to attract and retain quality employees) and from paying too much by product or service market pressures (the need to control labor costs because they are typically a substantial share of total cost and thus affect the price competitiveness of products/services.)

By contrast, two organizations that have the same pay-level targets may differ significantly in the basis for that same pay level. For example, some organizations may pay 10% to 20% above market pay for all jobs, regardless of performance, while other organizations pay below the market to reduce costs and be more competitive in their industry or, if they are profitable, provide a richer benefit package or higher levels of incentive. In the former case, a higher pay level may be deemed important to allow selectivity in hiring and to increase employee retention. In the latter case, the focus may be on cost savings, so the organization may be willing to tolerate higher levels of turnover. Yet another strategy, in the case of merit pay, is for an organization to only pay high-performing employees 10% to 20% above market pay while paying average performers at the market rate and below-average performers below the market rate. Such a strategy may provide a direct incentive for high performance, as well as encourage low performers to leave. To the degree that any of the previously mentioned strategies contribute to higher productivity, it may be that the organization that has a higher pay level per employee may actually have lower unit labor costs (i.e., labor cost per unit of output/revenue) because the higher productivity of its employees more than offsets their higher compensation levels. In other words, it is possible that more revenue can be generated using a smaller number of highly productive and highly paid employees than can be generated using a larger number of less productive, lower paid employees.

The key point then is that organizations not only have more flexibility (Gerhart & Milkovich, 1990) with respect to pay basis (i.e., how they pay) than pay level (how much they pay), but it is also the case that pay-level and pay-basis decisions are (or should be) interrelated and that paying high salaries and wages is not necessarily inconsistent with controlling costs and being efficient (Gerhart & Rynes, 2003). In the case of merit pay, however, it does assume that supervisors can accurately measure performance and are willing and able to provide meaningful rewards to employees who perform at higher levels.

FUNDAMENTALS

Two basic purposes of merit pay are to motivate employees to perform at a high level by recognizing and rewarding performance and to build the best workforce possible by attracting and retaining high performers. These are also known as incentive and sorting effects, respectively (Gerhart & Rynes, 2003; Gerhart & Fang, 2013). As shown in Table 5.1, the idea behind merit pay is to pay consistently high-performing employees above the average market salary, average performers at the average market salary, and low performers below the average market salary. By doing so, employees, it is believed, will have an incentive to perform at high levels and that high performers will be attracted and retained (or *sorted*; Lazear, 1999) by paying them a salary that is above the average for their occupation or skill set. Alternatively, it may be thought of as there being different sub-labor markets based

Table 5.1 Target Salary as a Percentage of Market Salary (Compa-Ratio) by Performance Rating

Performance Rating	Target Salary as a Percentage of Market Salary
Exceeds Expectations	110%–125%
Meets Expectations	90%–110%
Below Expectations	80%–95%

Barry Gerhart et al.

on performance and that the motivation and retention of high performers require that their pay be consistent with the submarket rate for high performers (Trevor, Gerhart, & Boudreau, 1997). As noted, paying for performance is also expected to help attract applicants with high potential for future performance and create a performance-driven culture.

A third objective of merit pay is cost-effectiveness. What does it cost the organization, and what is the organization receiving in return? For example, if cash compensation is at the 70th percentile among product market competitors, is productivity at higher level that justifies the increased labor costs? Are high-potential applicants interested in working in the organization, and are high-performing or high-potential employees retained in a cost-effective manner?

Ideally, the higher target salary levels for higher performing employees under merit pay are based on a pattern of *consistently* high performance. A standard way of putting this philosophy into practice is to move employees toward the target salary that corresponds with their most recent performance rating but not make all-or-nothing adjustments in any single year. If an employee consistently performs at a high level, then, based on the targets shown in Table 5.1, the organization will want the employee to earn between 110% and 125% of the market salary. However, if an employee has performed at an average level in previous years and receives a high-performance rating in the most recent year, that employee will not be immediately moved to 110% to 125% of market salary. Rather, the employee will be moved toward that part of their salary range but will have to perform at a high level consistently over time to reach that salary target (Gerhart, 2023).

Thus, as shown in Table 5.2, organizations often use a merit increase grid (sometimes also referred to as a merit matrix, salary matrix, or salary increase grid). As can be seen, a merit increase, when using such a grid, depends not only on the performance rating but also on the current position in the range, typically defined as the compa-ratio, the ratio of the employee's current salary to the midpoint of their salary range. In turn, the salary midpoint range would be set, based to an important degree, on external market pay surveys that report what other organizations pay for a particular skill set (Gerhart, 2023).

Table 5.2 Merit Increase Grid: Recommended Salary Increases by Performance Rating and Compa-Ratio

	Compa-Ratio[a]		
	80%–90%	91%–110%	111%–120%
Performance Rating			
Exceeds Expectations	8%	6%	4%
Meets Expectations	6%	4%	3%
Below Expectations	3%	2%	0%

[a] Employee salary/midpoint of their salary range.

A second and related reason for using position in range or compa-ratio as a factor in assigning merit increases is cost control. If an employee with a high compa-ratio were to continually receive high salary increases in percentage terms, then that employee's salary would soon exceed the market rate for high performers. Consider, for example, the *Rule of 72*, which comes to us from the finance and investing community. It says that to estimate the number of years it takes for an investment to double in size, divide the rate of return (or interest rate) into the number 72. Using this rule, an employee receiving a 6% salary increase each year would double their salary every 12 years. Clearly, labor costs could get out of hand quickly without the cost control aspect of the merit increase grid.

What this cost control mechanism means for an employee is that, after some point, the value of their contributions in the same job, as indicated by their salary increases is limited. To obtain further salary growth, the employee would need to seek to be promoted to a higher salary range. Alternatively, some organizations give merit bonuses that do not become part of the base pay to high-performing employees at the top of their range. Other organizations have gone to broadband programs that provide a higher maximum salary rate for their salary ranges. These programs are used by organizations that wish to de-emphasize promotion as a path toward salary growth and wish to emphasize rewarding contributions more strongly in the current job. The potential downside, of course, is weaker control of labor costs.

Budgeting for merit pay at the organization or business unit level and the distribution of this budget to supervisors who award merit increases to employees is another important tool for controlling labor costs. Given the amount and permanency of merit increases, senior management (often including the CEO or president, CFO, and CHRO) is involved in setting the annual merit pay budget for the organization. Typically, affordability, average pay increases in the labor market during the past year, and the firm's experience recruiting and retaining employees are key factors. Once a fiscally responsible merit budget has been established, it is distributed in fixed amounts to the supervisors of departments or work units where judgments will be made as to how much each employee will receive as permanent pay increases. The merit budget is most often distributed as a percentage of the total base pay paid to employees within that work unit or department. For example, if a department has 10 employees (not including the supervisor who reports to the next higher level), the salaries or wage for each of those employees is totaled, and the department supervisor will receive a percentage of the total department salary as the budget to be distributed among those employees. So, if salaries for the 10 employees totaled $800,000 and the budget was 4%, then the supervisor of that department would have $32,000 to distribute among the employees based on their performance as a permanent pay increase. Thus, since the maximum amount the supervisor can award is $32,000, if some employees are awarded an increase of more than 4%, other employees must get less.

As one can see, the use of fixed merit budgets requires managers to make trade-offs as to who within the unit or department gets a pay increase and what that amount will be. In other words, even if the performance appraisal process does not require managers to do a force rating, the merit budget, in fact, requires such judgments to be made because giving a larger increase to one employee means that other employees will get less.

The annual merit budget is a major expense permanently incorporated into future labor costs and, if awarded improperly, can limit an organization's ability to motivate employee performance and attract and retain high-performing employees. Furthermore, improperly awarded merit increases can result in lawsuits claiming illegal gender, race, age, and national origin bias. As such, systematic and periodic evaluations or merit pay programs are essential. Scott and Beck-Krala (2019) provide a model for evaluating merit pay programs from the perspective of (1) employee perceptions, understanding, and behavior; (2) financial and operational impact; (3) administrative reliability and efficiency; and (4) social responsibility and sustainability. A rigorous evaluation design, data collection methodology, and analysis process are described.

Global Perspective

Pay practices surveys consistently demonstrate that merit pay is firmly embedded in most pay structures in the United States (Scott, Somersan, & Repsold, 2015b; WorldatWork Total Rewards Association, 2021). Although merit pay programs are becoming more prevalent globally, substantial differences in how employees are paid remain, especially as related to rewarding performance (Bryson, Freeman, Lucifora, Pellizzari, & Perotin, 2012), although such differences are smaller (Gerhart, 2023) in companies that operate across borders (vs. local companies). The increased globalization of companies and workforces makes an understanding of how contextual factors affect the design, effectiveness, and employee acceptance of merit pay programs important. Substantial differences in employment regulations, institutions, and cultural norms affect the use, effectiveness, and employee perceptions of merit pay.

Employment regulations can have a direct impact on how companies award pay increases. Austria, for example, has the *distribution option* that requires pay increases be split into two components, with a general increase paid to all employees and another portion that can be distributed to employees based on a works agreement between management and the works council (Kaar & Grunell, 2001; Salimaki & Heneman, 2008). Thus, the size of merit awards is considerably less than merit awards in the United States, where the entire pay increase budget is often awarded through the merit pay program. Regulations also determine how much influence an individual firm has in establishing pay levels and methods for allocating pay. In the United States, the United Kingdom, and Japan, the organization has considerable influence, whereas in Sweden, Greece, and China, centralized bargaining with unions and government regulations restricts the influence that any one employer may have on pay increases

(Salimaki & Heneman, 2008). Furthermore, as discussed in the next section, regulations concerning pay transparency also differ substantially across countries (Veldman, 2017).

The institutional structure and regulation of unions also differ substantially and can affect the freedom of a company to use merit pay to reward performance and increase salaries. Additionally, unions frequently resist individual pay-for-performance programs because they create competition among employees and allow managerial judgments as to how much employees will receive. Bryson, Freeman, Lucifora, Pellizzari, and Perotin (2012) found union bargaining power is negatively related to performance-related and discretionary pay.

As we know from research conducted by Hofstede (1980), the GLOBE (Global Leadership and Organizational Behavior Effectiveness) Project (House et al., 2004), and others, cultural norms differ across countries and may affect employee perceptions of performance evaluation and merit increases (Goktan & Saatcioglu, 2011). Some theories and research have attributed cultural norms associated with individualism and collectivism, the need for achievement, power distance, and risk aversion to preferences for pay-for-performance reward programs. For example, employees in countries with a strong culture of collectivism may not perceive a pay program that rewards individuals, such as a merit pay program, as positively as will a more individualistic country, such as the United States. Likewise, people with a higher need for achievement and lower risk aversion may prefer jobs for which pay is linked more closely to performance than will those in countries low on these culture dimensions.

Importantly, however, country differences are not necessarily explained by national cultural differences because countries differ on multiple dimensions (see the previous discussion). In fact, Scott, Brown, Shields, Long, Antoni, Beck-Krala, Lucia-Casademunt, and Perkins (2015a) found that employee preferences for variable pay did differ across counties but not consistently with any one cultural attribute. Scott, Antoni, Grodzicki, Morales, and Pelaez (2020) found that employees in Australia had a higher level of preference for bonuses than those from Spain and Germany. Furthermore, they found that German employees had a lower preference for pay differences based on capability, pay variability, and bonus plans than those in all other countries included in this study. Furthermore, even when (mean) country differences exist and even when they are statistically significant, their practical significance may be limited. For example, in a meta-analysis of country differences in reward allocation (e.g., how much influence performance has), Fischer and Smith (2003) reported that country explained 3% of the variance in reward allocation decisions, leaving 97% unexplained by country (Gerhart, 2008).

As such, organizations with multiple global locations should be thoughtful about rolling out a merit pay program, carefully considering the degree to which it is in alignment with each location's cultural norms and employment practices. To the degree it is not, it should be due to a conscious decision to differentiate. There is a fundamental globalization versus localization issue that companies must consider once they have employees in multiple countries. In other words, is the multinational company going to create a uniform (standardized) set of compensation policies and programs to support a strategic plan and make it easier to move employees between countries (to the extent allowed by law), or is it going to develop customized compensation practices to align with the culture and other local labor market competitors? Of course, organizations within a country are typically not the same as we know from the fact that strategies and organization cultures also vary substantially within countries, as do the attributes of different organizations' workforces due related to attraction–selection–attrition processes, including sorting (Gerhart & Fang, 2013). Here, it is useful to keep in mind that even in the seminal Hofstede (1990) study, knowing a person's country explained only 2% to 3% of the variance in cultural values (Gerhart & Fang, 2005). That is because of the large variance in values within countries. Some evidence suggests that most global companies follow a strategy of standardization rather than localization when it comes to merit pay and compensation generally (Gerhart, 2023, Exhibit 16.17). The large amount of within-country variance helps organizations find enough employees who fit their compensation strategy.

PAY TRANSPARENCY CONSIDERATIONS

In recent years, pay transparency has become a major issue for governments and employers, both in terms of promoting

Barry Gerhart et al.

pay equity and as an indicator of an organization's commitment to open communications. If the goal is to motivate employees and encourage high performers to stay and poor performers to leave, employees must understand the message sent by the merit increase they receive. Thus, to correctly interpret a pay increase, employees need to know the amount of the average merit increase and their position in the pay range. In addition, the process by which the pay increase was determined through merit increase budgeting, performance evaluation, and the method by which the awards were distributed will provide information as to how employees should direct their future efforts. Furthermore, understanding the process can help reassure employees that the pay increase was based on merit as opposed to unfair biases held by their supervisor.

Scott, Somersan, and Repsold (2015b) found that rewards professionals believed pay communications to be an important element of effective compensation programs. However, this conflicted with findings that management shared little information about the merit pay program and how merit increases were determined. Only one-third of compensation professionals rated their rewards communications as effective (McMullen & Scott, 2020). Recent research examines the conditions under which pay transparency has positive or negative effects. For example, in terms of employee reactions (SimanTov-Nachlieli & Bamberger, 2021), higher paid employees react more favorably and lower paid employees, less favorably (due to low perceived distributive justice).

IMPLEMENTATION CHALLENGES

Although more than 85% of organizations report having merit pay programs, (WorldatWork Association, 2021 Compensation Programs and Practices Report), the literature consistently reports the challenges of implementing and administering merit pay programs that actually reward merit and that employees perceive as fair (e.g., Salimaki & Jamsen, 2010; Werner & Heneman, 2007). In many organizations, employees are not convinced that high performers receive salaries or salary increases that differ in a meaningful way from what average and lower performing employees receive. In that case, motivation and attraction or retention objectives are likely to be undermined.

Table 5.3 Distribution of Performance Ratings

Performance Rating	Frequency
Exceeds Expectations	40%
Meets Expectations	55%
Below Expectations	5%

The two culprits in employee skepticism are a lack of objectivity in merit pay dissemination or inadequate communication to employees, as discussed earlier.

One common problem with performance rating measures is that ratings are often clustered tightly and somewhat leniently. Table 5.3 provides an example of what this distribution might look like. This lack of variance in performance ratings translates directly into a lack of variance in salary increases, thus undermining the purpose of merit pay. This lack of variance arises due to a number of factors. First, supervisors may be reluctant to give different ratings to members of their workgroup because of a concern about the effect on workgroup cooperation or because managers may fear demotivating or angering people on whom they depend for future productivity. Second, in many organizations, supervisors are asked to explain low or high ratings but not other ratings. Third, the performance rating system may not be well designed and credible enough to support differentiation among employees. Among the ways this aspect can be improved are by setting specific performance goals in conjunction with employees, having multiple raters to reduce favoritism or idiosyncratic ratings, and involving employees in the design of the performance appraisal system.

Organizations have other tools at their disposal to increase differentiation in merit pay. In 1980, Jack Welch, CEO of GE (General Electric), championed the forced distribution of performance ratings, whereby a certain percentage of employees must fall into each of the performance rating categories. For example, rather than having a distribution that often comes out to be about 40%–55%–5% or some other distribution that results from individual managers having discretion, a forced distribution policy might require a distribution of 20%–70%–10%. Several companies instituted these forced distribution systems, and most, including GE, have encountered problems with employee morale and/or equal employment opportunity (e.g., age-related) litigation, leading them to discontinue their use of such programs.

Another potential drawback of a forced distribution system is that cooperation and teamwork may be harmed if the available pool of performance ratings and merit increases is fixed, regardless of the performance of the organization or units within the organization. This effect must be balanced against the hoped-for positive effects on attraction, motivation, and retention of top performers. If low performers are not satisfied with the system, that can be a positive if there is an effective performance management mechanism for terminating those low performers from the organization. The threat to teamwork/cooperation is likely to be greatest where there is greater interdependence among employees. The potential for problems is also likely to depend on whether the distribution is flexible and the degree to which competitive aspects are balanced by pay-for-performance programs (e.g., team, business unit, or organization-wide incentives) that provide an incentive for cooperation.

Another potential roadblock to paying for performance is the design of merit guidelines, including the merit increase grid discussed earlier (see Table 5.3). Obviously, even if performance ratings are differentiated, there will be little pay for performance if the size of merit increases does not differ significantly according to different performance ratings. Also, as discussed previously, merit increase grids are typically designed to give smaller merit increases to those already paid above the midpoint (i.e., those with higher compa-ratios) for cost control reasons and because those employees are thought to already be at the appropriate pay level, relative to the market. However, there is the potential for de-motivation for these employees, especially if opportunities for promotion based on performance are limited. In such cases, broadbands (see the earlier discussion) may be considered. Another possibility is the use of merit-based bonuses that do not become part of the base salary (e.g., Nyberg, Peper, & Trevor, 2016).

These features of merit pay programs can create a situation in which employees perceive there to be little in the way of pay for performance (Gerhart & Rynes, 2003; Scott, 2012). Consider the case of two employees, each earning $50,000 per year. Suppose that the first receives an *excellent* performance rating and a 6% merit increase, while the second receives a *very good* rating and a 5% increase. On an annual basis, the differential is only 1% or $500. On a weekly basis, the differential is $500/52 = $9.62. With a marginal tax rate of, say, 40%, the after-tax weekly differential is $5.77. Is this performance payoff sufficient to motivate Employee A to maintain the same level of high performance or motivate Employee B to aspire to higher performance? Many people would say no. Furthermore, given the imprecision of performance ratings, there is no assurance that better performance by Employee B would actually result in a higher rating and a modestly higher take-home pay.

Thus, it is easy to understand why employees are often skeptical about the real link between pay and performance. Consider, for example, a survey of employees in 335 companies conducted by the HayGroup (2002). Employees were asked whether they agreed with the statement "If my performance improves, I will receive better compensation." Only 35% agreed, whereas 27% neither agreed nor disagreed, and 38% disagreed with this statement.

Academics have also expressed skepticism regarding the effectiveness of merit pay (e.g., Deming, 1986; Pfeffer, 1998). A review of the arguments and counterarguments is not possible here. The interested reader is referred to Gerhart and Rynes (2003) for a review of merit pay and, more generally, incentive pay. Here, we note that Gerhart and Rynes concluded that, "despite considerable skepticism about merit pay, the actual evidence on merit pay is primarily positive" (p. 189). In addition, they argued that "important effects of merit pay have been largely ignored in the research literature" and upon accounting for these, "the evidence is bound to look considerably more positive" (p. 190). We discuss these ignored issues in the following section.

A FULLER PICTURE

Without in any way minimizing the challenges discussed earlier, it can be argued that the case for merit pay is stronger than usually believed for the following reasons:

First, small differences in merit pay can accumulate significantly over time. Returning to our earlier scenario, after

20 years, Employee A is earning $121,024, while Employee B is earning $101,078. Moreover, during that 20-year period, Employee A has earned $148,785 more than Employee B has, which is a substantial amount, even if adjusted to its present value ($76,690 using a 5% discount rate). If employees were informed that performing at a level consistently above average during the first half of their careers would yield this amount of extra cash, perhaps their instrumentality perceptions would be stronger, and they would react differently to merit pay, even at modest levels. This hypothesis, however, remains untested to date.

Second, merit pay is often defined too narrowly. Whether Employees A and B in our example receive significantly different pay increases in one year or over time is only part of the story. Rather, one must recognize that merit ratings not only influence annual salary increases (and/or bonuses) but also influence promotions (Gerhart & Milkovich, 1989).

Promotions, in turn, generally have a twofold effect on career earnings (Gerhart & Milkovich, 1992; Trevor, Gerhart, & Boudreau, 1997). First, there is typically a pay increase that goes along with the promotion and that may be considerably larger than the typical annual merit increase. The average pay increase due to promotion is in the range of 15% (Lazear, 1999; Gerhart, 2023, Chapter 10), which is considerably higher than the average within-grade merit increase (roughly 3% in recent years in the United States). Moreover, the pay increase due to promotion is considerably larger at top management levels, often more than 70% (Gerhart & Milkovich, 1990).

Second, a promotion usually moves the employee to a new pay grade at which they will have a lower compa-ratio. As we have seen, merit increase grids typically provide larger percentage increases to those with lower compa-ratios in the interest of moving their pay toward the target level for that position. Thus, the impact of performance on promotions can have significant consequences for the strength of pay-performance relationships, but these will be revealed only by examining the relationship over time.

Finally, sorting effects may also lead us to underestimate the true magnitude of the relationship between pay and performance

(Gerhart & Rynes, 2003). For example, in organizations that use selective and valid hiring procedures and that systematically *manage out* those who do not meet performance standards, those hired and those who remain employed will be more likely to perform at acceptable or higher levels (Boudreau & Berger, 1985). While there may be little variance in performance and/or pay within this group, this selected group of employees may have above-market pay, consistent with what may be their above-market performance. Thus, there are differences in pay based on performance, but it is a *between*-group difference (current employees vs. former employees) rather than a *within*-group (current employees) difference. Similarly, on the employee side of the decision, it may be that high performers are more likely to be interested in organizations that pay for performance and less likely to voluntarily exit from such organizations. In summary, even when there is little observed variance in performance ratings or pay within an organization, it may nevertheless be the case that sorting effects (and promotion can be included under this heading) have resulted in major differences in performance among organizations.

KEY DECISIONS

To summarize, the key decisions that should be considered in the design and implementation of merit pay programs or policies include the following:

1. *Performance Dimensions: What Criteria Are Included in Our Measure of Merit or Performance?* A job analysis is necessary to identify the key dimensions of job performance. Anything that is not measured and included in performance assessment risks being ignored. Equally problematic is having too many performance measures whereby an employee cannot prioritize their efforts.
2. *Pay for Performance Strength or Differentiation: To What Degree Are Pay and Performance Related?* As discussed, for merit pay to have incentive and sorting effects, the relationship between pay and performance must be meaningful. The reward, whether financial or recognition, must be substantial enough to motivate the desired behavior.

3. *Criteria Type: Results or Behaviors?* A balance between results and behavioral performance measures is important. Initially, the objective nature of results-oriented measures that include goal accomplishment (management by objectives), physical output, sales, and profits, may be seen as a major advantage; however, behaviorally based measures, while more subjective, can be used to verify that results are obtained in a way consistent with organizational values. Furthermore, behavioral measures provide an opportunity to coach employees in more effectively performing their jobs and earning merit increases because of this increased performance.

4. *Individual or Aggregate Performance Measures?* While merit pay is typically defined as individual-oriented (as with the results versus behavior issue), it must be recognized that, in practice, paying for performance may more broadly include individual and aggregate measures of performance. Thus, organizations may either include dimensions such as teamwork in merit ratings or seek to complement individual-level programs such as merit pay with programs that reward aggregate performance (e.g., profit sharing, stock plans).

5. *Sources of Performance Evaluation: Supervisor or Supervisor + Others?* Traditionally, the immediate supervisor has rated employee performance. Today, however, some organizations now use multisource programs (e.g., "360" programs that add feedback from subordinates, peers, and/or customers; London & Smither, 1995). Most organizations use multisource programs for employee development and career management rather than for pay and promotion decisions (Rynes, Gerhart, & Parks, 2005). Nevertheless, merit pay programs can have greater credibility and reliability if multiple raters are used. Most commonly, this would involve adding additional raters at the level of the employee's supervisor or above (rather than the peer, subordinate, or customer levels).

6. *Standards: Absolute or Relative (e.g., ranking, forced distribution)?* As discussed earlier, left to their own devices, managers tend to compress their distribution of assigned performance ratings, thus making it difficult to differentiate among employees in the merit pay process. A relative system, such as forced distribution, can efficiently change the distribution to have

more variance. Potential drawbacks include penalizing units that do, in fact, have many high performers and creating harmful competition among employees for the limited number of high ratings, which may harm cooperation and teamwork.

7. *Merit Salary Increases or Merit Bonuses?* Traditionally, most white-collar employees received annual merit increases that became a permanent part of their base salary. From an employer's point of view, these increases become part of long-term fixed labor costs. When sales decline, an employer's only option for reducing labor costs under this system is to reduce employment or cut employee pay. Alternatively, variable pay plans seek to have labor costs vary in alignment with variance in sales and/or profits. Such plans provide employee payments in the form of bonuses that do not become part of the base salary. A merit bonus would typically depend on both company performance (e.g., profits) and an individual employee's merit rating. Nyberg, Peper, and Trevor (2016) found that both merit pay increases and merit bonuses are positively associated with future employee performance. The cumulative (and thus larger) effect of merit ratings on salary over time, however, would be reduced by using merit bonuses, which, by design, do not accumulate. However, this strategy increases the risk that the organization will fall behind in its target competitive pay position in the labor market.

8. *Pay Transparency: How Much Information About Pay Should Be Shared With Employees?* Pay is important to employees, and it conveys an important message as to the value of an individual's performance. At a minimum, employees should receive the information needed to correctly interpret the message conveyed by a merit increase. However, the level of detail provided and employee privacy issues must be considered.

9. *Multinational Company Considerations: Should Merit Pay Program Design and Rewards Be Uniform Across Countries or Locally Responsive to Employment Traditions, Institutions, and Culture?* As discussed, individual rewards may not be well received by employees in some countries; regardless, a company may consider pay for performance as an important competitive advantage in terms of attracting, motivating, and retaining employees.

10. *Program Evaluation: Is a Periodic Merit Pay Program Evaluation Worth the Investment?* The purpose of merit pay programs is to increase individual and organizational performance, but they can be fraught with challenges and involve large expenditures that permanently increase labor costs. As such, the organization should consider the level and frequency of merit pay program evaluation.

CONCLUSION

Merit pay is a policy or program intended to differentiate pay increases to employees based on their performance. Over time, high-performing employees are expected to move to higher pay levels in a salary range than are low performers. Additionally, merit influences promotion, which typically results in still larger differences in pay levels as a function of performance over time. Another important, but often overlooked, effect of merit pay is to sort prospective and current employees (Cadsby, Song, & Tapon, 2007; Gerhart & Fang, 2013) such that high performers are more likely to be found at firms having stronger merit pay programs. These effects of merit pay depend on, first, a meaningful link being established between merit/performance ratings and pay and, second, employee understanding and a perception that the program is fair and credible. Merit pay programs differ significantly across organizations, and the 10 key decision areas represent the many ways in which the design of these programs can differ. Finally, it is important to recognize that merit pay programs are often combined with other pay-for-performance programs, including profit sharing, gain sharing, and sales bonuses.

For researchers, merit pay is an area that has been understudied, at least in terms of designs (Rynes et al., 2005) that include control groups (or significant variation across units or organizations in merit pay strength), intervening process variables (e.g., perceptions of merit pay strength), and/or careful longitudinal analyses (Rynes et al., 2005). Empirical work is also needed on the costs and benefits of forced distribution systems, on whether the merit pay and employee development aspects of performance management and appraisal should or should not be linked, and on the effects of merit pay when both sorting and incentive effects are examined and when merit pay is defined more fully to include not only merit increases for current performance but also the effect of merit ratings on promotion and overall pay growth over time. Finally, further research that focuses on quantifying the costs and benefits of merit pay decisions (e.g., Sturman, Trevor, Boudreau, & Gerhart, 2003) is needed.

Short Case

John Smith, president of a small company that provides software to corporate clients, wishes to make sure that his company's pay-for-performance system supports its strategic goals and their execution. Strategic goals include developing innovative software applications, customer satisfaction, and customer retention while keeping costs in check. Currently, salespeople are paid using a commission plan that determines payments based on quarterly revenues for each salesperson. Software engineers are currently covered by an incentive plan whereby payments depend on how much software code they write per quarter. Merit ratings are also conducted. Each employee is assigned an overall rating by the immediate supervisor once per year. These ratings have little impact on pay, however, because most people receive similar ratings, and there is also a belief that objective measures of performance are better.

QUESTIONS

1. Are the incentive programs in place aligned with the company's strategic goals? Is there any role for merit pay to play a greater role in achieving better alignment? Explain.
2. If merit pay is to play a larger role, what sort of changes to the current system may be necessary?
3. In addition to the sales and software engineers mentioned, what other employee groups would a merit pay plan likely cover, and what unique issues would be relevant to consider in designing merit pay for these different groups?

REFERENCES

Boudreau, J.W., & Berger, C.J. (1985). Decision-theoretic utility analysis applied to employee separations and acquisitions (Monograph). *Journal of Applied Psychology*, 70, 581–612.

Bryson, A., Freeman, R., Lucifora, C., Pellizzari, M., & Perotin, V. (2012). *Paying for performance: Incentive pay schemes and employee financial participation.* Centre for Economic Performance: London School of Economics and Political Science.

Barry Gerhart et al.

Cadsby, C.B., Song, F., & Tapon, F. (2007). Sorting and incentive effects of pay-for-performance: An experimental investigation. *Academy of Management Journal, 50,* 387–405.

Deming, W.E. (1986). *Out of the crisis.* Cambridge: MIT, Center for Advanced Engineering Study.

Fischer, R., Smith, P. (2003). Reward allocation and culture: a meta-analysis. *Journal of Cross-Cultural Psychology, 34,* 251–268.

Gerhart, B. (2008). Compensation and national culture. In S. Werner & L.R. Gomez-Mejia (Eds.), *Global compensation: Foundations and perspectives.* London: Routledge.

Gerhart, B. (2023). *Compensation,* 14th ed. Boston, MA: McGraw-Hill/Irwin.

Gerhart, B., & Fang, M. (2005). National culture and human resource management: Assumptions and evidence. *International Journal of Human Resource Management, 16,* 975–990.

Gerhart, B., & Fang, M. (2013). Pay for (individual) performance: Issues, claims, evidence and the role of sorting effects. *Human Resource Management Review, 24,* 41–52.

Gerhart, B., & Milkovich, G.T. (1990). Organizational differences in managerial compensation and financial performance. *Academy of Management Journal, 33,* 663–691.

Gerhart, B., & Milkovich, G.T. (1992). Employee compensation: Research and practice. In M.D. Dunnette & L.M. Hough (Eds.), *Handbook of industrial & organizational psychology* (2nd ed., pp 481–570). Palo Alto, CA: Consulting Psychologists Press, Inc.

Gerhart, B., & Milkovich, G.T. (1989). Salaries, salary growth, and promotions of men and women in a large, private firm. In R. Michael, H. Hartmann, & B. O'Farrell (Eds.), *Pay equity: Empirical inquiries.* Washington, DC: National Academy Press.

Gerhart, B., & Rynes, S.L. (2003). *Compensation: Theory, evidence, and strategic implications.* Thousand Oaks, CA: Sage.

Goktan, A.B., & Saatcioglu, O.Y. (2011). The effect of cultural values on pay preferences: A comparative study in Turkey and the United States. *International Journal of Management, 28*(1), 173–184.

HayGroup. (2002). Managing performance: Achieving outstanding performance through a "culture of dialogue". Working paper.

Hofstede, G. (1980). *Cultural consequences: International differences in work-related values.* Beverly Hills, CA: Sage.

Hofstede, G. (1990). A Reply and Comment on Joginder P. Singh: 'Managerial Culture and Work-Related Values in India'. *Organization Studies, 11*(1), 103–106.

House, R.J., Hanges, P.J., Javidan, M. Dorfman, P.W., & Gupta, V. (2004). *Culture, leadership, and organizations.* Thousand Oaks, CA: Sage.

Kaar, R.V.H., & Grunell, M. (2001). Eurofound report: Variable pay in Europe. April 27. https://www.eurofound.europa.eu/publications/report/2001/variable-pay-in-europe

Lazear, E.P. (1999). Personnel economics: Past lessons and future directions. *Journal of Labor Economics, 17,* 199–236.

London, M., & Smither, J.W. (1995). Can multisource feedback change perceptions of goal accomplishment, self-evaluations, and performance-related outcomes? Theory-based applications and directions for research. *Personnel Psychology, 48,* 803–839.

McMullen, T., & Scott, D. (2020). Findings from two decades of total rewards research. *Journal of Total Rewards, 29*(3), 6–13.

Nyberg, A.J., Peper, J.R., & Trevor, C.O. (2016). Pay-for-performance effect on future employee performance: Integrating psychological and economic principles toward a contingency perspective. *Journal of Management, 42*(7), 1753–1783.

Pfeffer, J. (1998). Six dangerous myths about pay. *Harvard Business Review, 76,* 108–120.

Pham, L.D., Nguyen, T.D., & Springer, M.G. (2021). Teacher merit pay: A meta-analysis. *American Educational Research Journal. 58*(3), 527–566.

Rynes, S.L., Gerhart, B., & Parks, L. (2005). Personnel psychology: Performance evaluation and pay for performance *Annual Review of Psychology*, 56, 571–600.

Salimaki, A., & Heneman, R.L. (2008). Pay for performance for global employees. In L.R. Gomez-Mejia & S. Werner (Eds.), *Global compensation: Foundations and perspectives* (pp. 158–166). Taylor & Francis Group.

Salimaki, A., & Jamsen, S. (2010). Perceptions of politics and fairness in merit pay. *Journal of Managerial Psychology*, 25(3), 229–251.

Scott, D. (2012). Blending general increases with a pay-for-performance policy. *Bloomberg BNA – Benefits and compensation update*. 20 17), 136.

Scott, D., Antoni, C., Grodzicki, J., Morales, E., & Pelaez, J. (2020). Global pay transparency: An employee perspective. *Compensation and Benefits Review*, 52(3), 85–97.

Scott, K.D. & Beck-Krala, E. (2019) Evaluating reward strategies, programs, and policies: Research and practice. In Stephen Perkins (Ed.), *The routledge companion to reward management* (pp. 97–111). London: Routledge, Taylor & Francis Group.

Scott, D., Brown, M., Shields, J., Long, R., Antoni, C., Beck-Krala, E., Casademunt, A.M.L., & Perkins, S. (2015a). A global study of pay preferences and employee characteristics. *Compensation and Benefits Review*, 47(2) 60–70.

Scott, D., Somersan, R., & Repsold, B. (2015b). Is there merit in merit pay? A survey of reward professionals. *WorldatWork Journal*. 24(1), 6–17.

SimanTov-Nachlieli, I., & Bamberger, P. (2021). Pay communication, justice, and affect: The asymmetric effects of process and outcome pay transparency on counterproductive workplace behavior. *Journal of Applied Psychology*, 106(2), 230.

Sturman, M.C., Trevor, C.O., Boudreau, J.W., & Gerhart, B. (2003). Is it worth it to win the talent war? Evaluating the utility of performance-based pay. *Personnel Psychology*, 56, 997–1035.

Trevor, C.O., Gerhart, B., & Boudreau, J.W. (1997). Voluntary turnover and job performance: Curvilinearity and the moderating influences of salary growth and promotions. *Journal of Applied Psychology*, 82, 44–61.

Veldman, A. (2017). Pay transparency in the EU: A legal analysis of the situation in the EU member states, Iceland, Liechtenstein and Norway. Report prepared for the European Commission, Directorate-General for Justice and Consumers, Directorate D–Equality Unit, Brussels. https://doi.org/10.2838/148250. Retrieved May 22, 2019, from https://publications.europa.eu/en/publication-detail/-/publication/329c3e47-2bd8-11e7-9412-01aa75ed71a1

Werner, J.M., & R.L. Heneman. (2007). "What have we learned about merit pay plans?" In Dow Scott (Ed.), *Incentive pay: Creating a competitive advantage* (pp. 29–41). Scottsdale, AZ: WorldatWork Press.

WorldatWork Total Rewards Association. (2021). Compensation Programs and Practices Annual Survey Results. September, 25.

A Model of the Appraisal Process

Kevin R. Murphy and Angelo S. DeNisi

Chapter 6

Over the years, a number of scholars have proposed models of the performance appraisal process, primarily as means of organizing past research and generating propositions for future research. Many of these models have focused on the rater as a decision maker who must acquire and process information in order to make appraisal decisions (e.g., DeCotiis & Petit, 1978; DeNisi, Cafferty, & Meglino, 1984; Feldman, 1981), while others have expended this view to consider organizational and contextual factors influencing appraisals in addition to rater decision-making activities (Landy & Farr, 1980; Murphy & Cleveland, 1995; Wexley & Klimoski, 1984). These models have generated a large amount of research and have generally served the field well in terms of suggesting new ideas for research. We do not mean to endorse or challenge any of these models or the ideas they have generated, but we have drawn on several of these to propose a model of the appraisal process that has a somewhat different goal.

The present volume deals with various perspectives on the processes of performance appraisal and performance management, prepared by scholars and managers from all around the world. Our goal, in this chapter, is to provide a set of unifying themes that can be used for the discussions of these perspectives.

DOI: 10.4324/9781003306849-6

That is, we do not propose a model to generate new research ideas (although we do discuss some possibilities along these lines later in the chapter), nor do we propose a model that is to replace any of the models already available. Instead, we propose a model that includes contextual factors that we believe influence appraisal decisions at various levels of analysis, as well as at individual-level cognitive and motivational factors that are likely to affect appraisals in a wide range of settings. Our goal is to provide a template for the various authors of the chapters in this volume that can be used to discuss the different systems using a set of common issues and topics. In particular, we propose a framework that can be used to compare performance appraisal and performance management systems across organizations, nations, and cultures.

We believe that all performance management systems, wherever they occur, can be analyzed in terms of the factors in our model. For example, in any country, in any setting, cultural norms, the legal system, and technology will play a role in determining how appraisals are done and how they are used. But, since the actual norms, systems, and technology will vary from setting to setting, the particular features of performance appraisal and performance management systems will almost certainly vary across industries, nations, and so on. We believe that analyzing diverse performance appraisal and performance management systems in terms of the models we present here will help illustrate the commonalities and explain the differences in systems. While we do not claim that our framework is comprehensive or universal, we do believe that it provides a basis for integrating global studies of performance appraisal and performance management systems.

THE PROPOSED MODEL: PART I

The model we use is presented in two parts, in Figure 6.1, and Figure 6.2. The first model (Figure 6.1) focuses on the performance appraisal process and ends with an evaluation that becomes part of the feedback to an individual employee (or team), as part of the performance management process aimed at improving performance at both the individual and organizational levels. The second model (Figure 6.2) deals with the performance management process and begins with the feedback provided in the appraisal process. We discuss this second model in more detail

Kevin R. Murphy and Angelo S. DeNisi

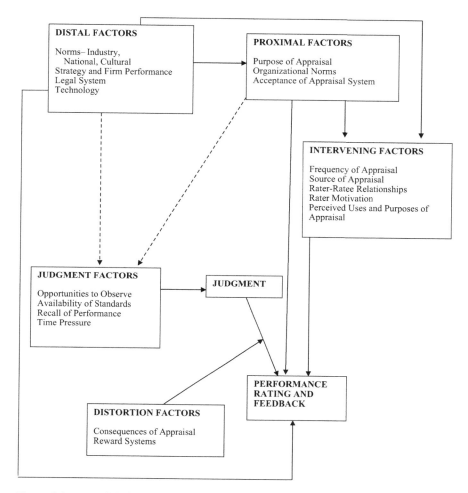

Figure 6.1   A Model of the Performance Appraisal Process

later, but we focus first on our performance appraisal model.
As can be seen in the figure, the first model is divided into several
distinct segments, and we describe each in turn.

Distal Factors

The model begins by acknowledging the role of distal factors
that operate at the level of the nation or region but that can still
influence the appraisal process. We discuss each of these in the
following sections, but these factors are things which are fixed,
for the most part, as far as the organization is concerned, and so
act as constraints or parameters for action the organization might

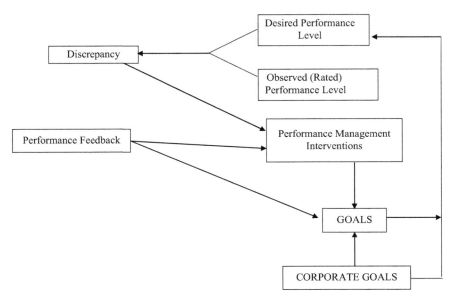

Figure 6.2   A Model of the Performance Management Process

take. Also included here are organizational factors at the most macro level of analysis, such as firm performance and firm strategy. These factors are somewhat under the control of the organization, but, even in cases where the factor can be changed (such as the strategy pursued), they are not likely to be changed simply to make the performance management process more effective, and so these, too, serve primarily as constraints or parameters within which the performance management system must operate.

Norms

Norms for behaviour exist at the level of the country, the industry, and the specific organization. For example, norms differ as to the way appraisals are used in organizations. In some organizations, it is the norm for all compensation decisions to be based on appraisals. This is also more likely to be the case in non-unionized sectors of the economy (e.g., service industries) and in individualistic societies, such as the United States. In these cases, appraisals are likely to be conducted once a year, since that is when permanent pay adjustments are likely to be made. Furthermore, the appraisals would likely occur at some point not far before the pay decisions must be made. However, in organizations where it

Kevin R. Murphy and Angelo S. DeNisi

was the norm for appraisals to be used for feedback purposes only, appraisals would likely occur more frequently and at less regular intervals.

Also, in societies where hierarchical relationships are more important (e.g., China), it is more likely that performance appraisals will be the sole province of the supervisor. In these societies, the notion that a subordinate might appraise their superior would be difficult to accept. Yet, in other societies, in which values such as power distance were low, it would be perfectly acceptable to have appraisals done by peers and even subordinates. In fact, in some societies where power distance was low and collaboration and collectivist views were valued, traditional supervisory performance appraisals might be seen as an illegitimate infringement on the rights of the workers or the work group, whereas in a culture with higher power distance, such supervisory appraisals would not only seem acceptable, but they might also be desired.

Thus, norms, whether they exist at the level of the organization, the industry, or the nation, can influence the appraisal process. These norms help to determine exactly which practices are acceptable and which are not, and so they serve as constraints on what the organization can realistically do with appraisals.

Strategy and Firm Performance

The strategy a firm pursues in competing also will affect the appraisal process. This link is actually readily observable, even though strategy is a distal factor in our model. For example, organizations that pursue an aggressive strategy of cost-cutting will probably develop appraisal (and performance management) systems that focus on behaviours that save money. Furthermore, one would expect to find performance management systems that reward employees or cost savings, such as Scanlon Plans (which are group incentive plans where employees are rewarded, financially, for proposals that lead to significant cost savings). Organizations that concentrate on providing stable service in a specialized niche would be likely to appraise things such as customer service and satisfaction and might even try to hire employees who fit the image of the niche in which the firm competes.

Different performance appraisal systems might be expected in an organization that has a long history of success and profitability than in an organization that is struggling to survive in a turbulent environment. In the former case, we would expect to have clear statements of standards and a shared understanding of how individual behaviour relates to firm performance. In the latter case, there might be few formal rules and perhaps even the absence of a formal appraisal system. Appraisals might be based more on short-term goals and objectives that would change frequently. But, the nature of the appraisal system might also be affected by where the firm is in the "organizational life cycle". Several scholars (e.g., Whetten, 1987; Whetten & Cameron, 1983) have discussed the stages in an organization's life, as well as its decline, and several others have suggested how this can influence the structure of the firm as well as how performance is defined and measured (see the review in Murphy & Cleveland, 1995, pp. 79–81).

Finally, firms that perform well are more likely to employ the latest innovations in appraisal systems, as opposed to less successful firms. In fact, this is related to one of the dilemmas facing scholars who work in the area of strategic human resource (HR) management (see, e.g., Collins, 2021). Specifically, these scholars have established relationships between firm performance and the presence of certain HR "best practices." But these two variables exist at the same time, and so it is difficult to determine if the adoption of certain HR practices leads to increased firm performance or if firms that perform well do many things well and can simply afford to adopt the best practices available.

Legal Systems

The legal system operating in a country, or a part of the country, also is likely to influence the way performance information is obtained and used. In the United States, a strong emphasis on litigation and accountability is likely to lead to an appraisal system that emphasizes detailed and specific record keeping and clear links between the behaviour of the ratee and the ratings they receive. But, even within the United States, state laws differ to a large enough degree that lawsuits dealing with unfair appraisal practices are more likely to be successful in some states than in others. In states where such suits are more successful, more detailed and well-documented appraisals are more likely to be found.

Kevin R. Murphy and Angelo S. DeNisi

Legal systems also differ in terms of the kinds of protection they offer employees. For example, in many Western European countries, employees' protection against being terminated is so strong that it makes little sense to try to use appraisals as a basis for termination. Also, in the United States, there are specific laws forbidding discrimination on the basis of race, religion, or gender. Other nations have similar laws, but still others have laws protecting some groups but not others, and there are still countries in the world where it is legal to discriminate against women in work settings. The greater the protection, and the more far-reaching the protection, the more likely it is that appraisal systems will be carefully designed and well documented.

Technology

Finally, technology can influence the type of performance information that is collected and how it is used. Computerization and the internet make it possible to appraise employees who cannot be observed directly, such as employees working in a different country. In such cases, it is unlikely that appraisals will focus on behaviours and more likely that they will focus on outcomes, since these are readily available at a distance. However, computer monitoring of performance does allow the appraisal of certain types of behaviours – even at a distance. These systems make it possible to monitor when a customer service representative is on the phone with a customer versus doing something else. This technology, then, can drive the content of the appraisal system itself, as well as that of the performance management system. For example, if it were easier to tell how many customers a service representative was speaking to, rather than how satisfied each customer was, the appraisals system and the performance management system would more likely focus on the number of calls handled or the length or the calls, rather than on the quality of service.

Also, the increasing affordability and ease of web-based information-collection systems make it more likely that some organizations will factor feedback from clients and customers into their normal performance appraisals, simply because it is so easy to collect the information. Such systems also make it easier for feedback to remain anonymous (if that is desirable) and for managers at different levels in the organization to share performance information about employees. Finally, improved technologies not only make it easier to document performance information but also make any such documentation easier to retrieve in court cases in which there is disagreement over what was said to whom about their performance.

These distal factors, then, are aspects of the situation that are not immediately associated with performance appraisals but can play an important role in the way appraisals are conducted and in how performance information is used. As noted earlier, these distal factors are not usually under the control of the person conducting performance appraisals, and some cannot easily be changed by anyone in the organization. These factors, therefore, act to set the parameters of what can be done in the area of performance appraisal and so function as constraints. But in order to fully understand appraisal systems in a global environment, it is critical that we appreciate the fact that such constraints do exist and that we try to understand exactly what effect they have on the resulting appraisal systems.

Proximal Factors

In addition to more distal factors, there are also a number of more proximal factors that exist at a more localized level and that affect the appraisal process. These factors exist primarily at the level of the organization or unit involved. These also serve as constraints for any performance management system, but these are things that are more closely under the control of the organization. They are also, of course, factors that will more directly affect the process and so are somewhat more critical to manage. There are three proximal factors which are likely to be particularly important for understanding performance appraisal systems.

Purpose of Appraisal

The purpose for which an appraisal is being conducted will likely have a major impact on the appraisal process. First, as noted earlier, the purpose of the appraisal is likely to have an impact on the frequency and timing of appraisals. This is true whether we are talking about norms regarding the use of appraisals or simply the ways in which appraisal information is used in a given firm. Purpose also is likely to affect who conducts the appraisals.

Kevin R. Murphy and Angelo S. DeNisi

Specifically, performance appraisals that are used to make administrative decisions about pay or promotion probably will draw heavily on annual evaluations from supervisors only. On the other hand, appraisals to be used primarily for feedback can (and probably should) come from subordinates and peers as well as supervisors.

The purpose of the appraisals also is related to a rater's motivation to provide accurate evaluations, and in particular, the rater's willingness to give high versus low ratings and to give ratings that discriminate among employees. Specifically, when appraisals are used for administrative decisions such as pay increases, raters might be motivated to give ratings that produce the desired distribution of these outcomes (e.g., similar raises to all members of a workgroup) rather than reflecting the performance levels of ratees. Thus, in this case, the ratings would be less accurate and there would be less willingness to discriminate among members of the work group (see, e.g., Varma & Budhwar, 2020).

Finally, the purpose of the appraisal can have an effect by changing the nature of the relationship between the rater and the ratee. In the case of appraisals that are to be used primarily for feedback, the rater takes on the role of a "coach" trying to help the subordinate develop. But, in the case of appraisals used for determining raises or promotions, the rater takes on more of the role of "judge" and he or she then hands down a judgement to the ratee. The nature of this relationship can have long-term implications for performance since the rater and ratee will continue to have to work together.

Organizational Norms

We discussed norms at the national or cultural levels as being distal factors influencing appraisals, but norms existing at the organizational level can be important as well, and they are more proximal. For example, both authors have encountered organizations where there was a strong norm to suggest that no one is rated "outstanding" or that no one is rated "poor". Other norms might dictate that the highest ratings go to the most senior people regardless of their true performance or that the true purpose of appraisals is to punish employees who do not follow group work rules. Some of these other purposes for appraisals are discussed in more detail in Cleveland, Murphy, and Williams (1989). In each case, these norms would have a direct effect on the nature of the ratings that were given and (probably) on how the ratings were interpreted by higher levels of management.

Acceptance of the Appraisal System

Acceptance of the appraisal system by employees (as well as by managers) is also an important factor to be considered. When an employee receives an evaluation suggesting they need to improve, this is done so that the employee will be motivated to change behaviour and improve their performance. But, if employees do not accept the appraisal system as legitimate, they are less likely to see the ratings as fair (cf. Folger et al., 1992), and rather than try to improve performance, the employees will resent the low ratings and will instead reduce their efforts at work. The knowledge that employees either accept or do not accept the legitimacy of the appraisal system can also influence raters' willingness to give low ratings. Finally, acceptance of the system by the raters/supervisors can also influence their rating behaviour such that they will rely on other means of changing behaviour outside the appraisal process if they do not see the process as legitimate. In this case, they would likely give all employees relatively positive evaluations regardless of their true levels of performance.

Intervening Factors

These are the result of the effects of distal and proximal factors and they can be viewed almost as mediator variables. That is, the factors we have listed as proximal and distal have an effect on the performance management process through these factors, as discussed earlier. For example, as noted, factors such as culture and norms will affect performance management processes through their effects on factors such as the frequency of appraisal and the reward structures in place. These factors will have a very strong and close relationship with the ratings made as part of the performance management process.

Performance appraisal systems ask raters to discriminate among ratees and to give high ratings to good performers and low ratings to poor performers. The rater's willingness to actually make these discriminations and identify good and poor performance might depend substantially on the norms of the

Kevin R. Murphy and Angelo S. DeNisi

organization (e.g., in many organizations, virtually everyone receives very positive performance appraisals, making it difficult for raters to signal truly good or truly poor performance) and the degree to which both raters and ratees accept the appraisal system as accurate and legitimate.

Judgements versus Ratings

In our discussion thus far, we have focused on how distal and proximal factors can affect the appraisal process, but it is important that we make another distinction now before proceeding further. Following the work of Murphy and Cleveland (1995), we distinguish between judgements and ratings in our model. A *judgement* is viewed here as a relatively private evaluation of a person's performance in some area. Accurate judgements require that raters observe and recall the actual performance of subordinates and that they compare their observations with appropriate and widely shared standards. This task is likely to be difficult under the best of circumstances and doubly difficult when raters are carrying out their evaluations under time pressure or under conditions where their attention is likely to be diverted from the task of performance appraisal. Nevertheless, a judgement is a cognitive process, and it is not really shared with anyone. *Ratings*, however, are a public statement of that judgement or evaluation which is made for the record. These ratings, then, are shared with others, but it is the central assumption of many models of a motivational process performance appraisal (e.g., LongeMnecker, Sims, & Gioia, 1987; Murphy & Cleveland, 1995) that the ratings individuals receive do not always correspond with the rater's private judgements about the performance levels of individual subordinates. We will discuss the factors that we believe lead to this discrepancy, but it is first necessary to establish the fact that we see these as two different outcomes, with different factors proposed to affect each one.

Judgement Factors

These are the factors we suggest affect the private judgements or evaluations raters develop concerning ratees. These judgement factors *may* be influenced by the distal and proximal factors proposed to affect the entire process, but it is more important to think about these as factors which, on their own, affect judgements.

Specifically, these are factors which research on cognitive processes involved in the appraisal process (e.g., DeNisi, 1996) has determined to affect those private cognitive judgements. These are presented in Figure 6.1 and are mostly self-explanatory. For example, if a rater does not have sufficient opportunity to observe a ratee performing all aspects of the job it will be impossible for the rater to form an accurate judgement of the ratee's performance. When an incident of performance *is* observed, the rater needs to have clear standards of performance available so that they can decide whether the incident was illustrative of good or poor performance. But rate performance is ongoing and so the rater must be able to store information (either behaviour or judgements) in memory over time, until they are needed to form an overall judgement. Unfortunately, information stored in memory can be forgotten or distorted over time so that the information available to the rater when a judgement is either limited or distorted (or both). Finally, time pressures, operating on the rater, who has additional responsibilities besides evaluating a given employee, will make it more likely that that information is never observed or is never evaluated correctly or is simply forgotten. Thus, these judgement factors really make it more or less likely that the judgement formed by the rater, of the ratee's performance, is accurate (i.e., reflects the ratee's *true* performance). Regardless of the accuracy of this judgement, however, it must still be made public as a rating on a scale. Our model proposes several factors that can distort the translation of a judgement into the rating so that public ratings can be quite different from private judgements.

Distortion Factors

There are a number of factors which might lead a rater to make a rating that is somehow different from the judgement they have formed. For this discussion, we assume that the underlying judgements are as accurate as they can be. That is, we assume that the extent to which the rater is able to do so, her or his judgements accurately reflect the ratee's performance. Distortion, then, indicates that the ratings provided do not reflect the judgements on which they should be based. Two factors strike us as particularly important in affecting this distortion: the reward systems of the organization and the consequences of the appraisal. The reward systems here refer to the issue of whether there are rewards for ratings that accurately reflect judgements and/or sanctions that follow ratings which do not reflect judgements. Organizational handbooks and mission statements often describe performance appraisals as critical to the organizations, but raters often reach the conclusion (usually a correct one) that organizations do not always value ratings that reflect accurate judgements.

Instead, there are many systems in which there are actually sanctions for providing ratings that reflect accurate judgements and/or rewards for ratings that do not reflect those judgements. For example, in organizations using forced distribution rating forms (i.e., forms that require certain percentages of ratees to each rating category), raters are "punished" if their ratings reflect judgements that all the ratees are performing well. Instead, they are *rewarded* if they adjust their ratings to fit the required distribution, even though they realize these do not accurately reflect their judgements. Other systems "punish" raters for ratings that accurately reflect their belief that some of their employees are weak performers, when other raters rate all of their employees as "outstanding", even if this does not reflect their judgements about those employees.

Although these rewards and sanctions can be important, in most situations, the motivation to either give accurate ratings (i.e., ratings that reflect judgements) or distort ratings is usually driven by the consequences associated with those ratings. For example, in an organization in which performance ratings have a strong impact on desired outcomes (e.g., promotions, raises), raters are often strongly tempted to inflate their ratings so that their ratees will not suffer. In some work groups, a rater might distort ratings so that each group member receives the same rating, even if the rater does not believe this to be the case. Here, a rater might believe that differentiating ratings could lead to dissension and competition within the team, and so the rater chooses to distort the ratings in order to keep the work group intact.

THE PROPOSED MODEL: PART II

The outcome of the performance appraisal model shown in Figure 6.1 is the public rating which is then shared with the employee or employees being evaluated. These evaluations often include a rating of overall performance, as well as ratings of tasks or traits or behaviours that are presumably related to overall performance. This evaluation could be considered the end of the performance appraisal process but the beginning of the performance management process. The desired outcome of the performance management process is an improvement in the performance of the employee being evaluated and, ultimately, in the performance of the organization, and that is the focus of the second part of our proposed model.

The Performance Management Process is modelled in Figure 6.2. Here we begin with the performance feedback given to the employee. This feedback generally indicates that there is some discrepancy between the observed level of performance in an area and the desired level of performance. This desired level of performance can be the result of established performance standards or earlier goal setting, but, in any case, the critical issue is how to move the employee closer to that desired goal. Figure 6.2 suggests that various performance management interventions are designed to influence either the employee's ability to improve, the employee's motivation to improve, or both.

The process begins with the employee's acceptance of the feedback and results in some change in performance that is (hopefully) closer to the desired performance level. Even if the employee is presently meeting her or his goals, the feedback might indicate that there is a need to increase those goals and so work harder. In any case, employee goals should determine (to a large part) the desired level of performance for the employee. Those goals, however, should also reflect larger corporate goals, or at least the goals of the next highest level in the organization. If this is done, then over time, the employee (hopefully) comes closer and closer to the desired level of performance, and so reduces the discrepancy between desired and observed performance. This progress is indicated by subsequent appraisals which produce subsequent feedback and closer approximations to the desired level of performance in a feedback loop similar to the type used in control theory (Carver & Scheier, 1981). As individual goals are met, then, corporate (or higher level) goals should also be met. Note that the system is not designed properly if individual goals can be met without there being any progress

Kevin R. Murphy and Angelo S. DeNisi

toward the achievement of organizational goals and, presumably, the improvement in organizational performance. In theory, the correct alignment of employee goals with organizational goals can then lead to improvements in organizational performance as well. This process continues until all goals are met. Then, the cycle begins again with new, more difficult individual goals that reflect new and more difficult corporate goals and that will result in even higher levels of corporate performance.

Note that, in our proposed model, discrepancies between observed performance levels and desired performance levels lead to both performance feedback and potential performance management interventions. Many performance management interventions involve some sort of goal setting, and ratees who receive unfavourable evaluations might set goals on their own that will influence their future performance. But, while goals are important, they are not the only mechanism by which performance management interventions might work. Changes in the reward structure could also help, especially when the reward system is set up so that it rewards the "wrong" behaviours.

However, most performance management interventions are focused on ways to motivate an employee to perform better. In some cases, the problem may not be one of motivation at all. Instead, the employee may not have been properly trained, or they may lack the basic ability or the skills needed to do better on the job. In other cases, the employee may lack to necessary skills or may need to overcome other constraints set by the organization. Thus, performance management interventions, especially those based on goals, may not always be the best way to improve performance.

There are many other factors that could limit the effectiveness of performance management interventions. For example, there is some evidence that performance feedback does not always have the desired effect on employee motivation and that, in some cases, the presence of feedback (regardless of the sign of the feedback) can actually hurt subsequent performance (e.g., Kluger & DeNisi, 1996). In addition, poor communication of goals and expectations or failure to monitor performance can result in failure, and ultimately, the employee must have some incentive to improve if the process is to be successful.

RECOMMENDATIONS FOR RESEARCH

As we noted at the outset that it was not our goal to propose a new model of the performance appraisal process. We discussed several such models earlier, and there are others not explicitly addressed here that have discussed appraisals within the framework of more global systems (e.g., Budhwar & Sparrow, 2002). Nor did we undertake a complete review of the relevant literature – such a goal would require far more than this chapter. Rather, we present a framework, based on appraisal research that can be used for discussing various appraisal systems. Nevertheless, the proposed model points to some directions for future research, and we turn to those to close this chapter.

Beginning with more distal factors, research aimed at describing "best practices" under different sets of circumstances would be useful. But in order to truly be instructive, it would first be important to develop a generalizable taxonomy of situational factors. Without such taxonomy, it might be difficult to determine exactly why a certain type of system is more successful in one country than in another and whether there are lessons to be learned from cross-country comparisons of appraisal systems. The factors proposed here could be the beginning of such taxonomy, but there are surely other models that could be used as well.

Factors such as those described as "proximal" in our model should also be related to different measures of appraisal effectiveness. Specifically, if an organization uses appraisals primarily for purposes seen as legitimate by most employees, and organizational norms are such that everyone seeks to be as fair and accurate in rating as they can be (which should lead to the widespread acceptance of appraisals), those appraisals should be more effective in reaching organizational goals than in organizational where these conditions are not met. Thus, we would expect appraisals to be associated with improved individual performance as well improved organizational performance. It may also be the case that perceived fairness and acceptability are the prerequisites for introducing changes in the way appraisals are conducted and used or for introducing less traditional appraisal systems.

There has already been substantial research on the role of our "intervening" factors (see, e.g., Murphy & Cleveland, 1995). There has also been a number of studies dealing with "judgement"

Kevin R. Murphy and Angelo S. DeNisi

factors (see, e.g., DeNisi, 1996), and there may be decreasing returns from carrying out more studies of the roles of these specific factors. However, we do believe that the interactions among the various factors identified in our model have been under-studied, and that considering the way these factors combine may still yield considerable benefits.

The area in our proposed model where there has been very little research, and yet there is the potential for many interesting ideas, lies in the translation of judgements into ratings and feedback. There has been almost no research on intentional distortion that might occur as part of this process. More important, although many authors have suggested that such distortion exists, there are almost no data suggesting the exact variables that lead to distortion or the specific nature of any distortion. This is fertile ground for future research in a national setting, as well as in a global setting, since different factors may lead to different types of distortion as we move around the world.

The benefit of developing an overall framework for discussing appraisal research and practice is that it provides a common language and frame of reference for making sense of the similarities and differences in appraisal systems across national and cultural boundaries. We hope the framework described here will prove useful for drawing insights from the chapters that follow.

REFERENCES

Budhwar, P., & Sparrow, P. (2002). An integrative framework for determining cross-national human resource management practices. *Human Resource Management Review*, 12: 377–403.

Carver, C.S., & Scheier, M.F. (1981). *Attention and self-regulation: A control theory approach to human behavior.* New York: Springer.

Cleveland, J.N., Murphy, K.R., & Williams, R.E. (1989). Multiple uses of performance appraisal: Prevalence and correlates. *Journal of Applied Psychology*, 74: 130–135.

Collins, C.J. (2021). Expanding the resource based view model of strategic human resource management. *The International Journal of Human Resource Management*, 32(2), 331–358.

DeCotiis, T., & Petit, A. (1978). The performance appraisal process: A model and some testable propositions. *Academy of Management Review*, 3: 635–646.

DeNisi, A.S. (1996). *Cognitive processes in performance appraisal: A research agenda with implications for practice.* London: Routledge Publishing, Ltd.

DeNisi, A.S., Cafferty, T., & Meglino, B. (1984). A cognitive view of the performance appraisal process: A model and research propositions. *Organizational Behavior and Human Performance*, 33: 360–396.

Feldman, J.M. (1981). Beyond attribution theory: Cognitive processes in performance appraisal. *Journal of Applied Psychology*, 66: 127–148.

Folger, R., Konovsky, M.A., & Cropanzano, R. (1992). A due process metaphor for performance appraisal. *Research in Organizational Behavior, 14,* 129–177.

Kluger, A.N., & DeNisi, A.S. (1996). The effects of feedback interventions on performance: Historical review, meta-analysis, a preliminary feedback intervention theory. *Psychological Bulletin, 119,* 254–284.

Landy, F.J., & Farr, J.L. (1980). Performance rating. *Psychological Bulletin,* 87: 72–107.

LongeMnecker, C.O., Sims, H.P., & Gioia, D.A. (1987). Behind the mask: The politics of employee appraisal. *Academy of Management Executive,* 1: 183–193.

Murphy, K.R., & Cleveland, J.N. (1995). *Understanding performance appraisal: Social, organizational, and goal-based perspectives.* Thousand Oaks, CA: Sage.

Varma, A., & Budhwar, P. (2020). Introduction – Performance management in context. In A. Varma & P. Budhwar. (Eds), *Performance management systems: An experiential approach* (pp. 1–14). London, UK: SAGE.

Wexley, K.N., & Klimoski, R. (1984). Performance appraisal: An update. In K. Rowland & G. Ferris (Eds.), *Research in personnel and human resources* (Vol. 2). Greenwich, CT: JAI Press.

Whetten, D.A. (1987). Organizational growth and decline processes. *Annual Review of Sociology,* 13: 335–338.

Whetten, D.A., & Cameron, K.S. (1983). *Organizational effectiveness: A comparison of multiple methods.* New York: Academic Press.

Performance Management in the United States

Elaine Pulakos, Rose A. Mueller-Hanson and Ryan S. O'Leary

Chapter 7

Nearly every type of industry and organization exists in the United States, from multibillion-dollar multinational corporations to government agencies employing hundreds of thousands of people to small nonprofit and family-owned businesses and everything in between. This diversity in organizational size, complexity, and mission has led to the use of many different types of performance management (PM) processes. While there has never been an "American style" of PM per se, a decidedly U.S. mindset and set of values have formed the underpinnings of PM since its inception.

U.S. history is a story of independence and self-determination. The country was born out of a desire for freedom from foreign rule and a belief that all individuals "are created equal" and endowed with certain inalienable rights, namely, "life, liberty, and the pursuit of happiness." As the United States has matured, these principles have endured. Despite diversity in its citizenry, the United States has retained the ideals on which it was built of individualism, capitalism, and democracy. These translate into several

DOI: 10.4324/9781003306849-7

commonly held beliefs, including the importance of "personal responsibility" for one's actions, the expectation that wealth and status can be achieved through education and hard work, and the right of individuals to determine their futures and elect their leaders.

The individualistic nature of U.S. culture is manifested in our PM systems. We see this first in their focus on *individual* evaluation and development. Although the importance of teams and teamwork has been acknowledged in the business environment, especially in recent years, U.S. PM nonetheless remains largely focused on evaluating individuals rather than teams or work units. The capitalist foundation of U.S. culture leads workers to expect rewards based on their individual contributions. As a result, most PM processes drive competition between team members, because top performers receive a larger share of limited reward pools. Because of the stakes involved, accurately identifying top performers and appropriately rewarding them have been enduring goals – and challenges – in the design of U.S. PM processes. Capitalism has likewise created a context of fierce competition at the organizational level. Pressure from investors, boards of directors, and executives with significant financial stakes in how well companies perform give rise to organizational climates in which growth and profitability are key priorities. These, in turn, lead to PM processes that similarly focus on how much individual team members are contributing to the organization's growth and success.

Another defining characteristic of U.S. PM processes is that they exist within a democracy in which everyone has a voice in government, and citizens expect transparent, fair, and unbiased systems and processes. This expectation has been reinforced by the U.S. legal system, which allows employees to seek redress if they feel they have been treated unfairly. The legal context in the United States, including precedents set through litigation, has led to a number of PM practices that are commonplace today, such as ensuring employees are evaluated against job-relevant criteria, upper level reviews of ratings to ensure fairness across employees, allowing employees input into their appraisals, and processes to appeal evaluations if employees feel their performance was not accurately rated.

Elaine Pulakos et al.

We have seen U.S. PM systems change significantly over time from relatively simple rating forms to complex automated systems to informal, ongoing performance conversations – and many combinations in between. Various trends have influenced PM characteristics at different points in time such as behavioral rating scales, competency modeling, cascading goals, and forced distributions, among others. These trends have reflected contemporary thinking at the time about how to design performance management processes to optimize individual and organizational performance. For example, in the early 2000s, cascading goals became popular as a strategy to align the activities of all organizational members so that everyone was working together in pursuit of the same critical goals. However, constant changes to PM philosophies and systems in the U.S. also reflect a long history of PM falling short of expectation, and there have been repeated efforts to fix what leaders and employees perceive as "broken" PM processes. The search for *effective* PM has sometimes been likened to the search for the Holy Grail. No other talent management system has been the focus of as much change, debate, or emotion as PM.

In this chapter, we examine the evolution of PM in the United States and the major trends that have impacted it over time. Despite strong ideals of self-determination, equal opportunity, and fairness, achieving effective PM in the United States has been an elusive goal. Initially promising ideas for how to conduct PM more effectively have ultimately proved disappointing. Managers and employees alike have reported constant dissatisfaction with their PM processes, and moreover, these have been shown to have little, if any, impact on individual or organizational performance. In the following, we tell the story of PM in the United States by examining the key factors and challenges that have driven its design over the last century. We conclude with a discussion of what we've learned and how U.S. organizations are thinking about PM today.

THE EVOLUTION OF PM IN THE UNITED STATES

The Early Years and First Rating Scales

The cornerstone of PM processes – using ratings to evaluate individual performance – began its genesis over 100 years ago.

The first large-scale use of ratings in work settings occurred in the late 1800s with efficiency ratings in the U.S. Federal Civil Service (Lopez, 1968). The subsequent emergence of scientific management theories in the early twentieth century (Taylor, 1911) highlighted the importance of individual productivity, and there was a corresponding use of ratings to drive higher performance (Grote, 1996; Murphy & Cleveland, 1995). The scientific management movement has been recognized as foundational in the evolution of today's PM processes (Muchinsky, 1997).

The idea of evaluating individual performance gained further traction during World War I (1914–1918) when Walter Scott and others conducted trait and ability assessments of army officers (Muchinsky, 1997; Scott et al., 1941). In 1922, Patterson introduced the Graphic Rating Scale (Patterson, 1922). This was the first rating scale in which different rating levels were anchored with verbal and numerical anchors. The idea was that rating accuracy would be improved by providing benchmarks, such as "excellent" and "poor," at appropriate points on the rating scale. While this was a step forward, these labels still left raters with considerable latitude to impose their own interpretations of what they meant (Borman, 1977; Landy & Farr, 1980). Hence, graphic rating scales did not improve rating accuracy as much as initially expected. But the idea that improvements in rating accuracy could be obtained through well-defined rating scales led to extensive research on rating formats (Austin & Villanova, 1992), which we discuss further later.

The U.S. Legal Context

The civil rights movement of the late 1950s and early 1960s brought attention to the fact that minorities had been systematically denied equal opportunity in areas such as housing, education, and employment. The Civil Rights Act of 1964 and subsequent legislation were passed to help rectify these inequities (e.g., Title VII of the Civil Rights Act, Equal Pay Act). These laws prohibited discrimination in employment practices and gave employees the right to challenge employment-related decisions. Many of these laws allow for jury trials and the collection of compensatory and punitive damages; they have led to some high-profile class-action lawsuits.

Table 7.1 Guidelines for Addressing Legal Requirements in the United States

- Employees must be evaluated on job-relevant factors.
- Employees must be told what is expected and the standards for evaluation.
- There must be a standard, documented procedure, with defined roles and responsibilities for employees and managers.
- Managers and employees should be trained to implement the process effectively.
- Managers should document effective and ineffective performance to substantiate their evaluations.
- Managers should be held accountable for providing feedback in a timely manner.
- Performance evaluations should be reviewed by a higher-level manager or panel.
- Employees should be allowed to comment on and appeal their performance evaluations.
- Employees should be notified of deficiencies and afforded opportunities to correct them.
- If performance evaluations are used for decision-making, the evaluation should be consistent with decisions (i.e., higher pay raises for higher-rated staff).

Since performance ratings provide the basis for making employment decisions, they are often the target of litigation. Procedural aspects of PM systems (e.g., specificity and subjectivity of performance criteria, procedural standardization) or outcomes (e.g., promotions, pay) can be challenged. It is thus important to be familiar with U.S. laws and professional guidelines that are relevant to PM design and implementation. More in-depth discussions of legal issues and associated case law can be found in Malos (1998, 2005), Kahn, Brown, and Lanzarone (1996), Martin, Bartol, and Kehoe (2000), Society for Industrial and Organization Psychology (2003) and UGESP (1978). Table 7.1 briefly summarizes guidelines from case law and professional practice that have implications for the design of PM systems in the United States.

A Focus on the Rating Format

Increasing legal challenges and concerns about discrimination in the 1970s and 1980s prompted the development of more structured performance evaluation processes. Attention shifted to a rating format design, based on the hypothesis that rating scales and criteria could be designed in a way that would yield accurate, unbiased ratings (Dunnette, 1963; Guion, 1961). Leveraging the critical incident technique (Flanagan, 1954), a new type of rating format was developed that gained tremendous popularity, behaviorally anchored rating scales, or BARSs. The idea was that anchoring different rating levels with specific work behaviors would help managers select a level of evaluation that accurately reflected each employee's performance (Borman, 1979; Latham & Wexley, 1977; Smith & Kendall, 1963). Researchers expected that the use of these rating scales would increase agreement, accuracy, and fairness, especially when their use was combined with rater training that taught raters how to avoid common rating errors, like leniency (Borman, 1975; Latham et al., 1975).

The rating format design and rater training continued to dominate efforts to improve PM for the next 20 years until Landy and Farr's (1980) game-changing review of the literature showed that no rating format yielded higher quality ratings than any others, irrespective of how well they were defined (Murphy et al., 1982; Saal & Landy, 1977). Landy and Farr (1980) called for a moratorium on rating format research and argued for a shift in focus to examining how human information processing and social, political, and environmental factors impact ratings. Although efforts to improve rating accuracy by changing the rating format proved unsuccessful, defining rating criteria has remained important to communicate what effective performance looks like and clarify what is expected of employees.

A Shift in Focus to the Human Rating Process

Using human information-processing models from cognitive psychology, researchers began to consider how humans attend to information, categorize that information to facilitate recall, and integrate different pieces of information over time to evaluate others. This line of research yielded new insights about why ratings are inherently inaccurate and ideas for how to improve accuracy through different types of training interventions. These included helping raters to develop job-relevant mental categories through which to observe and evaluate performance (Ilgen & Feldman, 1983). Rater training shifted its focus from reducing common rating errors such as halo and leniency (Cooper, 1981, Murphy & Balzer, 1989, Murphy et al., 1993) to focusing attention on relevant performance information and helping raters learn how to mentally store that information to facilitate accurate recall

(McIntyre et al., 1984; Pulakos, 1984, 1986). Information processing theories provided a greater understanding of how raters formulate their ratings but yielded few practical strategies for improving rating accuracy and PM effectiveness in organizations.

The Advent of Multisource Evaluations

In the 1960s and 1970s, about the same time as BARSs were gaining popularity, interest grew in examining the use of rating sources beyond supervisors, such as peers and customers (e.g., Lawler, 1967). The idea was that people with different role relationships to an employee would see different aspects of their performance (Borman, 1974). As an example, customers are usually in the best position to experience service effectiveness, whereas direct reports have unique views of supervisory effectiveness. By the early 1990s, the use of multisource or 360-degree rating processes exploded, driven by business trends that prioritized involving employees in rating processes, engaging customers in providing feedback, and enabling self-managed work teams (Hedge et al., 2001).

Multisource ratings have been used primarily for development purposes, rather than decision-making (Bracken et al., 2001; Smither et al., 2005). They are still commonly used today, especially for leaders. Ratings that are used for development purposes tend to be more accurate, reflecting strengths and development needs (Greguras et al., 2003). When these same ratings are used for decision-making, however, they become more lenient and less accurate, with most people rated at the higher end of the scale due to environmental. political, social, and interpersonal factors that we discuss in more detail later. Ratings that fail to reflect strengths and development needs are not useful for decision-making or development. This has been a long-standing challenge with ratings and one that continues to plague PM systems today.

A Focus on Setting Objectives and Evaluating Results

As discussed, the United States has a long history of being driven by bottom-line results. This focus has been reflected in the management strategies adopted by many U.S. companies and their PM systems. One of the first approaches to driving results was management by objectives (MBO). Introduced by Peter Drucker (1954), MBO focused on evaluating employees on the extent to which they achieved job-relevant performance objectives (Rodgers & Hunter, 1991). Ultimately, MBO systems were deemed too time-consuming and administratively burdensome to be sustainable (Jamieson, 1973, Strauss, 1972), but several of their features, like setting objectives and evaluating results, became common features of PM systems and are included in PM processes even to this day.

Cascading goals became popular in the early 2000s. The idea was to start with the organization's strategic goals and flow these down through the organization's levels, ultimately creating objectives for each employee that were directly tied to the organization's goals (Rodgers & Hunter, 1991). The idea was that such linkages would help employees understand how their work fit into the bigger picture and contributes to the organization's goals (Hillgren & Cheatham, 2000; Schneier et al., 1991). Leveraging principles from MBO, objectives state the outcomes each employee is expected to achieve in sufficient detail to judge whether the objective has been met. Employees and managers were frequently trained to set SMART (specific, measurable, aligned, realistic, and time-bound) goals. Although cascading goals were used extensively in U.S. organizations, several practical challenges with their use emerged as summarized in Table 7.2 (Pulakos & O'Leary, 2010).

Table 7.2 Practical Challenges with Cascading Goals

- Cascading goals take time and clear linkages can be difficult for managers to make who are not accustomed to translating goals from higher to lower levels.
- As goals are cascaded down, they often become disconnected from higher-level goals, like the game of telephone, in which retelling a story can alter it in ways not intended.
- Even with training, the quality of the objectives varies greatly from manager to manager. Sometimes managers set goals that are too easy or too hard.
- Objectives are rarely comparable across similarly situated employees, even when they occupy the same jobs.
- Objectives set at the beginning of the year cannot account for unexpected events during the year, and it is difficult to constantly update goals throughout the year.
- Evaluating the relative contributions of different employees can be difficult when their objectives are not comparable; for example, how does partial delivery of a hard goal compare to overachievement of an easy goal?
- Goal accomplishment is easier to evaluate in some cases than others, for example, when goals rely on quantity metrics versus quality judgments.

Elaine Pulakos et al.

The Adoption of Forced Distribution Ratings and Rankings

In the early 1980s, stemming from efforts to reduce rating leniency and drive higher organizational performance came the forced distribution rating method. Initially conceived of by General Electric (GE) CEO Jack Welch, forced distributions were ultimately adopted by many organizations. Employees were either ranked-ordered from top to bottom or categorized as top, middle, or bottom performers based on how their work compared to the work of others. The top group was often rewarded with promotions or higher pay, while the bottom group was frequently separated. In this manner, forced distributions helped raise the performance level and capabilities of the workforce overall.

An issue forced distributions posed, however, is that the top performers in a poorly performing group could be contributing the same as the bottom performers in a high-performing group. The fact that forced distributions compare people to each other rather than an absolute standard can yield inaccurate and unfair evaluations if the rankings of multiple groups are combined without considering how the top and bottom performers from different groups compare to each other. This issue can be addressed through calibration sessions in which employees are discussed and recategorized as necessary to ensure that the top and bottom performers are accurately identified across everyone considered. This can be a time-consuming process, however, that becomes more difficult as you move up the organization and the performance of those at lower levels becomes less well known. Forced distributions were used extensively in organizations for about 30 years, but their popularity began to wane around 2010 when many stopped using forced distributions, including GE.

A Shift to Competencies

By 2000, an increasingly popular trend in the United States was to evaluate individual performance using competency-based behavioral ratings. David McClelland is credited with introducing the idea of competency (Dubois, 1993), and competency-based talent management systems have proliferated, although there has been debate about exactly what competencies are and how to best measure them with some critical views. Boyatzis (1996) defined a competency as a combination of a motive, trait, skill, attribute, or a body of relevant knowledge; in other words, a competency is any individual characteristic that is required for effective performance on the job. Klein (1996) defined competencies as related, observable behaviors that represent common themes and differentiate effective from ineffective performers.

Following Klein's concept, competency models typically consist of behavioral performance factors that help communicate the organization's values, culture, and priorities. Initially, competency models were loosely developed, but over time, more rigorous development approaches that leverage job analytic methods were adopted to better support the use of competency ratings as a basis for decision-making (Schippmann, 1999). Like the rating format research discussed earlier, competency ratings have not proved to be more accurate or less biased than any other rating formats despite their popularity.

The Impact of Automation on U.S. PM

Along with the themes of maximizing performance and results that are prevalent in United States come the themes of continuous improvement and increased efficiency. From the advent of repetitive flow production in the early 1900s to the adoption of total quality management in the 1980s to recent trends to automate work, U.S. organizations continually look for ways to gain efficiencies. As organizations worked to address the Y2K problem in the late 1990s, we saw large-scale adoption of automated human resource information systems (HRISs). Several vendors (e.g., SAP, PeopleSoft, and Oracle) began offering HRISs that enabled tracking and managing employees throughout the employment lifecycle from pre- through post-hire. These systems automate human resources functions, such as time and attendance, leave, benefits, pay, recruiting, staffing, and PM (Dorsey, 2002).

Automating PM processes has yielded several positive outcomes. For example, automation has substantially reduced the paperwork and administrative burden associated with the PM workflow, especially for multisource feedback systems that are more complex to administer than supervisory evaluations. Automated systems allow for an efficient selection of raters (e.g., peers, customers, subordinates), the collection and integration of information from multiple raters, and the generation automated feedback reports (Summers, 2001). Automated PM systems also

Elaine Pulakos et al.

efficiently capture data and create a repository of accessible information that was previously more difficult to collect and centralize.

Initially, there was hope that automation would improve the quality, effectiveness, and impact of evaluations, but these hopes have not been realized. The implementation of automated PM systems did, however, increase attention to the importance of change management activities, such as building leadership support and employee buy-in, developing effective communication, training, and change management programs, and evaluating PM system effectiveness (Rodgers et al., 1993). Studies began examining the impact of the PM processes on employee engagement and performance, with the surprising results that they appeared to be having little if any impact on individual or organizational performance (CEB, 2004; Harter et al., 2002). At first, this led to the development of more elaborate PM systems. PM steps were broken down into more specific, structured, and scheduled activities, based on the idea that more steps and time devoted to PM would yield improved outcomes. This only resulted in more burdensome PM requirements that became increasingly disconnected from daily work (Pulakos & O'Leary, 2011), further turning PM into a set of disconnected, intermittent steps.

The PM Rule Book Goes Out the Window

More so than any other talent management system, PM has been characterized by an almost blind adoption of new PM trends that ultimately underdelivered on expectations (Pulakos & O'Leary, 2011). Organizations benchmark against companies they want to emulate and then attempt to replicate them, often without sufficient consideration of how well another's PM practices fit their organization's strategy, culture, and resources (Mueller-Hanson & Pulakos, 2018). As an example, Bock (2015) discussed how Google's culture supports paying high versus low performers very differently. It uses a data-driven process that is lengthy and results in highly differentiated rewards (Bock, 2015). While many companies want to emulate Google, its PM approach does not work well in contexts in which performance has not been well differentiated historically, the culture is egalitarian, and insufficient variable pay exists to make meaningful differentiated rewards.

Best practices that have gone in and out of favor over the years have included BARSs, forced distribution ratings, and cascading goals, among others. U.S. organizations have regularly reinvented their PM systems in hopes that the next new idea would better address the persistent challenges that have plagued PM – ratings that cluster toward the high end of the scale, dissatisfaction with performance reviews, and a dislike for the burdensome nature of PM processes. By 2010, negative attitudes toward PM rose to a fever pitch, especially concerning the PM review, which was seen as a waste of time and even harmful to employees. This resulted in emotional calls to eliminate them (Culbertson et al., 2013; Culbert & Rout, 2010).

Neuroscience research provided compelling evidence of brain changes that triggered automatic defensive reactions to feedback. These made performance reviews aversive, even for high performers (Rock, 2008, Rock & Jones, 2015). Further fueling the anti-PM sentiment were return-on-investment analyses that showed millions of dollars and excessive time spent on PM activities that were having no impact on individual or organizational performance (CEB, 2012). These factors sparked a massive movement to reinvent PM that surpassed any prior PM reform effort. But this time rather than following the latest PM trend, organizations began experimenting with substantially different and even radical changes to their PM processes. The decade from 2009 to 2019 brought out-of-the-box thinking and substantially different PM approaches. The amount of disruptive change that PM systems underwent during this period was unprecedented and spoke volumes about the extent of dissatisfaction that had developed toward them (Adler et al., 2016).

PM changes largely fell into two major approaches. The first focused on improving day-to-day manager and employee behaviors that research had shown were associated with higher performance and engagement. These included setting agile goals, providing informal feedback to employees in real time, and helping employees solve problems (Bryant, 2011; CEB, 2004). The second approach involved stripping down PM requirements and systems to reduce low-value, time-consuming activities. This was consistent with trends at the time to reduce talent management process complexity, which some argued had become too heavy, burdensome, and costly for its value. Some organizations focused on driving more effective PM behavior, some focused on streamlining PM processes, and some experimented with both approaches in tandem.

One practice that became a target of PM reform was goal setting. Many companies were spending countless hours cascading goals, only for these to become irrelevant within weeks or months as circumstances in the work situation were changing rapidly. Another target of PM reform was performance ratings. Several companies decided to eliminate ratings, which caused everyone to become obsessed with the question of whether they should keep or eliminate ratings (Adler et al., 2016). Many high-profile companies (e.g., Accenture, Deloitte, Microsoft, GAP) abandoned or substantially reduced their use of ratings (Culbert & Rout, 2010, Cunningham, 2015). Others held firm that ratings were important to retain. If the question of whether or not to keep ratings centered on their accuracy and fairness, the answer would be easy. Nearly a century of research had shown long-standing problems with rating fairness and accuracy (Bernardin & Beatty, 1984; DeCotiis & Petit, 1978; DeNisi, 2006; DeNisi & Murphy, 2017; Ilgen & Feldman, 1983; Landy & Farr, 1980; Murphy & Cleveland, 1991, 1995). But the question of what to do with ratings involved considerations that went beyond accuracy and fairness.

Those in favor of eliminating ratings did so on the basis that ratings were not providing accurate information about employees and so were essentially useless, and at the same time, rating processes were demotivating to everyone involved. On the side of retaining ratings, valid concerns were raised about the need for documentation to meet U.S. legal requirements. The most compelling rationale to keep ratings was the concern that without them, employees may receive no performance information whatsoever from their managers (Adler et al., 2016). Supporting this idea, CEB (2016) research showed that employees in rating-less organizations reported less engagement and perceived fairness than employees who received ratings. However, a cautionary note in interpreting these results is that CEB's research did not separately evaluate organizations that replaced ratings with regular check-ins, coaching, and feedback. Thus, although negative attitudes seemed to be associated with removing ratings, these may have resulted from poor PM practices that remained unaddressed when ratings were eliminated. Ratings or not, organizations need to have guardrails in place to ensure that employees are having performance conversations and receiving performance information.

By 2016, three new PM practices had been adopted by enough organizations that it was possible to begin examining their impact. These were rating-less reviews, ongoing feedback, and crowd-sourced feedback that leverages social media (Ledford et al., 2016). Based on survey feedback from 244 companies, 97% had adopted ongoing informal feedback, 51% had adopted rating-less reviews, and 27% had adopted crowdsourced feedback. These new practices did not always replace traditional PM processes. If one new practice was used, it was usually added to more traditional features like cascading goals, 360-degree feedback, competency assessment, and rating calibration. However, companies that adopted ongoing feedback and rating-less reviews in combination typically eliminated more traditional PM practices.

Results of this research showed that the combination of all three innovative practices had a significant positive impact on strategic alignment, motivating and developing employees, and rewarding top talent. The combination of ongoing feedback and crowdsourced feedback was more impactful than either ongoing feedback alone or ongoing feedback plus rating-less reviews. The new practices were perceived more favorably than traditional PM practices, suggesting promise for the direction companies were taking. Of course, the important question remained of how long the positive affect for these new practices would remain.

And Then the Pandemic

The COVID-19 pandemic that took the world by storm in early 2020 again shifted PM practices. Workers in most professional roles found themselves working from home (WFH). Many managers no longer had opportunities to observe employee performance directly; they had to trust their direct reports to work on their own and get things done without managers looking over their shoulders. Managers were called on to support their direct reports in new ways – by demonstrating caring and empathy to an extent that had not been asked of them before. Many of the things that research had shown were most important in driving performance – ongoing informal performance conversations, coaching, and helping employees solve problems – became more prevalent out of necessity due to the circumstances created by the pandemic. Organizations largely stopped focusing on the mechanics of their formal PM systems, and much of the debate about PM features and what to do about ratings subsided. Formal PM became less relevant during the pandemic, as organizations grappled to deal with their new realities and more significant challenges of safety, employee well-being, and WFH.

ENDURING CHALLENGES THAT CHARACTERIZE U.S. PM SYSTEMS

PM has been referred to as the "Achilles' heel" of talent management. No matter what system features, rating formats, and PM features have been tried, difficulties have arisen because at its core, performance management is inherently challenging. It relies on effective human interaction at the same time one person is required to evaluate another, which creates tension, distrust, and defensiveness. While many factors can undermine PM, three challenges have been enduring:

- organizational members viewing PM as an administrative system to be minimized rather than as a useful process for facilitating performance,
- difficulty engaging in effective and useful performance discussions, and
- human judgment and time factors that impact performance evaluations.

The View of Performance Management as an Administrative Burden

The prevailing opinion among most U.S. managers and employees is that the benefits of formal PM processes do not outweigh their costs. To the extent that PM systems are viewed as cumbersome, ineffective, and time consuming, they will be treated as an administrative chore to be minimized rather than a helpful tool for managing work and driving results. To gain value from PM, the research is clear that managers need to engage in the

PM *behaviors* (agile goal setting, informal feedback, and helping solve problems) that lead to high performance and engagement. Investments in system, tool, and process redesign are not nearly as important as leader enablement and training to drive effective PM behavior.

The Difficulty of Engaging in Productive Performance Discussions

The U.S. national culture tends toward egalitarianism and low power distance between supervisors and their team members. This creates reluctance on the part of managers to have honest performance discussions with employees for fear of damaging relationships with the very individuals they count on to get work done. In addition, the individualistic and achievement-oriented aspects of U.S. culture may be a factor in employee reluctance to admit any development needs for fear this will negatively impact their rewards and advancement. These tendencies are exaggerated when the primary purpose of PM is to make reward and promotion decisions.

Human Judgment and Time Factors

As Murphy and DeNisi (this volume) discussed, there are several human judgment factors that present challenges to effective PM, including managers' opportunity to observe performance, accurate recall of performance information, and time pressure. Although there is wide recognition in the United States that leadership is a critical function, but managers are frequently overworked and have numerous responsibilities aside from managing people. Additionally, most managers have multiple direct reports and when PM activities are separated by 6 months to a year, performance information becomes difficult to recall accurately. These factors contribute to managers basing their appraisals on general impressions of employees they have developed over time, which may be accurate or may be biased. Irrespective of how accurate these impressions are, providing feedback to employees based on impressions rather than actual performance examples causes difficulties when managers are asked to explain what the employee did that led to a certain rating.

Another factor that can interfere with accurate judgments is the opportunity to observe performance. With the sharp rise in telecommuting and WFH, especially since the pandemic, managers increasingly see only a fraction of employees' work behavior. The challenge is how to gain sufficient information on which to form a performance judgment and provide useful feedback when performance observations are limited.

WHAT WE'VE LEARNED ABOUT PM AND WHERE IT'S GOING

Over almost a century, PM in the United States has evolved from a narrow focus on performance ratings to the design of comprehensive, multifaceted, and automated annual PM processes. What was initially conceived of as a relatively simple problem of how to define rating scales that would enable managers to make accurate ratings turned into a more complex challenge of how to develop end-to-end PM processes that would enable setting expectations and evaluating, developing, and rewarding employees. Historically, attempts to improve PM in the United States have involved implementing more elaborate tools and processes – the hope was that these would serve to align work, improve rating accuracy, address performance gaps, and enable managers to make better decisions about employees. The problem – as we have learned – is that automated steps and tools can only help so much to improve an inherently human interaction and judgment process that is influenced by a vast array of political, social, motivational, environmental, and practical factors. Table 7.3 summarizes key conclusions from research and practice about PM (Pulakos et al., 2019).

Until about 10 years ago, most U.S. companies were using largely similar PM systems. These started with setting annual goals, often following a cascade from the organization's strategic goals down to each employee. After about 6 months, a formal midyear review would occur. At the end of the annual cycle,

Table 7.3 Conclusions about PM from Research and Practice

- Performance ratings are inherently limited in their value as performance measures.
- Managers can accurately place employees into general categories but cannot make nuanced performance judgments accurately due to human judgment and time factors.
- Rater–ratee relationship differences yield rating differences and performance differences.
- Political and social factors have strong impacts on ratings.

---

managers would rate employees – often using competency rating scales and evaluate the extent to which they met their annual goals. Managers would meet to discuss their ratings, calibrating these to ensure that employees were rated fairly compared to each other. Finally, managers would conduct formal reviews with their team members in which they would communicate the ratings and often information about pay and advancement for the next year. As we've discussed, these reviews were difficult and often demotivating for managers and employees. Moreover, these PM processes have been shown to have no impact on individual or organizational performance. Hence, substantial time was devoted to ineffective, even aversive, processes that yielded little value beyond administrative.

As dissatisfaction with traditional PM grew, PM researchers and thought leaders in the United States began arguing for increased attention to manager behaviors that had been shown to be associated with higher performance and engagement and calls to stop reinventing formal PM systems (Pulakos et al., 2019). As mentioned, three have proved to be the most important. The first of these is communicating clear goals and objectives to employees in real time with enough detail that people knew what to do and what good performance looked like in relation to that specific goal. This is different than annual goals that tend to be high-level and are set once annually and rarely revisited. Goals and objectives that drive performance need to be flexible and updated in real time as situations change so that they remain relevant and helpful for guiding performance. This is especially important in today's fluid, dynamic, and rapidly changing work environments.

The second important manager behavior is having regular informal performance conversations. These are important so that managers and employees can stay plugged in on what is happening, develop a common understanding of how work is progressing, and partner to overcome challenges. These change the nature of performance conversations from dreaded, stress-inducing yearly events to common, run-of-the-mill interactions. Both managers and employees become desensitized to the negative aspects of discussing performance as this becomes a routine part of work.

Elaine Pulakos et al.

The third important manager behavior is helping employees solve problems that are interfering with performance. As part of ongoing performance conversations, this means managers asking employees what challenges they are facing and assisting them in removing obstacles.

Increasing the frequency of the behaviors that matter most in driving performance and engagement helps overcome the enduring challenges that have plagued U.S. PM. Staying in touch through regular check-ins helps mitigate the human judgment and time factors that distort evaluations. Managers have more insight into how each employee is doing and armed with this information, they can form more accurate impressions about performance effectiveness. Managers can also help employees improve their performance in real time, enabling them to better achieve higher evaluations in the end. Managing performance as an intentional, daily activity has much more potential to positively impact performance than annual evaluations that occur too infrequently to be helpful and leave everyone on edge. Around 2010, organizations began showing more interest in enabling the key manager behaviors that drive performance and engagement.

While managers need to drive effective PM, they cannot do it alone. Employees have an important role to play in ensuring that PM processes are effective. They need to take responsibility for understanding their performance expectations, ask questions to clarify what's needed, and notify their managers when things interfere with achieving their objectives. Employees also need to react well to feedback and use it to their advantage. Table 7.4 summarizes the manager and employee behaviors that lead to effective PM.

While companies still benchmark and learn from each other, there has been a shift away from blindly adopting others' approaches to PM. During the last decade, organizations began experimenting with more bespoke PM processes that were fit to their cultures and values. We saw virtually nonexistent PM to highly structured PM processes that were tightly integrated with other talent management practices. A flavor for the range of different PM systems U.S. companies developed during the past decade can be found in Pulakos and Battista's (2020) recent book on PM transformation. Newer ideas included are playing to employee

Table 7.4 Manager and Employee Behaviors that Yield Effective PM

For Managers

- Set clear expectations, priorities, success criteria, and standards for the work being performed and revise expectations as needed in real time, so employees know what to do.
- Check in regularly to stay in touch with how employees are doing and provide regular, informal feedback to praise, coach, and course-correct.
- Coach and help employees solve problems that are blocking their performance.

For Employees

- Clarify performance expectations to ensure understanding, ask questions, and revisit as necessary.
- Set expectations with peers about who is doing what and by when.
- Ask for and accept feedback nondefensively and use feedback to course-correct and improve own performance.

Table 7.5 Where to Start PM Designs

- What business needs are we trying to address with the PM process?
- What must be evaluated to achieve our business goals?
- What values are most important to us and need to be reinforced?
- What are our beliefs about our managers and employees; how much trust is there in our environment?
- What is our philosophy about pay, and how much pay is at risk?
- How enthusiastic and able is our workforce to implement change?
- Will a common process work, or do we need different processes for different work and units?

strengths and accepting that everyone has limitations rather than imposing requirements to provide developmental feedback and improve performance in areas that may not be easily addressed by certain individuals. As organizations became flatter and more work was executed collaboratively through matrixed, cross-functional teams (CEB, 2012), some companies experimented with team-based PM processes. As suggested by Church et al. (2015), others developed multiple PM processes to reflect different work requirements, complexity, and goals across different organizational units. Pulakos et al. (2019) advocated that PM practices should be designed to fit the organization's strategy, culture, and goals, considering questions like those shown in Table 7.5.

A recent perhaps unexpected influence on PM has come from employees. Employees have found a stronger voice, and they are pressuring leaders to be more transparent, accessible, and helpful to them. Research from Perceptyx (2021) has shown that employees want to discuss their performance on a regular basis with their managers and are looking to leaders to provide them with rich, developmental feedback, learning experiences, and supportive coaching on a regular basis. Employees do not want to wait 6 months to a year to talk with their managers about their performance and development, and they don't want to be con-strained by the confines of a formal PM process. Instead, they want to be able to approach their leaders informally as needed. Leaders have been stepping up to meet these demands in part due to labor shortages and post-pandemic restlessness that has resulted in millions of American workers resigning to seek out new work opportunities. Perceptyx (2021) found that the informal PM behaviors we have been discussing here, along with attractive development opportunities, play an important role in delivering a positive employee experience and can fend off attrition. These influences are creating a new look for PM in organizations.

In conclusion, U.S. PM processes have taken many twists and turns. Achieving effective PM is not easy and continues to be a challenge. But organizations have begun taking more mindful approaches to PM, considering what features will best fit within their contexts. Things like the nature of the work, organizational philosophy and values about performance and rewards, climate and culture, maturity, and openness to change are all important considerations. From this perspective, there is no right, wrong, or one-way to design a PM process and no answer to questions like whether or not ratings should be eliminated. The points of reflection and mindset changes about work created by COVID-19 and subsequent restlessness have propelled more informal employee-centered, developmental, and compassionate perfor-mance conversations to occur between managers and employees. Whether or not these will become enduring, embedded fixtures in organizational cultures is yet to be determined, but the chances increase with continued pressure and demands from employees. It is unclear how PM may continue to morph and change into the future but as past history has shown, we will almost certainly see continued efforts to improve and gain more value from PM in U.S. organizations into the future.

REFERENCES

Adler, S., Campion, M., Colquitt, A., Grubb, A., Murphy, K., Ollander-Krane, R., & Pulakos, E. D. (2016). Getting rid of performance ratings: Genius or folly? A debate. *Industrial Organizational Psychology, 9*, 219–252.

Austin, J. T., & Villanova, P. (1992). The criterion problem: 1917 – 1992. *Journal of Applied Psychology, 77*, 836–874.

Bernardin, H. J., & Beatty, R. W. (1984). *Performance appraisal: Assessing human behavior at work.* Boston, MA: Kent.

Bock, L. (2015). *Work rules! Insights from Google that will transform how you live and lead.* New York: Twelve.

Borman, W. C. (1974). The rating of individuals in organizations: An alternate approach. *Organizational Behavior and Human Performance, 12*, 105–124.

Borman, W. C. (1975). Effects of instructions to avoid halo error on reliability and validity of performance evaluation ratings. *Journal of Applied Psychology, 60*, 556–560.

Borman, W. C. (1977). Consistency of rating accuracy and rating errors in the judgment of human performance. *Organizational Behavior and Human Performance, 20*, 238–252.

Borman, W. C. (1979). Format and training effects on rating accuracy and rating errors. *Journal of Applied Psychology, 64*, 410–421.

Boyatzis, R. E. (1996). Consequences and rejuvenation of competency-based human resource and organization development. In R. W. Woodman & W. A. Passmore (Eds.), *Research in organizational change and development* (Vol. 9, pp. 101–122). Greenwich, CN: JAI Press.

Bracken, D., Timmreck, C., & Church, A. (Eds.). (2001). *Handbook of multisource feedback.* San Francisco, CA: Jossey-Bass.

Bryant, A. (2011). Google's quest to build a better boss. *New York Times*, March 12. http://www.nytimes.com/2011/03/13/business/13hire.html?pagewanted=all&_r=0

Drucker, P. (1954). *The practice of management.* New York: Harper.

CEB (2004). *Driving employee performance and retention through engagement: A quantitative analysis of the effectiveness of employee engagement strategies.* Washington, DC: CEB. https://www.stcloudstate.edu/humanresources/_files/documents/supv-brown-bag/employee-engagement.pdf

CEB (2012). *Driving breakthrough performance in the new work environment.* Washington, DC: CEB. http://blueroom.neuroleadership.com/assets/documents/CEB%20-%20Driving%20Breakthrough%20Performance%20in%20the%20New%20Work%20Environment%20-%20Short%20Version.pdf

CEB (2016). *The real impact of eliminating performance ratings: Insights from employees and managers.* Washington, DC: CEB. https://www.cebglobal.com/human-resources/eliminating-performance-ratings.html

Church, A. H., Ginther, N. M., Levine, R., & Rotolo, C. T. (2015). Going beyond the fix: Taking performance management to the next level. *Industrial Organizational Psychologist, 8*, 121–129.

Cooper, W. H. (1981). Ubiquitous halo. *Psychological Bulletin, 90*, 218–244.

Culbert, S. A., & Rout, L. (2010). *Get rid of the performance review: How companies can stop intimidating, start managing—And focus on what really matters.* New York: Business Plus.

Culbertson, S. S., Henning, J. B., & Payne, S. C. (2013). Performance appraisal satisfaction: The role of feedback and goal orientation. *Journal of Personnel Psychology, 12*, 189–195.

Cunningham, L. (2015). In big move, Accenture will get rid of annual performance reviews and rankings. *Washington Post*, July 21. http://www.washingtonpost.com/blogs/on-leadership/wp/2015/07/21/in-big-move-accenture-will-get-rid-of-annual-performance-reviews-and-rankings/?tid=pm_pop_b

DeCotiis, T., & Petit, A. (1978). The performance appraisal process: A model and some testable propositions. *Academy of Management Review, 3*, 635–646.

DeNisi, A. S. (2006). *A cognitive approach to performance appraisal.* New York: Routledge.

DeNisi, A. S., & Murphy, K. R. (2017). Performance appraisal and performance management: 100 years of progress? *Journal of Applied Psychology, 3*, 421–433.

Dorsey, D. W. (2002). Information technology. In J. W. Hedge & E. D. Pulakos (Eds.), *Implementing organizational interventions* (pp. 110–132). San Francisco, CA: Jossey-Bass.

Dubois, D. D. (1993). *Competency-based performance improvement: A strategy for organizational change.* Amherst, MA: HRD Press.

Dunnette, M. D. (1963). A note on the criterion. *Journal of Applied Psychology, 47*, 251–254.

Flanagan, J. C. (1954). The critical incident technique. *Psychological Bulletin, 51*, 327–358.

Greguras, G. J., Robie, C., Schleicher, D. J., & Goff, M. (2003). A field study of the effects of rating purpose on the quality of multisource ratings. *Personnel Psychology, 56*, 1–21.

Grote, R. C. (1996). *The complete guide to performance appraisal.* New York: American Management Association.

Guion, R. M. (1961). Criterion measurement and personnel judgments. *Personnel Psychology, 4*, 141–149.

Harter, J. K., Schmidt, F. L., & Hayes, T. L. (2002). Business unit-level relationship between employee satisfaction, employee engagement, and business outcomes: A meta-analysis. *Journal of Applies Psychology, 87*, 268–279.

Hedge, J. W., Borman, W. C., & Birkeland, S. A. (2001). History and development of multisource feedback as a methodology. In D. W. Bracken, C. W. Timmreck, & Church (Eds.), *The handbook of multisource feedback* (pp. 15–32). San Francisco: Jossey-Bass.

Hillgren, J. S., & Cheatham, D. W. (2000). *Understanding performance measures: An approach to linking rewards to the achievement of organizational objectives.* Scottsdale, AZ: WorldatWork.

Ilgen, D. R., & Feldman, J. M. (1983). Performance appraisal: A process focus. In L. Cumings & B. Staw (Eds.), *Research in organizational behavior* (Vol. 5, pp. 141–197). Greenwich, CT: JAI Press.

Jamieson, B. D. (1973). Behavioral problems with management by objective. *Academy of Management Review, 16*, 496–505.

Kahn, S. C., Brown, B. B., & Lanzarone, M. (1996). *Legal guide to human resources.* Boston, MA: Warren, Gorham & Lamont, 6–2 to 6–58.

Klein, A. L. (1996). Validity and reliability for competency-based systems: Reducing litigation risks. *Compensation Benefits Review, 28*, 31–37.

Landy, F. J., & Farr, J. L. (1980). Performance rating. *Psychological Bulletin, 87*, 72–107.

Latham, G.P., & Wexley, K.N. (1977). Behavioral observation scales for performance appraisal purposes. *Personnel Psychology, 30*, 255–268

Latham, G. P., Wexley, K. N., & Pursell, E. D. (1975). Training managers to minimize rating errors in the observation of behavior. *Journal of Applied Psychology, 60*, 550–555.

Lawler, E. E. (1967). The multitrait-multirater approach to measuring managerial job performance. *Journal of Applied Psychology, 51*, 369–381.

Ledford, G. E., Benson, G. S., & Lawler, E. E. III (2016). *A study of cutting-edge performance management practices: Ongoing feedback, ratingless reviews and crowd-sourced feedback.* Scottsdale, AZ: WorldatWork.

Lopez, F. M. (1968). *Evaluating employee performance.* Chicago, IL: Public Personnel Association.

Martin, D. C., Bartol, K. M., & Kehoe, P. E. (2000). The legal ramifications of performance appraisal: The growing significance. *Public Personnel Management, 29*(3), 379–406.

McIntyre, R. M., Smith, D. E., & Hassett, C. E. (1984). Accuracy of performance ratings as affected by rater training and perceived purpose of rating. *Journal of Applied Psychology, 69*, 147–156.

Malos, S. (1998). Current legal issues in performance appraisal. In J. W. Smither (Ed.), *Performance appraisal: State of the art in practice* (pp. 49–94). San Francisco, CA: Jossey-Bass.

Malos, S. (2005). The importance of valid selection and performance appraisal: Do management practices figure in case law? In F. J. Landy (Ed.), *Employment discrimination litigation* (pp. 373–409). San Francisco, CA: Jossey-Bass.

Muchinsky, P. M. (1997). *Psychology applied to work: An introduction to industrial and organizational psychology*. Pacific Grove, CA: Brooks/Cole Publishing Company.

Mueller-Hanson, R. A., & Pulakos, E. D. (2018). *Transforming performance management to drive performance: An evidence-based roadmap*. New York: Routledge.

Murphy, K. R., & Balzer, W. K. (1989). Rater errors and rating accuracy. *Journal of Applied Psychology, 74*, 619–624.

Murphy, K. R., & Cleveland, J. N. (1991). *Performance appraisal. An organizational perspective*. Needham Heights, MA: Allyn and Bacon.

Murphy, K. R., & Cleveland, J. N. (1995). *Understanding performance appraisal: Social, organizational and goal-oriented perspectives*. Newbury Park, CA: Sage.

Murphy, K. R., Jako, R. A., Anhalt, R. L. (1993). Nature and consequences of halo error: A critical analysis. *Journal of Applied Psychology, 78*, 218–225.

Murphy, K. R., Martin, C., & Garcia, M. (1982). Do behavioral observation scales measure observation? *Journal of Applied Psychology, 67*, 562–567.

Patterson, D. G. (1922). The Scott Company graphic rating scale. *Journal of Personnel Research, 1*, 361–376.

Perceptyx. (2021, March 8). *The gender gap widens: Pnademic's impact on women in the owkrplace is far from over*. Cision, PR Newswire. https://www.prnewswire.com/news-releases/the-gender-gap-widens-pandemics-impact-on-women-in-the-workplace-is-far-from-over-301241819.html

Pulakos, E. D. (1984). A comparison of rater training programs: Error training and accuracy training. *Journal of Applied Psychology, 69*, 581–588.

Pulakos, E. D. (1986). The development of a training program to increase accuracy with different rating formats. *Organizational Behavior and Human Decision Processes, 38*, 76–91.

Pulakos, E. D., & Battista, M. (2020). *Performance management transformation: Lessons learned and next steps*. New York: Oxford University Press.

Pulakos, E. D., Mueller-Hanson, R., & Arad, S. (2019). The evolution of performance management: Searching for value. *Annual Review of Organizational Psychology and Organizational Behavior, 6*, 249–271. https://doi.org/10.1146/annurev-orgpsych-012218-015009

Pulakos, E. D., & O'Leary, R. S. (2010). Defining and measuring results of workplace behavior. In J. L. Farr & N. T. Tippins (Eds.), *The handbook of employee selection* (pp. 513–529). New York: Psychology Press.

Pulakos, E. D., & O'Leary, R. S. (2011). Why is performance management so broken? *Industrial Organizational Psychologist, 4*, 146–164.

Rock, D. (2008). SCARF: A brain-based model for collaborating with and influencing others. *NeuroLeadership Journal, 1*, 1–9.

Rock, D., & Jones, B. (2015). Why more and more companies are ditching performance ratings. *Harvard Business Review*, September 8. https://hbr.org/2015/09/why-more-and-more-companies-are-ditching-performance-ratings

Rodgers, R., & Hunter, J. E. (1991). Impact of management by objectives on organizational productivity. *Journal of Applied Psychology, 76*, 322–336.

Rodgers, R., Hunter, J. E., & Rogers, D. L. (1993). Influence of top management commitment on management program success. *Journal of Applied Psychology, 78*, 51–155.

Saal, F. E., & Landy, F. J. (1977). The mixed standard rating scale: An evaluation. *Organizational Behavior and Human Performance, 18*, 19–35.

Schippmann, J. S. (1999). *Strategic job modeling: Working at the core of integrated human resource systems.* Mahwah, NJ: Lawrence Erlbaum Associates, Inc.

Schneier, C. E., Shaw, D. G., & Beatty, R. W. (1991). Performance measurement and management: A tool for strategy execution. *Human Resources Management, 30*, 279–301.

Scott, W. D., Clothier, R. C., & Spriegel, W. R. (1941). *Personnel management.* New York: McGraw-Hill.

Smith, P. C., & Kendall, L. M. (1963). An approach to the construction of unambiguous anchors for rating scales. *Journal of Applied Psychology, 47*, 149–155.

Smither, J. W., London, M., & Reilly, R. R. (2005). Does performance improve following multisource feedback? A theoretical model, meta-analysis, and review of empirical findings. *Personnel Psychology, 58*, 33–66.

Society for Industrial and Organizational Psychology. (2003). *Principles for the validation and use of personnel selection procedures: Fourth edition.* Bowling Green, OH: Author.

Strauss, G. (1972). Management by objectives: A critical review. *Training and Development Journal, 26*, 10–15.

Summers, L. (2001). Web technologies for administering multisource feeback programs. In D. W. Bracken, C. W. Timmreck, & A. H. Church (Eds.), *The handbook of multisource feedback* (pp. 165–180). San Francisco, CA: Jossey-Bass.

Taylor, F. J. (1911). *The principles of scientific management.* New York: Harper & Brothers.

Uniform guidelines on employee selection procedures (1978). *Federal register, 43*, 38295–38315.

INTERNET RESOURCES FOR PERFORMANCE MANAGEMENT

www.gartner.com/en
www.opm.gov
www.shrm.org

Performance Management in Mexico

Jorge A. Gonzalez, Lorena Perez-Floriano and R. Aristeo Rodriguez

Chapter 8

INTRODUCTION

Performance appraisal (PA) is an integral part of organizational performance management (PM) systems. PA refers to activities used to assess employees, develop competencies, allocate rewards, and improve both individual and organizational performance. PM and PA scholarship and practice in Mexico have evolved to some extent since the publication of the first edition of this book. In the prior edition, Dávila and Elvira (2008) provide an overview of PM in Mexico, noting that PM systems and PA practices in Mexico date back to the 1970s, being mostly imported from North American systems. One major attribute of their analysis of PA included the wide variety of practices across organizational hierarchies, professions, and occupations. For instance, whereas management by objectives is used for senior management professionals, informal merit systems are used for clerical and manufacturing workers.

Despite challenges in PM design and implementation in Mexico, PM systems continue to be established in this country. Yet, cultural norms limit its implementation as a formal process (Rao, 2015). Although these challenges are global, they can be exacerbated by cultural, institutional, and structural misalignments (Aycan, 2005),

DOI: 10.4324/9781003306849-8

which is the case in Mexico. Here, we present a brief review of Dávila and Elvira's (2008) summary of PA practices in Mexico. Then, we describe the current distal (cultural, socioeconomic, legal/labor relations) and proximal (organizational) factors that surround PA practices in Mexico. Relying on this review, recent research on PA and cultural and socioeconomic trends in Mexico, as well as an additional interview with an executive and a personal communication with an HR consultant, we provide an updated account of PM and PA systems in Mexico. We follow this with an overview of recent academic research on PA in Mexico, discuss its implications for research and practice, and conclude with best-practice recommendations.

PA AND PM SYSTEMS IN MEXICO

Dávila and Elvira's (2008) overview of the state of the art of PA practices in Mexico portrayed a nascent human resource management (HRM) practice ripe with the promise of stimulating the performance of Mexican employees and the firms in which they work. In their literature review, they found only a few journal articles mentioning PA in Mexico. The sources of information they used came from professional and industrial associations, the written press, government statistics (INEGI), and authored books. Given the scarcity of scholarly research on the topic, six interviews with human resource (HR) professionals from Mexico were also included. From this work, the authors countered the prevailing notion that PA is rarely used as an incentive for individual performance in Mexico, instead finding evidence of PA being used effectively as a forum for employee expression of their views and career development aspirations rather than compensation adjustments (Milliman et al., 2002). Moreover, managers tend to overrate the performance of employees who meet their personal assumptions about proper employee behavior, highlighting the role of subjectivity (DeVoe & Iyengar, 2004). One reason is that Mexican managers do not generally receive prior training in management skills or the appropriate use of performance evaluation tools and mechanisms. In many organizations, managers are reluctant to provide direct feedback to their employees. Instead, both managers and employees prefer an informal, nonpunitive approach through which managers can provide genuine feedback (Brutus & Cabrera, 2004).

Following Murphy and DeNisi's (2008) model of the PA process, Dávila and Elvira (2008) organized their review into distal, proximal, internal, intervening, judgment, and distortion factors. Distal factors influencing PA processes received special attention as they include cultural and institutional factors in which nations differ, including the economy, culture, technological infrastructure, and labor systems. Distal factors also include organizational factors at a macro level of analysis, including the organization's strategy and performance.

The following statements summarize the implementation of PA practices in Mexico. For the most part, they comply with the cultural and institutional framework of the country, but some also represent faulty PA practices that demand reevaluation.

1. Performance evaluation rewards good (proper) behavior.
2. Performance evaluation is rarely related to individual performance.
3. PA has traditionally been used to make decisions about downsizing, promotions, and salary increases, as well as promote efficiency.
4. PA provides a safe space for employees to express their opinions and aspirations, enabling them to engage and communicate with upper management.
5. PA is used to evaluate rather than to develop employees.

THE ROLE OF CULTURAL FACTORS

Culture permeates all aspects of human life in Mexico. Major cultural aspects of this country as per cultural dimensions (Hofstede, 1980; Smith et al., 1996) include a collectivistic concern for the group over the individual, high power distance where people in power and resources are clearly distinct from those without it, uncertainty avoidance where people have a low tolerance for risk and ambiguity, emotionality whereby people display emotions freely, a particularistic approach to rules such that people in power can bend the rules, a sequential (relaxed, flexible, and circular) approach to time orientation, and a diffuse approach to space that blurs the line between public and private spaces. With more than 3,000 years of history, Mexican culture is hard to change. Mexico's history, based on colonial rule from Spain, characterizes it as a fusion of two cultures, or a torn culture rift between the culturally distant European and indigenous cultures (Gannon & Pillai, 2015). Equally, globalization trends and Mexico's geographic location just south of the United States renders it subject to trade, investment, and cultural influence from the United States, which influence employee behavior and the implementation and perception of PA and other HRM practices.

Despite the strong culture of Mexico, regional, organizational, professional, and demographic differences are ubiquitous. This degree of variety helps explain outliers and counterintuitive findings challenging traditional applications of culture. Scholars and managers should attend to internal variance attributed to regional differences, professional norms, socioeconomic status or social class, demographics (e.g., based on gender and generation; cf. Baeza et al., 2018), and corporate culture. For example, Pelled and Hill's (1997) study in Mexican *maquiladora* factory plants found that participative management practices enhanced individual performance, which counters expectations that align with high power distance cultural values. Pelled and Hill attributed such results to geographic location at the northern border and the corresponding corporate culture of maquiladoras – foreign manufacturing or assembly plants located along the U.S. border corridor that take advantage of the region's free-trade-zone laws, such as lower or no tariffs on finished goods.

Dávila and Elvira (2005) argued that cultural dimensions often have limited applications for understanding work behavior and instead proposed a hybrid view of Mexican work culture in which the national culture and the organizational culture nurture each other. The application to leadership, for example, explains the work culture of *benevolent paternalism*, whereby managers have a personal obligation to protect their employees and safeguard the personal needs of workers and their families. This cultural norm not only preserves social differentiation between managers and employees consistent with a high-power-distance culture but also hampers hierarchical communication and the potential for constructive conflict, which are key to the effective implementation of PA (Lindsley, 1999). Benevolent paternalism protects employees but also creates dependency behaviors among employees that limit decision-making ability (Martinez, 2005).

Historically, the benevolent paternalism leadership style heralds back to the *hacienda* paradigm in which the owner and boss (*patron*) not only paid wages but also provided protection to employees and their families in the form of housing, food, health care, and support in a welfare-type system that served to develop and strengthen familial bonds. This style of leadership may be more common in lower echelons and traditional organizations, but it also fits a *humanistic* style of leadership where employees are considered organizational stakeholders, and where there is a legitimate concern for employees and leaders and employees develop close relationships (Dávila & Elvira, 2012). Similarly, Ruiz et al. (2013) found that being supportive, fair, and caring was associated with effective managers in Mexico. Overall, these cultural elements create a Mexican leadership style characterized by mutual support between managers and employees as supervisors learn to give orders, criticize, and control employees. However, this approach to leadership also poses limitations to the application of PA derived from North American research and practice (Rao, 2015).

Aside from benevolent paternalism, Mexico is an honor culture in which values for dignity and honor shape people's cognitive style (Smith et al., 2017) and impression management is common (Rao, 2015). This means that workers tend to be very proud and suggests managers should be very sensitive to how they deliver performance feedback (Brutus & Cabrera, 2004). Such cultural characteristics present an obstacle for the implementation of PA systems, which require open communication and the ability to apply constructive feedback and criticism without taking it personally. Combined with other cultural attributes, such as collectivism, the cultural profile of Mexico promotes harmonious and nonconfrontational behavior in the workplace (Martínez & Dorfman, 1998; Brutus & Cabrera, 2004). This distinction suggests that Mexican workers are likely to perceive negative feedback as a personal attack such that delivering negative feedback may result in breaking the harmony of a relationship (Dávila & Elvira, 2007; Rao, 2015).

Mexico's collective and emotional cultural profile may also relate to an affiliative orientation that drives, high emotional involvement among coworkers, including managers with their employees.

This affiliative orientation can limit the implementation of PA systems that increase competition across coworkers and may instead harm a collaborative work environment (Ramirez & Zapata-Cantú, 2009). This premise was examined and contrasted with North American market orientation and Asia's familial collectivism style emphasizing sacrifice for the group through a study of managers' perceptions of their subordinates (DeVoe & Iyengar, 2004), which compared Citigroup workers from the United States, Asia, and Latin America, including Mexico. In this study, Mexican employees (along with employees from Brazil and Argentina) were perceived to be more intrinsically rather than extrinsically motivated, which differed from managers' perceptions of North American and Asian employees. Latin American managers' perceptions of their employees' motivation were also congruent with employees' own perceptions. Latin American employees likewise received higher performance evaluations than their counterparts; moreover, Latin American managers only weighed their perceptions of employees' intrinsic motivation when appraising performance. This implies that Mexican (along with other Latin American) managers overvalue employees who exemplify their assumptions about proper employee behavior.

THE ROLE OF SOCIOECONOMIC FACTORS

Mexico is a large developing economy. It is the second largest economy in Latin America, after Brazil. At the time of writing, Mexico had 128 million inhabitants. According to the International Monetary Fund (IMF), it has a nominal gross domestic product of 1.31 trillion US dollars, representing 2.61 trillion dollars in purchasing power parity. At the time of writing, Mexico ranked as the 15th-largest economy in the word, although this represented a rank of 95th in terms of nominal gross domestic product per capita (Recoveries, 2021). Mexico is the United States' second-largest trading partner, the second-largest purchaser of U.S. exports (after Canada), and the third-biggest exporter of goods to the United States (after Canada and China). Its economy is led by *Multilatinas*—Latin American multinational enterprises (Cuervo-Cazurra, 2016), such as CEMEX (cement and building materials), América Móvil (telecommunications), Grupo Alfa (diversified), Grupo Bimbo (food processing), and state-owned enterprises, including the oil company PEMEX. However, small and medium-sized enterprises (*Pequeñas y Medianas empresas* or *PyMEs*) and the informal economy represent a large portion of economic activity. Mexico's strategic geographic location and regional trade agreements such as the United States–Mexico–Canada Agreement (USMCA, formerly the North American Free Trade Agreement or NAFTA) and other treaties have helped globalize its economy.

Consistent with many other developing economies, Mexico has a small number of complex high-quality occupations and plenty of low-skilled occupations. Dávila and Elvira (2008) noted that the lack of formal PA systems influencing compensation may be one of the reasons for high turnover in the country, highlighting that almost half of Mexican workers leave their jobs due to low salaries. Although some employees join other organizations, many join the informal economy. This may also explain why more than half of the population works in informal occupations, a number that totaled 56% in 2021 (Cullell, 2021). Dávila and Elvira (2008) also cited a corporate report from HayGroup Mexico (Estrada, 2006) stating that two in three employees do not feel their contributions are recognized while almost half do not know what to expect during the PA interview. This report indicates that PA is applied erroneously in Mexico because managers do not understand its goals. Ultimately, managers tend to be good at developing plans and objectives but fail to communicate and establish agreement about such goals and objectives with their employees. Furthermore, Dávila and Elvira (2008) cited a survey from bumeran.com reporting that employees leave their jobs due to low compensation (46.5%) and poor organizational climate (28.3%). Similarly, media reports noted that six in ten workers perceive that their incomes do not align with the throughput and quality of their work and the need for organizations to align HR policies with suitable rewards and recognition. The need to align PA with work quantity and quality may be important to workers as the Organisation for Economic Co-operation and Development (OECD) ranks Mexico as one of the countries where employees work the most hours in a year (2,128 hours in 2021).

Dávila and Elvira (2008) espoused that organizations evolved to perform well in Mexico's weak economy and unstable political environment. The governance of Mexican business groups (*grupos*) is based on nuclear and extended family links, characterized by rigid bureaucracies, and favors collectivist versus individual values. These features make relational capital at the macro level a main competitive advantage (Sargent, 2005). Political instability has been linked to questionable ties with the government and corruption, both of which can influence the execution of strategy and measurement of performance at both the individual and firm levels (Nicholls-Nixon et al., 2011). Sentiments of corruption are also likely to influence perceptions of (lack of) accuracy and the existence of favoritism in the PA process of many organizations. This may be interpreted as an example of distortion factors (Murphy & DeNisi, 2008) that exist in PA meetings, including the potential to manipulate PA ratings and outcomes when the performance management system is not well understood in an organization, or when managers lack knowledge or training on how to implement effective PA practices.

LEGAL AND LABOR RELATIONS FACTORS

Mexico follows civil law, which is based on codified statutes. The Mexican judicial system establishes labor laws and employee rights. The Ley Federal del Trabajo regulates established laws and details the obligations and rights of both employees and employers as set forth in the Constitution since 1931. It establishes, for example, the minimum salary, which varies across geographic areas according to the state of development and cost of living (being higher in Mexico City and northern cities). Ley Federal del Trabajo also establishes regulations behind employment termination, a complicated legal process that favors employees, specifying just causes that employers must provide in writing to a worker to warrant termination.

Mexican legal codes are in constant revision. Global trends aimed at diminishing wage inequality have too influenced the Mexican labor relations environment. For instance, pressure from the United States conditioning the renewal of NAFTA led to changes in Mexican labor laws. The Nueva Ley Federal del Trabajo (NLTF; New Federal Labor Law) was signed in 2021 and focused on the following: (a) achieving decent and dignified work for workers by diminishing the practice of outsourcing, banning child labor; (b) facilitating unionization; (c) safer working conditions; (d) improving the administration of justice in labor disputes; (d) develop effective incentives to promote formal employment; and (e) increase productivity with government sponsored competency training and certifications. The NLFT establishes mandatory equal work for equal pay, aimed to disappear the appalling 34% gender gap wage differences, which is composed of a 25% gap for professional men and women, and 80% for domestic staff (Redacción Factor Capital Humano, 2020).

Unionism

Constitutional law allows Mexican workers to unionize, bargain collectively, and strike. Labor law establishes specific rules regarding the organization and registration of a labor union. The Confederation of Mexican Workers (CTM) is the largest confederation of labor unions in the country. Historically, the CTM had strong ties to the PRI (Institutional Revolutionary Party) political party, which ruled Mexico for most of the 20th century (Bensusán & Middlebrook, 2012). Despite recent changes in the political landscape of the country, the CTM remains a powerful confederation of labor unions, representing about 70% of collective bargaining agreements (Rao, 2015). Many other union confederations exist in Mexico, with many employees enjoying their protection. For example, about two thirds of public school teachers are unionized in the National Syndicate of Education Workers (SNTE). Despite data showing a high union density relative to other OECD countries, this density is declining.

The Mexican labor union system has traditionally been associated with worker complacency and characterized by corruption and media scandals (Caulfield, 2004; Greer et al., 2007; Lévesque et al., 2015). For instance, while many employees enjoy genuine protection, some industries are characterized by *sindicatos blancos* (i.e., "white unions"), created and managed by employers, and *sindicatos fanstasma* (i.e., "ghost unions), which are union facades. The rationale behind the legality of such unions is to circumvent involvement by political parties that may not represent workers' interests, but the corollary is that white unions represent organizational interests and that ghost unions are registered with the government but do not represent workers' interests and prevent real unions from being established (Rao, 2015). The NLFT constitutes a strong reformation to unionism in Mexico. Before the reform, once a company union was registered at the secretary of labor, it was almost impossible for workers to create or enroll in other unions. With the NLFT reform, white unions are bound to disappear by 2024, strengthening the power of worker unions in Mexico. At the time of this writing, these changes had slowly started to occur and should be achieved nationwide by 2024. These reforms promise to increase fairness and transparency in the administration of PA in Mexico, but the effects remain to be seen.

Profit Sharing

In Mexico, labor law requires employers to distribute a percentage (10% at the time of writing) of their profits (*Reparto de Utilidades*) on an annual basis. This legal practice establishes an institutional link between individual and organizational performance, although it also poses several challenges. The practice accounts for an important proportion of workers' salaries, especially in large financial *grupos*. Miguel Ángel Durazo, a retired HR executive and seasoned HR consultant in Mexico, concurred with these statements in a personal communication. Nonetheless, Durazo acknowledged that whereas this link is common in large companies, it is not always the case for many small and medium size companies. He further states that some small companies tend to avoid the responsibility of redistribution by spending their profits before the start of a new fiscal year (expanding their operations, hiring new people, buying new machinery or technology, or outsourcing part of their labor operations, among others). Therefore, the link between organizational performance and individual pay is present in many executive and managerial positions in large companies as their rewards are usually tied to firm performance. Nonetheless, this relationship is unpredictable for most workers in lower-level positions.

Other legal factors involve benefits to which employers are obligated to contribute, including the Mexican Institute for Social Security (IMSS) and Services for State Workers or Civil Service Social Security and Services Institute (ISSSTE), which administer the health and social security systems for Mexican private (IMSS) and public (ISSSTE) workers. Laws have also established a savings retirement system (SAR) through which employers contribute 2% of an employee's base pay and a fund that promotes housing (Infonavit) for which employees pay approximately 5% of base pay.

PROXIMAL (ORGANIZATIONAL) FACTORS

Proximal factors refer to localized factors that exist at the level of the organization or unit involved, such as organizational norms, and the purpose and acceptance of the PA system (Murphy & DeNisi, 2008). According to Dávila and Elvira (2008), combining psychosocial recognition and financial rewards may help foster a climate conducive to workers' loyalty and commitment in Mexican companies. Nevertheless, managing both individual and firm performance through PA practices requires fostering a culture in which performance management and evaluation systems are established, understood, and accepted.

Dávila and Elvira (2008) also described several PA practices used by multinational company operations in Mexico. Practices included the use of Six Sigma methodology for continuous improvement, common in GE (General Electric); however, there is evidence that the program is falling out of favor despite evidence that it works to improve performance. Another example is the PA system of American Express based on individual and group activities and dialog between managers and employees. It consists of several subprocesses, including the establishment of objectives, individual career development, coaching, feedback, a performance evaluation comparing current with past performance levels, and an assessment of individual and group contributions toward objective accomplishment. The American Express PA practice is implemented twice a year. Dávila and Elvira also delineate the management by objectives program applied by the hotel NH Kristal Mexico, which links individual compensation strategies with the organization's financial objectives through variable pay for its executive employees. One key aspect of the program specifies that global business results are the responsibility of all executives. According to Dávila and Elvira's six interviewees, the instruments used to appraise performance indeed vary to depending on hierarchical level. Top managers tend to be evaluated in terms of their contribution to organizational performance, whereas clerical and manufacturing-level workers are evaluated based on merit and mastery of job tasks.

Jorge A. Gonzalez et al.

TECHNOLOGY FACTORS

At the time of writing, complex information technology (IT) tools played only a limited role in HR practices. However, IT utilization has the potential of informing workers of their performance while avoiding confrontation with managers. In an interview, a former director of health and safety at CEMEX, and a seasoned HR executive and consultant, was asked to describe the major changes in PA over the last 10 years. On the use of digital tools to perform PA, he stated, "The major shift has been in assessing if the person's responsibilities match their competencies versus focusing on their performance." The former director stated that this type of evaluation involves many competencies such as ethics, negotiation skills, and team management. The evaluation of performance is done in a separate meeting and executives are evaluated according to "both the individual development objectives and the business unit objectives ...., and each of these factors has a loading of 50% percent. Fulfilling the individual development objectives may require extensive travelling to learn or adapt different business practices." This PA experience nurtures the development of competencies and helps the employee achieve their assigned objectives. Notably, PA rating sources involve both internal and external customers.

RECENT RESEARCH ON PA IN MEXICO

Research on PA in Mexico since the publication of the first edition of this book has only included a few studies. Nonetheless, these new studies do present evidence that the transferability of U.S. PA practices can be successfully implemented, particularly in professional settings. They also suggest novel strategies for successful PA implementation and design of PM systems. Altogether, these points advance the idea that Mexican organizations are experiencing a shift from labor and manufacturing toward knowledge and professional work.

Shortly after the publication of the first edition of this book, Dávila and Elvira (2009) assessed the performance management system of CompuSoluciones, a medium-sized knowledge-intensive firm (KIF) from Guadalajara, Mexico. The case is based on qualitative interviews with managers and employees and focuses on how PA practices can influence knowledge transfer and the performance of knowledge workers. The authors focused on two PM system challenges—defining the content of performance and subjective judgments in PA. Knowledge work complicates PA practices because firms need to retain highly qualified knowledge workers, motivate them to apply their intellectual skills, and encourage employees to be loyal and committed to the firm (Alvesson, 2004). Resultantly, PA practices and associated rewards should be oriented toward work quality and motivation. This feat, however, remains a central challenge in Mexico, where merit increases are often not related to performance ratings or performance.

PM practices in the firm CompuSoluciones are part of a holistic PM system that links individual and firm performance through financial, operational, and personnel indicators with challenging but attainable goals. The PM system initiates wth staffing practices, including recruitment and selection, based on organizational values to stimulate harmony. Such values were determined by a committee seeking to rescue the firm's roots of participation, integrity, trust, service, dedication, loyalty, and innovation. The individual PA system consists of objectives proposed by the employee and reviewed by the supervisor monthly. Meeting objectives were tied to 15% of pay and the annual evaluation. A third-level program was also implemented—an interview with the supervisor's manager every 6 months. Moreover, a peer recognition program (*Aros* or rings; based on the firm's logo) was instituted, signaling appreciation of employees who uphold firm values. Employees may give the rings to colleagues in exchange for rewards such as time off, training courses, or movie tickets. In the annual 360-degree survey, employees are also appraised by 12 people (the immediate supervisor, third-level supervisor, colleagues, other members). Unlike other Mexican firms, the 360-degree survey is tied to salary raises and managers leverage it to discuss feedback and employee development plans. The PM system did incur criticism, nonetheless, including too many and redundant questions, matching feedback statements across employees, inconsistent follow-ups on personal development plans, and notable recency effects (incidents closer to the appraisal date are mentioned more often). However, both employees and managers expressed satisfaction with the system.

Using a sample of Mexican managers, Selvarajan and Cloninger (2012) explored the relationship between PA source, purpose, and feedback richness with perceived fairness and accuracy, satisfaction with the PA, and motivation to improve. They expected that Mexico's paternalistic and high-power-distance culture implied that employees may be more accepting of their bosses' evaluations. Relying on theory (e.g., DeNisi & Pritchard, 2006), they posited that single-source PA can be subject to bias and political objectives, whereas multisource PA (e.g., 360 degree) is more culturally appropriate and hence considered fairer. In the study, a tripartite conceptualization of organizational justice as distributive, procedural, and interactive was implemented (cf. Colquitt et al., 2001). The authors purport that PA with administrative purposes (e.g., compensation and promotions) is subject to favoritism, friendships, and politics and may be perceived to lack distributive justice, whereas developmental PA triggers less comparative information seeking and is perceived to be fairer.

Such findings can be compared with PA practices at CEMEX, the cement giant, where managers strive to avoid favoritism and employees' PA is performed solely for developmental purposes. Meanwhile, salary and promotions involve a separate process altogether. Based on one of the interviews conducted for this chapter, employees' performance at CEMEX was evaluated every 3 months to assess people's advancement on their set individual and business goals. The company supports extensive traveling in supporting competency development. During the last 15 years, the conversation at CEMEX shifted to competency development and assessment, along with the increasing role of IT systems in the appraisal process that has allowed CEMEX to perform 360-degree PA across the company. Such practices are aligned with theoretical prescriptions based on findings that developmental PA can result in positive supervisor–subordinate interactions, interactional fairness, and that perceived accuracy of ratings together with frequent, timely, and specific feedback can be considered sufficiently trustworthy to drive employees toward following PA prescriptions (Kinicki et al., 2004).

Overall, the findings of Selvarajan and Cloninger (2012) reveal that multisource appraisals and feedback-rich appraisals were positively related to procedural and interactive fairness, but not to distributive fairness. Also, procedural and interactive justice, but not distributive justice, were positively related to PA satisfaction and motivation to improve performance. Interestingly, appraisal purpose was not related to fairness perceptions. Such outcomes are consistent with established findings that Mexican employees are motivated by intrinsic factors instead of extrinsic rewards based on PA ratings, that Mexican workers are concerned with psychological contracts in terms of loyalty, and that employees expect to be assessed by their cooperation instead of competition (DeVoe and Iyengar, 2004).

In a comparative study, Selvarajan et al. (2018) explored the relationship between PA fairness, leader–member exchange (LMX), and motivation to improve performance. The authors expected that this relationship would be stronger in both Mexico and the United States but weaker in Mexico on the basis that LMX, the quality of exchange between leader and follower, is a source of motivation through a sense of obligation for reciprocity. PA essentially involves dyadic exchanges dependent on LMX, which can influence fairness perceptions. The authors noted that if the employee is satisfied with PA through a positive perception of fairness and LMX, they would be intrinsically motivated and self-determined to improve performance. That is, if supervisors treat their subordinates with fairness and honesty, they earn subordinates' respect and are also able to influence superior–subordinate behaviors. Owing to a higher-power-distance culture, the authors expected Mexican employees to defer to higher authorities for decision-making, preferring to keep a safe distance from superiors and reacting less negatively to justice violations.

Selvarajan et al. (2018), however, did not expect Mexican employees to have strong expectations to be treated with dignity and respect in their interactions with management. They argued that since Mexican employees are less sensitive to reciprocal norms of LMX, the quality of LMX would be less important to employee outcomes such as motivation to improve performance, relative to their U.S. counterparts. Their results showed that LMX was significantly related to employees' motivation to improve performance in both Mexico and U.S. samples, but LMX did not

Jorge A. Gonzalez et al.

mediate the role of fairness of this outcome as it did in the United States. Furthermore, neither procedural nor distribute fairness influenced LMX or motivation to improve performance in Mexico. Interactive fairness did show a positive relationship with motivation to improve performance, albeit slightly less for Mexican workers than their U.S. counterparts. LMX, the authors discovered, was not responsible for carrying the effect of fairness on this outcome. This pattern of results supports the idea that Mexican employees may not expect distributive or procedural fairness from PA and instead are motivated by intrinsic factors such as recognition for their loyalty and familiar collegiality.

Rodriguez Montaño and Ordaz Álvarez (2021) examined PA applications to the public sector, a trend also common in other countries (Boselie et al., 2018). They noted that one of the challenges in using PA to improve government functions is that it is often perceived as a punishment, but it has nonetheless become institutionalized since the 1980s thanks to political legitimacy implementation efforts by President Miguel de La Madrid, and by new governmental transparency legislations during President Vicente Fox in the early 2000s. In governmental organizations, PA is closely linked to the two logics of public administration (Bailleres, 2016): (a) ex ante or a priori, which precedes the execution of public administration and where public policies are examined and evaluated prior to their implementation, and (b) during or concomitant, which it is applied during the implementation and execution of the public action.

Concomitant PA in public organizations is important since it allows for the detection of deviations from the goals, programs, objectives, and resources, establishing corrective measures, when necessary, during public management execution (Erales, 2019). For example, a supervisor's failure to perform the annual PA of their subordinates is a cause for an investigation and a potential report of misbehavior in the *Plataforma Nacional de Transparencia* (National Transparency Platform; PNT). The PNT reports are not very detailed (2 or 3 lines maximum), which means that reports of embezzlement may be triggered by minor errors, such as failing to account for a building or a desk. The lack of detailed information makes people suspicious of anyone who has their name appear in the PNT database, which has the corollary effect of driving detailed reporting and accounting because, for a public manager, having their name appear in the PNT is a cause of disgrace equivalent to a red flag in a criminal background check (Ramos, 2020).

Citizens' lack of trust in government institutions is one driver for the increasing implementation of PA in the public sector as proponents advocate for its implementation, including those based on "new public administration theory" (Cabrero, 2005) and efforts to evaluate public administration results (Caiden & Caiden, 2001; Arellano-Gault, 2012). Given the prevalence of corruption in Mexico's public sector, increasing effectiveness and efficiency through transparency management of the public budget and spending has been the primary goal of public PM systems. PA has also been applied in Mexican universities since the 2000s (Rueda Beltrán, 2008; Hernández Mosqueda et al., 2016) with the goals of performance improvement, development of "soft" skills, resource distribution, accountability, and institutional accreditation. Mexico and the rest of Latin America likewise offer opportunities to study HRM practices in hybrid public–private organizations and collaborations, including transitions across organizational forms (Aguinis et al., 2020). Future research may show how PA practices and their outcomes compare across public, private, and hybrid organizational forms.

PRACTICAL IMPLICATIONS FROM RECENT RESEARCH

Recent research increasingly shows that some U.S. PA practices can be imported to Mexico, but some modifications should be made, and that locally grown practices can be effective to improve employee performance. This hybrid approach to PA practices is common in other countries, including Latin American ones (Morley et al., 2021). The CompuSoluciones case is a good example to follow for Mexican firms, particularly KIFs and other professional settings. Meanwhile, results from Selvarajan and Cloninger (2012) suggest that HR managers implement frequent multisource (360-degree) appraisals with rich feedback. Such results fit in with the Mexican distal context, which emphasizes relationships and where administrative decisions, including compensation and promotions, are often based on seniority. One point to note is that whereas 360-degree PA involves self-assessments, one can expect self-ratings to be inflated (Goris, 2014). The studies by Selvarajan and colleagues (Selvarajan & Cloninger, 2012; Selvarajan et al., 2018) also suggest that Mexican employees may not expect distributive or procedural fairness from PA but rather are motivated by intrinsic motivation factors and being recognized by their loyalty and collegiality. However, these results counter the idea that Mexican employees do not expect dignity and respect from their supervisors or PAs. Instead, they align with Smith et al.'s (2017) expectations about honor cultures and PA practices that emphasize dignity and respect. For example, the Balance Scorecard methodology, which is based on respect and trust, has been successfully applied by a Danish firm in Mexico and a maquiladora (Gordon, 2006; Ramirez & Zapata-Cantú, 2009). Overall, recent research shows that PA practices are being successfully implemented in Mexican businesses, as well as in the public sector, albeit with different goals.

Combining these results with Mexico's style of collectivism imply that group-based PA can be successfully implemented with the goal of increasing individual and team performance, whereas individual-based PA is best used for administrative purposes. This can be particularly effective if employees perceive that the PA process is not competitive against coworkers, is not affected by personal favoritism of the supervisor, and has at least a small impact on compensation (e.g., raises or a periodic bonus). The implementation of a PA-based bonus would not need to be implemented on a yearly basis, as more frequent assessments and rewards would better fit the time orientation of Mexican employees. Frequent informal performance interviews or "check-ins" can be used instead. The low role of distributive and procedural justice on PA outcomes, including motivation to improve performance and actual performance, indicates that many employees will have a certain disdain for formal PA and will expect them to be tainted by favoritism and the personal opinions of their superiors, even when multiple sources are implemented. Despite Mexico's high-power-distance culture, employees value the dignity, honor, and respect of interactional justice in PA. Elements tied to cooperation with familiar collegiality, such as organizational citizenship and helping behaviors, as well as loyalty and commitment to the company, should be included in PA ratings.

REFERENCES

Aguinis, H., Villamor, I., Lazzarini, S. G., Vassolo, R. S., Amorós, J. E., & Allen, D. G. (2020). Conducting management research in Latin America: Why and what's in it for you? *Journal of Management, 46*(5), 615–636.

Alvesson, M. (2004). *Knowledge work and knowledge-intensive firms*. Oxford: Oxford University Press.

Arellano-Gault, D. (2012). The evaluation of performance in the Mexican federal government: A study of the monitoring agencies' modernization process. *Public Administration Review, 72*(1), 135–142.

Aycan, Z. (2005). The interplay between cultural and institutional/structural contingencies in human resource management practices. *The International Journal of Human Resource Management, 16*(7), 1083–1119.

Baeza, M. A., Gonzalez, J. A., & Wang, Y. (2018). Job flexibility and job satisfaction among Mexican professionals: A socio-cultural explanation. *Employee Relations, 40*(5), 921–942.

Bailleres, H. J. E. (2016). El Sistema de Evaluación del Desempeño en México: Realidades, quimeras y perspectivas. In *XXI Congreso Internacional del CLAD sobre la Reforma del Estado y de la Administración Pública* (pp. 8–11). Santiago. Retrieved from: http://www2.congreso.gob.pe/sicr/cendocbib/con4_uibd.nsf/E597D3AE66E4D838052580B5005B14B6/$FILE/baillhel.pdf

Bensusán, G., & Middlebrook, K. J. (2012). Organized labor and politics in Mexico. In Roderic Ai Camp (comp.), *Oxford Handbook of Mexican Politics* (pp. 335–364). New York: Oxford University Press.

Boselie, P., Farndale, E., & Paauwe, J. (2018). Comparing performance management across contexts. In *Handbook of research on comparative human resource management* (pp. 164–183). Cheltenham: Edward Elgar Publishing.

Brutus, S., & Cabrera, E. F. (2004). The influence of personal values on feedback-seeking behaviors. *Management Research, 2*(3), 235–250.

Cabrero, E. (2005). Between new public management and new public governance: The case of Mexican Municipalities. *International Public Management Review, 6*(1), 76–99.

Caiden, N. J., & Caiden, G. E. (2001). Strategies for meeting the challenges of diversity management in the civil service. In *Managing diversity in civil service*, United Nations Department of Economic and Social Affairs (UNESA) and the International Institute of Administrative Services (IIAS) (pp. 123–136). Amsterdam: IOS Press.

Caulfield, N. (2004). Labor relations in Mexico: Historical legacies and some recent trends. *Labor History, 45*(4), 445–467.

Colquitt, J. A., Conlon, D. E., Wesson, M. J., Porter, C. O., & Ng, K. Y. (2001). Justice at the millennium: A meta-analytic review of 25 years of organizational justice research. *Journal of applied psychology, 86*(3), 425.

Cuervo-Cazurra, A. (2016). Multilatinas as sources of new research insights: The learning and escape drivers of international expansion. *Journal of Business Research, 69*(6), 1963–1972.

Cullell, J. M. (2021). La desocupación continúa en descenso, pero todavía es superior a la de los primeros meses de 2020. [Unemployment continues to decliate, but it's still higher than in the first months of 2020]. *El País*, Madrid. Retrieved from: https://elpais.com/mexico/2021-10-25/la-informalidad-laboral-en-mexico-vuelve-a-los-niveles-anteriores-a-la-pandemia.html.

Dávila, A., & Elvira, M. M. (2005). Culture and human resource management in Latin America. In M. M. Elvira& A. Dávila (Eds.), *Managing human resources in Latin America: An agenda for international leaders* (pp. 3–24). London: Routledge.

Dávila, A., & Elvira, M. M. (2007). Psychological contracts and performance management in Mexico. *International Journal of Manpower, 28*(5), 384–402.

Dávila, A., & Elvira, M. M. (2008). Performance management in Mexico. In A. Varma, A. P. S. Budhwar, & A. S. DeNisi (Eds.), *Performance management systems* (pp. 115–130). New York: Routledge.

Dávila, A., & Elvira, M. M. (2009). Theoretical approaches to best HRM practices in Latin America. In A. Dávila & M. M. Elvira (Eds.), *Best human resource management practices in Latin America* (pp. 180–188). Oxford: Routledge.

Dávila, A., & Elvira, M. M. (2012). Humanistic leadership: Lessons from Latin America. *Journal of World Business*, *47*(4), 548–554.

DeNisi, A. S., & Pritchard, R. D. (2006). Performance appraisal, performance management and improving individual performance: A motivational framework. *Management and Organization Review*, *2*(2), 253–277.

DeVoe, S. E., & Iyengar, S. S. (2004). Managers' theories of subordinates: A cross-cultural examination of manager perceptions of motivation and appraisal of performance. *Organizational Behavior and Human Decision Processes*, *93*(1), 47–61.

Erales, C. A. B. (2019). La transparencia como constructor de confianza e inhibidor de los hechos de corrupción. *Revista Mexicana de Ciencias Penales*, *2*(7), 57–74.

Estrada, J. (2006). Satisface más al empleado el clima laboral que salario. [Work climate is more satisfactory to the employee than is salary] In *ISI emerging markets*. Guadalajara. Retrieved from: http://www.securities.com/doc.html?pc=MX&sv=CORP&doc_id=117697271.

Gannon, M. J., & Pillai, R. (2015). *Understanding global cultures: Metaphorical journeys through 34 nations, clusters of nations, continents, and diversity*. Thousand Oaks, CA: Sage.

Gordon, G. (2006). Uniform maker sews up success with scorecard. *Quality progress*, *39*(10), 37.

Goris, J. R. (2014). Self-appraisals in Mexico: Assessing the self-enhancing tactician perspective. *International Journal of Commerce and Management*, *24*(2), 152–166.

Greer, C. R., Stevens, C. D., & Stephens, G. K. (2007). The State of the Unions in Mexico. *Journal of Labor Research*, *28*(1), 69–92.

Hernández-Mosqueda, J. S., Tobón-Tobón, S., & Guerrero-Rosas, G. (2016). Hacia una evaluación integral del desempeño: las rúbricas socioformativas. *Ra Ximhai*, *12*(6), 359–376.

Hofstede, G. (1980). Culture and organizations. *International Studies of Management & Organization*, *10*(4), 15–41.

Kinicki, A. J., Prussia, G. E., Wu, B. J., & McKee-Ryan, F. M. (2004). A covariance structure analysis of employees' response to performance feedback. *Journal of Applied Psychology*, *89*(6), 1057.

Lévesque, C., Bensusán, G., Murray, G., Novick, M., Carrillo, J., & Gurrera, M. S. (2015). Labour relations policies in multinational companies: A three-country study of power dynamics. *Journal of Industrial Relations*, *57*(2), 187–209.

Lindsley, S. L. (1999). Communication and "the Mexican way": Stability and trust as core symbols in maquiladoras. *Western Journal of Communication*, *63*(1), 1–31.

Martinez, P. G. (2005). Paternalism as a positive form of leadership in the Latin American context: Leader benevolence, decision-making control and human resource management practices (pp. 75–93). In M. M. Elvira and A. Dávila (Eds.), *Managing human resources in Latin America: An agenda for international leaders*. Oxford: Routledge.

Martínez, S. M., & Dorfman, P. W. (1998). The Mexican entrepreneur: An ethnographic study of the Mexican empresario. *International Studies of Management & Organization*, *28*(2), 97–124.

Milliman, J., Nason, S., Zhu, C., and De Cieri, H. (2002). An exploratory assessment of the purposes of performance appraisals in North and Central America and the Pacific Rim. *Human Resource Management*, *41*(1), 87–102.

Morley, M. J., Murphy, K. R., Cleveland, J. N., Heraty, N., & McCarthy, J. (2021). Home and host distal context and performance appraisal in multinational enterprises: A 22 country study. *Human Resource Management, 60*(5), 715–736.

Murphy, K. R., & DeNisi, A. (2008). A model of the appraisal process. In A. Varma, A. P. S. Budhwar, & A. S. DeNisi (Eds.), *Performance management systems* (pp. 81–94). Oxford: Routledge.

Nicholls-Nixon, C. L., Davila Castilla, J. A., Sanchez Garcia, J., & Rivera Pesquera, M. (2011). Latin America management research: Review, synthesis, and extension. *Journal of Management, 37*(4), 1178–1227.

Pelled, L. H., & Hill, K. D. (1997). Participative management in Northern Mexico: A study of maquiladoras. *International Journal of Human Resource Management, 8*(2), 197–212.

Ramirez, J., & Zapata-Cantú, L. (2009). HRM systems in Mexico: The case of Novo Nordisk. In A. Davil & M. M. Elvira (Eds.), *Best human resource management practices in Latin America* (pp. 111–126). Oxford: Routledge.

Ramos, T. D. (2020). El derecho de acceso a la información pública. La ineficacia de su ejercicio en México. *Ciencia jurídica, 9*(18), 21–39.

Rao, P. (2015). *Human resource management in Mexico: Perspectives for scholars and practitioners*. Charlotte: International Age Publishing.

Recoveries, M. D. (2021). *World economic outlook*. International Monetary Fund.

Redacción Factor Capital Humano. (2020). Reformaran 14 leyes para garantizar igualdad salarial entre mujeres y hombres. [14 laws to guarantee equal pay between women and men to be reformed]. Retrieved September 15, 2022, from https://factorcapitalhumano.com/leyes-y-gobierno/reformaran-14-leyes-para-garantizar-igualdad-salarial-entre-mujeres-y-hombres/2020/11/.

Rodríguez Montaño, L. C., & Ordaz Álvarez, A. (2021). La evaluación del desempeño, una nueva herramienta de la cultura de la transparencia aplicada al sector público en México. *Trascender, contabilidad y gestión, 6*(18), 28–40.

Rueda Beltrán, M. (2008). La evaluación del desempeño docente en las universidades públicas en México. [The evaluation of teaching performance in public universities in Mexico]. *Revista Iberoamericana de Evaluación Educativa, 1*(3), 8–17.

Ruiz, C. E., Wang, J., & Hamlin, R. G. (2013). What makes managers effective in Mexico? *Leadership & Organization Development Journal, 34*(2), 130–146.

Sargent, J. (2005). Large firms and business groups in Latin America: Towards a theory based, contextually relevant research agenda. *Latin American Business Review, 6*(2), 39–66.

Selvarajan, T. T., & Cloninger, P. A. (2012). Can performance appraisals motivate employees to improve performance? A Mexican study. *The International Journal of Human Resource Management, 23*(15), 3063–3084.

Selvarajan, T. T., Singh, B., & Solansky, S. (2018). Performance appraisal fairness, leader member exchange and motivation to improve performance: A study of US and Mexican employees. *Journal of Business Research, 85*, 142–154.

Smith, P. B., Dugan, S., & Trompenaars, F. (1996). National culture and the values of organizational employees: A dimensional analysis across 43 nations. *Journal of Cross-Cultural Psychology, 27*(2), 231–264.

Smith, P. B., Easterbrook, M. J., Blount, J., Koc, Y., Harb, C., Torres, C., … Rizwan, M. (2017). Culture as perceived context: An exploration of the distinction between dignity, face and honor cultures. *Acta de investigación psicológica, 7*(1), 2568–2576.

Performance Management Systems in the UK

*Maranda Ridgway, Helen Shipton and Paul Sparrow**

Chapter 9

This chapter covers four main areas. First, it summarizes the socio-economic and legal context surrounding the employment relationship, followed by a historical review of performance management systems (PMSs) development in the UK. Second, it identifies the key comparative factors that impact PMS practices in the country. Third, when appropriate, it links to the Murphy and DeNisi model presented in Chapter 6 throughout these opening sections. Fourth, the chapter summarizes the challenges facing effective PMS in the UK as identified by the research and practitioner communities, using the evidence base of a library search through Web of Science from 2017 to 2022.

THE UK'S SOCIO-ECONOMIC, LEGAL AND POLITICAL BACKGROUND

UK employment levels have risen over the last decade from 29.7 million in 2013 to 32.8 million in 2022. As of July 2022,

* This chapter has been updated based on Paul's work in an earlier edition.

DOI: 10.4324/9781003306849-9

75.9 per cent of people of working age were employed, and official unemployment as a percentage of the economically active is 3.8 per cent. In 2021, 'professionals' were the largest occupational group in the UK, with 25.7 per cent of people employed, followed by 'associate professional and technical occupations', with 14.6 per cent, and 'administrative and secretarial occupations', with 10.6 per cent employed. The lowest occupation group was 'process, plant and machine operatives', with 5.6 per cent employed. Employment in the public sector stands at 5.7 million. The COVID-19 pandemic dramatically affected remote work, with 24 per cent hybrid working and 14 per cent working exclusively from home.

Three imperatives govern the employment relationship: (1) a complex mix of individual and collective agreements, (2) implicit and explicit understandings, and (3) rights and obligations enshrined in legal statutes. A legal framework underpins the employment contract and the implied and express terms. Contract and common law (established by judges' decisions, not statute) are used to establish whether a person is regarded as an employee in the first place, whether the employer is entitled to exercise control over what the employee does, whether the employee is integrated into the structure of the organization, whether there is a mutual obligation to supply and accept work, and, if yes, whether they can be considered an employee and so claim entitlements. In the UK, there has long been a principle of 'voluntarism' and state abstention from the employment relationship. British statute law impinges on the nature of PMSs through a 'floor of rights' established, structural support for collective bargaining, and restrictions on boundaries of lawful action. The floor of rights covers rights for the individual on matters such as unfair dismissal, redundancy, equal opportunities, maternity leave, employment rights for the disabled, confidentiality of computerized data, and health and safety at work.

The UK's former membership of the EU had two primary legal effects: regulations which affected member states, overriding domestic law, and directives concerning employees' social rights and interests. These regulations are applied directly in the public sector but indirectly in the private sector, where national courts consider a directive's purpose when interpreting national

Maranda Ridgway et al.

legislation. Therefore, some statutory principles have been enacted in response to European directives, and some employee protection existed in parallel with rights accumulated through common law precedents. Here, rights had been established through judicial reviews over time.

Before the UK's exit from the European Union (Brexit), European directives had introduced a range of regulatory effects on UK employment, including measures relating to works councils, maximum working hours, full employment rights for part-time work, and parental leave. In addition, health and safety had been elevated as a policy area demanding systematic and planned approaches on the part of employers, and the broadened definition of health concerns encompassed factors such as stress, smoking, and harassment. Finally, discrimination legislation was extended from sex, race and disability into the arena of age discrimination, all of which have since been captured along with broader categories of difference under the Equality Act 2010. The legal context surrounding the employment relationship in general and, therefore, the conduct of PMSs is complex, especially since Brexit. At the time of writing, although the UK is no longer bound by EU employment law, there was no intention to reduce the level of social protection.

HISTORICAL DEVELOPMENT OF PERFORMANCE MANAGEMENT IN THE UK

The original Harvard model of human resources (HR; Beer et al., 1984) stressed four outcomes against which an HR system should be judged: cost-effectiveness, competence, commitment, and coherence. Of course, there are still many UK organizations today that struggle to implement even the most basic PMS, and there were some organizations back in the 2000s that could claim sophisticated systems. Nonetheless, if we look back over the main developments in practice among UK organizations, it has evolved through successive attention to several factors: first, in the early years of the century, cost-effectiveness (exerted in the form of top-down systems based on narrow specifications of performance as measured through outputs such as objectives); second, a more developmental agenda focused on enabling competence and broader performance specifications; third, more significant concern about the need for mutual employer – employee understanding about – and commitment to – performance, often in the context of engagement programmes. Finally, streamlining - removing low-value effects – is linked with concern about broad strategic imperatives; it is increasingly recognized that poorly designed PMSs might hinder coherence between PMSs and other HR agendas such as talent management and total rewards management.

The 1980s – The Importance of PMSs

Concerning Murphy and DeNisi's model (see Table 2.1), the norms relating to the distal factor of purpose (the frequency, source, and use of PMSs) have developed over time. The importance of PMS in the UK was first highlighted in the 1980s. UK organizations were subjected to considerable competitive threats at the time, and HR systems were developing under this impetus (Hendry, Pettigrew & Sparrow, 1989). Performance management was one of the many US concepts that began to influence UK practice. Existing thinking about the nature of PMSs was already relatively advanced and quickly incorporated into professional training. However, of course, there was a significant gap between the intent behind systems and the quality of their execution (problems were experienced with Murphy and DeNisi's proximal factors of both the purpose and acceptance of systems).

Highlighting its importance gave more attention to the different purposes PMSs might serve. Randall et al. (1984) distinguished between three roles typically seen in UK firms at the time: performance (concentrating on, improving, and maintaining performance); potential (assessing what individuals were capable of in the future and giving attention to development needs); and reward (allocation of monetary and nonmonetary rewards). It was pointed out that most organizations (inappropriately) attempted to handle all three decisions in a single process, such as the appraisal interview, and that the efficiency of the process was very dependent on the manager's skills. In practice, appraisers tended to use different appraisal styles such as "tell and sell", "tell and listen", "listen and support", and "joint problem-solving" (these relate both to Murphy and DeNisi's proximal factor of purpose and to how judgements were made). Joint problem-solving is the recommended approach and textbook solution. However, in practice, surveys of the time showed that 61 per cent of UK organizations were using performance appraisal for management training and development needs and 57 per cent for assessing potential. In addition, about 40 per cent of organizations used appraisals for clerical staff (Neale, 1991; Torrington & MacKay, 1986).

The 1990s – Broadening PMS Conceptualizations

Given early concerns about the capability of narrowly defined appraisal processes to handle the complex decisions needed of a PMS, the conceptualization of PMSs was soon broadened. Murphy and DeNisi's language made the distal factor of strategy and firm performance more visible within systems. Philpott and Sheppard (1992) identified eight successive layers of activity, each making its contribution to human resource management (HRM): mission statements (defining the business territory and necessary direction), business strategies and objectives (providing explicit guidance on future behaviours), values statements (saying what was important to the organization in terms of how it conducted its affairs), critical success factors (spelling out factors that contributed to effective performance), performance indicators (where job-level critical success factors were translated into individual-level factors), appraisal processes (the forum in which individual performance, qualities, and competencies were evaluated), pay reviews (where performance might be explicitly linked to rewards), and performance improvement processes (where training, career development, coaching, and counselling could be used to handle under-performance). PMSs were then seen as part of a top-down cascading process that carried the advantages of clarifying the nature of individual support for strategic objectives, educating the workforce about the nature of business performance, monitoring such performance, and identifying factors that accounted for overachieving and under-achieving performance.

However, there were soon debates about the most appropriate performance criterion that might be used for PMSs. Organizations began to identify the most appropriate contingencies that supported the use of systems (Sparrow & Hiltrop, 1994) which could be output-based (measuring what was achieved through objectives, standards and targets), input-based (measuring how employees performed through behaviours, values and competencies), stakeholder-based (measuring the expectations of key stakeholders such as the internal teams that received the output of an individual or customers), or simpler task/process-based (measuring the conduct of prioritized sequences of activities). There was much experimentation with systems that combined these elements with different weightings. In terms of Murphy and DeNisi's judgement factors, the opportunity to observe performance ("who says" you are doing a good job) requires the involvement of different sets of people. Attention was also given to the source of evidence on which performance assessment was based (Redman & Snape, 1992), which in practice could be grand-parent (skip-one-level manager), aunt/uncle (internal customer), client (external customer), subordinate (upward), other managers (peer), parent (immediate supervisor), or manager (self-appraisal). Again, multiple variations existed regarding how these sources of evidence were combined. In short, complexity was the order of the day, and surveys that assessed the presence or not of a PMS were of limited value. This approach still carries implications for many survey-based comparative studies of HRM, which inevitably can only make high-level comparisons of practice.

Although by this time, it was accepted (reluctantly in some sectors such as public services) that appraisal systems were a feature of HRM, Murphy and DeNisi's intervening factors of a rater–ratee relationship, motivation, and quality of leader–member exchange, and judgement factors in terms of standards, still presented problems. Two adages characterized UK thinking about PMSs within professional training circles at the time: (1) "there is nothing better than a well-designed PMS, but there is definitely nothing worse than a poorly designed one," and (2) "even the best-designed PMS will be destroyed by incompetent managers". Regarding the last quip, line managers were considered to need a series of competencies to be able to "handle" even a simple PMS: objective setting, assessment, coaching, delegated, sup-porting, communication, and motivation. Therefore, the practical introduction of a PMS was considered part of a politically deter-mined HR strategy, crucially dependent upon the prior demon-stration of basic HR capabilities. The PMS of the time typified the nature of the more complex systems. Four outputs influenced an organizational capability review from the appraisal process: a personal job improvement plan (where the appraisal process highlighted deficiencies in the business process, not the person), a career development plan, a training plan, and a performance

Maranda Ridgway et al.

rating. The performance rating was fed into a separate (in time) pay review. The organization capability review formed one of the significant inputs into the business-strategy-setting process so that strategy was always analysed in the context of capability limitations. The following year's objective-setting process then flowed top-down from the business strategies. There was widespread dissatisfaction with PMSs in the UK, especially the appraisal element, with surveys showing that 68 to 80 per cent of organizations using appraisal were dissatisfied with it (Bowles & Coates, 1993; Fletcher, 1993).

By the early to mid-1990s, some new life was put into PMSs via the growth of management competencies and the pursuit of values-based HR strategies. These developments created a new context for PMSs. Organizations were giving more attention to the nature of effective (managerial) performance and had initially introduced competencies into their resourcing processes (notably in external recruitment and internal career assessment processes). The competency approach proved very popular but naturally led to the argument amongst line managers that "if you are going to decide whether or not to recruit me on competencies, and whether I get promoted on this basis, then I assume that you believe that they are good enough to pay me for them?" In short, the pressure was exerted on PMSs to make sure that they did not just measure outputs (e.g., the achievement of objectives, targets, or standards) but also inputs (such as the values that an employee brought to a job or the behaviours or competencies), they could demonstrate. Attention was given to PMSs' role in competency-based HR strategies (Torrington & Blandamer, 1992). There was a difference between PMSs that were competency-linked (somewhere within the performance appraisal, an assessment of behaviours or competencies might be made, and this number, in conjunction with other factors such as the achievement of outcomes, might influence the final assessment of performance in some unprescribed way) and PMSs that were competency-based (where the effective display of competency led to a score that was directly linked towards a final performance and rewards outcome; Sparrow, 2002). Whether competency-based or more indirectly competency-linked, PMSs were seen to serve a robust developmental agenda.

By the late 1990s, the context for PMSs shifted again (there was another shift in Murphy and DeNisi's strategy and firm performance factor). Organizations paid attention to the link between values and strategy execution and the need for person–organization fit. The introduction of values (a "how you do it" or input-type performance outcome) into PMSs was motivated by the idea that strategy could only be executed through the display of values (a typical example would be customer service values); that is, there was no choice but to inculcate the values, and the task of the PMS was to "educate" managers and employees into this reality.

In the context of discussions about a changing psychological contract at work and ever-increasing demands for flexibility, it was appreciated that while line managers may be able to direct the performance of their employees, they often had minimal insights into the personal needs and desires of their employees and the factors that might, or might not, persuade them to commit firmly to the organization. More attention was therefore given to Murphy and DeNisi's rater–ratee relationship factor. In addition, organizations began to understand the power of their PMSs as a vehicle for re-engaging their workforce behind a "new deal" at work. For example, NatWest, a major UK retail bank, pioneered a renegotiating the "deal" process at work with their employees – what the organization expected of employees and what the employees expected of the organization in return. This new deal was established through a one-off process of focus groups and one-to-one interviews with staff. However, it was understood that to sustain the relevance of a more individualized performance negotiation, line managers would need to adopt and adapt existing HR processes to understand and manage employee sentiment. Improving the quality of the PMS in terms of the honesty of the dialogue it contained seemed an obvious mechanism for achieving this (Herriot, 1998). In general terms, the focus had shifted from the need for PMS to provide sophisticated evaluation and appraisal skills towards a broader agenda of improving performance and then into a mechanism for enabling more open and honest communications about behaviours and outcomes, issues, and problems surrounding the execution of strategy, and the need to engage and motivate employees behind this.

The 2000s – The Shifting Focus of PMSs

Three other HR developments reinforced this shift in focus: talent management, employee segmentation, and total rewards management models. The first was the growth of talent management. The developmental agenda PMS had served so well in the early 1990s was being replaced by attention to a much narrower cadre of "talented" employees. McKinsey's work on the War for Talent proved influential. In the US, this was associated with a greater emphasis on PMSs that differentiated performance through lavishing significant rewards at the high end of the performance and exerting more punitive control over poor performance (the "rank and yank" systems that were to cause much controversy in terms of their potential for discrimination). In the UK, the political debates were quite similar, and the absence (at the time) of age discrimination might have made the introduction of such systems more straightforward, but what appeared to happen was that the more contentious issues were removed from PMSs. Decisions about identifying talent (and, by default, likely access to development resources) were increasingly made through separate talent management forums or processes. The PMS was instead mobilized as a way of helping think about a more individualized performance contract.

The second point was focused on employee segmentation (Matthewman, 2003). Under this philosophy, organizations identify those segments of their employees whose performance drives return on investment. It involves the application of customer relationship management principles to the organization's workforce and is used to identify the optimal workforce required to match customer expectations. It is important to note that Murphy and DeNisi's factor of rater–ratee relationship is too narrow to capture this development – this is an employee-as-consumer-to-organization relationship. Large UK employers such as Tesco, Marks and Spencer, Vodafone and Royal Bank of Scotland have pursued this strategy. For example, in 2003, Tesco, the leading UK supermarket and food retailer, acknowledged that it knew more about its customers than its employees. Based on consumer research, staff were placed into five categories or employee segments (want it all, live to work, work to live, pleasure-seekers, and work–life balancers) to be more receptive to employees' needs (Watkins,

2003). They ascertained what staff wanted from a career in Tesco and provided a series of "for me" solutions to enable staff to tailor their hours and employment relationship to their needs. Staff was surveyed twice a year to link their engagement scores to improvements in other areas. In short, PMSs were part of a two-way communication process that played an essential role in building levels of employee engagement.

The third development was the growth of "total rewards management" models. Closely linked to the need to develop more idiosyncratic or individualized "deals" within the employment relationship, it was considered necessary to reward performance through a total assessment of desired rewards, which in practice might include tangible factors (competitive pay and benefits, ownership potential, recognition and fairness), quality of work (perceived value, challenge, autonomy, quality of work relationships), growth opportunities (quality of feedback, learning and development opportunities beyond the job), work–life balance demands, and inspirational/emotional needs (the quality of leadership; the values and behaviours lived by the organization; communication, risk sharing; and the potential for reputation enhancement).

Compare the factors argued here as essential ingredients of a PMSs with the 1984 model of Randall et al. that differentiated discussion about performance, potential, and reward. In theory, PM discussions, at least in the more sophisticated UK organizations, had become highly integrated with higher-level organizational concerns of employee engagement and individualized reward.

The 2010s (and Beyond) – Emerging PMSs Debates

PMSs have continued to evolve into three broad debates. The first of these debates contends that the informal aspects of a PMSs, such as employee communication and the manager–employee relationship, were more important than the formal aspects, such as objective setting (Schleicher et al., 2018). In some cases, frontline managers felt conflicted about balancing expectations to adopt more informal approaches to managing performance while following robust PMSs (Saundry, Jones & Wibberley, 2015). However, as Perkins (2018) indicated, the informal aspect required attention balanced alongside the formal PMSs and should form part of line manager capability development.

Maranda Ridgway et al.

A second debate argues for the departures from performance ratings, which are neither accurate nor valuable (Schleicher et al., 2018). For example, Smith and Bititci (2017) suggested that how performance measures and targets are used could adversely impact employee engagement. Murphy (2020) takes the argument further, suggesting that regular performance evaluations should be abolished altogether in favour of performance leadership.

In the final debate, there is an argument for removing "low value" aspects of performance management (Schleicher et al., 2018), such as an incoherent system, poor feedback loops, and no accountability (Broad & Goddard, 2010). This argument extends to examining the negative effect of excessively directive PMSs on employee well-being (Franco-Santos & Doherty, 2017), enforcing standardized systems and approaches to performance management in complex employment contexts (Waring, 2017), and challenging resource-intensive processes in resource-poor settings (Moxham, 2010).

It is important to note that these debates have not been resolved. They do, however, bring into focus contemporary factors impacting PMSs in the UK and hint at what the future of PMSs may entail.

CONTEMPORARY FACTORS IMPACTING PERFORMANCE MANAGEMENT IN THE UK

From a comparative HRM perspective, Cranet data from 2009/10 shows that 85.5 per cent of UK organizations formally assess managers using a performance appraisal scheme, compared to 80 per cent in Greece, 78.9 per cent in Germany but only 34.1 per cent in Bulgaria (Boselie, Farndale & Paauwe, 2018). What sorts of factors account for such differences? There are obvious issues such as levels of organizational autonomy and the consequent ability to introduce more flexible HR systems with less concern about industrial relations issues. In addition, demographics associated with the industrial sector play an essential role, seen, for example, the significant size of the public sector (which began to implement PMSs at about the same time that such systems had come into criticism in the private sector) and a relatively high number of large organizations on the one hand and small and medium-sized enterprises on the other (which impacts the level of formality of HR). Sparrow and Hiltrop (1994) also identified three comparative HR features linked to the nature of PMSs that we suspect, based on recent research, still hold today: (1) country-specific cultural values, (2) the efficiency of the manager–subordinate relationship, and (3) the level of strategic integration and devolvement of HRM (Shipton, Whysall & Abe, 2021).

Macro Level

At a macro level, two of Hofstede's cultural dimensions (uncertainty avoidance and power distance) can be associated with the nature and conduct of PMSs in the UK. Not only are there cross-national differences in the efficiency of the dialogue (Murphy and DeNisi's rater–ratee relationship factor), but national cultures impact the nature of the dialogue (their perceived use and purpose). The dialogue that takes place in the appraisal process becomes what Sparrow (1998) called the "stake of a different game". As noted earlier, early performance appraisal systems in the UK were characterized as a "joint problem-solving" activity with decentralized responsibility over how individual objectives may be met (Randall et al., 1984). From a cultural point of view, this was not surprising. In the UK and the US (Denmark, Sweden, Norway, the Netherlands), the national culture combines low power distance with low uncertainty avoidance. Power distance touches on the extent to which superiors can influence the behaviour of subordinates and vice versa. Low power distance is associated with a greater acceptance of equality, participation, and cooperation between those in higher and lower organizational positions (Sanders, Yang & Li, 2021). It also means that the boss can be bypassed and rules bent so that the employee can get things done. Therefore, the independence and self-realization of the employee is an issue. The "boss", therefore, may need to find out the detail of the subordinate's tasks (again, the role of managers in a UK context is to manage and be an effective manager, you do not have to know the technical detail of your subordinate's tasks, whereas in for example France, managers are expected to be able to answer detailed questions about their subordinates' jobs). In the UK, the low power distance is blended with low uncertainty avoidance, which is associated with a higher tolerance of risk and acceptance of dependencies in performance, a reliance on resourcefulness and adaptability in achieving goals and a tendency to be reactive, rather than proactive, feedback (Shipton et al., 2021).

It is unsurprising that in this "game", it is legitimate to make the performance appraisal discussion a joint problem-solving activity. Moreover, British organizations should consider a process such as psychological contracting as critical within their existing PMS (Perkins, 2018). Bechter, Brandl, and Lehr (2022) also draw attention to the role of Hofstede's individualism–collectivism construct, with individualism being associated with people acting more in their self-interest and initiative.

Institutional Level

At an institutional level, the efficiency of the manager-subordinate relationship (Murphy and DeNisi's rater–ratee relationship) has a powerful impact on the nature of PMSs, as does the level of devolvement of HR. Bournois and Chauchat (1990) gave attention to the presumed efficiency of the manager–subordinate relationship. They mapped European countries on two dimensions: the estimated level of management talent and levels of worker motivation. At the time, the UK scored poorly on both dimensions, underperformed only by Spain, Greece, and Portugal. Concerning PMSs, at the time, four out of five PMSs were failing (Fletcher & Williams, 1992) because the system was not used, modelled, or supported at the top of the organization; line managers viewed the system as an administrative burden; performance objectives were subjective and subject to change; or managers were incapable of giving practical and constructive feedback or dealing with conflict. Marchington (2015) has since argued that the devolvement of HR to line managers in the UK was still associated with a sense that HR managers had not just given personnel management away but had given it up, with evidence of poor legitimacy of HR, among other stakeholders. Since this period, much activity inside UK organizations may be seen in attempting to improve the efficiency of the employment relationship and historically high levels of PMS failure. Although, it could also be argued that UK managers were somewhat more honest about the failings of PMSs!

The Strategic Role of HR Functions

The third comparative factor concerns the strategic role of HR functions. Using data from the Cranet survey, the UK initially had a "professional mechanic" approach to HR strategy (Brewster & Larsen, 1993). As a result, the strategic integration of HR into the business strategy was low, and the level of devolvement of HR to the line was also low. Since this time, there has been considerable devolvement of HR to line managers, fuelled by shared service HR models and the growth of business partner roles. In modern HR functions, the capability of line managers to conduct effective performance appraisals is a significant determinant of the ultimate credibility of the system.

However, such macro factors aside, the best way to understand which factors impact the nature of PMSs in the UK is to consider the main "design choices" that organizations make when thinking about the shape of their systems and then look at the factors that most likely influence these choices.

CRITICAL CHALLENGES IN PERFORMANCE MANAGEMENT IN THE UK

As should be evident throughout this chapter, PMSs have long represented a mature HR technology in the UK (Freemantle, 1994; IRS, 1994, 1999; Industrial Society, 1997) but are not without challenges (Sayers et al., 2018). By the 1990s, they were widespread in the UK. For example, a 1994 Industrial Relations Service survey (IRS is an employment intelligence provider) reported that 90 per cent of respondents used an appraisal system, and by 1999, this figure had reached almost 100 per cent. However, the design of PMSs is still debated regarding issues of fairness, assessment validity, and strategic sensemaking. The issue of fairness has been discussed in terms of designing PMSs which are absent of bias or discrimination (Beck, Brewis & Davies, 2021; Williams & Beck, 2018).

Despite remaining issues relating to fairness, the design of PMSs is often judged more in terms of coherence – how it supports macro-corporate imperatives, such as the delivery of an appropriate customer experience. To identify the evidence base and challenges in the UK performance management context, a keyword search using Web of Science was carried out using performance management and appraisal lexemes from 2017 to 2022. This period captures the upheaval caused by the UK's departure from the EU. The most influential papers (i.e., those published in journals ranked highly in the Academic Journal Guide) set within a UK context are reported here. In addition, publications by the UK professional body, the Chartered Institute of Personnel Development (CIPD), have been searched to assess the developing professional debate.

The professional rhetoric around the topic has become increasingly sceptical. For example, Gifford 2016, p. 8) noted that "an increasing number of employers appear to be questioning the value and relevance of traditional performance management processes" and "while the narrative accounts help us understand why and how employers have taken a different approach to managing performance, they do not give much if any evidence on whether these new practices improve performance". The need to realign PMSs after the damage created by ill-thought-out processes of downsizing, outsourcing, in-sourcing, acquisition, or cost-cutting has also been discussed by Drumm (2005). This need for realignment brought heightened importance to PMS elements that signalled the (new) job purpose and the (often poorly understood) consequences of performance in the surviving roles. Perhaps not surprisingly, the quality of management is considered key to transforming performance in organizations (Mahony, 2003), and this has led to "an evolutionary change in this area, with organizations seeing it as an opportunity for coaching rather than judging individuals ... performance management systems went hand in hand with a leadership and communications programme" (Glover, 2003, p. 9). As a result, much of the professional focus has moved away from the issue of performance management towards that of talent management. Moreover, PMSs are an HR process that can be digitized, so attention to it has been subsumed within a broader move to automated transactions, capability development, and strategic support.

In many senses, the academic research needs and priorities that surround performance management have remained the same as they ever were. However, Fletcher (2001, p. 473) noted that as "performance appraisal ... widened as a concept and as a set of practices and ... the form of performance management [became] part of a more strategic approach to integrating HR activities and business policies" research has shifted away from its traditional focus on measurement issues and accuracy towards more social and motivational aspects. Reviewing the most influential papers published through Web of Science, it was clear that in the English language management journals, there is still a predominance of US writers on the topic, followed by the UK, India, Australia, and China. Focusing on the UK specifically, there are three broad (yet unsurprising) emergent themes: (1) contextualization of PMSs, (2) digitization of PMSs, and (3) PMSs during disruption.

Contextualization of PMSs

The importance of context has garnered increasing attention in academic and practitioner-orientated research (DeNisi & Murphy, 2017; Ferris et al., 2008; Murphy et al., 2018; Pichler, 2012). For example, a recent study by Hodgkinson et al. (2018) utilized postal survey data for English leisure providers to determine how organizational ownership type (i.e., private or public) influences its antecedents and performance outcomes. A notable finding from their research was that performance appraisals appeared as an antecedent for affective commitment only in privately owned organizations. They concluded that PMSs must be context specific, recognizing the nuances of different service settings.

Digitization of PMSs

Digital technologies and data analytics have advanced rapidly in recent years, and many organizations are reaping benefits from the efficiencies such technologies bring. Therefore, it is unsurprising that digitization elements have seeped into people management practices to influence employee performance. On one hand, Gifford (2016) notes that feedback delivered electronically, for example, via a PMSs application, is as effective as when delivered through face-to-face discussions. On the other hand, the advancement of technology in this context has not been exclusively positive, and research has paid attention to some of the unintended consequences of digitization. For example, using a UK-based professional Rugby Union club as a case study, Manley and Williams (2022) found tensions emerging among employees due to intense performance surveillance. Integrating surveillance technology into the workplace resulted in employees feeling heightened anxiety and performance fatigue.

Similarly, Kayas et al. (2019) report on the introduction of PMSs within a UK local authority, propagated by the central government and in response to austerity measures. Their study found that the PMS was transformed into a surveillance system to inform employment termination decisions. Recently, Kougiannou and Mendonça (2021) found from their work with food couriers that digital technology intended to manage and organize gig workers translated into managerial silencing of workers' voices. Furthermore, although digital technology can play an important role in organization performance, it may also divide workers, thus hindering performance (Mendonça & Kougiannou, 2022).

Volatility, Uncertainty, and PMSs

It is almost impossible to ignore the effect of COVID-19 on (working) lives and how practices and systems, such as performance management, have rapidly adjusted consequently. The pandemic has paved the way for debate and highlighted the emergent challenges of operating in an environment of continual and unpredictable disruption and how this influences PMSs. For example, Bindl et al. (2019) explain how employees have adjusted to changing circumstances brought about by the pandemic. Simultaneously, HR practitioners must guide how to manage employees during such uncertain and volatile times (Barclay, Kiefer & El Mansouri, 2022). Furthermore, the increase in remote working in response to COVID-19 has led to organizations rethinking how to manage staff performance from a trust perspective (Pass & Ridgway, 2022).

CONCLUSION

The field of PMSs in the UK is a mature one. Organizational practice has evolved through successive concerns for cost-effectiveness, competence, commitment, and coherence. The recent focus on values-based HRM and person–organization fit brings three potentially different "faces" for PMSs. From a comparative HRM perspective, a range of factors can be linked to the nature of PMSs in the UK, including individual values orientations, the (in)efficiency of the employment relationship, and levels of devolvement of HR to line management. The professional dialogue has become increasingly sceptical, but new avenues of practice that serve performance management aims are opening. The interests of UK academics are unique and have moved away from the US dialogue around accuracy and fairness towards political context and user acceptability. The focus of study (but equally validity and generalizability of the dialogue) has also moved away from private towards public sector settings. However, even from existing work, several issues surrounding PMSs remain broadly untested. Notably, these include

1. the varied motivations to introduce PMS (which may be cloaked under headings such as self-development, culture change, or performance and linked explicitly to other strategic outcomes).
2. the level of internal consistency (such as the range of competencies in other parts of the HR system and total-system alignment with the logic contained in the PMS initiatives).
3. the ability of new PMSs to produce higher levels of employee engagement (as opposed to just more self-awareness or measurement accuracy).
4. the level of alignment between rewards (in their broadest sense) produced by the PMSs and the varied needs of diverse employee segments may be working to very different psychological contracts.
5. the extent to which standalone PMSs contribute directly to value creation in the organization or instead serve more to protect value by managing only marginal risks (extraordinarily high or low performance, the identification or management of which may well be handled through other processes such as business process modifications, team socialization processes, or talent management/calibration exercises).

The management field in the UK will contain many lively debates for several years.

REFERENCES

Barclay, L.J., Kiefer, T., & El Mansouri, M. (2022). Navigating the era of disruption: How emotions can prompt job crafting behaviors. *Human Resource Management*, 61(3), 335–353.

Bechter, B., Brandl, B., & Lehr, A. (2022). The role of the capability, opportunity, and motivation of firms for using human resource analytics to monitor employee performance: A multi-level analysis of the organizational, market, and country context. *New Technology, Work and Employment*, 37(3), 1–27.

Beck, V., Brewis, J., & Davies, A. (2021). Women's experiences of menopause at work and performance management. *Organization*, 28(3), 510–520.

Beer, M., Spector, B., Lawrence, P., Mills, D., & Walton, R.E. (1984). *Managing human assets*. New York: Free Press.

Bindl, U.K., Unsworth, K.L., Gibson, C.B., & Stride, C.B. (2019). Job crafting revisited: Implications of an extended framework for active changes at work. *Journal of Applied Psychology*, 104(5), 605–628.

Boselie, P., Farndale, E., & Paauwe, J. (2018) Comparing performance management across context. In C. Brewster, W. Mayrhofer, & E. Farndale (Eds.) *Handbook of research on comparative human resource management.* Edward Elgar Publishing, pp. 164–183.

Bournois, F. & Chauchat, J.H. (1990). Managing managers in Europe. *European Management Journal,* 8(1), 3–18.

Bowles, M.L. & Coates, G. (1993). Image and substance: The management of performance as rhetoric or reality? *Personnel Review,* 22(2), 3–21.

Brewster, C. & Larsen, H.H. (1993). Human resource management in Europe: Evidence from ten countries. *International Journal of Human Resource Management,* 3(3), 409–434.

Broad, M. & Goddard, A. (2010). Internal performance management with UK higher education: An amorphous system?. *Measuring Business Excellence,* 14(1), 60–66.

DeNisi, A.S. & Murphy, K.R. (2017). Performance appraisal and performance management: 100 years of progress? *Journal of applied psychology,* 102(3), 421–433.

Drumm, G. (2005). Putting the pieces back together to realign performance in the organization. *Performance Improvement,* 44(6), 26–30.

Ferris, G.R., Munyon, T.P., Basik, K., & Buckley, M.R. (2008). The performance evaluation context: Social, emotional, cognitive, political, and relationship components. *Human Resource Management Review,* 18(3), 146–163.

Fletcher, C. (1993). Appraisal: An idea whose time has gone? *Personnel Management,* September, pp. 34–37.

Fletcher, C. (2001). Performance appraisal and management: The developing research agenda. *Journal of Occupational and Organizational Psychology,* 74(4), 473–487.

Fletcher, C. & Williams, R. (1992). The route to performance management. *Personnel Management,* 24(10), 42–47.

Franco-Santos, M. & Doherty, N. (2017). Performance management and well-being: A close look at the changing nature of the UK higher education workplace, *The International Journal of Human Resource Management,* 28(16), 2319–2350.

Freemantle, D. (1994). *The performance of "performance appraisal" – an appraisal.* Windor: Superboss Ltd.

Gifford, J. (2016). Could do better? Assessing what works in performance management. *Chartered Institute of Personnel and Development Research Report,* December.

Glover, C. (2003). Performance is key to success. *People Management,* 17 April, p. 9.

Hendry, C., Pettigrew, A. & Sparrow, P.R. (1989). Linking strategic change, competitive performance and human resource management: Results of a UK empirical study. In R. Mansfield (Ed.) *Frontiers of management research.* London: Routledge.

Herriot, P. (1998) The role of the HR function in building a new proposition for staff. In P.R. Sparrow & M. Marchington (Eds.) *Human resource management: The new agenda.* London: Financial Times Pitman Publications.

Hodgkinson, I.R., Hughes, P., Radnor, Z., & Glennon, R. (2018). Affective commitment within the public sector: Antecedents and performance outcomes between ownership types, *Public Management Review,* 20(12), 1872–1895.

Industrial Relations Service (1994). Improving performance: A survey of appraisal arrangements. *Employment Trends,* 556, 5–14.

Industrial Relations Service (1999). New ways to perform appraisal. *Employment Trends,* 676, 7–16.

Industrial Society (1997). *Appraisal. Report No.37.* London: Industrial Society.

Kayas, O.G., Hines, T., McLean, R., & Wright, G. (2019). Resisting government rendered surveillance in a local authority, *Public Management Review,* 21(8),1170–1190,

Kougiannou, N.K. & Mendonça, P. (2021). Breaking the managerial silencing of worker voice in platform capitalism: The rise of a food courier network. *British Joural of Management,* 32, 744–759.

Mahony, C. (2003). On good authority. *People Management*, 6 March, p. 28.

Manley, A. & Williams, S. (2022). We're not run on Numbers, We're People, We're Emotional People': Exploring the experiences and lived consequences of emerging technologies, organizational surveillance and control among elite professionals, *Organization*, 29(4), 692–713.

Marchington, M. (2015). Human resource management (HRM): Too busy looking up to see where it is going longer term?. *Human Resource Management Review*, 25(2), 176–187.

Matthewman, J. (2003). Strong division. *People Management*, 20 February, p. 34.

Mendonça, P. & Kougiannou, N.K. (2022). Disconnecting labour: The impact of intraplat-form algorithmic changes on the labour process and workers' capacity to organise collectively. *New Technology, Work and Employment*. Advanced online publication. https://doi.org/10.1111/ntwe.12251

Moxham, C. (2010). Help or hindrance? *Public Performance & Management Review*, 33(3), 342–354.

Murphy, K.R. (2020). Performance evaluation will not die, but it should. *Human Resource Management Journal*, 30(1), 13–31.

Murphy, K.R., Cleveland, J.N., & Hanscom, M.E. (2018). *Performance Appraisal and Management*. Thousand Oaks, CA: Sage.

Neale, F. (Ed.) (1991). *Handbook of performance management*. Wimbledon: Institute of Personnel Management.

Pass, S. & Ridgway, M. (2022). An informed discussion on the impact of COVID-19 and 'enforced' remote working on employee engagement. *Human Resource Development International*, 25(2), 254–270.

Perkins, S.J. (2018). Processing developments in employee performance and reward. *Journal of Organizational Effectiveness: People and Performance*, 5(3), 289–300.

Philpot, I. & Sheppard, L. (1992). Managing for improved performance. In M. Armstrong (Ed.) *Strategies for human resource management*. London: Kogan Page.

Pichler, S. (2012). The social context of performance appraisal and appraisal reactions: A meta-analysis. *Human Resource Management*, 51(5), 709–732.

Randall, G.A., Packard, P.M., Shaw, R.L., & Slater, A.J. (1984). *Staff appraisal*. London: Institute of Personnel Management.

Redman, T. & Snape, E. (1992). Upward and onward: Can staff appraise their manag-ers? *Personnel Review*, 21(7), 32–46.

Sanders, K., Yang, H., & Li, X. (2021). Quality enhancement or cost reduction? The influence of high-performance work systems and power distance orientation on employee human resource attributions. *The International Journal of Human Resource Management*, 32(21), 4463–4490.

Saundry, R., Jones, C., & Wibberley, G. (2015). The challenge of managing informally. *Employee Relations*, 37(4), 428–441.

Sayers, E., Benson, A., Hussey, D., Thompson, B., & Irdam, D. (2018). Improvement required? A mixed-methods study of employers' use of performance management systems. *Advisory, Conciliation and Arbitration Service*. Retrieved August 2, 2022 from: https://www.acas.org.uk/improvement-required-a-mixed-methods-study-of-employers-use-of-performance-management-systems

Schleicher, D.J., Baumann, H.M., Sullivan, D.W., Levy, P.E., Hargrove, D.C., & Barros-Rivera, B.A. (2018). Putting the system into performance management systems: A review and agenda for performance management research. *Journal of Management*, 44(6), 2209–2245.

Shipton, H., Whysall, Z., & Abe, C. (2021) Turnover and retention in the United Kingdom: Change, uncertainty and opportunity. In D.G. Allen & J.M. Vardaman (Eds.) *Global talent retention: Understanding employee turnover around the world (Talent Management)*, Emerald Publishing Limited, Bingley, pp. 17–39.

Smith, M. & Bititci, U.S. (2017). Interplay between performance measurement and management, employee engagement and performance. *International Journal of Operations & Production Management*, 37(9), 1207–1228.

Sparrow, P.R. (1998). Re-appraising psychological contracting: Lessons for employee development from cross-cultural and occupational psychology research. *International Studies of Management and Organisation*, 28(1), 30–63.

Sparrow, P.R. (2002). To use competencies or not to use competencies? That is the question. In M. Pearn (Ed.), *Handbook of individual development in organizations*. London: Wiley.

Sparrow, P.R. & Hiltrop, J.M. (1994). *European human resource management in transition*. London: Prentice-Hall.

Torrington, D. & Blandamer, W. (1992). Competency, pay and performance management. In R. Boam & P.R. Sparrow (Eds.) *Designing and achieving competency: A competency based approach to developing people and organizations*. London: McGraw-Hill.

Torrington, D. & MacKay, L. (1986). Will consultants take over the personnel function? *Personnel Management*, 18(2), 34–37.

Waring, M. (2017). Management and leadership in UK universities: Exploring the possibilities of change, *Journal of Higher Education Policy and Management*, 39(5), 540–558.

Watkins, J. (2003). Tesco tailors working conditions. *People Management*, 29 May. p. 10.

Williams, G. & Beck, V. (2018). From annual ritual to daily routine: Continuous performance management and its consequences for employment security. *New Technology, Work and Employment*, 33(1), 30–43.

Performance Management in France and Germany

Cordula Barzantny and Marion Festing

Chapter 10

INTRODUCTION

Performance management has been described in many ways. There is no single definition that scholars working in this field have agreed on, and the advances in the field continue in various directions. In recent years, an increasing amount of studies have been conducted in the public sector, also in France and Germany (Helmig, Michalski, & Lauper, 2008; Carassus, Favoreu, Gardey, & Marin, 2012; Falzon, Nascimento, Gaudart, Piney, Dujarier, & Germe, 2012; Boitier & Rivière, 2013; Kroll & Proeller, 2013; Carassus, Favoreu, & Gardey, 2014; Kroll & Vogel, 2014; Jantz, Christensen, & Lægreid, 2015; Wegrich, 2015; Grossi, Hansen, Johanson, Vakkuri, & Moon, 2016; Grossi, Reichard, & Ruggiero, 2016; Weiss, 2020; Kroll & Pasha, 2021; McMullin, 2021). The performance domain thus seems to be multifaceted (Cascio, 2006) and has not evolved much for a more standardized approach inside and across borders (Cascio, 2012). Armstrong and Baron (1998: 7) have defined performance management as "a strategic and integrated approach to delivering sustained success to organizations by improving the performance of the people who work in them and by developing the capabilities of teams and individual contributors."

DOI: 10.4324/9781003306849-10

As with many other human resource measures, performance management follows very much the example of US American companies (see for example Pudelko, 2005; 2006; Claus & Briscoe, 2006). This can be observed in large companies in Europe, among them those in France and Germany as well, which are the two countries of investigation within this chapter. It seems that a kind of best-practices system has emerged (Brewster, 1996). It has become popular, especially in multinational organizations, to define a common set of values or competencies, which are supposed to apply within the worldwide organization. Based on these criteria selection, appraisal, development and compensation practices are designed (Festing, Eidems, Royer, & Kullak, 2006).

Another very common approach is the use of the balanced scorecard (Kaplan & Norton, 1992, 2006) in performance management. This measure, which also originated in the United States, is adapted to the needs of human resource management (HRM) and furthermore to the respective corporate and local contexts (Becker, Huselid, & Ulrich, 2001; Phillips, Stone, & Phillips, 2001; Huselid, Becker, & Beatty, 2005). For the French context, Bourguignon et al. (2004) discuss the balanced scorecard, which has not received a particularly warm welcome and where the *tableau de bord* has been used for at least 60 years. This may be explained in terms of ideological assumptions, since these management tools tend to be somewhat coherent with the local ideologies in the countries of origin. Therefore, mainly larger, multinational corporations have introduced the balanced scorecard in France.

In order to address the criticism and hindrances of the balanced scorecard implementation in the French corporate context, Oriot and Misisazek (2004) furnish an interesting case study of a European space company. They found that despite the estimated influences of national culture, the most important factor posing barriers to balanced scorecard implementation was the professional context. This is linked to a strong engineering background with a lack of short-term cost-consciousness in the observed company.

In an empirical study comparing Germany, China and the United States, Festing and Knappert (2014) corroborated that *both the institutional and cultural contexts are relevant for a complete understanding of Performance Management* (p. 345). These authors show that there are country-specific profiles, but they do not differ as much as expected, a higher number of performance management features (6 out of 10) are universally applicable and tend towards similarities across countries in their sample of HR and middle MNC managers. Regarding the measures applied for performance management in large French and German organizations, at the first view, it is difficult to identify significant differences from the measures in the Anglo-American performance management literature. However, this does not mean that the system is identical. On the contrary, country-specific dimensions can be identified (Dowling, Festing, & Engle, 2023), especially in the way performance management processes are carried out. While we find the same vocabulary and similar agendas, the different environments firms are operating in have a strong influence on the implementation process (Radin, 2003). The aim of this chapter is to describe and explain different country-specific approaches for dealing with performance management and to outline their possible implications as well as recent evolutions and developments, if any. In this chapter, we particularly address the various factors highlighted in the model proposed by Murphy and DeNisi, since their model is designed to analyze in detail performance appraisal, performance process, and performance management systems across organizations, nations and cultures.[1]

First of all, the European context is described, with France and Germany as rather important countries that are closely tied together in European history and in the present. Then we will analyze some particularities in the examples of France and Germany. The approach is to take first a broader look at the underlying HRM model and then concentrate on the performance management field, which we will outline in the context of the respective institutional and cultural environments. The Murphy and DeNisi model provides an excellent basis for summarizing our findings while structuring the possible commonalities and differences in the systems with respect to distal, proximal, intervening, judgment and distortion factors. At the end of the chapter, a discussion about possible convergent or divergent developments concludes the analysis.

Cordula Barzantny and Marion Festing

THE EUROPEAN CONTEXT FOR PERFORMANCE MANAGEMENT IN FRANCE AND GERMANY

Based on the model outlined by Murphy and DeNisi it can be argued that the European context includes *distal* factors, which may have an impact on European performance management systems. However, Europe is far from being a homogeneous group of countries. Although the EU is striving for common, supranational regulations its countries include differences in the ideological, political, legal, social and cultural environment (Brewster, 1994; Nikandrou, Apospori, & Papalexandris, 2005). Nikandrou et al. state that Europe is "characterized by internal variation among various clusters of countries and, at the same time, by external uniformity compared to the rest of the world" (2005: 542).

Within the course of discussions centering on the concept of HRM in the 1990s, it became clear that this concept is difficult to apply in the same way that it is used in the US, where the concept was developed (Guest, 1994; Brewster, 1995). Guest (1994) states that the unitarist perspective contradicts the prevailing European tradition of pluralism. Furthermore, the strong individualist orientation inherent in this concept is difficult to realize in societies characterized by a higher degree of collectivism and more emphasis on social welfare and social responsibility for the more disadvantaged in society. Other barriers include differences in the ownership and control systems of organizations in Europe and the strong legal environment in many countries (Guest, 1994). Brewster (1994) suggests that limited organizational autonomy is of major importance, too (see also Lawrence, 1993).

Brewster (1994, 1995, 1999) and Brewster, Mayrhofer and Smale (2016) emphasize the need to pursue a contextual paradigm, that is, addressing explicitly the external context of firms. Other researchers have confirmed the impact of the country-specific institutional or socioeconomic background (see, e.g., Gooderham, Nordhaug, and Ringdal, 1999) or of cultural values (see, e.g., Lindholm, 2000; Papalexandris & Panayotopoulou, 2004; Cascio, 2006) on HRM. To sum up, it can be said that "a single universal model of HRM does not exist" (Pieper, 1990: 11).

Clearly, the European evidence suggests that management can see the unions, for example, as social partners with a positive role to play in HRM: and the manifest success of many European firms which adopt that approach shows the, explicit or implicit, anti-unionism of many American views to be culture-bound.

(Brewster, 1994: 81; see also Pudelko, 2005)

With respect to performance management, this research perspective has led to the development of the Murphy and DeNisi model outlined earlier in this book. It provides a broad framework that takes into account a variety of factors in which European diversity can be expressed.

Although France and Germany are neighboring European economies, sharing a common border and strong economic ties (half of all intra-EU Community trade is with the other partner), there is no common understanding of HRM: The historical, cultural and environmental factors in each country still play decisive roles which account for differences, despite continuing EU harmonization and standardization inside the single European market. Historically, Germany and France grew as competitors and enemies until the industrial revolution. Nationalist ideologies threw Europe and notably France into conflict and war against Germany several times until the end of World War II, and then the daring project of European integration saw its inception in the treaties of Paris (1951) and Rome (1957). Ever since, the French and German economies have played a major role in European integration and economic cooperation. However, both countries have different backgrounds since World War II because France was among the victorious countries whereas Germany was defeated. This had an important impact on the social, corporate and industrial relations systems: France continued the historically more hierarchical and conflict-intensive governance and behavioral mechanisms while (Western) Germany had to completely recreate all political, social and economic systems, assisted by the governance examples in the allied countries, notably the Anglo-Saxon ones such as the US and UK.

As an example, in Europe, social factors play an important role in career systems (Alexandre-Bailly, Festing, and Jonczyk, 2007). There is a high emphasis on a broad general education (Pudelko, 2000b), which becomes especially visible in the French system of the *classes préparatoires* providing general knowledge for another two years after the *baccalauréat* which is equivalent to a high school degree in the US. Only students who have success-fully completed a corresponding exam get the chance to study in the prestigious *Grande Ecole* system. Furthermore, empirical studies have shown that social class still matters to a high extent with respect to careers (Hartmann, 2003). In contrast, in Germany paths to higher education follow a more egalitarian principle, offering the same chances to every person. The reputation of the universities is not as important as in France, but individual performance counts. The emphasis is much more on technical knowledge than on social networks. However, this does not mean that social networks do not play a role in career systems, but the role is less important than in France (Alexandre-Bailly et al., 2007). Additionally, Germany appears to be linked to the Northern European tradition that, when compared to Southern European countries, also tends to be driven more by equality and consen-sus (Festing, 2012).

SPECIFICITIES CHARACTERIZING PERFORMANCE MANAGEMENT IN FRANCE

HRM in France started from a personnel administration and legal background position. The primary mission was to ensure that the firm complies with all legal provisions and avoids lawsuits and government inspections. Therefore, the personnel departments of corporations have been obliged to maintain a high level of legal expertise (Gooderham et al., 1999). In a rather conflict-driven tradition of labor relations where union power is restrained to collective bargaining, cooperation with unions is limited. Training is another important aspect of HRM in France, since to avoid penalty taxes there exists a legal obligation for firms to invest annually 1.68 % of payroll into the training of employees (1%) and apprenticeship support tax (0,68%) These obligations have been reformed several times in the last decade and apply to all enter-prises with at least 11 employees, below this employee threshold the obligation is reduced to 0, 55% of the total payroll for training and still 0,68% for apprenticeship taxes in 2022. With the short-ening of business cycles, the skills and competencies seem to have also shorter half-lives for maintaining overall employability of employees, hence the sustained effort in professional training and a lifelong learning approach. Overall French HRM and its evolution is described by Jenkins and van der Wijk (1996) as "*hesitant innovation*". The management of performance in this context entered rather late into the area of people management and HRM. Historically, performance management in France was either linked to the physical and mechanical performance of processes in industrial manufacturing or, since the 1960s, to stock market portfolios of shares. Performance management – particularly its measurement at the level of the firm – is mainly developed in accounting and executive remuneration. It is in the 1980s that performance management entered into HRM on a larger scale, notably with a more structured performance appraisal and the evaluation of employees. Since then, performance management in French organizations has seen an evolution from a tool based on measurement toward an instrument used for motivating people in the firm as well as evaluating intellectual capital. More recent evolutions of performance management integrate aspects of coaching, competence-based management and the knowledge worker in the wider area of HRM (Devillard, 2001; Klarsfeld & Oiry, 2003; Defélix, Klarsfeld, & Oiry, 2006). Particularly emphasizing the measurement aspects, performance management using the balanced scorecard is also related to quality in the French management literature (Iribarne, 2003). Today, performance management is strongly linked to employee involvement as well as governance aspects. In this context, performance management is further related to the individual's responsibility, accountability and trust (Saglietto & Thomas, 1998) and reemerges as an important motivational instrument of HRM.

Meysonnier (1994), for example, proposes a model tested with a sample of 271 French small and medium-sized enterprises (SMEs) where the economic performance of the firm is influenced by the social performance of the human resources. He shows that quality in HRM seems to matter for the firm's general outcome in the largely independent family-owned sample. Therefore, strategic HRM with its drive for social performance, which means fostering mainly the nonfinancial 'people' relationships for higher organizational achievements, is a determinant of firm performance increasing the motivation and involvement of employees on the individual, as well as on the team level (Côté & Tega, 1980; Besseyre des Horts, 1988; Kieser & Kubicek, 1992).

In their empirical study on performance measurement in French companies, Bescos and Cauvin (2004: 195) state that the four perspectives of the balanced scorecard (BSC; financial, customers, internal processes, learning and growth) tend to be rather an example of the relations between financial and nonfinancial measures but differ from a model of a performance measurement system. The authors underline that "this implies an adaptation of the Balanced Scorecard to the context of a firm or a country." Interestingly, the study shows that indicators related to employee satisfaction or shareholder value do not play an important role in France as they do elsewhere. More recent empirical work by Bouamama, Basly and Zian (2021) showed that French intermediate-sized financial managers do not use, to the same extent, all the indicators constituting the four dimensions of BSCs.

The French context appears rather specific, notably regarding cultural norms as a critical factor of differentiation. France is one of the most inventive countries with respect to high-technology research and development (4th rank in the world according to the Organisation for Economic Co-operation and Development (OECD) and Eurostat in 2006; at the 11th world rank in 2021 (Invest in France, 2022; WIPO, 2022) and still among the top country to attract investors in Europe (EY, 2022), more particularly in life sciences and biotechnology as well as in computer sciences with new information and communication technologies (ICTs; Bpifrance, 2022). This also leads to a high acceptance of technology in the workplace in general. The use of ICT is fostering innovative collaborative work and management and tends to enhance productivity, which gives a direct link toward performance. Interestingly, the Latin world appeals more to direct and face-to-face contacts and not the dialogue through keyboard and screen; nevertheless, the use of ICT enables managers to deal with the traditionally significant amount of administrative and procedural issues particular to the French system. ICT also helps by offering some sort of 'playground' for using and supporting French creativity; the very conceptual and continuous modeling emphasis in the educational system of France also drives the use of electronic simulation tools. Hence, the COVID-19 pandemic has fostered particularly the use and development of ICTs and with the high social protection level in France, businesses were enabled to strengthen their investments in innovation and entrepreneurship, despite the pandemic. Here it may be of interest that the major share of French corporations is led by CEOs with an engineering background and engineering graduate training is perceived as the most prestigious and desired qualification for a professional career in French business (see also Maurice, Sellier, & Silvestre, 1982; Alexandre-Bailly et al., 2007).

Another important factor to be observed is the country-specific legal, as well as institutional, system. Its impact is developed in the next section, also as part of the *distal* factors outlined in the Murphy and DeNisi model, which have implications for other model-related factors.

IMPACT OF THE LEGAL ENVIRONMENT ON PERFORMANCE MANAGEMENT IN FRANCE

In France, the impact of the legal environment on performance management can be seen as minimal if there is any impact at all. French labor law gives large flexibility to assess and evaluate the performance of employees so long as the basic principles of merit and nondiscrimination are respected. In a comparative study, the French system has been attributed to the group of moderately regulated countries in Europe. In contrast, the German legal system, which is described in the next section, is in the group of highly regulated countries (Nikandrou et al., 2005).

From the institutional side, the French Ministry of Industry is calling attention to quality and performance by offering a prize to the best performers in industry and services since 2006 (Prix Français de la Qualité et de la Performance). The idea behind this prize is to involve not only large corporations but also SMEs in industry and services and support a comprehensive overall drive toward excellence in quality and performance in organizations. Performance is still strongly related to quality, notably if it is considered on the level of the whole organization. While large corporations seem to follow more global approaches of performance management systems, dominated mostly by US American standards, SMEs in France appear to be more reserved with respect to the implementation of those systems. Particularly, performance appraisal systems and their strategic HRM elements tend to be generated, if at all, by visionary individuals at these firms, notably the founders or the head of the organization. Meysonnier's study

Cordula Barzantny and Marion Festing

(1994) has demonstrated the positive effect of a qualitative HRM strategy on firm performance by testing a model of interdependencies between social, organizational and economic performance in SMEs. Regarding careers and training, France represents, on one hand, employees with poor basic and manual skills training at the bottom of the corporate ladder and, on the other hand, very high-brow generalists, notably engineers, as leaders of the firm, also with global profiles.

In conclusion, we can see that the particularities of various factors, not only for the French case of performance management systems but, more generally, also play a crucial role, as we emphasize with the framework of Murphy and DeNisi's model along the different groups of distal, proximal, intervening, judgment and distortion factors in the next section.

IMPACT OF THE CULTURAL ENVIRONMENT ON PERFORMANCE MANAGEMENT IN FRANCE[2]

According to Hofstede's dimensions (1980, 1991; see also https://geerthofstede.com), France is characterized as high on power distance, high on uncertainty avoidance, high on individualism and moderate on the masculinity index with a rather feminine attitude. The first and the last dimension differentiate France very clearly from Germany. Such dimensions as part of the *distal* factors seem to be identified with the least difficulties per country and society. It is important to note that companies engaging in international business such as multinational enterprises (MNEs) have to consider the interplay of various distal factors (Morley, Murphy, Cleveland, Heraty, & McCarthy, 2021). A study focusing on French multinationals' approach in the Middle East provides some examples (Yahiaoui, Nakhle, & Farndale, 2021).

As has been shown in the historical developments, the French culture is – compared to other European countries – relatively high on power distance (Hofstede, 1991), valuing hierarchy (House et al., 2004), manifested by a rather unequal power distribution in society. High power distance leads to an elite system that still prevails in education, administration, the management of organizations and overall society. Appreciation and appraisal of performance, for example, are strongly influenced by this context.

Regarding *proximal* factors, many French firms dispose of appraisal schemes with formal annual interviews and assessments. The respective outcomes have an impact on remuneration and other benefits of the appraised individual (Rojot, 1990). But how the process of appraisal is finally carried out seems to show the variance between formally acclaimed performance management systems and processes and the reality in French organizations, which leads to the intervening factors of Murphy and DeNisi's model.

An example of the *intervening* factors, according to Murhy and DeNisi's model, understood as results of the effects of distal and proximal factors, is the fact that performance appraisals, as well as complete talent management systems, in France tend to be influenced by the prevailing elite system (see Brunstein, 1995) with her chapter on France for an overview of an elitist and Tayloristic approach in French firms; see also Bonneton, Festing, & Muratbekova-Touron, 2020). This is manifest in the following way: if the individual to be evaluated comes from a more prestigious background, the performance appraisal will be more positive because of a priori more favorable expectations. This effect is even stronger when both the evaluator and the person to be evaluated share a similar higher educational background. Therefore, the often-used management by objectives as a base for measuring possible performance indicators seems to be subjective according to this context following the national ranking of higher education establishments (*Grandes Ecoles* & universities). The basis of a fair performance management for equal HRM (Besseyre des Horts, 1991) is the measurement and the possible measurability of objective indicators. Therefore, the appraisal mechanisms and systems enter into the focus of attention (Longenecker et al., 1987). Unfortunately, in France they are also often used with the aim to confirm and to justify the impact on someone's remuneration of rather subjective criteria and their evaluation (see also Bourguignon, 1998, with her study supporting that rather subjective perceptual elements play an important role for performance evaluations). This leads sometimes to limited motivation of individuals who have high performance potential despite the fact that their graduate studies were achieved in a second-tier school in France. The outcome may be that organizations are pulling themselves away from people performance inside their own firm. On higher levels of the organization, this is, for example, often vested in countervailing power games. Here we observe an interesting

Cordula Barzantny and Marion Festing

impact of *judgment* factors with private evaluation of a person's performance in some area (Murphy & Cleveland, 1991; see also Bourguignon, 2004).

High power distance in France leads to a very low degree of openness and lack of transparency between both parties in the evaluation processes. "*French companies are described as being based on the principle of control with power concentrated at the top*" (Gooderham et al., 1999: 513, emphasis added). Overall, the employee-manager relationship is characterized by a lack of trust and circumvention of direct feedback. According to van der Klink and Mulder (1995) and Lane (1994) the lack of trust manifests itself through the managers' reluctance to share information "*since asymmetric information is a precondition for maintaining power*" (Gooderham et al., 1999: 513–514, emphasis added). This affects the objective-setting process as well as performance feedback, often leaving employees with a feeling of ambiguity and unfairness in the process and its outcomes and a perception of special, more favorable treatment for certain individuals according to the superior's will, mood and network. In performance appraisals a manager tends to have the final word with a strong tendency to assign job objectives (Schuler, Jackson, & Luo, 2004) without clear negotiation, leading to a more ambiguous formulation and, furthermore, a fuzzier relationship.

The difference in power distance may also explain the stratification of average income from bottom to top across industrial organizations varying by a ratio of 1 to 15 in France whereas Germany displayed a factor of 6 as studied by Maurice, Sellier and Silvestre (1982).

As in most continental European countries, French employees value stability and longer lasting, stable employment relationships. France is one of the EU countries with the highest percentage of civil servants among the working population (Eurostat 2021). People have a rather adverse attitude to change which impacts their preference and choice of employers as well as types of employment desired (public vs. private sector). These facts might reflect a high level of uncertainty avoidance.

The more feminine score of France compared to Germany is reflected in the definition of careers and the importance of professional progression. In a quasi-Latin environment like France's work climate, quality of life and work–life balance tend to be higher valued than basic economic considerations. This also has an influence on cooperation at work; French employees, on average, prefer a job placement with challenging interpersonal interaction and a positive climate since they focus on people relationships. Since interpersonal ties and networks tend to be very important, open criticism of others, notably along the hierarchical line, is avoided in order to have at least superficial harmony prevailing in work groups. This also impacts feedback, which is often only given when improvements and corrections are requested by the superior. The more qualified the professional category of employee, the fuzzier the goals and objective-setting become. Since in France the generalist profile prevails, the appraisal process takes this into account and expects a rather diverse human development potential.

Since organizational norms do not necessarily contribute significantly to the accuracy of the performance appraisal process and overall performance management, we observe a stronger impact from the rater–ratee relationship as well as the rater motivation, which represent *intervening* factors in Murphy and DeNisi's model. The perceived uses of a performance rating system lead to a rather average rating of all employees in a department, firm or corporation, with little discrimination among ratees.

Regarding *distortion* factors, we see a rather low impact of performance appraisal on promotion, pay raises and so on in the traditional French company and corporate hierarchy because of the social differentiation between employees already existing independently from actual professional performance. Interestingly, the variance of performance ratings tends to be small and around the average per professional group. Nevertheless, higher qualified and more prestigious graduate degrees influence performance raters more positively and work experience with demonstrated performance often counts less than social and educational background!

The fact that most private organizations in France have introduced performance appraisal schemes is corroborated by the Cranet data (Hegewisch & Larsen, 1996; Brewster, Mayrhofer, & Morley, 2004). Interestingly, this was not necessarily valid for the public sector following a much slower evolution, which has only recently introduced new performance appraisals (Grossi, Reichard, & Ruggiero, 2016). Overall, "effectiveness and further uptake in France have been hampered by both management and trade union opposition, who see appraisal as a threat to their traditional autonomy" (Hegewisch & Larsen, 1996: 13; see also Bournois, 1996; Doellgast & Marsden, 2019).

Performance-based pay is introduced in France mainly for senior managerial staff and follows US examples (see, e.g., Bournois & Tyson, 2005; Peretti & Roussel, 2000) in order to give performance incentives to corporate leaders. Interestingly, the acceptance of variable pay schemes appears rather high in private companies and French managers display a willingness to take risks in this regard, because the basic social security and safety net ensure a rather high level of assistance for the individual (Sire & Tremblay, 1996, 1998).

In sum, we perceive the French historical cultural underpinning as a major influence on performance management systems as well as performance appraisal processes. Influences of globalization, corporate culture and organizational norms appear to be rather weak in the French case, even if corporations in France, particularly larger ones, formally adopt the US and Anglo-Saxon example of performance management systems.

To contrast two European countries, in the next section the German specificities will be covered highlighting again the factors of Murphy and DeNisi's model.

SPECIFICITIES CHARACTERIZING HRM AND PERFORMANCE MANAGEMENT IN GERMANY

The main elements of the institutional framework in Germany are the German labor market institutions of collective bargaining, codetermination and vocational training (Müller, 1999; Festing, 2012). Considering these factors, it has to be stated that Germany provides not only important differences compared to the US or Japan but also when looking at other European countries (Pudelko, 2000a, 2000b, 2000c). As Dickmann (2003) states, the historical evolution, the cultural and institutional environment, as well as the industry structure – that is, the *distal* factors as identified by Murphy and DeNisi – are features that clearly distinguish Germany also from other European countries. He identifies the rather collectivist culture combined with the tight institutional framework as a major feature of the German system. Gooderham et al. (1999: 513) conclude that "German work life is characterized by powerful labor representative bodies and strong work legislation, and the personnel function has to deal with detailed and comprehensive regulations and is therefore highly operative oriented."

However, it cannot be said that the German HRM model is characterized by outstanding specificities that have had a direct influence on HRM role models in other countries such as the US. The German model seems to be less subject to stereotypical consideration than, for example, the American model, which can be described as "short-term performance efficiency based on flexible market structures and profit orientation" or the Japanese model interpreted as "long-term behavioral effectiveness based on cooperative clan structures and growth orientation" (Pudelko, 2005: 2067). According to Pudelko (2005, 2006), this is mainly due to a lack of information, which makes it even more important to take a special look in this chapter at the HRM practices of this country, focusing on performance management.

Insofar as HRM in Germany is concerned, there is always a special interest in the legal system as part of the institutional environment of German firms. Very often the system of codetermination is in the center of interest (see for example, Wächter & Stengelhofen, 1992; Warner & Campbell, 1993; Pudelko, 2005; Festing, 2012). These aspects are described in the next section.

IMPACT OF THE LEGAL ENVIRONMENT ON PERFORMANCE MANAGEMENT IN GERMANY

As has been outlined in the introduction about the specificities of the HRM system in Germany, the German situation is characterized by a rigid legal environment. As in France, it also emphasizes nondiscrimination. However, complex labor laws, contractual agreements with the unions, a system of codetermination including participation, consultation and information rights on the level of the works councils (*Betriebsrat*) limit managerial discretion (Conrad & Pieper, 1990; Müller, 1999; Tempel, 2001; Wächter & Müller-Camen, 2002; Pudelko, 2005; Doellgast & Marsden, 2019).

In Germany, five levels of regulation concerning the industrial relations system can be identified: the state level, the collective

Cordula Barzantny and Marion Festing

bargaining level, the company level, the plant level and individual workplace and work contracts. "The German state guarantees unions' and employers' associations freedom in concluding collective labor contracts and does not interfere actively in day-to day activities" (Conrad & Pieper, 1990: 124). This is the most important precondition for the functioning of the German industrial relations system.

With respect to performance management, the most important industrial relations level is the plant level. Here, the system of legally guaranteed codetermination is relevant.

> Employees may exercise their influence through elected works councils. ... Works councils have almost no rights in the economic management of the company but have various options in influencing a company's HRM policy. Whereas in some matters they only have to be consulted, they may participate in the decision-making process in others (participation rights) or even have to approve management decisions (genuine co-determination rights).
>
> (Conrad & Pieper, 1990: 126)

The latter is the case when regulations for assessment and thus for performance management are concerned. This means that any introduction or change of a performance management system including all details is subject to codetermination, that is, needs the approval of the works councils. According to Dickmann (2003), this should lead to cooperative behavior and thus to the consensus orientation further discussed in later (Festing, 2012).

Besides the industrial relations system, the social market economy is an important feature of the German economy. It is seen as the basis for a "consensus philosophy, self-reinforcing socio-cultural institutions and a distinct approach to business management" (Dickmann, 2003: 266). It aims at a high level of job security for staff members and "acts as an incentive for companies to use long-term career and succession planning and puts an onus on vocational training and staff development to increase functional flexibility" (Dickmann, 2003: 267). Performance management is a central element of the previously mentioned features such as career and succession planning. Thus, there is a strong link between the social market economy system and the importance of performance management in the German economy, associated with long-term developmental strategies in international HRM. These may even be fostered by the quality orientation typically associated with German firms (Vitols et al., 1997) leading to highly valued specialist knowledge, often acquired within so-called chimney careers (Dickmann, 2003), that is, the career of a specialist (see also Alexandre-Bailly et al., 2007).

To sum up, the insights gained from the short discussions about the industrial relations system, as well as the social market economy, indicate that a cooperative orientation and long-term developmental HR strategies are a central feature of the German HR system indicating the strategic importance of performance management systems (see also Child, Faulkner, & Pitkethly, 2001). This is underlined by an extensive vocational training system, which provides employees with broad basic qualifications and should indicate a long-term perspective in the employment relation (Conrad & Pieper, 1990; Warner & Campbell, 1993; Brewster, 1995; Rowold & Kauffeld, 2009). The strong developmental orientation is a key characteristic of the German business system (Festing, 2012, 2017).

IMPACT OF THE CULTURAL ENVIRONMENT ON PERFORMANCE MANAGEMENT IN GERMANY

There is evidence that cultural differences have an impact on HRM and on the specific field of performance management (Conrad & Pieper, 1990; Lindholm, 2000). In terms of the four original dimensions identified by Hofstede (1980, 1991), the German culture can be described as relatively low on power distance, high on uncertainty avoidance, high on the masculinity index and high on individualism. In this section, we outline the impact of cultural values on selected *proximal*, as well as *intervening*, factors.

Power distance seems to have an impact on the process of how an agreement on job objectives is reached. In German companies, objective settings in the performance appraisal process are the result of a negotiation between superior and employee (for this relationship, also see Schuler, Jackson, & Luo, 2004). The same is the case, for example, in Sweden (Tahvanainen, 1998).

Cordula Barzantny and Marion Festing

Both countries are characterized by a relatively low power distance (Hofstede, 1980). The low degree of power distance is also associated with a rather high degree of openness between both parties in the rater-ratee relationship, not only during the objective setting process but also when performance feedback is concerned (Schneider, 1988). In Germany, performance feedback seems to be an ongoing process of a dialogue between superior and subordinate, including also many informal elements (Pudelko, 2000b). In contrast, in many Asian countries, a high level of power distance leads to a clear assignment of job objectives by the manager and often to a more formal relationship between superior and employee (Lindholm, 2000). This more formal relationship is also valid for France.

The highly regulated work environment is often attributed to a high level of uncertainty avoidance in Germany (Conrad & Pieper, 1990; Warner & Campbell, 1993). With respect to performance management, Germans expect such a system to be highly integrated in a set of precise rules: performance evaluations should be formalized in terms of defining goals or criteria, time frames, measurement methods and consequences, for example, for training or pay decisions. According to an interview with a German HR expert, the system is close to being overregulated.[3] The standards set for this process are important *judgment factors* in the sense of Murphy and DeNisi's model.

Feedback is provided in a way that includes open confrontations – an approach, which would not be acceptable, for example, in Asian countries. In Germany, it is mainly based on individual achievements. Individual achievements often can be clearly measured, for example in measurement-by-objectives (MBO) systems. *Distal* factors such as strategic goals of firms are transferred into goals relevant for the individual depending on their position. This reflects a high level of individualism in German culture. In summary, the role of performance management is significant for German managers. It indicates a high importance of career progression for the individual as well as within the society, which reflects the high score on Hofstede's masculinity index (Lindholm, 2000). From an organizational perspective, the major goal is coordinating all activities according to the major strategic goals of the firm.

Another feature, which may explain the high importance of performance management in German companies, is the aforementioned long-term orientation in Germany (Dickmann, 2003; Ferner, Quintanilla, & Varul, 2001; Festing, 2012). Many Germans still value long-term employment relationships (Child, Faulkner, & Pitkethly, 2001; Festing, Müller, & Yussefi, 2007). In this context, seniority plays an important role as in many German companies there is a comparatively high number of managers who still pursue lifelong careers within one firm (Pudelko, 2000b, 2000c). Performance management has a central function here in providing feedback and especially in outlining avenues for future development within the firm. This indicates the importance of the strong link between performance appraisal and human resource development. Performance management would have a different meaning in a culture characterized by a short-term orientation.

In contrast, the link to performance-based pay has to be seen critically: while in the last decades performance-based pay has also been of increasing importance to German firms (Brewster & Hegewisch, 1994; Müller, 1999; Child, Faulkner, & Pitkethly, 2001), it does not have the same meaning as in other countries. This may be due to the fact that German companies – as most of their European counterparts (Ferner & Varul, 2000) – have introduced performance-related pay practices much later than British and US American firms, probably also due to the respective institutional and cultural environment.[4] One of the major reasons for this is that in German companies the introduction of performance-based pay systems needs to be approved by the works council (Müller, 1999). However, performance-based pay is also an expression of a rather short-term orientation (Pudelko, 2005), which contradicts the assumption that Germans are rather long-term oriented. Thus, in many companies, here we rather see the adoption of a typical feature of the Anglo-Saxon HRM system. However, as it is not fully compatible with German traditions and values its adoption seems to have been realized only to a modest extent. In summary, although there is a high acceptance of a performance management system and its impact on career development the direct link to performance-based pay at this stage cannot be described as typical for all companies.

Cordula Barzantny and Marion Festing

This might be different in multinational corporations where there is a need to have worldwide standards in executive compensation (Festing, Eidems, & Royer, 2007, Dowling et al., 2023). While there are country-specific differences in performance management a study comparing Germany, China and the US indicates that they are not as important as expected (Festing, Knappert, Dowling, & Engle, 2012).

Concerning pay distribution, we usually find a normal distribution centering on the 100% mark with a low standard deviation. This is in line with information from a German HR expert who states that the willingness to discriminate between ratees is still low compared to other countries such as the US. This also leads to evaluations that are closer to the average than to the extreme poles of the evaluation scale. The underlying reason for this result may also lie in the highly egalitarian German system described earlier.

To sum up, it can be said that in German firms, performance appraisal is of high importance in the context of long-term employment relationships. It has a long tradition in Germany (Oechsler, 2006) and very often includes behavioral dimensions (input factors) as well as output factors (Pudelko, 2000b). However, the emergence of integrated performance management systems is rather recent. In integrated performance management systems (Verweire & van den Berghe, 2004) appraisal is usually linked to the fields of management development and managerial pay. The investment in training based on performance appraisal results, especially seems to differentiate Germany from other countries such as the US, where often up-or-out systems are favored (Pudelko, 2000b). The consequences of performance appraisal are discussed as *distortion* factors in the Murphy and DeNisi model. It becomes clear that especially the financial consequences may not be as important as in other countries (Child, Faulkner, & Pitkethly, 2001).

While the German system seems to be very close to the Anglo-Saxon system, the preceding analysis has revealed a number of German particularities. In the French case, representing a different approach compared to the German system, management is still able to pursue a tradition of autonomous, non-consultative decision-making (Gooderham et al., 1999: 514).

CONCLUDING REMARKS ON FUTURE DEVELOPMENTS OF THE GERMAN PERFORMANCE MANAGEMENT SYSTEM

Some researchers have found evidence that the German HRM model is in a process of change. While for a long time after World War II, the economic conditions were more or less stable (Streeck, 1997, 2001) and characterized by growth, enabling the development of a social market economy, recently, external factors inducing change have emerged. Among these are the German reunification and the opening of new markets for labor as well as for products in Central and Eastern Europe and, of course, the worldwide-encompassing phenomenon of globalization (Ferner & Varul, 2000). These factors seem to be forcing German companies to intensify their internationalization processes, which compared to their US and UK counterparts have only started comparatively late (Ferner, Quintanilla, & Varul, 2001). There are indicators that this process is associated with a further adoption of Anglo-Saxon HRM practices, partly starting in subsidiaries outside Germany and then being transferred back to the headquarters in the sense of reverse diffusion (Ebster-Grosz & Pugh, 1996; Müller, 1999). A long list of examples is given based on case study research in German MNEs by Ferner and Varul (2000). They state that

> as German companies move beyond their classic export platform strategy to become international players, they are much more likely to absorb the prevailing business-cultural practices of companies well versed in the deregulated rules of the international economy than they are to transmit their own peculiarities to others.
>
> (Ferner & Varul, 2000: 136)

Due to globalization, firms feel a need to standardize their HRM practices on a worldwide level, and this is also true for performance management (Festing, Eidems, & Royer, 2007; Festing, Knappert, Dowling, & Engle, 2012). Thus, as has been discussed before, in large MNEs there may be more evidence for integrated global performance management systems following the same pattern worldwide.

However, it has to be considered that in the European Economic Area, less than 1 per cent of enterprises are large ones; the rest are SMEs. Two thirds of all jobs in this region are in SMEs, while one third is provided by large enterprises (UNECE, 2007). In Germany, the percentage of jobs in SMEs rises to almost 60 per cent (Institut für Mittelstandsforschung, 2021). Consequently, in these companies, performance management rather follows a local pattern, being mainly based on performance appraisal. Although it is recommended that SMEs offer systematic career management related to a performance management system, this area very often is neglected due to a lack of resources (Festing, 2007); on the contrary, talent management systems in German SMEs and family businesses rather focus on the development of all employees and have an inclusive focus (Festing, Schäfer, & Scullion, 2013; Harsch & Festing, 2019). Consequently, there are still German particularities deeply rooted in cultural values and in the specific institutional context, which lead to a different performance management reality than in other countries although the measures and agendas might have similar names. Pudelko speaks about a "compromise formula" (2005: 2067), which is difficult to describe and distinguish. We will come back to this point in the next section when discussing the tendencies for convergence and divergence in Europe.

CONCLUSION

The presentations and discussions of the performance management systems in France and Germany have clearly shown that it is most important to include environmental factors in order to understand the particularities of each system as indicated by the contextual paradigm by Brewster (1999) or as in the model developed by Murphy and DeNisi in this book with particular focus on performance appraisals (Chapter 6 in this volume; see also Boselie, Farndale, & Paauwe, 2018). In the following, key arguments concerning the impact of the French and German institutional and cultural environment on performance management are summarized and structured according to the dimensions outlined by Murphy and DeNisi. At the end of the conclusion, we briefly discuss possible tendencies of convergence or divergence of HRM systems and especially performance management systems in Europe.

From the analysis, it has become clear that the *distal factors* differ to a high extent between France and Germany. The legal environment with the system of codetermination in Germany has a strong influence on the emergence of performance management systems while in France legal aspects play only a minor role. Thus, discretionary choices seem to be higher in France. With respect to national educational institutions, we can observe a far stronger tradition in Germany than in France to invest in the training and professional development of employees. This may stem from the German "dual vocational training system" of alternating on-the-job training and formal education in professional schools (apprenticeships), which offers well qualified intermediate professionals. This may explain the strong link between performance appraisal, training and career development as well. Such training and development systems have been lacking in France and are currently developed. Besides the analysis of the institutional environment, the specificities of the German and French cultures have also led to important insights into the performance management process in both countries. It has been outlined that major differences were related to the power distance and femininity/ masculinity dimensions identified by Hofstede (1980). For example, while the high power distance in France leads to objectives set by the superiors, the rather low power distance in Germany is associated with negotiations in the objective setting process in the context of performance management. The strong masculine dimension attributes a high importance on the notion of vertical careers in Germany. For the individual and the status within the society, this is most important. While career success is important in France as well there is another dimension resulting from the high degree of femininity. Well-being in the working environment seems to play a relatively more critical role in France than in Germany. This may explain why one very important goal in the performance management discussion is not to damage the personal relationship. Lebas (1995) has argued that performance measurement is intertwined with performance management and cannot be separated. The context of the management relationships has a decisive impact that seems to be more personalized in France compared to more factual and task-orientated relationships in Germany. As outlined in the model by Murphy and DeNisi, the distal factors have an impact on the proximal factors as well as on the intervening factors related to performance management systems. This is highlighted in the following discussion.

With respect to the *proximal factors* the purpose of appraisal seems to be more control-oriented in France while the emphasis in

Germany is on coordination and cooperation for reaching common organizational and, in the best case, also individual goals. This, of course, is reflected in the rater–ratee relationship which, due to cultural differences, has a high potential to differ between Germany and France. Furthermore, it indicates differences in rater motivation. However, in both countries, the willingness to discriminate among ratees is low. In France it is very common from school age on to give average grades, even if the performance is outstanding. Similar tendencies can be observed in Germany. It seems that appraisal systems are accepted to a higher degree in Germany than in France because they have a direct individual value if they are well managed. Differentiated open, direct and fair *feedback* is very much appreciated by individuals in the German context.

More similarities were found when analyzing the *intervening factors* in both countries. The frequency of appraisal is, of course, very much dependent on the organizational system and inherent norms. As has been mentioned earlier, the organizational size and the degree of internationalization play important roles here as well. However, in many cases there seems to be a performance appraisal at least once a year in German and in French organizations, which is carried out by the superior. Depending on the purpose, this information can be used for making decisions about promotion, performance-based pay and personnel planning. This is for example the case in the "Leadership Evaluation and Development" concept of DaimlerChrysler Corporation. Here, individual assessments by the superior are a next step discussed in Performance Validation Meetings on higher hierarchical levels. Furthermore, this information is used in Executive Development Conferences and supports succession planning procedures (Ring, Groenewald, & Varga von Kibed, 2003). However, as we have outlined earlier, there are many cases where performance appraisal is not directly linked with other HR decisions, and this is sometimes perceived as being free from *distortions* that may occur due to the consequences of appraisals such as forced distribution because of certain budget constraints. In the first case, the *judgment* is based on the individual and less on the organizational requirements.

Using the model developed by Murphy and DeNisi we were able to draw a differentiated picture of the commonalities and differences in performance management systems in France and in Germany. The question that emerges from the identification of the differences in the performance management practices in Germany and France is whether signs of convergence or divergence of the different systems can be identified. Gooderham et al. (1999: 526) state that *"the German regime … appears to be relatively unreceptive to international developments within the personnel management in general and collaborative practices in particular."* Katz and Darbishire (2001), Streeck (2001) and Pudelko (2006) discuss converging divergences in employment systems. With respect to the employment system within each country, they see an increasing divergence. However, in terms of workplace patterns at least Katz and Darbishire (2001) have identified a growing convergence. This is confirmed by research from the Cranet network, mainly focusing on Europe (Brewster, 2006). Brewster, Mayrhofer, and Morley (2004) give a more differentiated perspective. They distinguish between directional convergence and final convergence. The first is concerned with the question of whether the same trends can be observed in different countries; the latter addresses the results. Their conclusion, based on the Cranet data, is as follows:

> From a directional point of view, there seems to be a positive indication of convergence. However, when one looks at the question from a final convergence point of view, the answer is no longer a clear positive one. None of the HR practices converged at the end of the decade. Rather, the maximum point of convergence is reached in the middle of the decade with signs of divergence after that.
>
> (Brewster, Mayrhofer, & Morley, 2004: 434)

Thus, the results concerning the convergence or divergence of HRM systems including performance management systems are mixed. There is no clear tendency, although in an empirical study concerning the convergence–divergence debate in HRM, Pudelko (2005) concludes that the majority of the HR managers investigated (originated from Germany, the US and Japan) expect a convergence of HRM systems.

These results of the convergence/divergence discussion are very much in line with the findings of this chapter indicating an isomorphism, maybe even a mimetic isomorphism (DiMaggio & Powell, 1983), with respect to the adoption of performance

Cordula Barzantny and Marion Festing

management systems especially in large multinational organizations in Europe taking the example of the Anglo-Saxon world. However, there seems to be room for local adaptations in this process. As Fletcher (2001) has stated in his seminal article, the context is important and requires adaptation to make sense of professional performance management systems in respective environments (see also Delery, 1998). This poses ongoing challenges for strategic human resource management with global thinking and local action (see also DeNisi, Murphy, Varma, & Budhwar, 2021).

NOTES

1 For a detailed description, see Chapter 6.
2 Our analysis and observations were corroborated during six interviews of HRM professionals of MNCs based in France and who are in charge of implementing and managing performance management systems at corporate and business unit levels in 2006 and 2022. The interviews consisted of open-ended questions concerning the performance management practices in the firms.
3 The interviews were conducted by one of the authors with an HR manager of a German MNE who is involved in the development and application of the company performance management system at the corporate and business unit level. The interview mainly consisted of open-ended questions concerning the performance management practices and the impact of differing institutional and cultural environments within the respective MNE. They took place in October 2006 and 2022 and lasted for approximately one hour each.
4 For an analysis of the institutional environment with respect to the development and spread of stock options in Germany, see Sanders and Tuschke (2007).

REFERENCES

Alexandre-Bailly, F. with Festing, M., & Jonczyk, C. (2007). Choix et formation des dirigeants en France et en Allemagne. In F. Bournois, J. Duval-Hamel, S. Roussillon, & J. L. Scaringella (Eds.) *Comités exécutifs* (pp. 245–250). Paris: Groupe Eyrolles.
Armstrong, M., & Baron, A. (1998). *Performance management. The new realities.* London: Institute of Personnel and Development.
Becker, B. E. with Huselid, M. A., & Ulrich, D. (2001). *The HR scorecard: Linking people, strategy, and performance.* Boston, MA: Harvard Business Press.
Bescos, P.-L., & Cauvin, E. (2004). Performance measurement in French companies: An empirical study. In M. J. Epstein & J.-F. Manzoni (Eds.) *Performance measurement and management control: Superior organizational performance, studies in managerial and financial accounting* (Vol. 14, pp. 185–202). Oxford: Elsevier Jai.
Besseyre Des Horts, C.-H. (1988). *Vers une gestion stratégique des ressources humaines.* Paris: Les Editions d'Organisation.
Besseyre Des Horts, C.-H. (1991). *L'appréciation comme pratique fondamentale de développement de l'équité en GRH.* Paris: cahier de recherche CCI.
Boitier, M., & Rivière, A. (2013). Freedom and responsibility for French universities: From global steering to local management. *Accounting, Auditing & Accountability Journal*, 26(4), 616–649.

Bonneton, D., Muratbekova-Touron, M., & Festing, M. (2020). Exclusive talent management unveiling the mechanisms of the construction of an elite community. *European Management Review*, 17(4), 993–1013. DOI: 10.1111/emre.12413.

Boselie, P., Farndale, E., & Paauwe, J. (2018). Comparing performance management across contexts. In Brewster, C., Mayerhofer, W. & Farndale, E. (Eds.) *Handbook of research on comparative human resource management* (2nd ed., pp. 164–183). Cheltenham: Edward Elgar.

Bouamama, M., Basly, S., & Zian, H. (2021). How do contingency factors influence the content of balanced scorecards? An empirical study of French intermediate-sized enterprises. *Journal of Accounting & Organizational Change*, 17(3), 373–393.

Bourguignon, A. (1998). *L'évaluation de la performance: un instrument de gestion éclaté*, Rapport de recherche ESSEC-CR-DR – 98-042.

Bourguignon, A. (2004). Performance management and management control: Evaluated managers' point of view. *European Accounting Review*, 13(4), 659–687.

Bourguignon, A, with Malleret, V., & Nørreklit, H. (2004). The American balanced scorecard versus the French tableau de bord: The ideological dimension. *Management Accounting Research*, 15(2), 107–134.

Bournois, F. (1996). Industrial relations, source of economic and social performances of a company. In A.-M. Fericelli & B. Sire (Eds.) *Performance et Ressources Humaines*. Paris: Economica.

Bournois, F., & Tyson, S. (2005). *Top Pay and Performance - Strategy and Evaluation*, Oxford: Butterworth-Heinemann.

Bpifrance (2022). https://www.bpifrance.com/

Brewster, C. (1994). European HRM. Reflection of, or challenge to, the American concept. In P. S. Kirkbride (Ed.) *Human resource management in Europe. Perspectives for the 1990s*. London & New York: Routledge.

Brewster, C. (1995). Towards a "European" model of human resource management. *Journal of International Business Studies*, 26(1), 1–21.

Brewster, C. R. (1996). Restoring childhood: Saving the world's children from toiling in textile sweatshops. *Journal of Law and Commerce*, 16, 191.

Brewster, C. (1999). Strategic human resource management: The value of different paradigms. *Management International Review*, 39, 45–64.

Brewster, C. (2006). *International Human resource management: If there is no "best way", how do we manage?*, Inaugural Lecture, Henley Management College UK.

Brewster, C., & Hegewisch, A. (Eds.) (1994). *Policy and practice in European human resource management. The price waterhouse cranfield survey*. London & New York: Routledge.

Brewster, C., Mayrhofer, W., & Smale, A. (2016). Crossing the streams: HRM in multinational enterprises and comparative HRM. *Human Resource Management Review*, 26(4), 285–297.

Brewster, Ch., Mayrhofer, W., & Morley, M. (Eds.) (2004). *Human resource: Evidence of convergence?* London: Elsevier.

Brunstein, I. (1995). France. In I. Brunstein (Ed.) *Human resource management in Western Europe* (pp. 59–88). Berlin, New York: Walter de Gruyter.

Carassus, D., Favoreu, C., & Gardey, D. (2014). Factors that determine or influence managerial innovation in public contexts: The case of local performance management. *Public Organization Review*, 14(2), 245–266.

Carassus, D., Favoreu, C., Gardey, D., & Marin, P. (2012). La caractérisation et le management des déviances organisationnelles liées à la mise en œuvre d'une démarche de performance publique: Application au contexte public local français. *Management International / International Management/Gestión Internacional*, 16(3), 102–117.

Cascio, W. F. (2006). Global performance management systems. In *Handbook of research in international human resource management* (pp. 176–196). Cheltenham and Northampton: Edward Elgar Publishing Ltd.

Cascio, W. F. (2012). Global performance management systems. In G. Stahl, I. Björkman, & S. Morris (Eds.) *Handbook of research in international human resource management* (2nd ed., pp. 176–196). Cheltenham: Edward Elgar.

Child, J. with Faulkner, D., & Pitkethly, R. (2001). *The management of international acquisitions.* Oxford: Oxford University Press.

Claus, L., & Briscoe, D. (2006). Employee performance management across borders: A review of relevant academic literature. *Paper presented at the Annual Conference of the Academy of Management,* Atlanta, GA.

Conrad, P., & Pieper, R. (1990). Human resource management in the Federal Republic of Germany. In Pieper, R. (Ed.) *Human resources management. An international comparison* (pp. 109–139). Berlin: de Gruyter.

Côté, M., & Tega, V. (1980). *La démocratie industrielle.* Montréal: Les Presses HEC et les Editions agence d'Arc Inc.

Defélix, C. with Klarsfeld, A., & Oiry, E. (Eds.) (2006). *Nouveaux regards sur la gestion des compétences.* Paris: Vuibert.

Delery, J. (1998). Issues of fit in strategic human resource management: Implications for research. *Human Resource Management Review,* 8(3), 289–309.

DeNisi, A., Murphy, K., Varma, A., & Budhwar, P. (2021). Performance management systems and multinational enterprises: Where we are and where we should go. *Human Resource Management,* 60(5), 707–713.

Devillard, O. (2001). *Coacher, efficacité personnelle et performance collective.* Paris: Dunod.

Dickmann, M. (2003). Implementing German HRM abroad: Desired, feasible, successful? *International Journal of Human Resource Management,* 14(2), 265–283.

DiMaggio, P., & Powell, W. (1983). The iron cage revisited: Institutional isomorphism and collective rationality in organisational fields. *American Sociological Review,* 48(4), 147–160.

Doellgast, V. & Marsden, D. (2019). Institutions as constraints and resources: Explaining cross-national divergence in performance management. *Human Resource Management Journal,* 29(2), 199–216.

Dowling, P. with Festing, M., & Engle, A. (2023 forthcoming). *International human resource management* (8th ed.). Andover: Cengage.

Ebster-Grosz, D. & Pugh, D. (1996). *Anglo-German business collaboration. Pitfalls and potentials.* Basingstoke: Macmillan.

Eurostat (2021). Government employment. https://ec.europa.eu/eurostat/cache/digpub/european_economy/bloc-4d.html?lang=en

EY (2022). Europe Attractiveness survey 2022. How will Europe compete for investment amid ongoing turbulence? https://www.ey.com/en_gl/attractiveness

Falzon, P., Nascimento, A., Gaudart, C., Piney, C., Dujarier, M.-A., & Germe, J.-F. (2012). Performance-based management and quality of work: An empirical assessment. *Work,* 41, 3855–3860.

Ferner, A., with Quintanilla, J., & Varul, M. (2001). Country-of-origin effects, host-country effects, and the management of HR in multinationals. *Journal of World Business,* 36(2), 107–127.

Ferner, A., & Varul, M. (2000). "Vanguard" subsidiaries and the diffusion of new practices: A case study of German multinationals. *British Journal of Industrial Relations* 38(1), 115–140.

Festing, M. (2007). Globalization of SMEs and implications for international human resource management. *International Journal of Globalisation and Small Business,* 2(1), 5–18.

Festing, M. (2012). Strategic human resource management in Germany: Evidence of convergence to the U.S. Model, the European Model, or a Distinctive National Model? *Academy of Management Perspectives,* 26(2), 37–54.

Festing, M. (2017). Learning about Talent retention in times of crisis – Opportunities for the Robert Bosch group in the context of the German Industrial relations system. In Liza Castro Christiansen, M. Biron, E. Farndale & B. Kuvaas (Eds.) *The global human resource management casebook* (2nd ed., pp. 22–31). New York: Routledge.

Festing, M., with Eidems, J., & Royer, S. (2007). Strategic issues and local constraints in transnational compensation strategies: An analysis of cultural, institutional and political influences. *European Management Journal*, 25(2), 118–131.

Festing, M., with Eidems, J., Royer, S., & Kullak, F. (2006). *When in Rome Pay as the Romans Pay. Considerations about transnational compensation strategies and the case of a German MNE*, Working Paper No. 22: ESCP-EAP European School of Management Berlin.

Festing, M., & Knappert, L. (2014). Country-Specific Profiles of Performance Management in China, Germany, and the United States-An Empirical Test. *Thunderbird International Business Review*, 56(4), 331–351.

Festing, M., with Knappert, L., Dowling, P. J., & Engle, A. D. (2012). Global performance management in MNEs – Conceptualization and profiles of country-specific characteristics in China, Germany, and the United States. *Thunderbird International Business Review*, 54(6), 825–843.

Festing, M., with Müller, B., & Yussefi, S. (2007). *Careers in the auditing business – Still ballroom dance?! Static and dynamic perspectives on the psychological contract in the up-or-out system*, Paper to be Presented at the 23rd EGOS Colloquium, Vienna, July 2007.

Festing, M., Schäfer, L., & Scullion, H. (2013). Talent management in medium-sized German companies – an explorative study and agenda for future research. *The International Journal of Human Resource Management*, 24(9), 1872–1893.

Fletcher, C. (2001). Performance appraisal and management: The developing research agenda. *Journal of Occupational and Organizational Psychology*, 74, 473–487.

Gooderham, P., with Nordhaug, O., & Ringdal, K. (1999). Institutional and rational determinants of organizational practices: Human resource management in European firms. *Administrative Science Quarterly*, 44, 507–531.

Grossi, G., Hansen, M. B., Johanson, J.-E., Vakkuri, J., & Moon, M. J. (2016). Introduction: Comparative performance management and accountability in the age of Austerity. *Public Performance & Management Review*, 39(3), 499–505.

Grossi, G., Reichard, C., & Ruggiero, P. (2016). Appropriateness and use of performance information in the budgeting process: Some experiences from German and Italian municipalities. *Public Performance & Management Review*, 39(3), 581–606.

Guest, D. (1994). Organizational psychology and human resource management: Towards a European approach. *European Work and Organizational Psychologist*, 4(3), 251–270.

Harsch, K., & Festing, M. (2020). Dynamic talent management capabilities and organizational agility—A qualitative exploration. *Human Resource Management*, 59(1), 43–61.

Hartmann, M. (2003). Nationale oder transnationale Eliten: Europäische Eliten im Vergleich. In S. Hradil & P. Imbusch (Eds.) *Oberschichten? Eliten? Herrschende Klassen* (pp. 273–298). Opladen: Leske und Budrich.

Hegewisch, A., & Larsen, H. H. (1996). Performance management, decentralization and management development: Local government in Europe. *Journal of Management Development*, 15(2), 6–23.

Helmig, B., Michalski, S., & Lauper, P. (2008). Performance management in public & non-profit organisationen. Empirische Ergebnisse zum Teilaspekt performance appraisal. *Zeitschrift Für Personalforschung*, 22(1), 58–82.

Hofstede, G. (1980). Motivation, leadership, and organization: do American theories apply abroad? *Organizational Dynamics*, 9(1), 42–63.

Hofstede, G. (1991). *Cultures and organizations: Software of the mind*. London, UK: McGraw-Hill.

House, R., with Hanges, P. J., Javidan, M., Dorfman, P. W., & Gupta, V. (Eds.) (2004). *Culture, leadership and organizations. The GLOBE study of 62 societies*. Thousand Oaks, CA: Sage.

Huselid, M. A., Becker, B. E., & Beatty, R. W. (2005). *The workforce scorecard, managing human capital to execute strategy*. Boston, MA: Harvard Business Press.

Institut für Mittelstandsforschung (2021). *The German Mittelstand a s a model for success*. Bonn: Institut für Mittelstandsforschung. https://www.bmwk.de/Redaktion/EN/Dossier/sme-policy.html [consulted 30/08/2022].

Invest in France (2022). https://investinfrance.fr/france-ranked-the-worlds-11th-most-innovative-country/, last consulted 13/09/2022.

Iribarne, P. (2003). *Balanced Scorecard et qualité, le couple gagnant*. Paris: AFNOR.

Jantz, B., Christensen, T., & Lægreid, P. (2015). Performance management and accountability: The Welfare Administration Reform in Norway and Germany. *International Journal of Public Administration*, 38(13/14), 947–959.

Jenkins, A., & van der Wijk, G. (1996). Hesitant innovation: The recent evolution of human resources management in France. In Timothy Clark (Ed.) *European human resource management* (pp. 65–92). Oxford: Blackwell.

Kaplan, R., & Norton. D. (1992). The balanced scorecard. Measures that drive performance. *Harvard Business Review*, 70(1), 71–79.

Kaplan, R., & Norton. D. (2006). *Alignment: Using the balanced scorecard to create corporate synergies*. Boston, MA: Harvard Business Press.

Katz, H., & Darbishire, O. (2001). Review symposium. Converging divergences: Worldwide changes in employment systems. *Industrial and Labor Relations Review*. 54(3), 681–716.

Kieser, A., & Kubicek, H. (1992). *Organisation*. 3rd ed. Berlin, New York: Walter de Gruyter.

Klarsfeld, A., & Oiry, E. (Eds.) (2003). *Gérer les compétences: des instruments aux processus : cas d'entreprises et perspectives théoriques*. Paris: Vuibert.

Kroll, A., & Pasha, O. (2021). Managing change and mitigating reform cynicism. *Public Money & Management*, 41(5), 395–403.

Kroll, A., & Proeller, I. (2013). Controlling the control system: Performance information in the German childcare administration. *International Journal of Public Sector Management*, 26(1), 74–85.

Kroll, A., & Vogel, D. (2014). The Psm-leadership fit: A model of performance information use. *Public Administration*, 92(4), 974–991.

Lane, C. (1994). Industrial order: Britain, Germany & France. In Richard Hyman & Anthony Ferner (Eds.) *New frontiers in European industrial relations* (pp. 167–195). Oxford: Blackwell.

Lawrence, P. (1993). Human resource management in Germany. In S. Tyson, P. Lawrence, P. Poirson, L. Manzolini, & C. F. Vicente (Eds.) *Human resource management in Europe* (pp. 25–41). London: Kogan Page Limited.

Lebas, M. (1995). Performance measurement and performance management. *International Journal of Production Economics*, 41(1/3), 23–35.

Lindholm, N. (2000). National culture and performance management in MNC subsidiaries. *International Studies of Management & Organization*, 29(4), 45–66.

Longenecker, C. O., with Sims, Jr., H. P., & Gioia, D. A. (1987). Behind the mask: The politics of employee appraisal, *Academy of Management Executive*, 1(3), 183–193.

Maurice, M., with Sellier, F., & Silvestre, J.-J. (1982). *Politique d'éducation et organisation industrielle en France et en Allemagne*. Paris: Presses Universitaires de France.

McMullin, C. (2021). Challenging the necessity of New Public Governance: Co-production by third sector organizations under different models of public management. *Public Administration*, 99(1), 5–22.

Meysonnier, F. (1994). *Stratégies de gestion des ressources humaines et performance dans les PME –Résultats d'une recherche exploratoire*. Rapport de recherche FR CESREM – CR-94-12.

Morley, M., Murphy, K., Cleveland, J., Heraty, N., & McCarthy, J. (2021). Home and host distal context and performance appraisal in multinational enterprises: A 22 country study. *Human Resource Management*, 60(5), 715–736.

Müller, M. (1999). Unitarism, pluralism and human resource management in Germany. *Management International Review*, special issue. 39(3), 125–144.

Murphy, K., & Cleveland, J. (1991). *Performance appraisal: An organizational perspective*. Boston, MA: Allyn& Bacon.

Nikandrou, I., with Apospori, E., & Papalexandris, N. (2005). Changes in HRM in Europe. A longitudinal comparative study amont 18 European countries. *Journal of European Industrial Training*, 29(7), 541–560.

OECD (n.d.). http://www.oecd.org/

Oechsler, W. (2006). *Personal und Arbeit – Grundlagen des Human Resource Management und der Arbeitgeber-Arbeitnehmer-Beziehungen* (8th ed.). München: Oldenbourg.

Oriot, F., & Misisazek, E. (2004). Technical and organizational barriers hindering the implementation of a balanced scorecard: The Case of a European Space Company. In M. J. Epstein, & J.-F. Manzoni (Eds.) *Performance measurement and management control: Superior organizational performance, Studies in Managerial and Financial Accounting* (Vol. 14, pp. 265–301). Oxford: Elsevier Jai.

Papalexandris, N., & Panayotopoulou, L. (2004). Exploring the mutual interaction of societal culture and human resource management practices; Evidence from 19 countries. *Employee Relations*, 26(5), 495–509.

Peretti, J.-M., & Roussel, P. (Eds.) (2000). *Les Rémunérations. Politiques et pratiques pour les années 2000*, collection Entreprendre. Paris: Vuibert.

Phillips, J. J. with Stone, R. & Phillips, P. (2001). *The human resources scorecard (Improving Human Performance)*. Woburn, MA: Butterworth-Heinemann.

Pieper, R. (1990). Human resource management as a strategic factor. *Human resources management, an international comparison*. Berlin: de Gruyter.

Pudelko, M. (2000a). *Das Personalmanagement in Deutschland, den USA und Japan*. Band 1: Die Bedeutung gesamtgesellschaftlicher Rahmenbedingungen im Wettbewerb der Systeme. Köln: Jörg Saborowski Verlag.

Pudelko, M. (2000b). *Das Personalmanagement in Deutschland, den USA und Japan*. Band 2: Eine systematische und vergleichende Bestandsaufnahme. Köln: Jörg Saborowski Verlag.

Pudelko, M. (2000c). *Das Personalmanagement in Deutschland, den USA und Japan*. Band 3: Wie wir voneinander lernen können. Mit einer empirischen Studie über die 500 größten Unternehmen der drei Länder. Köln: Jörg Saborowski Verlag.

Pudelko, M. (2005). Cross-national learning from best practice and the convergence-divergence debate in HRM. *International Journal of Human Resource Management*, 16(11), 2045–2074.

Pudelko, M. (2006). A comparison of HRM systems in the USA, Japan and Germany in their socio-economic context. *Human Resource Management Journal*, 16(2), 123–153.

Radin, B. (2003). A comparative approach to performance management: Contrasting the experience of Australia, New Zealand, and The United States. *International Journal of Public Administration*, 26(12), 1355–1376.

Ring, M., with Groenewald, H., & Varga von Kibed, G. (2003). "Leadership Evaluation and Development" – die Einführung des LEAD-Konzeptes bei DaimlerChrysler Japan. In W. Dorow & H. Groenewald (Eds.) *Personalwirtschaftlicher Wandel in Japan* (pp. 457–475). Wiesbaden: Gabler.

Rojot, J., (1990). Human resource management in France. In R. Pieper (Ed.) *Human resources management, an international comparison* (pp. 87–107). Berlin: de Gruyter.

Rowold, J., & Kauffeld, S. (2009). Effects of career-related continuous learning on competencies. *Personnel Review*, 38(1), 90–101.

Saglietto, L., & Thomas, C. (1998). Gestion des ressources humaines et enjeux de l'économie post-industrielle : L'histoire d'une reconquête de la performance fondée sur la responsabilisation et la confiance. *Revue de gestion des ressources humaines*, 28, 15–25.

Sanders, W. M. G., & Tuschke, A. (2007). The adoption of institutionally contested organizational practices: The emergence of stock option pay in Germany. *Academy of Management Journal*, 50, 33–56.

Schneider, S. (1988). *National vs. corporate culture: Implications for human resource management*. Fontainebleau: Insead.

Schuler, R. S., with Jackson, S. E., & Luo, Y. (2004). *Managing human resources in cross-border alliances*. London/New York: Routledge.

Sire, B., & Tremblay, M. (1996). Perspective sur les politiques de rémunération des dirigeants en France. *Revue Française de Gestion*, No. 111, Nov./Dec, 230–238.

Sire, B., & Tremblay, M. (1998). Éclatement des politiques de GRH selon l'espace culturel: Une comparaison Internationale des politiques de rémunération In J. Allouche & B. Sire (Eds.) *Ressources Humaines : Une gestion éclatée* (pp. 335–352). Paris: Economica.

Streeck, W. (1997). German capitalism: Does it exist? Can it survive? *New Political Economy* 2(2), 237–257.

Streeck, W. (2001). High Equality, low activity: The contribution of the social welfare system to the stability of the German collective bargaining regime. *Industrial and Labor Relations Review*. 54(3), 698–706.

Tahvanainen, M. (1998). Expatriate *Performance Management*. Helsinki: Helsinki School of Economics Press.

Tempel, A. (2001). *The cross-national transfer of human resource management practices in German and British multinational companies*. München/Mering: Hampp Verlag.

UNECE (2007, 17 February). UN-*ECE Operational Activities: SME – Their role in foreign trade*. Available http://www.unece.org/indust/sme/foreignt.html

van der Klink, M., & Mulder, M. (1995). Human resource development and staff flow policy in Europe. In Anne-Wil Harzing & Joris van Ruysseveldt (Eds.) *International human resource management* (pp. 156–178). London: Sage.

Verweire, K., & van den Berghe, L. (2004). *Integrated performance management – A guide to strategy implementation*. London: Sage.

Vitols, S., with Casper, C., Soskice, D., & Woolcock, S. (1997). *Corporate governance in large British and German companies: Comparative institutional advantage or competing for best practice*. London: Anglo-German Foundation for the Study of Industrial Society.

Wächter, H., & Müller-Camen, M. (2002). Co-determination and strategic integration in German firms. *Human Resource Management Journal*, 12(3), 76–87.

Warner, M., & Campbell, A. (1993). German management. In D. J. Hickson (Ed.) *Management in Western Europe: Society, culture and organization in twelve nations* (pp. 89–108). Berlin: de Gruyter.

Wächter, H., & Stengelhofen, T. (1992). Human resource management in a unified Germany. *Employee Relations*, *14*(4), 21–37.

Wegrich, K. (2015). Accommodating a Foreign Object: Federalism, coordination and performance management in the reform of German employment administration. *Public Management Review*, 17(7), 940–959.

Weiss, J. (2020). Managing performance and strategy: Managerial practices in German local governments. *Public Performance & Management Review*, 43(5), 1129–1149.

WIPO (2022). World intellectual property organization: *Global Innovation Index*. https://www.wipo.int/global_innovation_index/en/2021/ [consulted 10/09/2022].

Yahiaoui, D., Nakhle, S. F., & Farndale, E. (2021). Culture and performance appraisal in multinational enterprises: Implementing French headquarters' practices in Middle East and North Africa subsidiaries. *Human Resource Management*, 60(5), 771–785.

Performance Management Systems in Turkey

Gaye Özçelik, Zeynep Aycan and Serap Keleş

Chapter 11

TURKEY IN BRIEF: SOCIO-ECONOMIC AND POLITICAL BACKGROUND

Located at the crossroads of civilizations bridging the East and the West, Turkey has been an emerging economy, attracting significant attention for its geo-political and strategic importance. The country is classified among the 20 emerging and growth-leading economies (G20 major economies) and is the 23rd-largest in the world by nominal gross domestic product (GDP) and the 11th-largest by purchasing power parity (PPP). As of September 2022, Turkey has a population of 86.4 million (Worldometer, 2022) and is considered among the world's leading producers of agricultural products, textiles, motor vehicles, transportation equipment, construction materials, consumer electronics and home appliances. The country's political system shifted from a parliamentary system to a presidential system in 2017. Today, Turkey is known to be a presidential representative democracy and a constitutional republic.

After the deep economic crisis in February 2001, and September 11th events, the single-party government had taken

DOI: 10.4324/9781003306849-11

strong structural and social steps for the recovery of the economy in 2002 which enabled the country to elevate its outlook in the following years. For instance, the economy witnessed a drop in inflation – which was as high as 110.2 percent in the early 1980s – to almost single-digit around 2007. However, considering recent years, unexpected challenges experienced globally, such as the outbreak of the COVID-19 pandemic and its lasting for more than 2 years, the rising energy prices, and the war between Russia and Ukraine and global food shortage have led up to rising inflation rates all around the globe as well as Turkey. Nevertheless, amidst the COVID-19 pandemic, Turkey experienced an economic recovery of 11 percent in 2021 (Butler and Küçükgöçmen, 2021). In this respect, looking back to the very recent times, due to the worldwide soaring prices, the economic achievements in Turkey have been overshadowed making inflation rates rise as high as 80.2 percent in August 2022 (Trading Economics, 2022). Data from Reuters have shown that the annual growth in the first quarter of 2022 was revised to 7.5 percent from 7.3 percent (Devranoğlu and Küçükgöçmen, 2022).

HRM AND PERFORMANCE MANAGEMENT SYSTEM IN TURKEY: 2000s AND ONWARDS

The development and application of human resource management (HRM) practices in general have become more widespread in Turkey for about a decade and a half or two. This section focuses on the latest developments in the field of HRM regarding the emergence of the strategic view of HRM function, advancements in organizational HRM practices, as well as contemporary trends and changing approaches to PMS in Turkey

With the accelerated change and complexities of the business environment, such as intense competition, technological advancements, the emergence and development of artificial intelligence (AI), availability or knowledge-based workforce and talent, diversity issues, many large-sized enterprises (LSEs) in the Turkish business market have recognized HRM departments playing a key strategic role for achieving and sustaining competitive advantage. (Cranet, 2017; Gürbüz and Mert, 2011; Gürol, Wolff, and Berkin, 2011). A majority of large-sized companies have moved improvements in aligning their human resource (HR) functions with the mission, vision and strategies of the organizations. The HRM perspective of the latest decade required HRM to hold a strategic partnership role in the organizations and thereby coordinating many HRM functions (i.e. recruitment, selection, training, performance, compensation) and elevating the organizational strategies by attracting and retaining qualified and talented workforce.

In the meantime, there is a need to mention the differentiated HR approach and the HRM practices between small and medium-sized enterprises (SMEs) and those of LSEs. SMEs in Turkey represent 99.8 percent of all registered entities in the country and comprise 73 percent of its workforce, constituting a vital role in economic growth and employment creation (TOBB, 2020). SMEs generally implement HRM practices in a different way than LSEs do. For instance, training activities are generally executed via on-the-job training, which is not necessarily based on formal training needs analysis (Çetinel et al., 2008). Several SMEs are more likely to value performance appraisal and conduct job analysis only if there is a requirement and therefore are found to take a rather disoriented approach to these practices.

However, some national LSEs and multinational organizations with foreign capital in the Turkish business are more likely to adopt North American–based HRM practices (Tüzüner, 2014: 439). In essence, the basic motivation for Turkey's move from 'Personnel Affairs' or 'Personnel Department' to 'HR management' was the adoption of the American model (Tüzüner, 2014). This trend has continued to dominate HRM practices as well as performance management systems even until recent years.

As the main subject of discussion of this chapter, while some research and data on performance management systems (PMSs) are evident, access to a comprehensive set of findings about this specific and fundamental practice that feeds other HRM practices is still not abundant. Nevertheless, the most recent findings available on PMSs in Turkey will be explained. Longitudinal survey data from the Cranfield Research Report (2017), as well as available scholarly research findings on performance management (PM), will be helpful in understanding the developments of PMSs in recent years in Turkey. These studies include findings on some aspects influenced by PMSs, including performance appraisal, training and development, career management and performance-reward contingency.

CONTEXTUAL FACTORS DRIVING HRM AND PMSS IN TURKEY
Cultural Context

According to Hofstede's (1980) well-known research findings, Turkey was situated in the cluster of high-power-distance and collectivist countries. However, subsequent studies have reported that the socio-cultural environment of Turkey is changing towards being less collectivistic (e.g., Aycan et al., 2001; Karabat and Calis, 2014), somewhat less hierarchical (Aycan et al., 2000; Karabat and Calis, 2014) and less uncertainty avoiding (e.g., Kabasakal, Dastmalchian, Karacay, and Bayraktar, 2012). In addition, the GLOBE (Global Leadership and Organizational Behavior Effectiveness) Project also demonstrates that Turkey is below the world average on performance and future orientation. Another salient and still relevant cultural characteristic of Turkey is paternalism (see Pagda 2019).

Over the past decade and a half, there have been major changes in the political, economic and social aspects of Turkey, which might have altered the national cultural dynamics of the country as well as the management perspectives in organizations. Recent research has aimed at identifying whether macro-environmental changes lead to differences in cultural values which might give rise to different management styles. The main motivation is to provide any clues about the impact of culture on the management of organizations (i.e., Beydilli and Kurt, 2020). As one of the last comprehensive series of studies, the GLOBE Project, conducted in 1995 and 2019, aimed to identify how different cultural characteristics can impact leadership, management and approaches to performance on the basis of nine cultural dimensions namely, performance orientation, uncertainty avoidance, power distance, institutional collectivism, in-group collectivism, assertiveness, gender egalitarianism, future orientation and humane orientation (Alipour, 2019; House et al., 2004).

A crucial premise of the GLOBE study is to take into consideration the Eastern beliefs, cultures and values which have largely been ignored in other research settings before the GLOBE Project (Kabasakal et al., 2012). In this respect, the project involved the

Middle East as an additional cluster of countries in which Turkey is embedded. The results of the survey in 2019 have found that scores with regard to *uncertainty avoidance* (the extent to which a society is looking for orderliness, consistency, structure, formalized procedures and laws), *humane orientation* (the extent to which societies appreciate their members for being fair, altruistic, friendly, generous, caring and kind to others), *future orientation* (the extent to which a society tends to be averse to risk-taking and opportunistic decision-making) have been relatively low and these scores did not significantly differ from those in 1995. In the meantime, Turkish society has been found to have a moderate level of *institutional collectivism* (collective distribution of resources and collective action). The country shows collectivist examples in a couple of areas but not all as mentioned in previous Hofstede's (1980) study. For example, co-worker relationships were found to be individualistic in corporate settings. However, sharing of material resources, feeling of involvement in others' lives and susceptibility to social influence have been evident. Turkish society is more likely to pursue a collectivist tendency in the areas of self-presentation and sharing of outcomes with their colleagues. There is a strong sense of nationalism but a low level of trust in society which can be attributed to the reduced level of trusting others, group solidarity and association with others in teamwork in institutional settings.

In the meantime, Turkey has had one of the highest *in-group collectivism* scores (the degree to which individuals express pride, loyalty and cohesiveness in their organizations or families). A high level of trust in family members and mutual trust within the family are imperative in both rural and urban families. In Turkish society, children are taught to support and help their family members, which creates interdependence among family. The comparison of 1995 and 2019 scores demonstrated that there is no major shift in Turkish culture (Pagda, 2019).

Considering *power distance*, Turkey has been found to have a high score in line with previous cross-cultural studies (Hofstede, 2011, 2001). Power distance refers to the degree to which employees are free to express their ideas and disagree with their supervisors and obey them (House et al., 2004). In organizational settings, power distance was defined with representations of very steep hierarchical organizational structures (Trompenaars and Hampden-Turner, 1998). In Turkish society, power and resources are allocated according to hierarchy rather than an egalitarian distribution. In a similar vein, Aydınlı (2010) found that banking organizations in Turkey are more likely to have complex organizational structures which are representations of hierarchy and the existential inequality between lower and higher organizational levels.

Many of the organizations in the Turkish business, in particular LSEs and multinationals with foreign capital, have tried establishing a performance culture (Tower Watson Consulting, 2012) or at least using some type of system (Aguinis, 2013). They are more likely to put efforts to implement the classical proverbial performance management system as an integrative process comprising goal setting, clarification of expectations, coaching, performance appraising and providing resources and assistance, regular performance reviews and rewards for performance (Süzer, 2004; Tüzüner, 2014). Similarly, most multinational Turkish companies aim to establish accountability through ever-present performance management processes through which both quantifiable objectives and competencies of employees are evaluated via formal people reviews (Bigan, Decan, and Korkmaz, 2017). These organizations determine their KPIs (key performance indicators) to set their goals, achieve strategic goals and evaluate employees vis-à-vis the goals. The outputs of these appraisals have provided input, especially for their reward accomplishments, training and development, and shape top management decisions on their career mobility. Bigan et al. (2017) have further emphasized the crucial need for these organizations to embrace and celebrate cultural diversity, strive to create an inclusive environment and strengthen performance in order to become among the world-class companies in talent attraction, engagement and retention.

In the meantime, the fact that personal relationships play an important role in Turkish culture giving rise to avoidance of confrontation, the implementation of valid, reliable and fair PMSs still might pose an important challenge (Aguinis, Joo, and Gottfredson, 2012). From another perspective, the way the PMSs are implemented in organizations has been found to vary due to the assumptions and values of managers about their employees no matter how established the organizational systems and rules are (Keles and Aycan, 2011). In their study, Keles and Aycan (2011) found that managers who held positive beliefs about employees (i.e., they are goal-oriented) are more likely to implement structured and participative performance management practices and value high performance orientations. In the meantime, managers who held paternalistic and collectivist values were less likely to consider employees to be goal-oriented and proactive. They were held responsible towards others only to fulfill their obligations. Managers tended to implement non-participative PM practices (i.e., employees' opinions are not asked based on the assumption that they expected close guidance and supervision). The study has its implications such that the successful implementation of PMSs varies by the values held by those managers who put these systems into practice.

Furthermore, these values become espoused in time, and not only the managers but the employees as well develop beliefs about the extent to which their manager appreciates their performance and their work. One recent in-depth study with a multinational subsidiary operating in Turkey by Özçelik and Uyargil (2019) found that the alignment of perceptions and interpretations of performance management as well as other HRM practices among employees, managers, as well as HR professionals, would appear to indicate an internally coherent and integrated system of HR practices from the perspective of different workforce groups. Employees will develop their own perceptions and evaluations about the organization's HRM practices through the managers' attitudes and behaviours (i.e., employees take initiative, are goal-oriented) while implementing these practices. For instance, with positive managerial values, employees are found to perceive HR practices as fair, providing growth and development opportunities and enabling employee participation (Nishii et al., 2008; Piening et al., 2014). In this sense, it is also necessary to build an attributional alignment about the way HR practices are implemented across different employee levels. In this regard, establishing a perfect PM process certify neither its successful implementation nor a positive interpretation of it by all members of the organization.

Gaye Özçelik et al.

Institutional Context

PMSs serving as important "feeders" (Aguinis, 2013) to other HRM practices have made great progress regarding its formal development and implementation in the recent decade or two in a developing country like Turkey (Turan, 2021). One of the most important factors and a driving force that influence the development and implementation of performance appraisal in Turkey took place around the legal framework, namely the Labour Act Law No 4857, which took effect in 2003. The law requires that employers evaluate employees' performances systematically and objectively because in the case of termination of any employment contract by the employer, the reason for termination must be clearly stated, and any legal rights arising from the termination must be paid to the employee on the date of termination. If any employer terminates the employment contract of any employee based on their performance, it is essential that the employee's defence is taken, and if necessary, the person is given a period of time to monitor one's performance. For this reason, in performance-based terminations, the PMs that form the basis for the termination must be based on concrete and measurable data. PMs based on subjective evaluations cannot form the basis for the termination of the employment contract. Termination of the employment contract based on performance evaluations that are far from objective measurements enables employees to apply to the judicial remedy with the request for invalidity of the termination and reinstatement which can lead the court to decide to re-instate the employee (Erdem, 2015). Therefore, the performance management system of a company has become a legal platform for both employees and employers.

The continuously rising dynamic and competitive national and international markets and the accelerated shift to an industrialized and service-based economy, an increased importance of the country's geopolitical position and its young and dynamic workforce require Turkish business organizations to be more profit-oriented and maintain competitiveness locally as well as globally. Turkish organizations facing these challenges eventually realize the critical role HRM, as well as PM and development, plays for their survival in fierce global competition.

There are also some organizational-level variables that are related to the use of effective PMSs. The private sector accounts some 80 percent of Turkey's economy in which the majority is composed of family-owned SMEs. Due to the dominance of informal family norms (rather than institutional norms) in these family-owned organizations, basic HRM functions such as PMSs cannot be implemented properly (Karartı, 2014). A key controversy is going on between top management and the HR department as to the former focusing on work output and the latter aiming at employee development and satisfaction. For example, in these family-owned organizations, a family-like environment and relationship-oriented organizational norms may result in subjective and less formal PMSs rather than more objective and formal ones that aim at identifying and differentiating good versus poor performers. It is very difficult to replace the traditional management approach in these family-owned businesses with the modern one involving a PMS. Hence, in comparison to private-sector organizations and multinational corporations (MNCs), SMEs and family-owned organizations are more likely to implement traditional stand-alone performance appraisal rather than an integrative PMS (Aycan and Yavuz, 2008).

Cranfield Human Resource Management Survey of 2017

The comprehensive and longitudinal survey carried out by Cranfield Network on Comparative Human Resource Management (Cranet) provides data on HRM practices across the world that are collected by an international team of collaborators from top business schools and academic institutions (www.cranet.org). Cranet aims at providing a coherent and accurate picture of international and comparative HRM. Turkey has been included in a number of waves, collected in 1992, 1995, 2000, 2005 and 2017, in the Cranet survey. PM data were collected from mainly private-sector organizations in Turkey operating in various sectors. It should be noted that the profile of organizations that agreed to participate in this survey does not represent Turkish business organizations in general. In the meantime, unfortunately the survey did not involve those performance management-related questions in 2017, and therefore, the findings regarding PMSs were highly scarce concerning the 2017 survey. The report generally presents organizational reports of performance data to identify training needs and making pay decisions, as well as the degree to which training was effective and some career development methods that can be considered beneficial for individual's performance development. The available findings are discussed here.

According to the findings for 2017, more than 90 percent of the organizations in Turkey benefit from appraisal data to identify training needs. The interesting finding is that this result (about 90 percent) is much higher than the average of EU countries (74 percent), non-EU European countries (72 percent) and non-European countries (80 percent). This is an interesting finding for Turkey when compared to the survey held in 2000.

Of the respondent organizations from Turkey, 43.6 percent report that their organizations assessed their performance before and immediately after training. Whereas, 50.9 percent of those have mentioned that employees' job performance have been assessed a few months after training. In addition, 80 percent of those organizations reported that employees receive informal feedback from their managers. The interesting finding is that informal feedback from employees (83.8 percent) is highly common which might indicate the changing nature of the workforce who are less prone to criticism but open feedback. The findings of subordinate and peer evaluation being promising might bear positive implications for performance appraisal as well.

Regarding the development methods which are crucial for career management as well as performance development, a majority of the participating organizations reported that employees receive coaching (73.5 percent) and mentoring (83.8 percent), making Turkey's score way higher than those EU countries and non-EU European counties average. The findings about subordinate and peer evaluation were also promising. The percentage of organizations that reported the use of subordinate and peer evaluation tripled in 5 years and increased to 38 percent, although it is still far from being at the desired level. In addition, the findings from participating organizations in Turkey show that 72.1 percent prefer development centres, making it to be the highest rate when compared to average of EU-countries

(35.9 percent), non-EU European countries (43.2 percent) and non-European countries (41.2 percent).

Considering performance-based pay, 69 percent of the participating organizations in private organizations and mixed sectors in Turkey report that performance results were used in performance-related pay. When bonuses based on individual and team goals are examined, 68 percent of the organizations report that they implement bonus payments based on individual goal accomplishments. In the meantime, the rate of organizations which reward employees via bonuses based on team goal accomplishment is 59 percent. The rate of use of bonuses based on team-based pay is found to be much higher than average rates of EU countries (43 percent), non-EU European countries (45 percent) and non-European countries (45 percent). The findings particularly regarding bonuses based on team performance can indicate the collectivistic nature of Turkish society in support of maintaining group harmony (Aycan, 2005; Pagda 2019). Another remarkable implication can be that the use of an integrated PMS seems to gain prevalence in Turkey.

Organizations in Turkey have been likely to show particular improvements in utilizing the data drawn from performance appraisals for training needs assessments and investing in training and development activities. Furthermore, the findings regarding the adoption and acceptance of informal feedback from managers as well as peers might bear positive implications of PMSs, enabling employee development in the organizations. Although businesses in Turkey have quite a long way to go to improve their PMSs, all the developments can promise hope for organizations to gain and sustain their competitive advantage by adding value to members of the workforce and enhancing their complex skills, thereby retaining talent.

PMSS: FUTURE WAYS FORWARD

In the very recent years, not only Turkey as well as the whole world have been going through volatile technological (i.e., increased digitalization in particular after the onset of COVID-19) enhancements, slowing down of the economy and political crises as well as environmental problems (i.e., climate change) which brings out serious challenges for organizations to be able to foresee the future and determine specific business goals as the environment is currently hardly allowing them to do so. In particular to the HRM function, all these developments force organizations to change their approach to any prevailing practices and processes in PMS for the fact that it becomes harder day by day for enterprises to stay with the goals determined without revising them, cascading them down to departments, units and employees and appraising employees' performance against these goal accomplishments. Therefore, organizations are looking for ways to be more agile and creative.

What comes along with these changes for today and the future is a shift toward people-oriented PMSs from a profit-oriented one and maintaining the welfare of all parties involved in an organizational relationship. We see that PM has actually long been in the way to be redesigned as early as 2002 by Brian Jensen. An important development in this area took place when Jack Welch, the CEO of General Electric, left the company in 2005. The company quietly abandoned its system of grading employee performance because the system had increased internal competition and started to damage cooperation. Another significant abandonment of the traditional PMS was due to the agile practices led by the company Adobe which began to run frequent regular review meetings rather than yearly administrations. Therefore, annual performance reviews have begun to be replaced by more frequent informal meetings between managers and employees for more than a decade (Cappelli and Tavis, 2016). In fact, we are experiencing a period of increasing unhappiness with the traditional performance process. Reflexes such as acting more agile, self-organizing, determining one's own direction and responding instantly to customer feedback and changes in needs are now in conflict with the traditional performance evaluation process that is conducted once a year. Goals are short term and tend to change frequently in the process (Buckingham and Goodall, 2015; Cappelli and Tavis, 2016). For many businesses, the ability to innovate quickly and act in alignment with what change provides will be a serious competitive advantage now and then. It has become difficult to evaluate the past or present performance of employees because companies do not have clear annual periods as they used to in the recent past.

Global companies like Intel, Google, Twitter and LinkedIn are the very first organizations that started implementing an innovative management system called OKR (objectives and key results) with the aim of staying agile. OKRs were invented and promoted by Andrew Grove, one of the founders and the former CEO of Intel, in 1968. OKR is a management system that aligns the company's goals with each employee's goals and sets a clear focus for the long term (Grove, 1995). OKRs are different from KPIs which are standalone metrics indicating the degree to which employees make progress. On the other hand, objective describes those measurable goals that teams set. OKRs emerge as the driving force that produces tangible results aiming for a company's development. Because it motivates both the company and the employees to achieve their goals. In addition, the OKR approach offers the opportunity to monitor their progress with measurable results. Today, many successful companies such as Google, Intel, Linkedin, ING Bank and many others are using the OKR management method. The OKR system focuses on continuous and timely feedback which means end-of-year or closing-period evaluations tend to be abandoned.

In alignment with the technological disruptions, breakthrough innovations, changing stakeholders (i.e., consumers, employees) expectations and decision-making processes accompanied by the aforementioned shifts in the global business world, many LSEs in Turkey have been questioning, discussing as well as looking for ways to move beyond the so-called 'conventional' PMSs to a 'new generation' PM approach. Examples in Turkey stand out with the practices and discussions of organizations and professional business enterprises via their summits and meetings. The main motive behind this shift has been the agile business world which forces many business enterprises to establish systems that can better see the future (Harvard Business Review Turkey, 2020). With the rising young workforce, there has been a wide necessity to tear down the 'silo' mentality of the organizations via enabling transparent cross-company communication and team collaboration, facilitating internal workforce mobility, employee ownership of responsibilities, skills development and advancement opportunities which can lead to greater employee engagement (Harvard Business Review Turkey, 2022; YGA, 2021). It has become important for organizational leaders to both set objectives and enable employees to figure out their milestones that indicate how they can accomplish each objective. Companies have also been

Gaye Özçelik et al.

focusing on leaders to make skill alignments across management, take a visionary perspective and change the organizational culture in alignment with their purpose. In this respect, a culture of continuous feedback and development has started to gain some importance. A considerable number of LSEs have figured out the importance of the compatibility of the leader's visionary approach and competencies of managers as well as the vitality of seeing the process as a culture change, supporting it with new technology and training employees to achieve new competencies. One of the largest Turkish-origin international organizations, Koç Holding,[1] has been one of group of pioneering companies that extensively worked on the new-generation PMSs by taking a wholistic organizational change management approach. The main pillars that enabled the success of the new PMSs were involving all people in the process; listening and understanding their needs, expectations and skill requirements; and supporting them with continuous training and communication (Harvard Business Review Turkey, 2022).

Recently, the concept of customer experience has been already on the corporate agenda (SabancıDx, 2020). In today's experience economy, leaders recognize that in order for an elevated customer encounters, the practices focusing on employee experience – the culmination of every interaction and touchpoint that an employee encounters in a given company – should be improved. For instance, according to Randstadt Employer Brand Research Global Report (2022), more than half of the participants in the research ask for a positive and pleasant work atmosphere. Airbnb, the first company in the world to appoint a global head of employee experience, has now been followed by many large companies. What is becoming more visible day by day is the reengineering of all HR processes with a focus on experience and the appointment of "Employee Experience Managers" at different levels by leading organizations both their headquarters and regional organisations which is as well a rising common policy by the large business organization in Turkey Many LSEs such as Apple Turkey, L'Oréal Turkey, Turkcell,[2] Koç Holding and HepsiBurada[3] are implementing various employee experience projects such as office-free working, 6 weeks paternity leave in line with the principles of equality and inclusion, provision of 'welcome box' to new employees (Çalışan Deneyim, 2021). The main motivation for this new initiative is to empower people and to work under an interactive and a development-oriented context and thereby create a positive employee experience.

As can be seen from the previous sections, a number of scholarly studies conducted in Turkey portrayed the current situation in private-sector organizations. However, almost no study investigated the PMSs in public-sector organizations. Most large-scale private-sector organizations and MNCs adopt Western-style PMSs. Despite limited data, there is evidence that public-sector organizations in Turkey are also becoming aware of the importance of effective PMSs. Nevertheless, recent positive developments have been taking place in Turkey, including scientific and technological improvements and the changing nature of market structures. The establishment of the Presidency of the Republic of Turkey Human Resource Office[4] is an apparent development for the public sector, in particular. The HR Office aims to create projects for enabling the improvement of HR in accordance with Turkey's vision, objectives and priorities. It aspires to be an important catalyst for such organizations allowing them to acknowledge the vitality of executing people-oriented HRM practices and thereby achieve and maintain their competitive advantage. This development will also reinforce the initiatives of domestic private-sector organizations (i.e., SMEs and other large Turkish domestic enterprises) towards building and implementing more effective HRM and practices.

In sum, Turkey as well as the world have been undergoing significant transformations in economic, political, technological and environmental aspects. While PMSs used to be a difficult practice for countries like Turkey defined by a collectivist, high-power-distance and paternalistic culture, it seems that the traditional methods to assess and rate employee performance are losing their emphasis. The new reflections in PMSs (i.e., increased focus on employee experience, involvement and taking initiative to handle agile work requirements) necessitates more frequent, regular and open communication and feedback sessions among employees and managers as well as peers and other stakeholders. Although MNCs and corporate LSEs can again take the lead for such implementations, the remaining majority of SMEs and other domestic Turkish organizations may lag behind in this regard. The new paradigm poses yet another challenge for enterprises and

HR professionals in the Turkish cultural context to clearly articulate and explain these changes and what lies behind them to the managers as well as employees.

NOTES

1 Koç Holding AS is **Turkey's leading investment holding company**. and Koç Group is Turkey's largest industrial and services group in terms of revenues, exports, number of employees, taxes paid and market capitalization. It operates through the following segments: Energy, Automotive, Consumer Durables, Finance, and Other. The Energy segment operates in refinery, fuel distribution, LPG distribution, power generation, natural gas and other industries. The Automotive segment operates in various industries such as passenger cars, commercial vehicles, farm tractors and defence. The Consumer Durables segment involves white goods and consumer electronics. The Finance segment engages in banking, leasing, insurance, real estate investment trust, pension funds, factoring, brokerage, asset management and consumer finance activities. The Other segment includes other lines of business, which include food production, food production distribution, retailing, tourism, marine operations, information technology, and ship and yacht construction. The company was founded by Vehbi Koç on December 6, 1963, and is headquartered in Istanbul, Turkey.
2 A converged telecommunication and technology services provider, founded and headquartered in Turkey. It serves its customers with voice, data, TV and value-added consumer and enterprise services on mobile and fixed networks. Mobile communication in Turkey began when Turkcell commenced operations in February 1994.
3 One of the greatest marketplace organization in Turkey leading the development and digital transformation of the e-commerce sector in Turkey providing 130 million types of products in 32 categories to our customers.
4 Presidency of the Republic of Turkey Human Resource Office, https:// www.cbiko.gov.tr/en/institutional/presidential-decree-no-1-organisation-of-the-presidency, Retrieved on September 15, 2022.

REFERENCES

Aguinis, H. (2013). *Performance Management* (3rd ed.). Upper Saddle River, NJ: Pearson Prentice Hall.
Aguinis, H., Joo, H., & Gottfredson, R.K. (2012). Performance management universals: Think globally and act locally, *Business Horizons*, 55(4), 385–392.
Alipour, A. (2019). The conceptual difference really matters: Hofstede vs GLOBE's uncertainty avoidance and the risk-taking behavior of firms. *Cross Cultural & Strategic Management*. Published online ahead of print doi:10.1108/CCSM-04-2019-0084.
Aycan, Z. (2001). Human resource management in Turkey: Current issues and future challenges. *International Journal of Manpower*, 22(3), 252–260.
Aycan, Z. (2005). The interface between cultural and institutional /structural contingencies in human resource management. *International Journal of Human Resource Management*, 16(7), 1083–1119.
Aycan, Z., Kanungo, R., Mendonca, M., Yu, K., Deller, J., Stahl, G., & Kurshid, A. (2000). Impact of culture on human resource management practices: A 10-country comparison. *Applied Psychology*, 49(1), 192–221.

Aycan, Z., & Yavuz, S. (2008). Performance management in Turkey. In A. Varma, P.S. Budhwar, & A. DeNisi (Eds.), *Performance Management Systems: A Global Perspective* (1st ed.). Routledge. https://doi.org/10.4324/9780203885673.

Aydınlı, A. (2010). Converging human resource management: A comparative analysis of Hungary and Turkey. *The International Journal of Human Resource Management*, 21(9), 1490–1511. doi:10.1080/09585192.2010.488453.

Beydilli, E.T., & Kurt, M. (2020). Comparison of management styles of local and foreign hotel chains in Turkey: A cultural perspective. *Tourism Management*, 79, 104018.

Bigan, I., Decan, S., & Korkmaz, B. (2017). How Turkish companies can become global successes. *Mc Kinsey& Company*, 6, 1–6. Retrieved on September 17, 2022, https://www.mckinsey.com

Buckingham, M., & Goodall, A. (2015). Reinventing performance management system. *Harvard Business Review*, 93(4), 40–50.

Butler, D., & Küçükgöçmen, A. (2021). Turkey's economy boomed 11% last year, most in a decade. Retrieved on July 24, 2022, https://www.reuters.com/markets/asia/turkish-economic-growth-surges-11-last-year-expected-2022-02-28/

Calışan Deneyim (2021). Öne Çıkan Çalışan Deneyimi Projeleri (Öne Çıkan Çalışan Deneyimi Projeleri). Retrieved on October 20, 2022, https://www.calisandeneyimi.io/

Cappelli, P., & Tavis, A. (2016). The performance management revolution. *Harvard Business Review*, 94(10), 58–67.

Çetinel, F., Yolal, M., & Emeksiz, M. (2008). Human resources management in small- and medium-sized hotels in Turkey. *Journal of Human Resources in Hospitality & Tourism*, 8(1), 43–63.

Cranet. (2017). *International executive report 2017, Cranet survey on comparative human resource management*. Cranfield, UK: Cranet-Cranfield University.

Devranoğlu and Küçükgöçmen (2022). Turkey's economy grew 7.6% in Q2 driven by domestic demand, exports. Retrieved on July 12, 2022, https://www.euronews.com/next/2022/09/01/turkey-economy-gdp

Erdem, H. (2015). Termination of an employee's contract due to poor performance, HR Dergi. Retrieved September 21, 2022, https://hrdergi.com/is-sozlesmesinin-performans-dusuklugu-nedeniyle-feshi.

Grove, A. (1995). *High Output Management*, New York: Vintage.

Gürbüz, S., & Mert, I.S. (2011). Impact of the strategic human resource management on organizational performance: Evidence from Turkey. *The International Journal of Human Resource Management*, 22(8), 1803–1822.

Gürol, Y., Wolff, R.A., & Berkin, E.E. (2011). E-HRM in Turkey: A case study. In Information Resources Management Association (Ed.), *Encyclopedia of e-business development and management in the global economy* (Chapter 6.4, pp. 1633–1634). Hershey, PA: IGI Global. DOI: 10.4018/978-1-60960-587-2.ch604.

Harvard Business Review Turkey (02.07.2020). "Agility Panel", You Tube. https://youtu.be/DLaEuxY65CY.

Harvard Business Review Turkey, 2022 (19.09.2022). "Gelenekselden Geleceğe Performans Kültüründe Değişim" (Changing Performance Culture from Traditional to Future), You Tube. https://youtu.be/gZGLBzeqNY8.

Hofstede, G. (2001). *Cultural consequences*. Thousand Oaks, CA: SAGE.

Hofstede, G. (2011). Dimensionalizing cultures: The Hofstede model in context. *Online Readings in Psychology and Culture*, 2, 8. http://dx.doi.org/10.9707/2307-0919.1014.

House, R. J., Hanges, P. J., Javidan, M., Dorfman, P. W., & Gupta, V. (Eds.). (2004). *Culture, leadership, and organizations: The GLOBE study of 62 societies*. Thousand Oaks, CA: SAGE.

Kabasakal, H., Dastmalchian, A., Karacay, G., & Bayraktar, S. (2012). Leadership and culture in the MENA region: An analysis of the GLOBE project. *Journal of World Business*, 47, 519–529. DOI: 10.1016/j.jwb.2012.01.005.

Gaye Özçelik et al.

Karabat, B., & Calis, S. (2014). Changing Face of performance appraisal in Turkey: A research within the scope of international studies. *International Business Research*, 7(11), 117–125.

Kararti, T. (2014, March). *Convergence or divergence? Analysis of human resource practices in SME Turkey* (MPRA Paper No. 54389). Munich Personal RePEc Archive. https://mpra.ub.uni-muenchen.de/54389/1/MPRA_paper_54389.pdf

Keles, S., & Aycan, Z. (2011). The relationship of managerial values and assumptions with performance management in Turkey: Understanding within culture variability. *International Journal of Human Resource Management*, 22, 1–17. 10.1080/09585192.2011.599952.

Nishi, L.H., Lepak, D.P., & Schneider, B. (2008). Employee attributions about the 'why' of HR practices: Their effects on employee attitudes and behaviours, and customer satisfaction. *Personnel Psychology*, 61, 503–545.

Özçelik, G., & Uyargil, C.B. (2019). Performance management systems: task-contextual dilemma owing to the involvement of the psychological contract and organizational citizenship behavior. *European Management Review*, 16(2), 347–362.

Pagda, Z. (2019). The replication of the GLOBE study in Turkey: Understanding the effects of social, economical, and political changes on cultural dimensions and leadership ideals: A mixed methods study (Dissertations, University of San Diego), 159. https://digital.sandiego.edu/dissertations/159.

Piening, E.P., Baluch, A.M., & Ridder, H.-G. (2014). Mind the intended-implemented Gap: understanding employees' perceptions of HRM. *Human Resource Management*, 53(4), 545–567.

Randstadt (2022). Employer Brand Research Global Report. Retrieved on September 25, 2022, https://workforceinsights.randstad.com/hubfs/REBR%202022/rebr%20 2022%20global%20report.pdf?hsLang=nl.

SabancıDx (May 22, 2020). "The Day After Tomorrow" - Serdar Turan 'Yeni Dünya, Yeni Düzen, Yeni Liderlik, You Tube. https://www.youtube.com/watch?v=N_cB0CNMLYM.

Süzer, H.D. (2004, October). A'lari sirkete cek ve B ve C'yi gelistir. (Recruit As and develop Bs and Cs). *Capital Monthly Business and Economy Journal*. Retrieved from the World Wide Web on August 29, 2006. http://www.capital.com.tr/haber. aspx?HBR_KOD=1113

TOBB, (The Union of Chambers and Commodity Exchanges of Turkey) (2020). SMEs of Turkey. Retrieved on June 12, 2022. https://tobb.org.tr/KobiArastirma/Documents/ SMEs%20of%20Turkey%20Report%202020.pdf

Towers Watson Consulting. (2012). Türkiye Işgücü Araştırması Raporu. Retrieved on September 15, 2022, https://www.wtwco.com/tr-TR/

Trading Economics. (2022). Turkey Inflation Rate. Retrieved on September 1, 2022, https://tradingeconomics.com/turkey/inflation-cpi

Trompenaars, A., & Hampden-Turner, C. (1998). *Riding the Waves of Culture: Understanding Diversity in Global Business*. London: Nicholas Brealey.

Turan, S. (2021). A transformation in the performance management: More flexibility and agility. *Harvard Business Review*, Video Recording. Retrieved on September 10, 2022, https://youtu.be/3cHMpnZuE_8.

Tüzüner, L. (2014). Human resource management in Turkey. In B.E. Kaufmann (Ed.), *The Development of Human Resource Management across Nations* (pp. 437–460). Massachusets: Edward Elgar Publishing.

Worldometer (2022). Turkey's population. Retrieved on September 18, 2022, from https://www.worldometers.info/world-population/turkey-population/

Young Guru Academy (YGA) (December 14, 2021). Bugün Olsun, Benim Olsun Değil; Yarın Olsun, Bizim Olsun (Let Tomorrow Be Ours, Not Today Be Mine; Let Tomorrow Be Ours), You Tube. https://youtu.be/KzSBlDaP09w.

Performance Management in India

Tanuja Sharma, Pawan S. Budhwar, Arup Varma and Peter Norlander

Chapter 12

INTRODUCTION

India presents a multitude of economic, political, cultural, and social contexts. This puts one of the fastest-growing economies in a unique position differentiating it from the rest of the world. The fast-paced gross domestic product (GDP) growth of almost 9% has encouraged the rise of the entrepreneurial wave in India (World Bank, 2021). Tech start-ups have increased rapidly in the period between 2013–2018 with roughly 7200–7700 start-ups being launched in the period (NASSCOM, 2022). In addition to start-ups, India continues to be a hub for foreign MNE subsidiaries which exploit the cost-efficiencies the market provides (Björkman and Budhwar, 2007). The workplace in India constitutes a multigenerational workforce with baby boomers, Gen X, millennials, and Gen Z working in the same organization. In addition to these unique complexities, the Indian business landscape is also affected by the global COVID-19 pandemic, geopolitical disruptions (Russia–Ukraine war), and fluctuations in the international markets. Indian businesses now operate in an extremely volatile, uncertain, complex, and ambiguous (VUCA) world, and this has necessitated a need for organizations to revisit their systems to stay competitive and compete on the global stage.

DOI: 10.4324/9781003306849-12

In this chapter, we present a critical overview of the Indian context regarding one of the most crucial HR systems in organizations, namely, the performance management system (PMS). A large variety of both forms and designs of PMSs are in use in Indian organizations. However, as one might expect, the nature and content of PMS in the Indian context differ in different types of organizations, that is, private, public, and foreign firms (Amba-Rao et al., 2000; Budhwar & Boyne, 2004; Saini & Budhwar, 2007). With the growth of the Indian economy, more and more Indian organizations are emphasizing the development of effective PMSs. While there are some commonalities in the practice of performance management, it is rather difficult to generalize, given the scope of a diverse and varied country like India. Although India has emerged as a leading exporter of computer software and a major global outsourcing hub for information technology (IT) and IT-enabled services, the economy continues to be a mixture of traditional village farming and handicrafts, on one hand, and a wide range of modern industries including chemicals, food processing, steel, and a multitude of other services, on the other (Budhwar, 2001). Ironically, the existing literature on performance management is rather scarce and fails to provide a clear picture of the PMSs in use in Indian organizations. We believe our chapter helps fill this gap. A review of the existing literature (e.g. Basu, 1988) reveals that PMS practices in India range from "no appraisal" to "sophisticated multipurpose, multi-component web-based performance management systems." Performance management practices in India range from annual confidential reports (ACRs) used by the Armed Forces to annual performance assessment reports (APARs) used by government departments. In addition, both the public and private sectors use key performance indicators/key result areas (KPIs/KRAs)–based PMSs, 360-degree appraisal and balanced scorecards (BSCs). Some of the key factors influencing performance appraisal (PA) management in India are (1) changes in the economic environment resulting from the integration of the Indian economy into the global economy, (2) cultural diversity, and (3) the ongoing technological revolution. Furthermore, Indian organizations are facing several challenges as they attempt to establish formal PMSs. These include, although are not limited to, (1) transparency in the appraisal process, (2) establishing clear linkages between performance evaluation and rewards, and (3) a multitude of labour laws, some of which have not been updated for decades.

In this chapter, we initially outline the history of the development and acceptance of PA/management systems in India. This is followed by a discussion of the current scenario of PMSs in Indian organizations. Next, we explore the key factors that impact PMSs in India, and finally, we highlight the challenges faced by organizations in establishing effective PMSs.

HISTORY OF PMSs IN INDIA

The literature (e.g. Basu, 1988) reports that leading private-sector organizations such as Union Carbide started using PAs for managerial personnel as far back as 1940, followed by other well-known organizations, such as the Tata Iron and Steel Company, Voltas, and Bata India, which introduced such systems in the 1950s. However, public-sector enterprises adopted a confidential reporting system, which has been used by the government to evaluate its bureaucrats since India achieved independence in 1947. Furthermore, personality- and trait-based systems of evaluation were in use before 1947 in the Indian armed forces and civil services, although these were primarily used for merit pay and promotion-related decisions.

In a 1968 survey (Bolar, 1978), 49 of 82 companies reported having some form of formal performance evaluation system in place, although 20 of the 49 companies reported that while they had the systems in place, these systems were rarely used. Furthermore, graphic rating scales were the most popular form of evaluation in use at the time. In the mid-1970s, Rao and Pareek (1996) developed an open-ended PAS that included performance planning and analysis, identification of development needs, participatory planning, culture building, competence building, and upward appraisal and review for Larsen and Toubro. Although this system was simply called performance appraisal, its focus was on managing overall performance and development. Many other organizations subsequently developed and implemented open-ended appraisal systems similar to the one in use at Larsen and Toubro (for details see Rao, 2004). In the late 1970s and early 1980s, most Indian organizations were using performance appraisals (PAs) to regulate employee behaviour and help develop employee capabilities. These were known by various names, such as "work planning and review system" in the Life Insurance Corporation, and "performance planning and review system" in the National Dairy Development Board. In later years, performance appraisal systems were revamped to incorporate quality initiatives such as total quality management. Indeed, organizations such as Xerox (India) became well known for incorporating quality dimensions into their performance review systems, whereby individual performance reviews reflected the input of customers (both internal and external) and "quality of work" and "customer service" were some of the critical dimensions on which both employees and executives were appraised (Parker & Datta, 1996). By the late 1980s, some clear trends in PMSs began to emerge – such as a shift away from closed and confidential evaluations to open dialogue and discussion-based systems.

In addition, there was a discernible move from a purely numeric evaluation format to qualitative, interactive, and improvement-oriented systems (Rao & Pareek, 1996). Overall, performance appraisal/management had been an under-emphasized function in Indian businesses until very recently (e.g. Amba-Rao et al., 2000). It was only in the early twenty-first century that most Indian organizations started emphasizing the development of effective PMSs (Rao et al., 2001). As these authors note, it was around this time that the performance management processes started incorporating development-oriented tools, as well as feedback and counselling systems. By 2004, with continuing economic liberalization and enhanced competition, a majority of Indian organizations reported using various methods of performance appraisals/management. Indeed, numerous organizations such as Infosys, Titan, Tata Steel, Bharat Petroleum, Dr. Reddy's Lab, and the National Stock Exchange are known to use some of the most sophisticated forms of PMSs. For example, the appraisal system in Voltas recognizes communication and counselling as important aspects of development through self-improvement and encourages raters to be objective during the evaluation process. At Larsen and Toubro, the use of facilitators is a unique part of the evaluation and development system. Furthermore, peer rating and an assessment of values and potential are also incorporated into the PMS (Rao & Rao, 2006).

Ironically, despite the major changes sweeping the Indian economy, and the consequent professionalism introduced by these changes, informal and confidential appraisals by the immediate supervisor continued to be a part of the evaluation process, especially in public-sector organizations. However, there were some notable exceptions, such as the Life Insurance Corporation, the National Dairy Development Board, and the National Thermal Power Corporation. These public-sector organizations used progressive, open-ended performance appraisal/management systems for almost three decades (Rao, 2004). Sixth Central Pay Commission in India and the Department of Public Enterprise (DPE) guideline 2008 mandated the use of bell curve and performance-related pay (PRP) in the public sector. The use of e-PMS and online performance management has become a new normal for most government organizations in the current decade. Over the past few years, the MNE subsidiaries and start-ups have also begun experimenting with their PMS processes, adopting more agile and flexible systems like objectives and key results (OKR). First introduced by Intel, this novel system aims as setting significant, concrete, and measurable goals with 3–5 key results that are periodically tracked within an assessment year. Firms like Google, Netflix, Adobe, and Paytm have been the frontrunners in adopting the new PMS with an audacious team and individual goals and more frequent review cycles (SHRM, 2020).

CURRENT SCENARIO

The world has been struggling with the COVID-19 health pandemic and consequent lockdowns. Firms were mandated to move to work-from-home set-ups and geographically concentrated virtual teams were created everywhere (Chamakiotis et al., 2021). This brought about an absolute overhaul in the traditional work, workforce, and workplace. The move to digitalization was augmented by the pandemic and emerging technologies like artificial intelligence (AI), machine learning (ML), and robotic process automation (RPA) made their way into the human resource processes. Digital human resource (HR) technologies have transformed the way HR processes are implemented in the workplace and have a favourable impact on business outcomes (Jani et al., 2021).

Tanuja Sharma et al.

There has also been a considerable shift towards environmental consciousness and sustainability in organizational practices. Given the global climate change crisis and rising inequality in the nation (Lawson & Martin, 2019), organizations have attempted to take corrective actions and broadened their performance measurement criteria to encompass environmental performance (Ahmad et al., 2020; Chaudhary, 2019). Environmental, social, and corporate governance (ESG) outcomes also feature in the scorecards of top executives in the firm which ultimately impacts their variable pay component (Bhattacharyya & Vijayaraghavan, 2021).

There has been a rather impressive move by Indian companies to go global. From major international acquisitions by leading organizations such as Tata Steel and United Breweries to operations in numerous countries, the truly global Indian corporation is now a reality. A logical outcome of this is the need to manage performance in numerous countries, as well as the need to manage a multicultural workforce. Many HR professionals now admit newfound respect for PMSs in India, viewing them as a tool for transforming the organization by promoting a high-performance culture. As an example, the HR team at Ranbaxy Laboratories, an Indian pharmaceutical multinational, uses an electronic performance management system for development purposes by incorporating their "Values-in-Action" leadership competencies into the PMS. The company is also using PMSs for promoting the notion of employee ownership of tasks, by linking the PMS with its business processes and providing employee mentoring through coaching. Not surprisingly, almost all IT and IT-enabled organizations in India now use e-PMS (for details, see Budhwar et al., 2006).

Recently, Aon conducted a comprehensive salary increase survey for 2021–22, covering 1350 organizations across all industries and business sectors in India. The report suggested that bell curves and 5-point rating scales remain the preferred mode of evaluation, with over 53% using them. They also reported that only 5% of organizations have completely moved away from ratings and are now leveraging contextualized feedback and developmental conversations. Further firms are using non-traditional methods like (1) gamified performance metrics using badges, leader boards, and the like; (2) strength-based assessments instead of rating scales; and (3) 10/100/200-point rating scales

Bonus Payout over the years

Bonus Payout as a percentage of fixed pay ▇ 2019 ▨ 2020 ▇ 2021

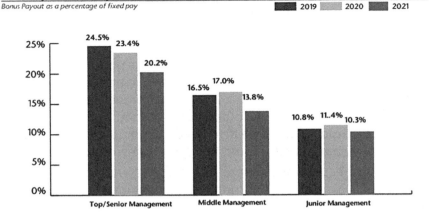

Figure 12.1   Bonus pay-out over the years (Aon India, 2022)

as an alternative to the bell curve that allows extensive options accounting for "in-betweens".

Trends on variable bonus pay-out highlighted in the report suggested the sharpest decline in senior management pay-out and an overall decline of 15% in 2021 as compared to variable bonus pay-outs in 2020 (See Figure 12.1). Although the amount was relatively lower, however, 85% of the firms still paid variable bonuses during the pandemic.

Given the pressures of the pandemic and budgetary constraints, firms were pushed to adopt more innovative ways of retaining top talent. Additionally, India has a high majority of young, skilled individuals in the workforce who values non-monetary benefits more. Given this context, firms invested in reinventing their pay communication philosophy and adopted more transparent communication. They also conducted extensive manager training to ensure appropriate messages were percolated down in the firm. Performance coaching and feedback systems have been instituted in most firms. The use of analytics for performance management is a common practice due to enterprise resource planning implementation. Research also corroborates that the use of HR analytics makes the feedback more objective (Sharma & Sharma, 2017). Research has established that appropriately designed manager coaching has a positive and sustainable impact on team performance (Nyfoudi, Shipton, Theodorakopoulos, & Budhwar, 2022).

Tanuja Sharma et al.

Another interesting finding in the Aon India report was the organizational responses to hybrid workplaces. They reported that 14% of organizations are revisiting their rewards and benefits policies for the virtual workspace and another 14% are focusing on manager capability development. There is also a growing consensus in India Inc. that the earlier ways of working and HR processes need to be reconfigured for hybrid workplaces.

PMSs OF MNCs IN INDIA

The preceding discussion concentrated on PMSs in Indian organizations in general; however, it is important that we separately examine PMSs in multinational corporations (MNCs) operating in India. In this connection, Budhwar and Singh (2004) conducted an in-depth study of HRM systems in 102 MNCs operating in India. Concerning PMSs in MNCs, they report that (1) most MNCs in India follow a formal and structured approach to performance appraisal; (2) the appraisal or assessment system is typically developed in their corporate office(s) and imported, and adapted, for use in India; and (3) in most cases, the appraisals are conducted once a year. It should be noted that some firms (e.g. Hyundai) conduct bi-annual appraisals, while others (e.g. GlaxoSmithKline Beecham) conduct quarterly appraisals. There has also been a recent shift towards feedback conversations instead of formal appraisals which happen on a more ongoing basis. Firms like EY have introduced a "Feedback Friday" system where weekly feedback is shared by managers regarding project updates. All participating firms have a structured format and a clear set of parameters for appraisals. In many cases, the ratee is required to fill out a self-appraisal, whereby they can list their achievements and plans/goals for development. Next, the rater (i.e., the immediate supervisor) is required to meet with the ratee to discuss his/her performance, compare the ratee's self-appraisal with the rater's evaluation, and arrive at mutually accepted ratings and evaluation(s). This discussion is designed to help resolve the discrepancy between the ratee's own evaluation and that of the rater as well as allow the ratee to explain contextual factors that may have affected their performance. In practice, of course, things often work out differently. The general trend seems to be that the immediate supervisor of the employee fills out the form, allows the employee to read it, and then asks them to countersign it, after which the form is sent to the head of the department/division. In addition to the evaluation of performance for the period under review, most organizations also use the appraisal system to identify employee training needs. In order to ensure that limited time is spent on filling forms and focus is on actionable feedback, Deloitte introduced the four-question PMS wherein managers respond to four behavioral questions regarding the performance (compensation range, promotion readiness, team behaviour, probability of low performance). This reduces the administrative tasks associated with the PMS while ensuring the relevance of the system for decision-making and downward HR processes.

With the growing trend of start-ups and multinational enterprises (MNEs) in the country, the importance of favourable behaviours and soft skills has taken precedence in the workspace. Organizations have adopted some form of competency-based evaluations. These competencies go beyond the technical skills required for the job and instead are behavioural skills required to thrive in the organizational culture. These include elements like leadership skills, communication and influencing skills, change leadership, client excellence, and the like. These competencies draw from organizational vision and serve as a base for potential and performance assessment. Most organizations use these competency-based assessments to identify their high-potential employees and develop training and succession plans for them. Public enterprises like Indian Oil Corporation Limited and National Thermal Power Corporation use these competencies to make promotion decisions while private Indian MNCs like Airtel, Reliance, and HUL use them for development need identification. The variability also occurs across the management levels, with senior executives assessed more on behavioural competencies than technical skills (Kamjula & Narendar, 2022).

Finally, most MNCs have an individual-based PMS, although some (e.g., Whirlpool) also use team-based evaluations. Almost all the firms use some kind of rating scale, grading or ranking system, and set targets for appraisals. For senior managers, many firms employ more comprehensive evaluation systems, such as the 360-degree feedback mechanism. Such a comprehensive PMS has some drawbacks as summarized in the comments of the HR manager from Hughes Software Systems:

> What happens is that implementation of appraisal is something that nobody likes, it is almost like a necessary evil that everyone has to see. I have not seen in my career someone willing to do that. So we have to at times give the bad news or we have to be tough, which people do not like doing. So no matter how objective it becomes, or how transparent it becomes, doing a tough part of evaluating a person is something that people do not like. That is the bad part of the whole thing.

The preceding quote is the "bad news" as some continue to feel that appraisals (and all that goes with appraisals) are a waste of time. The good news is that a majority of HR managers are convinced of the utility of comprehensive PMSs, and report that most employees seem to accept the system rather quickly and treat it as a "way of life" in their organizations. However, what is clear is that the system can be further improved. For example, the way PMSs are currently implemented in MNCs, the ratee's involvement is rather limited, especially in terms of goal setting despite the organizations claiming that the process is expected to be fully participative. This is further true in the Indian business process outsourcing sector where systems are strongly data-driven (see Budhwar et al., 2006). Perhaps this is reflective of the hierarchical nature of Indian society (see Kakar, 1971; Sparrow & Budhwar, 1997). To help us better understand how factors such as power distance affect the Indian workplace, the following section presents a discussion of the key factors influencing PMSs in India.

FACTORS INFLUENCING PMSs IN INDIA
Economic Factors

As mentioned earlier, over the last few years, India has emerged as one of the fastest growing economies in the world (with an average annual growth rate of 8% over the past three consecutive years). The fundamentals of the Indian economy are being reported as strong and stable as measured by indicators such as growth rates, foreign exchange reserves, foreign direct investment, and inflation and interest rates. Indeed, several key forecasting agencies such as the Economist Intelligence, the Confederation of Indian Industry, and Citigroup have predicted sustained GDP growth of 7.5–8% in FY 2022 (PTI, 2022).

Furthermore, as is now globally acknowledged, the service industry in India is the fastest-growing sector and the most consistent performer, particularly the IT/information technology-enabled services sectors, which have recorded 15.5% year-on-year growth by FY 2022 (NASSCOM, 2022). Overall, the key environmental factors shaping the Indian economy are globalization, profitability through growth, technology, and intellectual capital. The continued growth of the Indian economy, and the need to sustain this rate of growth, are putting tremendous pressure on industry leaders and HR professionals to better manage both their financial and human resources (e.g. Budhwar & Sparrow, 1998; Saini & Budhwar, 2007). As a result, many organizations are recognizing and emphasizing the critical role played by various HR processes, including PMSs.

Relatedly, the contribution of initiatives such as goal setting, decision-making, conflict resolution, and OCTAPACE (openness, confrontation, trust, autonomy, pro-action, authenticity, collaboration, experimentation) in helping increase motivation and maintain the morale of employees is being appreciated by the Indian organizations. Indeed, the use of the PMS as a mechanism to improve a firm's performance has increased drastically over the past few years (e.g., Amba-Rao et al., 2000; Bordia & Blau, 1998).

In this connection, the relationship and impact of distal factors like norms, strategy, and firm performance (Murphy & DeNisi, 2008) on performance appraisal are being revisited and defined and communicated to employees during the initial stages of their employment. Furthermore, both private- and public-sector organizations are clearly setting individual and department goals (KPAs), and the use of appraisal information for decision-making is on the increase (Rao, 2004). Moreover, positive correlations have been indicated in a study conducted on tracing linkages between the employee's perceptions of PMS in the use and external customers' perceptions of service quality delivered to its customers in the banking sector (Sharma, 2006, 2008).

Cultural Factors

The impact of cultural factors on both macro (distal factors) and micro levels (proximal factors) of PMSs is also increasingly evident in the Indian workplace (see Budhwar, 2000). India represents a "major socio-historic entity representing one idea of one civil society that is composed of a small set of closely interrelated attributes" (Kothari, 1997: 7, cited in Chhokar, 2007). As a result, the business environment in India is not only complex but also full of contrasts; for example, there are significant variations between industry sectors (see Budhwar, 2001; Budhwar & Boyne, 2004).

The extremely rich history and cultural heritage of the country coupled with its recent economic successes have added to the complexity and diversity of Indian society and culture. In this connection, several scholars (e.g. Sinha, 2004; Sparrow & Budhwar, 1997) have written extensively on leadership, motivation, PMS, and compensation philosophy in the Indian business context. Furthermore, scholars (e.g. Gupta, 2000) have conducted in-depth studies of concepts such as "nurturing-task leadership" and "araam" (leisure, relaxation), to better understand the evolving Indian workplace culture and ethos. In order to better understand how the Indian culture affects individuals and their workplace experience, it is important that we explore India's standing relative to other nations on critical contextual factors that may influence business decisions.

In this connection, the GLOBE (Global Leadership and Organizational Behavior Effectiveness) Project, a major cross-cultural study covering 63 countries, has observed that in India "it is not easy to find manifestations of 'Indian' culture which are: (a) common to the entire country without exception, and (b) unique to the country insofar as these are not found in other countries" (Chhokar, 2007).

Based on continuing traditional rituals and ceremonies, the concept of time, respect for age, and the prevalence of family-owned businesses, India is often categorized as a traditional and collectivist society. Indeed, the GLOBE Project results place India high on collectivism and humane orientation. Furthermore, it is placed in the top one-third among all nations in terms of performance orientation, future orientation, and power distance.

In terms of gender egalitarianism, India seems to continue to be a male-dominated society. India ranks 26 out of 53 nations on the measure of uncertainty avoidance. Given the preceding, it is not surprising that Trompenaars (1993) classifies India as a "family culture," marked by a person-oriented and hierarchical culture which tends to be power oriented. Here, the leader, or manager, is seen as a caring parent, and power tends to be moral and social in nature and is rooted in broad status. In addition, the corporate culture tends to be high in context, and the thrust is on intuitive development.

Finally, the focus is on effectiveness and not efficiency (Pattanayak et al., 2002: 474–5). Overall, the few published studies on India indicate a presence of collectivist and individualist values and the adoption by many Indian organizations of the formal systems of management in a vertical collectivist culture. This often creates unpredictability in managerial and decision-making styles, whereby the practices may seem similar to many Western managerial practices, though their basic causes or driving forces are quite different, given the diversity of the Indian nation. It should be noted, for example, that Indians are very proud of their "secular," multireligious, multicultural, and multilingual country (e.g., Budhwar, 2001). The multiplicity of languages (e.g., 15 official languages recognized by the Indian constitution and hundreds of dialects) adds to the complexity of the nation and its workplace. Also, in the absence of a strong legal system and its clear implementation which can define the scope of various HR policies and practices, it is rather difficult to develop a common and comprehensive PMS for such a diverse nation.

In summary, performance management in India, particularly in local and national public- and private-sector firms, is deeply affected by the high-context, power-oriented, hierarchy-driven mindset of Indian managers. As the literature documents, their style of leadership and management is paternalistic in nature and often causes employees to look for detailed and continuous guidance in order to achieve the defined goals (Sparrow & Budhwar, 1997). Thus, adherence to norms and managerial directives is emphasized. Furthermore, supervisor–subordinate relationships play a huge role in determining the ratings of individual

Tanuja Sharma et al.

employees (Varma, 2022). In this connection, Varma, Pichler, and Srinivas (2005) reported that subjectivity in ratings had a significant impact on the ratings awarded to employees, such that raters tended to inflate ratings of poor performers whom they liked. Performance is linked to both compensation and promotions; however, all performance rewards must be validated by the senior management team and HR department.

Finally, the confidentiality of information is maintained at many levels in the entire process, thus depriving individual employees of a clear understanding of the process and the outcomes. At a macro level, distal factors like norms, strategy, and firm performance clearly have played a role in the evolution of industry in India and HR practices and policies. For example, public-sector units in the country are an outcome of India's first prime minister Jawaharlal Nehru's vision of a mixed economy, emphasizing both private and public enterprise. The Indian public-sector units are governed by welfare objectives and tend to focus on generating employment, skilling Indian labour and making India self-reliant by producing and distributing goods and services. In addition, the policy of lifetime employment and the active participation of unions have had the effect of taking away the focus from productivity and profits, instead emphasizing sustenance and governance (also see Budhwar & Boyne, 2004). As a result, HR systems in the public sector units are often maintenance-oriented, rather than progressive. For example, PMSs in public-sector units are typically used only for promotion purposes, and reward/outcomes are often not clearly linked to performance and productivity. As a result, the acceptance of the PMS is extremely low, further confounded by the fact that PMSs in PSUs are typically operated under a "closed system." Also, many researchers have reported distortions in rating and promotion decisions (e.g. Amba-Rao et al., 2000; Sharma, 2006).

However, findings of an empirical study conducted on Indian banks to map the role of PMSs (Sharma, 2006) indicate that the private banks (both foreign banks and Indian private banks) show a higher correlation with the four important dimensions of the PMS – performance planning, feedback and coaching, performance review and rewards with internal service climate and external customer's perception of service quality.

Focus on performance planning has been the strength of private banks. Performance orientation and training given for communication during induction also played an important role. However, nationalized banks follow the policy of considering seniority as the main factor for promotions, and performance review only has a limited role in supporting such decisions.

KEY CHALLENGES FACING EFFECTIVE PMSs IN INDIA

As is clear from the preceding discussion, performance appraisal/management practices have been continually improving, with considerable innovations and changes, but can be further improved by new interventions (see Bolar, 1978). Based on the earlier discussion, we present a list of key action items that can help further improve PMSs in the Indian context.

For one, mismanagement of the PMS is sometimes in evidence (Varma & Budhwar, 2020). There is also scanty literature on measuring the effectiveness of PMS and its consequent impact on workplace outcomes like engagement and productivity (Sharma et al., 2016, 2021). An interesting study on new ventures found a strong significance of perceived total rewards with the employees' work engagement and happiness at work (Gulyani & Sharma, 2018). Research also indicates that very few managers are proficient in performance planning. Typically, organizations attach higher priority on acquiring technical competencies (such as in the fields of operations management, accounting, and marketing) rather than on HR competencies of determining performance objectives, providing feedback, and administering performance-contingent rewards. These activities are often seen as unnecessary and time-consuming by both managers and employees. In addition, the haphazard administration and confidential nature of PMSs lead to conflict between raters and their ratees. One key factor that is often overlooked is that Indian organizations are not homogenous. Thus, although all types of Indian firms implement PMSs, the process varies significantly depending on the nature and size of the firm. Perhaps the biggest challenge before Indian organizations today is to ensure that the whole process of performance management is not reduced to a simple form-filling exercise, a mistake repeatedly made by managers (Rao, 2004).

Furthermore, the dyadic nature of performance seems to have been almost completely ignored, for the most part, with most evaluation and feedback mechanisms being top-down. Not surprisingly, there are numerous issues related to problems with ratings. For example, ratings are subject to bias and often coloured by the nature of the relationship between supervisors and subordinates. Also, supervisors are often willing to inflate ratings to avoid having to give negative feedback. Clearly, this is an area that needs attention from both managers and HR departments so that feedback can be used as a mechanism to help improve performance (Sharma, 2006).

Another challenge facing organizations is performance management in a team environment. Effective systems need to be developed so that individuals in teams can receive fair and equitable evaluations. In this connection, Rao and Pareek (1996) have argued that in order to draw the best from employees, the following attributes need to be in place: (1) a high degree of entrepreneurship and global thinking, (2) cost-effectiveness and high-performance standards, (3) quality-consciousness in products and services to match international standards, and (4) an emphasis on values that help kindle hidden talent. They maintain that "performance appraisal systems have a catalytic role to play" (1996: 7) to meet the objective of putting these attributes in place. These authors also emphasize that to meet international standards, the integration of quality into performance development has been a challenge for all Indian organizations.

Next, the confidential nature of appraisals and the lack of direct and obvious connection between one's performance and the rewards remain as strong de-motivating factors. Organizations need to establish transparent systems such that employees can see the link between performance and rewards and trust the system to be fair to them. With globalization and liberalization sweeping India, the optimum use of money and machines has more or less been achieved. Technological developments have accelerated this achievement manifold by creating a global village. Competitive advantages are being actualized by outsourcing work and processes throughout the world.

The major challenges before firms are to maximize employee performance and achieve the highest level of quality output.

Perhaps this is clearly evident in the Indian BPO sector which is now maturing and where firms are having a difficult time retaining employees and consistently improving their performance (Budhwar et al., 2006). This requires an intrinsically motivated workforce in a more meaningful context, which helps them grow in self-esteem while simultaneously allowing for the growth of business enterprises. Thus redefined, the role of management clearly becomes that of a provider of correct and timely information about organizational goals, resources, technology, structure, and policy. This would create a context that has a multiplicative impact on employees, their individual attributes, competencies, and willingness to perform; goal clarity; and sense of ownership, by the continuous participation of employees in work efforts and feedback, together with outcomes and rewards, leading to higher self-esteem and greater involvement. Systemic support in terms of performance planning, coaching, feedback and a correlation between performance and the desired rewards or outcome thus would seem critical.

Thus, a well-designed PMS which can act as a strategic tool for attaining employees' quality output, leading to their retention and continued association and involvement of both internal and external customers, which significantly contributes to the sustainability of the organizations, should be the aim in the long run.

REFERENCES

Ahmad, S., Abdullah, A., & Talib, F. (2020). Lean-green performance management in Indian SMEs: A novel perspective using the best-worst method approach. *Benchmarking: An International Journal* (ahead-of-print). https://doi.org/10.1108/bij-05-2020-0255

Amba-Rao, S.C., Petrick, J.A., Gupta, J.N.D., & Von der Embse, T.J. (2000). Comparative performance appraisal practices and management values among foreign and domestic firms in India. *International Journal of Human Resource Management*, 11(1), 60–89.

Aon India. (2022). AON India's 26th salary increase survey Prepared by rewards solutions rewards solutions proprietary & confidential. https://img.response.aonunited.com/Web/AonUnited/%7Bcc3a2269-c5aa-4ac7-abc8-b9c5a32f898b%7D_Aon_India_Salary_Increase_Survey_Phase_I_2021-22_-_Insights_Report.pdf

Basu, M.K. (1988). *Managerial Performance Appraisal in India*. Delhi: Vision Books.

Bhattacharyya, R., & Vijayaraghavan, K. (2021). Firms plan to link investment in social good to CEO salary. *The Economic Times*. https://economictimes.indiatimes.com/news/company/corporate-trends/firms-plan-to-link-investment-in-social-good-to-ceo-salary/articleshow/87196247.cms

Björkman, I., & Budhwar, P. (2007). When in Rome …? Human resource management and the performance of foreign firms operating in India. *Employee Relations*, 29(6), 595–610.

Bolar, M. (Ed.) (1978). *Performance Appraisal: Readings, Case Studies and a Survey of Practices.* New Delhi: Vikas Publishing.

Bordia, P., & Blau, G. (1998). Pay referent comparison and pay level satisfaction in private versus public sector organizations in India. *International Journal of Human Resource Management,* 9(1), 155–167.

Budhwar, P. (2000). Factors influencing HRM policies and practices in India: An empirical study. *Global Business Review,* 1(2), 229–247.

Budhwar, P. (2001). Doing business in India. *Thunderbird International Business Review,* 43(4), 549–568.

Budhwar, P., & Boyne, G. (2004). Human resource management in the Indian public and private sectors: An empirical comparison. *International Journal of Human Resource Management,* 15(2), 346–370.

Budhwar, P., & Singh, V. (2004). Dynamics of HRM systems of foreign firms operating in India. Paper presented at the *Annual Academy of Management Conference,* 6–11 August, New Orleans.

Budhwar, P., & Sparrow, P. (1998). Factors determining cross-national human resource management practices: A study of India and Britain. *Management International Review,* 38(Special Issue 2), 105–121.

Budhwar, P., Varma, A., Singh, V., & Dhar, R. (2006). HRM systems of Indian call centres: An exploratory study. *International Journal of Human Resource Management* 17(5), 881–897.

Chamakiotis, P., Panteli, N., & Davison, R.M. (2021). Reimagining e-leadership for reconfigured virtual teams due to Covid-19. *International Journal of Information Management,* 60, 102381. https://doi.org/10.1016/j.ijinfomgt.2021.102381

Chaudhary, R. (2019). Green human resource management in Indian automobile industry. *Journal of Global Responsibility,* 10(2), 161–175. https://doi.org/10.1108/jgr-12-2018-0084

Chhokar, J.S. (2007). India: Diversity and complexity in action. In J.S. Chhokar, F.C. Brodbeck, & R.J. House (Eds.), *Culture and Leadership across the World: The Globe Book of In-depth Studies of 25 Societies* (pp. 971–1020). Mahwah, NJ: Lawrence Erlbaum Associates; Sage.

Gulyani, G., & Sharma, T. (2018). Total rewards components and work happiness in new ventures: The mediating role of work engagement. *Evidence-Based HRM: A Global Forum for Empirical Scholarship,* 6(3), 255–271.

Gupta, R.K. (2000). *Requisite Organizational Design in Towards the Optimal Organization: Integrating Indian Culture and Management.* New Delhi: Excel Books.

Jani, A., Muduli, A., & Kishore, K. (2021). Human resource transformation in India: Examining the role digital human resource technology and human resource role. *International Journal of Organizational Analysis* (ahead-of-print). https://doi.org/10.1108/ijoa-08-2021-2886

Kakar, S. (1971). Authority pattern and subordinate behaviours in Indian organisation, *Administrative Science Quarterly,* 16(3), 298–307.

Kakkar, S., & Vohra, N. (2021). Self-regulatory effects of performance management system consistency on employee engagement: A moderated mediation model. *American Business Review,* 24(1), 225–248. https://doi.org/10.37625/abr.24.1.225-248

Kamjula, N., & Narendar, K. (2022). Competency mapping – A tool to measure Employee Performance for Gen – Y. *Journal of Advanced Research in Dynamic and Control Systems,* 11(05-Special Issue), 1634–1639. https://www.jardcs.org/abstract.php?id=1558

Lawson, M., & Martin, M. (2019, October 9). *The Commitment to Reducing Inequality Index 2018.* Oxfam International. https://www.oxfam.org/en/research/commitment-reducing-inequality-index-2018

Murphy, K.R., & DeNisi, A. (2008). A model of the appraisal process. In A. Varma, P.S. Budhwar, & A.S. DeNisi (Eds.), *Performance Management Systems* (pp. 81–94). London: Routledge.

NASSCOM. (2022, February 15). *Technology Sector in India 2022 : Strategic Review.* NASSCOM. https://nasscom.in/knowledge-center/publications/technology-sector-india-2022-strategic-review

Nyfoudi, M., Shipton, H., Theodorakopoulos, N., & Budhwar, P. (2022). Managerial coaching skill and team performance: How does the relationship work and under what conditions? *Human Resource Management Journal.* Advanced online publication. https://doi.org/10.1111/1748-8583.12443

Parker, M., & Datta, R. (1996). Performance management system in Modi Xerox. In T.V. Rao & Udai Pareek (Eds.), *Redesigning Performance Appraisal Systems*, New Delhi: Tata McGraw-Hill.

Pattanayak, B., Gupta, V., & Niranjana, P. (2002). *Creating Performing Organizations: International Perspective for Indian Management.* New Delhi: Response Book-Sage.

PTI. (2022, April 25). India's GDP likely to grow 7.5-8 pc in FY23: CII President. *The Economic Times.* https://economictimes.indiatimes.com/news/economy/indicators/indias-gdp-likely-to-grow-7-5-8-pc-in-fy23-cii-president/articleshow/91073932.cms?from=mdr

Rao, T.V. (2004). *Performance Management and Appraisal Systems – HR Tools for Global Competitiveness.* New Delhi: SAGE.

Rao, T.V., & Pareek, U. (1996). Performance appraisals in the new economic environment. in T.V. Rao & Udai Pareek (Eds.), *Redesigning Performance Appraisal Systems.* New Delhi: Tata McGraw-Hill.

Rao, T.V., & Rao, R. (Eds.) (2006). *360 Degree Feedback and Performance Management System* (Vol. 1). New Delhi: Excel Books.

Rao, T.V., Rao, R., & Yadav, T. (2001). A study of HRD concepts, structure of HRD departments, and HRD practices in India. *Vikalpa*, 26(1), 49–63.

Saini, D., & Budhwar, P. (2007). Human resource management in India. In R. Schuler & S. Jackson (Eds.), *Strategic Human Resource Management* (pp. 287–312). Oxford: Blackwell Publishing.

Sharma, A., & Sharma, T. (2017). HR analytics and performance appraisal system: A conceptual framework for employee performance improvement. *Management Research Review*, 40(6), 684–697.

Sharma, N.P., Sharma, T., & Agarwal, M.N. (2016). Measuring employee perception of performance management system effectiveness: Conceptualization and scale development. *Employee Relations*, 38(2), 224–247. https://doi.org/10.1108/ER-01-2015-0006

Sharma, N.P., Sharma, T., & Agarwal, M.N. (2021). Relationship between perceived performance management system (PMS) effectiveness, work engagement and turnover intention: Mediation by psychological contract fulfillment. *Benchmarking: An International Journal* (ahead-of-print). https://doi.org/10.1108/bij-01-2021-0008

Sharma, T. (2006). A comparative Audit of Performance Management System of selected banks in India and its contribution in delivering quality service to its Internal and External customers. Paper presented at 21st Workshop at Strategic Human Resource Management, March 30–31, Aston Business School, Birmingham, U.K.

Sharma, T. (2008). Exploring linkages between employees' perception of performance management practices, service climate and their customers' perceptions of service quality. *Journal of Applied Management and Entrepreneurship*, 13(3), 47.

SHRM. (2020, September 3). *OKR Implementation Handbook.* SHRM. https://www.shrm.org/shrm-india/pages/peoplestrong-okr-.aspx

Sinha, Jai B.P. (2004). *Multinationals in India – Managing the Interface of Cultures*, New Delhi: Sage.

Sparrow, P., & Budhwar, P. (1997). Competition and change: Mapping the Indian HRM recipe against world-wide patterns. *Journal of World Business*, 32(3), 224–242.

Trompenaars, F. (1993). *Riding the Waves of Culture. Understanding Cultural Diversity in Business.* London: Economist Books.

Varma, A. (2022). Case 16: Performance management systems at V-Pharmel. In A. Malik (Ed.), *Strategic Human Resource Management and Employment Relations.* Cham: Springer Texts in Business and Economics. Springer https://doi.org/10. 1007/978-3-030-90955-0_32

Varma, A., & Budhwar, P.S. (2020). *Performance management systems: An experiential approach.* North Tyneside, UK: SAGE Publications Limited.

Varma, A., Pichler, S. and Srinivas, E.S. (2005). The role of interpersonal affect in performance appraisal: Evidence from two samples – U.S. and India, *International Journal of Human Resource Management,* 16 11), 2029–2044.

World Bank. (2021). *GDP growth (annual %) | Data.* Data.worldbank.org. https://data. worldbank.org/indicator/NY.GDP.MKTP.KD.ZG?locations=IN

Performance Management Systems in China*

Fang Lee Cooke

Chapter 13

INTRODUCTION

A variety of performance management techniques is promoted as modern western human resource management (HRM) techniques in China. This is in spite of the fact that performance appraisal practices have long existed in China with strong Chinese characteristics. This chapter first provides an overview of the human resource environment in China through a summary of the main characteristics of HRM and employment profiles in China. It then traces the historical development of the performance appraisal system during the state-planned economy period and the ensuing economic reform period. A number of key characteristics and pitfalls in performance appraisal practices are identified. Some of them are generic in many parts of the world; others are unique to the Chinese cultural context. A most notable difference between the Chinese style of performance appraisal and that promoted in Western HRM literature is the relatively narrow focus of the former. The adoption of the Western approach in China is further hampered by the lack of strategic orientation of many Chinese firms and the deficiency of human resource (HR) skills to design

---

* This chapter focuses on mainland China.

DOI: 10.4324/9781003306849-13

and implement an effective performance management system. The utility of the Western approach to performance management is questioned.

While a level of simplicity is inevitable in a chapter that is to summarize the performance management practices of a vast country, this chapter avoids a broad-brush approach as far as possible by drawing specific examples from primary and secondary empirical data collected by the author. Primary data include interviews with government officials and civil servants, senior managers and HR managers in commercial businesses in the private sector. Secondary empirical data came from studies published in academic and practitioners' journals as well as scholarly books in both English and Chinese. Together, these primary and secondary empirical data sets provide balanced information that covers organizations of different sizes and ownership forms and different categories of employees and sectors. This spread of coverage is essential because these contingent factors may have a significant influence on the way the performance appraisal system is designed, implemented, utilized and perceived by both the appraisers and appraisees. For example, performance appraisal may be more widely used in government and civil service organizations in part because it is an established part of their HRM system, but performance measurement can be more subjective due to the perceived need to emphasize the ideological dimensions and the difficulties to quantify performance level compared with enterprises. It is these nuances that make the comparisons of performance appraisal systems across different organizations and sectors in China more interesting and revealing.

OVERVIEW OF CHINA'S HUMAN RESOURCE ENVIRONMENT

Founded in 1949, socialist China has over 70 years of history. For the first three decades until the end of the Cultural Revolution in 1976, the personnel management system in China was highly centralized under the state-planned economy regime. As of 1978, the state sector (government organization, public-sector organization and state-owned enterprises) employed nearly 80 per cent of the urban workforce (National Bureau of Statistics of China, 2021). Personnel management during this period exhibited two major features in terms of its governance structure and the substance of the personnel policy. First, the personnel policy and practice of organizations were strictly under the control of the state through the regional and local personnel and labour departments. Centralization, formalization and standardization of the personnel policies and practices were the primary tasks of the Ministry of Labour (for ordinary workers) and the Ministry of Personnel (for professional and managerial staff). It was these ministries' responsibility to determine the quantity to be employed and sources of recruitment as well as the pay scales for different categories of workers. State intervention was also extended to the structure and responsibility of the personnel functions, including performance management, at the organizational level. Managers of all levels were only involved in the administrative function and policy implementation under rigid policy guidelines (Child, 1994; Zhu and Warner, 2019). Second, job-for-life was the norm for the majority of employees in urban areas disregarding the work attitude and performance outcome of the individual (Warner, 1996). Wages were typically low with only a small gap between each grade as a result of the egalitarian approach to redistribution. Monetary incentives and personal advancement were regarded as incompatible with the socialist ideology.

These characteristics were dominant in the personnel management system of the country because, until the 1980s, the state was the employer of the majority of the urban workforce. The situation of state dominance started to change in the late 1970s, following the country's adoption of an 'open door' policy in 1978 to attract foreign investment and domestic private funds in order to revitalize the nation's economy. In parallel with this economic policy, the state sector has witnessed radical changes in its personnel policy and practice, as part of the Economic Reforms and the Enterprise Reforms that began in the early 1980s (Child, 1994). One of the major changes has been the rolling back of direct state control and the consequent increase of autonomy and responsibility at the enterprise level in major aspects of their personnel management practice, including the wide adoption of performance-related bonus schemes to subsidize the low wages. These changes were followed by several rounds of radical downsizing in the state-owned enterprises and, to a lesser extent, in the public sector and government organizations throughout the

1990s. This has led to a significant reduction of the state sector and the radical growth of businesses in a variety of forms of business ownership (Hassard et al., 2007). As of 2020, the state sector only employed less than 12 per cent of the urban workforce (National Bureau of Statistics of China, 2021).

Meanwhile, China's economic structure has undergone significant changes. Some industrial sectors have experienced slow growth or even contraction, whereas other sectors have seen rapid expansion during different periods. Construction, finance and insurance, real estate, retail and catering are amongst the industries that have expanded significantly. In general, the weight of China's economic structure has been moving from agriculture and heavy industry towards the service sector. In 1978, the gross domestic product (GDP) of the secondary industry (i.e. the industrial sector) made up 47.7 per cent of the national GDP whereas the GDP from the tertiary industry (the service sector) was only 24.6 per cent; in 2020, 54.5 per cent of the national GDP was contributed by the tertiary industry whereas GDP contributed by the secondary industry was reduced to 37.8 per cent[1] (National Bureau of Statistics of China, 2021). The growing diversity of ownership forms and business nature has different implications for performance management as part of human resource management in different firms in China.

HISTORICAL DEVELOPMENT OF THE PERFORMANCE MANAGEMENT SYSTEM

In line with the development of its personnel management system, the development of the performance management system in China can be divided into two broad periods.[2] The first period was the state-planned economy period during which performance appraisal for ordinary workers mainly focused on attendance monitoring and skill-grading tests. The former was used as the basis for wage deduction whereas the latter was for a pay rise. Since wage increases were frozen during the Cultural Revolution period (1966–1976), skill-grading tests were in effect not carried out. In addition, personal character traits were used as part of the criteria for evaluating an employee's performance. For the professional and managerial staff (broadly classified as state cadres), performance appraisal was used primarily as a means for selecting and developing cadres and as evidence for promotion (Zhu and Dowling, 1998). In the early years of socialist China, ideological (i.e. those who conform to the morals and values of the socialist regime) and technical elites were promoted. However, during the Cultural Revolution period, political performance (e.g. loyalty to the Communist Party) and moral integrity were the key criteria of performance measurement instead of technical competence and output. Organizational leaders were not enthusiastic about conducting performance appraisals in part because they lacked informative job specifications and performance indicators, and in part, they found the exercise time-consuming (Chou, 2005).

The second period started from the early 1980s till now, that is the period of market economic development. During this period, and particularly since the 1990s, performance appraisal systems have been more widely adopted by organizations. For example, Björkman and Lu's (1999) study of 72 foreign-invested enterprises in China found that nearly half of them had adapted their Western performance appraisal system to suit the Chinese culture. Ding et al.'s (1997, p. 611) study of 158 foreign-invested enterprises in southern China showed that 'regular evaluation of individual employee performance and setting employee pay levels based on individual performance have become organizational norms'. They also found that workers were receptive to individual-oriented performance measurement and rewards in order to maximize their income. However, it must be noted that performance review here is mainly used to determine pay. Performance-related pay is the main method for setting pay rates in the majority of foreign-invested manufacturing plants where workers, many of whom are rural migrant workers, work excessively long hours in order to increase their wage income.

Lindholm et al.'s (1999) survey of 604 Chinese managerial and professional employees from MNCs in China found that they were satisfied with the Western-style performance management system adopted in their company. They particularly liked the developmental approach in the system and were keen to participate in setting their performance objectives and receive formal performance feedback. It must be noted that prestigious multinational corporations (MNCs) in China are attractive to those who have strong career aspirations and desire development opportunities.

Bai and Bennington's (2005) study of the Chinese state-owned enterprises in the coal mining industry revealed that as a result of increasing pressure from intensified market competition, Chinese state-owned enterprises were utilizing modern performance appraisal measures as effective tools to enhance their management efficiency and productivity. Their study showed that whilst differences from Western performance appraisal practices persist, significant changes were taking place in performance appraisal practices in China that depart from their traditional form.

Performance management also became a top priority in the management of government and civil service organizations since the mid-1990s, as part of the state's broader initiative of reforming its civil service function (Burns and Zhou, 2010; Liu and Dong, 2012; Wang et al., 2019; Zhang and Zhou, 2017). In particular, the 'Provisional Regulations for State Civil Servants' was implemented in 1993 (hereafter 'Regulations'). The Regulations placed great emphasis on recruitment, performance appraisal and assessment, promotion, reward and disciplinary procedures in order to improve the transparency and efficiency of the personnel administration. The Regulations were replaced by the first Civil Servant Law of China which took effect on 1 January 2006.[3] The government officials and civil servants whom the author interviewed commonly reported that their municipal governments have adopted a type of 'management by objective' scheme where performance targets are cascaded down from each level and reviewed on an annual basis. Since the 2010s, the performance management of government officials (also classified as civil servants) has been tightened even more, especially during crises such as COVID-19, and they are 'accountable for anything that goes wrong', as some of the interviewees remarked.

KEY FACTORS INFLUENCING THE PERFORMANCE MANAGEMENT SYSTEM

A number of key factors influence the performance management systems in China, mainly in the design of the performance indicators and the process of conducting performance appraisals. While some factors are generic to performance management in many countries, others are specific to the Chinese cultural and institutional context.

The influence of organizational size, ownership and business nature

Variations in HRM practices tend to exist as a result of differences in organizational size, ownership forms and business nature of the firm. The same is true in the performance management system in China (distal factors). For example, Wang *et al.*'s (2019) study found that political, cultural and institutional contextual factors tend to affect performance appraisal practices in Chinese public sector organizations. Chen *et al.*'s (2004) study of 100 enterprises of various sizes in the information technology (IT) industry found that, compared with larger firms, smaller enterprises tended to focus on individuals' quality and competence in their appraisal system, including attitude, work intensity, moral integrity and position and neglect the evaluation of team performance or the quality of customer services. The study also revealed that employees in smaller firms paid more attention to the utilization of their competence, had lower demands for and expectations from the performance appraisal system and were more easily satisfied and motivated than their counterparts in larger firms. In addition, appraisal outcomes in smaller firms were more heavily influenced by the subjective impression of the superior (rater), whereas the intervention of subjectivity was better avoided in larger firms.

While sharing some similarities, the performance management system applied to ordinary employees tends to differ from that for professional/managerial staff. These differences become even more significant between enterprises and government, civil services and public-sector organizations. Generally speaking, performance appraisal for ordinary employees in China was mainly about linking their productivity and level of responsibility with their wages and bonuses in order to motivate them to work towards the organizational goals and generate profits (see Table 13.1). This is in spite of the fact that an employee's moral behaviour continues to be part of the appraisal in many state-owned enterprises. By contrast, results of performance appraisals for professional and managerial staff, particularly those in government and civil service organizations, are often linked to annual bonuses and promotions. The state also has a much more hands-on role in designing the performance indicators for

Fang Lee Cooke

government officials and civil servants. In 1998, the Ministry of Personnel introduced a new performance appraisal scheme for evaluating civil servants (Chou, 2005). The scheme focused on four main performance indicators as criteria for assessing civil servants' performance: *De* (morality), *neng* (competence/ability), *qin* (diligence/work attitude) and *ji* (achievement). Many organizations added another indicator, *lian* (honesty/non-corrupted), to the four as corruption opportunities became relatively widespread amongst government officials and civil servants. Similar criteria for performance appraisal apply in public-sector organizations (Wang *et al.*, 2019).

In principle, performance appraisal for all employees focuses on two aspects: behaviour measurement and outcome measurement. These include the employee's moral and ideological behaviour, competence, skill level and ability to apply skills and knowledge to work, work attitude, work performance and achievement, personal attributes, physical health and so forth. It has been noted (e.g. Chou, 2005) that the importance of political integrity has been since the early 2000s significantly downplayed by leaders in government organizations because of the need to have competent cadres to deliver government functions effectively. However, the intensifying Sino-US politico-economic-technological war and the rise of nationalism means that the political stance of government officials has become a key focus. The continuing anti-corruption campaign under the Xi Jinping government has also put government officials and civil servants on their toes (Vyas and Wu, 2020).

Broadly speaking, performance appraisals for non-managerial employees in enterprises tend to be held on a more regular basis than that for government officials and civil servants. This is mainly because the outcome of the former is often directly linked to their financial reward and job security (proximal factors; see Table 13.1). The methods of assessment/appraisal used for non-managerial employees in enterprises are also simpler, mainly between the supervisor and the individual being appraised. The practice of the last one out is commonly adopted by well-performing private enterprises in which the last 10 per cent or so performers may be given counselling by their appraiser and training for improvement. Failure to do so

Table 13.1 Key characteristics in performance assessment/appraisal practices in China

	Main characteristics of enterprise workers	Main characteristics for government officials and civil servants
Purposes of assessment (proximal factors)	Financial reward, job grading, job retention	Financial reward, routine appraisal, promotion and grading
Measurements of performance (proximal factors)	More quantifiable hard targets Effort (e.g. attendance, work attitude), output (e.g. productivity),	Hard as well as 'soft' criteria Four or five norms *De* (morality), *neng* (competence/ability), *qin* (diligence /work attitude), *ji* (achievement), *lian* (honesty/non-corruptness)
Methods of assessment	Top-down assessment, self-evaluation Tests to compete for posts – 'last one in the assessment out' practices Digital technology and data analytics	Self-appraisal, collective/ peer appraisal discussion meetings as acts of democracy, top-down assessment, bottom-up appraisal
Frequency of assessment (intervening factors)	Monthly, quarterly, six-monthly, and annual (end-of-the-year) appraisals	Six-monthly and annual (end-of-the-year) appraisals
Implementation process (intervening factors)	Relatively easier to conduct appraisal/ assessment due to a more specific purpose and outcome	More problematic to conduct appraisal due to less quantifiable criteria, more complex relationships with peers/superiors, and organizational politics A greater level of subjectivity and intervention
Utilization of outcome (distortion factors)	Linked to financial reward Little link to training and development Little feedback from superior	Linked to bonus and promotion Little link to training and development Little feedback from superior
Persistent cultural influence v. adaptation of western HR practices (distal factors)	Harmonization, egalitarian norm More widespread adaptation of performance appraisal of western style as part of modernized HR practices to enhance organizational performance	Harmonization, egalitarian norm Less influenced by individualistic performance-related reward pressure More cautious adaptation of western HR practices due to sectoral and ideological differences

(Continued)

Fang Lee Cooke

Table 13.1 (Continued)

	Main characteristics of enterprise workers	Main characteristics for government officials and civil servants
Acceptance of performance appraisal practices (proximal factors)	More receptive to performance-related rewards due to job insecurity and the financial pressure of individuals	More resistant to performance appraisal due to a greater level of subjectivity in appraisal criteria and intervention in the process

in the next round of appraisal may lead to these employees being demoted, retrained, and dismissed if underperformance persisted. By comparison, annual performance appraisal (at the end of the year) is the norm in government and civil service organizations. The performance appraisal procedure adopted is more sophisticated. It normally involves the initial self-appraisal, followed by a peer appraisal discussion meeting held collectively in the department as an act of democracy. Finally, the department leader will sign the form and submit it to the personnel department for record keeping.

Business nature, broadly defined, further influences the performance management system. This is often the case across different departments within the same organization. For example, an observation shared by many government officials whom the author has interviewed was that it is easier for the heads of revenue-generating departments to get a good rating for their performance than those who are in charge of departments that are prone to public complaints no matter how hard they have worked and how much they have achieved. Police forces and municipal environment cleaning and protection units are cases in point. However, interviewees also reported that municipal leaders are acutely aware of the need to 'balance the situation' so that staff in the complaint-prone departments are not demotivated because their performance forms a vital part of the overall performance of the municipal government. Municipal leaders may intervene in the performance appraisal outcomes by rotating the top prize between departments (the leaders of which will be rewarded accordingly) or by offering some concessions or other benefits discretely to those departments that are given lower ratings.

The declining but enduring influence of Chinese culture

Performance appraisal (and rewards associated with it) is perhaps one of the HRM practices that display the most enduring influence of Chinese culture (distal factor). It has been widely noted that the Chinese culture respects seniority and hierarchy, values social harmony, and adopts an egalitarian approach to distribution (Hofstede, 1991; Takahara, 1992; Yu, 1998). It is a well-known fact that the Chinese respect age and seniority. In an organizational environment, this is often translated into the following assumption: Older age → seniority → higher grade and higher organizational position → higher level of contribution and more value-added to the organization → higher income. Similarly, egalitarianism has long been recognized as a unique Chinese societal culture and continues to be used by some as a yardstick of fairness and equity in rewards, especially in the distribution of bonuses. It has been reported that those who were rated for the top prize had to share their bonuses with their colleagues in order to avoid jealousy and resentment in the public sector. Employees have also been known to rotate the top award amongst themselves (Cooke, 2004). Since performance appraisal in China is often narrowly related to financial reward and promotion instead of training and development needs, these Chinese norms play a particularly influential role throughout the appraisal stages. The Chinese cultural norm of modesty and self-discipline (Bailey *et al.*, 1997) is also reflected in the appraisal system because self-evaluation and criticism often form part of the appraisal process and content, particularly in government and civil service organizations. In addition, Chinese employers tend to attach considerable weight to their employees' work attitude and the effort they have made in their work, often disregarding the outcome of their work. This norm is typically applied in the selection for promotion and bonus allocation.

The strong influence of the Chinese culture on performance appraisal has been confirmed by the findings of a number of empirical studies. For example, Easterby-Smith *et al.*'s (1995) comparative study of eight matched Chinese and UK companies revealed that appraisal criteria in Chinese organizations focus on not only hard tasks but also 'moral' and ideological behaviour. Self-evaluation and democratic sounding of opinions by peers and subordinates are the commonly used appraisal methods. Studies on performance appraisal practices in MNCs and joint ventures in mainland China further highlighted the tension between what is required to be effective in implementing the western approach to performance appraisal and the Chinese cultural tradition (e.g. Child, 1994; Lindholm *et al.*, 1999). Whilst the former requires individualistic goal setting, face-to-face feedback/criticism and employee involvement, the latter respects age, hierarchy and values collectivism and emphasizes the importance of maintaining 'face' and harmonious relationships at the workplace (e.g. Bozionelos and Wang, 2007; Hofstede, 1991; Lockett, 1988).

However, changes in the cultural outlook are taking place in China, as mentioned earlier. For example, Bailey *et al.*'s (1997) comparative study of managers in the US, Japan and mainland China found that whilst the collectivist culture remained pertinent amongst the Chinese managers surveyed, there was a discernible new trend for endorsing individual accountability and initiative in the Chinese enterprises as a result of transformational changes in China's economic policy since the late 1970s. Bai and Bennington's (2005) study also revealed that Chinese cultural values did not impede the implementation of individual performance-related reward schemes, suggesting that the new materialism has overtaken traditional cultural forces. In the private sector, the traditional Chinese cultural norms of egalitarianism and seniority are significantly diluted by the constant pressure for employees to exceed their performance, often tied to performance-related pay, in order to for the business to remain competitive. Despite stipulations of the labour law, many private firms do not offer permanent employment contracts and continuing employment is underpinned by the individual's performance record. In the state sector, however, cultural values still hold strong. As Gu and Nolan's (2017, p. 1433) study of the performance appraisal system of three banks in China shows, while the Chinese banks are converging towards western practices, they retain strong Chinese cultural characteristics in that the 'perceived influence of *guanxi* [interpersonal relationships] on performance appraisal was strongest in the state-owned bank and weakest in the foreign-owned bank'. Specifically, the generational effect of cultural values, the international experience of the employees and managers in the state-owned bank and the alignment between the senior managers and others over the purpose of the performance appraisal were the main reasons for the differences observed between the state-owned and foreign-owned banks (Gu and Nolan, 2017). As a result, the state-owned bank 'was perceived as significantly less fair in its appraisal procedures than both its city-commercial and foreign-owned counterparts' (Gu et al., 2020).

MAJOR CHALLENGES TO EFFECTIVE PERFORMANCE MANAGEMENT

Performance management in China encounters a number of pitfalls and challenges, as it does in other countries. Some of these are universal, and others are accentuated by Chinese cultural values and organizational characteristics. This section discusses some of these issues.

Lack of strategic HRM, understanding of and managerial competence for performance management systems

An important element of a performance management system is the alignment of the system with the strategic goals of the organization because a fundamental task for the former is to ensure the fulfilment of the latter (Williams, 2002). However, the majority of Chinese organizations do not have clear strategic goals, let alone cascade these goals to departmental and individual levels and design comprehensive performance indicators based on these strategic goals (Yu, 2006). As Liu and Dong (2012) argued, despite considerable progress since the 1993 reforms, the performance appraisal system for civil servants needs to be better connected with the human resource management system and the performance budget system and improve on the appraisal technics. Moreover, performance measures are increasingly focusing on relatively short-term financial targets.

Since the 2000s, many HRM concepts and practices were introduced as advanced Western management philosophy and techniques, including performance management, performance appraisal, management by objective, balanced scorecard, key performance indicators and so on. Organizations started to apply these new HRM concepts and tools to their organizations

Fang Lee Cooke

without a real understanding of what they mean and how they can be adapted to suit their organizational environment. An increasing number of organizations are reported to have adopted performance management schemes and implemented performance appraisal practices. However, the majority of appraisers and appraisees are not aware of what is being assessed and for what purposes. An important part of the performance management system is to utilize the appraisal outcome to inform various aspects of the HRM, including career planning, employee training and development, job allocation and reward. However, the majority of Chinese firms still lack a strategic and integrated approach to HRM, particularly in using performance appraisals to inform employee training and development. As a result, performance appraisal is often narrowly focused on reward (proximal factors) instead of utilizing the result to inform career planning and training and development (e.g. Chen *et al.*, 2004).

There is insufficient managerial thinking and skill in designing a performance management system and conducting performance appraisals. Discrepancies in performance measure criteria and standards often exist across departments within the same organization, causing grievances from employees when a similar level of performance is given different scores and financial rewards (Liu, 2005).

Performance management has not been fully accepted by managers as an effective tool for managing human resources. According to a study conducted by Zhang (2005) who surveyed the managers and workers across the five subsidiaries of a large stock market–listed state-owned enterprise, junior managers appeared to be more conservative and resistant than workers in terms of implementing a new performance management scheme which is aimed to relate performance more closely to financial rewards. More specifically, whilst 90 per cent of the mid-ranking managers believed that differential rewards would be more effective than an egalitarian distribution system, over half of the junior managers believed that differential rewards should only be implemented when egalitarian elements were also incorporated in the differential scheme. While over 80 per cent of the mid-ranking managers believed that recognition and incentive would have motivational effects, only 12 per cent of junior managers felt this was the case. By contrast, over half of the workers surveyed had a positive attitude towards performance-related pay, and only a small minority of 10–15 per cent felt that competition pressure and distributional variations should be minimized. In addition, whilst 64 per cent of the workers believed that their reward was closely related to their group performance, the rest felt that their reward had nothing to do with group performance. This indicates that the alignment of goals and performance levels has yet to be made at all levels within the organization.

Performance appraisal seen as a formality

A related problem is that performance appraisal is often seen as a waste of time and not taken seriously by either the appraisers or the appraisees (e.g. Chou, 2005; Cooke and Huang, 2011). A manager from a tax bureau whom the author interviewed disclosed that he distributed the annual appraisal forms to his staff for them to fill in rather than conducting the appraisal and writing the comments himself. All he did was sign his name on the forms without checking them and forward the forms to the personnel department for record keeping.

> I am too busy to do all that rubbish, especially at the end of the year. I don't want to upset my staff by giving them negative feedback. It is just a formality we have to go through once a year. It is not real work.

A common feature in the performance appraisal is that the appraisal outcome is rarely fed back to the appraisee in qualitative comments and is seldom used for training and development purposes (Chen *et al.*, 2004; Easterby-Smith *et al.*, 1995). This is in part because line managers are reluctant to provide negative feedback to subordinates in order to avoid causing resentment and resistance from the staff concerned which may impede motivation and performance further. It is also related to the narrow use of performance appraisal for financial rewards as a prevailing practice in China.

Avoiding criticism of bad behaviour reflects the Chinese culture of neutrality which leads to the tolerance of poor performers, thus demotivating good performers. The egalitarian and neutral approach to managing workplace relationships further results in the adoption of a broadband approach to performance rating. In most organizations, a quota system is imposed by the senior authority in classifying employees' performance in their annual performance reviews. For example, according to the state guideline for government and civil service organizations, no more than 10 per cent of civil servant employees should be rated 'excellent' for symbolic purposes, the same is true for the last category 'unacceptable'. This broadband system and the small differentials in prize awards do not provide sufficient motivational or punitive effects to enhance performance levels.

For some appraisees whose wage is not related to performance, the incentive impact of receiving a good rating is so small that it falls short of being inspirational, to say the least. A mid-ranking civil servant (a department chief of a traffic bureau) whom the author interviewed held this view, which was shared by some other civil servants interviewed:

> Our annual performance appraisal is a pointless exercise. It has no value at all. I was rated as the best employee of the year by my colleagues in the bureau last year, but I did not want to take the title, because the reward was so trivial and meaningless. I did what I need to do and what I think I should do, not because I wanted to get the prize. I feel more comfortable without it.

The lack of utility of performance appraisal as perceived by appraisers and appraisees remains a severe barrier (intervening factor) to the effective implementation of performance appraisal, particularly in the public sector.

Subjectivity and the increasing role of digital technology

It is recognized that subjectivity exists in performance appraisals, especially for jobs the performance of which is difficult to quantify and measure. The impartiality and competence of the appraiser in conducting appraisals also play an important part in controlling the level of subjectivity. Since the majority of Chinese managers have limited HR training and knowledge, the level of subjectivity may be relatively high when they use their own judgement, experience and preference in conducting the performance appraisal and distributing rewards. On one hand, certain types of employees may be rated and rewarded favourably;

on the other hand, Chinese managers may continue to feel the pressure to adopt a broad band in assessing performance levels and an egalitarian approach to the distribution of rewards in order to maintain workplace harmony.

An added dimension of subjectivity in performance appraisal in China is the way performance measurement criteria are set. As discussed earlier, performance measurement criteria in China tend to focus on effort and behaviour instead of/as much as the outcome. There is a lack of individualized performance measurement indicators to reflect the specific characteristics of different posts in the public sector where performance is less quantifiable. The five major criteria for performance appraisal for government officials and civil servants are a case in point (see Table 13.1). The high level of subjectivity is reflected in a sarcastic saying that is going around: 'If the leader says you are good, then you are good even if you are no good. If the leader says you are no good, then you are no good even if you are good'. This subjectivity encourages some people to pretend to be busy and cultivate their relationships with their superiors to gain promotion.

Not all jobs would allow the worker to pretend to be busy. The performance management of certain categories of the workers, such as takeaway riders and cleaners in the public domain, has become much more transparent and instantaneous by using digital technology, such as GPS. Tightening performance surveillance has been a salient feature for workers whose productivity can be measured easily. This happens not just in China but also in other parts of the world, including large multinational firms such as Amazon. The growing use of digital technology and artificial intelligence in performance management means that the level of subjectivity interjected by the managers may be reduced, but at the same time, work pace is intensifying and individuals relying on performance-related pay are under pressure to work faster and longer hours, resulting in health problems, burnout and overwork-related deaths (Wang and Cooke, 2021).

Interventions in the appraisal process

Ironically, the biggest hurdle in making performance appraisal really effective is perhaps the adoption of the collective peer appraisal method. It requires colleagues from the same group/department to gather together to give a self-appraisal and to

Fang Lee Cooke

appraise each other's performance, including that of their superior, in a face-to-face meeting. The collective peer appraisal, known as the 'democratic life meeting' during Mao's era, is often no more than a show. It provides *prima facie* evidence of fairness and transparency in the process. In reality, peers are unwilling to say anything negative to others face-to-face as a Chinese norm of face-saving for both parties. They are even less willing to criticize their superiors for fear of revenge. Fear of negative consequences of appraisal (e.g. revenge by a superior if criticizing his conduct or reduced bonus as a result of self-criticism) is an important distortion factor in the performance appraisal process. Finally, it has been observed that annual appraisal report writing can be a literary exercise for supervisors, and it may be the supervisor's literary skills, rather than the civil servants' performance *per se*, that determines the appraisal results. 'Moreover, supervisors were not held responsible for falsifying civil servants' performance records' (Chou, 2005, p. 47). However, performance supervisors may exercise leniency bias when rating their employees due to contextual uncertainty (i.e. supervisors' span of control vs. employees' job non-routineness) and prior employee performance (Gong *et al.*, 2021).

Elitism and high-performance culture

Marchington (2015) was highly critical of the direction that HRM research and practice has been heading, namely the obsession with strategic HRM to prove the legitimacy of HRM as an organizational function and the increasing focus on talent management as a small group of elites who are believed to create value for the organization and thus need to be nurtured (see also Harney and Collings, 2021). This trend is becoming more and more evident and widespread in China. Elitism is very much part of the Chinese traditional culture that has been revived after three decades of suppression during the state-planned economy period (1949–1978). Increasingly, companies adopt an elitist approach to HRM by considering highly educated and top-performing employees as talents to focus on for recruitment and then find the most effective way to incentivize their management (Cooke et al., 2014).

Leading private companies like Huawei and Tencent are constantly searching for an effective performance management system and fostering a high-performance culture for employees to increase their performance levels continuously. Others are exploring innovative ways to improve employee performance. For example, Song *et al.*'s (2019, p. 1) study also found that a large financial service firm in China was using work-oriented social media (DingTalk) and socialization-oriented social media (WeChat) as complementary resources to 'generate synergies to improve team and employee performance'. As such, the firm was using information technology investments to create business value.

Having tried various Western performance techniques such as 360-degree feedback, key performance indicators and objectives and key results with limited success, some companies have turned to a narrow focus on the financial target and cascade the target down to each department and, subsequently, each team and individual. It is short term and narrow, with little consideration of the long-term development needs of employees. Poor performers are simply dismissed or encouraged to exit the company. It is a simplistic and pragmatic approach adopted by companies to remain competitive. In this approach, performance is managed with financial mechanisms, entrenching the annual performance appraisal exercise as a formality to show that the company has such an HR policy and practice.

Common in performance appraisal techniques is the need to assign the appraised employees to a performance category or rank them in a performance spectrum. The bell curve technique or a forced distribution evaluation system is often used by organizations in China. Ge *et al.*'s (2022) study reveals that the implementation of the forced distribution evaluation system has a negative impact on the individual innovation performance of employees and that although the implementation of the forced distribution evaluation system improves the innovation performance of low-performance employees, it reduces the innovation performance of elite employees, which is contrary to the original intention of some companies to pursue elite culture by implementing this system. In addition, the results show that the degree of employee cooperation plays a moderating role in the implementation of the forced distribution evaluation system and employee innovation performance in that the higher the degree of employee cooperation, the greater the negative impact of the company's implementation of the forced distribution evaluation system on employee innovation performance.

Employee retention

The organizational behaviour and HRM literature have long suggested that intrinsic rewards are the most effective mechanisms to motivate and retain employees, whereas extrinsic rewards such as bonuses and subsidies are hygiene factors (Herzberg, 1987). However, research evidence and fieldwork conducted by the author show that material incentives remain crucial in retaining talents. The younger generation of Chinese has been identified to be more demanding and eager to succeed, in large part as a result of the 'one-child' policy enforced from the 1980s to the mid-2010s (Connor, 2013). In particular, the role of employee share ownership plays a critical role in incentivizing employees' organizational behaviour and performance in some firms, whereas performance-related bonuses and other material incentives have been heavily used to retain and motivate employees. Huawei is an exceptional example, in which the founding CEO, Ren Zhengfei, holds only less than 1 per cent of Huawei's shares, and its employees hold the majority of shares.

The story of NetEase, where the author conducted fieldwork in 2019, illustrates the important role of material incentives and career paths in managing young talents, in addition to a mix of other 'human-centred' and 'cost-centred' HRM practices. NetEase Inc., founded in 1997 and based in Guangzhou, is a Chinese IT company that develops and operates online PC and mobile games, advertising services, email services and e-commerce platforms in China. It is one of the largest internet and video game companies in the world. According to the managers interviewed by the author, due to the nature of the business, the majority of the workers are young university graduates in their early to mid-20s. They not only are highly talented with creative ideas but are also rather individualistic in their preferences. HRM programmes are therefore developed to cater to individual strengths to maximize their satisfaction of working with the company, performance, and retention. There is a sophisticated initial training system to identify high-potential employees and enable them to complete the training quickly and be promoted to more value-added positions to fulfil their potential. A mentor system is adopted to coach new staff. Staff turnover is one of the key performance indicators of team leaders. Emotional control mechanisms are implemented to deal with 'bad' customers, for example, exchanging bad customers amongst peers, turning to peers for help to deal with the bad customer, and having tea parties in the afternoon to overcome stress and share positive energy. An employee is expected to work in a certain position for two to three years and is then promoted to another position before they are fatigued and let them see the career progression path. Moreover, a rich welfare and benefits programme is available, from which employees can choose their preferred welfare schemes. In short, according to the managers interviewed, NetEase tries all sorts of ways to please the employees, including, for example, finding out what their interests are and then pleasing them by having parties, games and so forth and then giving them prizes. However, these seemingly human-centred HRM practices are a means to maintain and improve employee performance.

CONCLUSION

This chapter has provided an overview of the historical development of performance management systems in China. It has revealed that some form of performance appraisal has long existed in a Chinese style, with a narrower purpose and a different focus on its content (e.g. moral behaviour) than what is being promoted in the Western literature on the performance management system. In recent years, performance management as a modern western HRM concept and technique is being embraced by an increasing number of Chinese firms. Chinese employees in enterprises are becoming more receptive towards performance-oriented rewards and welcome career development opportunities through the implementation of a performance management system.

However, the implementation of a performance appraisal system in China is challenged by a number of factors that are universal as well as cultural- and organizational-specific. In particular, Chinese cultural values seem to have a profound and enduring influence throughout the various stages of the performance appraisal system. This is especially the case in government and civil service organizations where state intervention remains relatively strong and performance outcomes are more difficult to quantify. It is perhaps in this sector where performance appraisal is more seen as a formality and punctuated with a greater level of subjectivity, compared with the reward-driven performance appraisal system in enterprises, especially in the private sector.

Fang Lee Cooke

In general, the performance appraisal system in China is reward-driven and tends to focus on the person and behavioural performance, whereas the performance appraisal system promoted in the Western HRM literature takes a developmental approach and focuses on the alignment between individual performance and organizational goals. Nevertheless, recent studies on performance appraisal practices in China show that an increasing number of Chinese organizations are experimenting with some Western performance management techniques. Whilst a total transfer of Western practices is not found, or indeed plausible, a unique blending of both modernizing and traditional forces is at play in shaping the performance management practices in China (Bailey et al., 1997; Song et al., 2019; Wang et al., 2019). The continuing trend of adaptation of Western performance management practices is likely to lead to further behavioural changes from Chinese managers and employees that depart from traditional Chinese cultural norms exhibited in the Chinese-style performance appraisal system. At the same time, firms are increasingly adopting an elitist approach to recruiting and managing high-performing employees to remain competitive. This high-performance culture and management practices have implications for human resource development and employee well-being.

NOTES

1 In statistical terms, the primary industry refers to the agricultural sector, secondary industry refers to the industrial sector and the tertiary industry refers to the service sector (see *China Statistical Yearbook*).
2 Also see Zhu and Dowling (1998) for a summary of the history of performance appraisal in China.
3 The Civil Servant Law (2006) applies to the management of government officials and civil servants in other public-funded organizations. There were nearly 6.4 million civil servants and more than 30 million personnel working in the public-funded organizations in China by the end of 2003 (*China Daily*, 27th April 2005).

REFERENCES

Bai, X. and Bennington, L. (2005) 'Performance appraisal in the Chinese state-owned coal industry', *International Journal of Business Performance Management*, 7, 3, pp. 275–287.
Bailey, J., Chen, C. and Dou, S. (1997) 'Conceptions of self and performance-related feedback in the US', *Journal of International Business Studies*, 28, 3, pp. 605–625.
Björkman, I. and Lu, Y. (1999) 'A corporate perspective on the management of human resources in China', *Journal of World Business*, 34, 1, pp. 16–25.

Bozionelos, N. and Wang, L. (2007) 'An investigation on the attitudes of Chinese workers towards individually based performance-related reward systems', *The International Journal of Human Resource Management*, 18, 2, pp. 284–302.

Burns, J. P. and Zhou, Z. R. (2010) 'Performance management in the government of the Peoples Republic of China: Accountability and control in the implementation of public policy', *OECD Journal on Budgeting*, 10, 2, pp. 1–28.

Chen, M. Z., Wang, L. P. and Dai, H. R. (2004) 'Performance appraisal criteria and implementation in small IT enterprises in China', *Development and Management of Human Resources*, 3, pp. 36–39.

Child, J. (1994) *Management in China during the Age of Reform*, Cambridge: Cambridge University Press.

Chou, B. (2005) 'Implementing the reform of performance appraisal in China's civil service', *China Information*, XIX, 1, pp. 39–65.

Connor, S. (2013) 'One-child policy: China's army of little emperors', *The Independent*, 10 January.

Cooke, F. L. (2004) 'Public sector pay in China: 1949–2001', *International Journal of Human Resource Management*, 15, 4/5, pp. 895–916.

Cooke, F. L. and Huang, K. (2011) 'Post-acquisition evolution of the appraisal and reward systems: A study of Chinese IT firms acquired by US firms', *Human Resource Management*, 50, 6, pp. 839–858.

Cooke, F. L., Saini, D. and Wang, J. (2014) 'Talent management in China and India: A comparison of management perceptions and human resource practices', *Journal of World Business*, 49, 2, pp. 225–235.

Easterby-Smith, M., Malina, D. and Lu, Y. (1995) 'How culture-sensitive is HRM?' *International Journal of Human Resource Management*, 6, 1, pp. 31–59.

Ge, C. M., Zhan, M. M., Deng, H. Q. and Jiang, J. H. (2022) 'Research on the impact of mandatory distribution evaluation system on employee innovation performance', *China Human Resource Development*, 39, 3, pp. 6–22.

Gong, N., Boh, W. F., Wu, A. and Kuo, T. L. (2021) 'Leniency bias in subjective performance evaluation: Contextual uncertainty and prior employee performance', *Emerging Markets Finance and Trade*, 57, 8, pp. 2176–2190.

Gu, F. and Nolan, J. (2017) 'Performance appraisal in Western and local banks in China: The influence of firm ownership on the perceived importance of guanxi', *The International Journal of Human Resource Management*, 28, 10, pp. 1433–1453.

Gu, F., Nolan, J. and Rowley, C. (2020) 'Organizational justice in Chinese banks: understanding the variable influence of guanxi on perceptions of fairness in performance appraisal', *Asia Pacific Business Review*, 26, 2, pp. 169–189.

Harney, B. and Collings, D. G. (2021) 'Navigating the shifting landscapes of HRM', *Human Resource Management Review*, 31, 4, p. 100824.

Hassard, J., Sheehan, J., Zhou, M., Terpstra-Tong, J. and Morris, J. (2007) *China's State Enterprise Reform: From Marx to the Market*. Cheltenham, UK: Routledge.

Herzberg, F. (1987) 'One more time: How do you motivate employees?', *Harvard Business Review*, 65, 5, pp. 109–120.

Hofstede, G. (1991) *Cultures and Organizations, Software of the Mind*. New York: McGraw-Hill.

Lindholm, N. (1999) 'Performance management in MNC subsidiaries in China: A study of host-country managers and professionals', *Asia Pacific Journal of Human Resources*, 37, 3, pp. 18–35.

Lindholm, N., Tahvanainen, M. and Björkman, I. (1999) 'Performance appraisal of host country employees: Western MNEs in China', in Brewster, C. and Harris, H. (eds.), *International HRM: Contemporary Issues in Europe* (pp. 143–159). London: Routledge.

Liu, H. X. (2005) 'Who should appraise the appraisers and who should monitor the monitors', *Development and Management of Human Resources*, 11, pp. 40–41.

Liu, X. and Dong, K. (2012) 'Development of the civil servants' performance appraisal system in China: Challenges and improvements', *Review of Public Personnel Administration*, 32, 2, pp. 149–168.

Lockett, M. (1988) 'Culture and the problems of Chinese management', *Organisation Studies*, 9, pp. 475–496.

Marchington, M. (2015) 'Human resource management (HRM): Too busy looking up to see where it is going longer term?', *Human Resource Management Review*, 25, 2, pp. 176–187.

National Bureau of Statistics of China (2021) *China Statistical Yearbook 2021*, http://www.stats.gov.cn/tjsj/ndsj/2021/indexeh.htm.

Song, Q., Wang, Y., Chen, Y., Benitez, J. and Hu, J. (2019) 'Impact of the usage of social media in the workplace on team and employee performance', *Information & Management*, 56, 8, pp. 1–20.

Takahara, A. (1992) *The Politics of Wage Policy in Post-Revolutionary China*. London: Macmillan.

Vyas, L. and Wu, A. M. (2020) 'Anti-corruption policy: China's Tiger Hunt and India's demonetization', *International Journal of Public Administration*, 43, 11, pp. 1000–1011.

Wang, M., Zhu, C. J., Mayson, S. and Chen, W. (2019) 'Contextualizing performance appraisal practices in Chinese public sector organizations: the importance of context and areas for future study', *The International Journal of Human Resource Management*, 30, 5, pp. 902–919.

Wang, T. Y. and Cooke, F. L. (2021) 'Internet platform employment in China: Legal challenges and implications for gig workers through the lens of court rulings', *Relations Industrielles/Industrial Relations*, 76, 3, pp. 541–564.

Warner, M. (1996) 'Human resources in the People's Republic of China: The "Three Systems" Reforms', *Human Resource Management Journal*, 6, 2, pp. 32–42.

Williams, R. (2002) *Managing Employee Performance: Design and Implementation in Organisations*, London: Thomson Learning.

Yu, H. (2006) 'Performance management of the Chinese style', *Development and Management of Human Resources*, 1, pp. 34–35.

Yu, K. C. (1998) 'Chinese employees' perceptions of distributive fairness', in Francesco, A. M. and Gold, B. A. (eds.), *International Organisational Behavior* (pp. 302–313). New Jersey: Prentice Hall.

Zhang, L. H. (2005) 'A case study analysis of the remuneration change strategy of a state-owned enterprise', *Development and Management of Human Resources*, 11, pp. 47–49.

Zhang, M. and Zhou, W. (2017) 'Civil service reforms in Mainland China', In *Public Administration in East Asia* (pp. 145–164). London: Routledge.

Zhu, C. and Dowling, P. (1998) 'Performance appraisal in China', in Selmer, J. (ed.), *International Management in China: Cross-Cultural Issues* (pp. 115–136). London: Routledge.

Zhu, C. J. and Warner, M. (2019) 'The emergence of Human Resource Management in China: convergence, divergence and contextualization', *Human Resource Management Review*, 29, 1, pp. 87–97.

USEFUL WEBSITES

http://www.chinaHR.com
http://www.ChinaHRD.net
http://www.china-hr.org
http://www.800hr.com

Performance Management Systems in South Korea

Hyuckseung Yang and Chris Rowley

Chapter 14

INTRODUCTION

Performance management systems (PMSs) in South Korea (hereafter Korea) can be best understood in the context of the transformation companies have gone through in the nature of their relationship with their human resources (HR) and HR management (HRM) as a whole within Korea's institutional and cultural context. This has several aspects to it, including the underpinning and content of HRM, and the PMSs within it, and three critical junctions in time – 1987, 1997 and 2016. We deal with these in the following sections. As such our chapter deals with the development, features and issues of PMSs and factors that are evaluated to influence their changing nature. It should be noted, however, that all the dimensions of PMSs are not included, but the typical features, issues and factors conspicuous in Korea are explored.

BRIEF SOCIO-ECONOMIC AND POLITICAL BACKGROUND

Korean society is influenced by its Confucianist traditions and background. This impacts national and corporate culture, management and business from values and norms such as

DOI: 10.4324/9781003306849-14

hierarchical paternalism, kinship and collectivism (Rowley, 2002; Rowley and Bae, 2003; Yang, Chang and Song, 2005). Emerging from under-development, poverty and the ruin of Japanese occupation and the Korean War, the post-1960s Korean economy boomed and transformed from an agricultural basis to manufacturing successes and social development. Korea was seen as one of the Asian 'miracles', albeit its underpinnings and sustainability have been challenged (see Rowley and Fitzgerald, 1996; Rowley and Bae, 1998; Rowley et al., 2002). We step aside from such debates and note Korea has emerged as a producer of a range of products from 'ships to chips' in global markets from particular forms of capitalism, the *chaebol*, large, diversified, family-owned conglomerates. Korea recorded high economic growth from 1960 to 1997 during which the gross domestic product (GDP) grew at an average annual rate of about 7%.

However, the 1997 Asian financial crisis seemed to expose these achievements and structures as a 'mirage' (Rowley and Bae, 2004). The crisis led to the bankruptcy of some *chaebols* such as Daewoo, and the surviving *chaebols* became vulnerable. Banks' lending standards were strengthened due to the financial crisis, and above all, the International Monetary Fund (IMF) imposed liberalization of the 'direct investment market' in exchange for bailouts. As a result, the maximum share of stocks that foreign investors can hold increased from 26% in 1997 to 50%, and from 50% to 55% in 1998. The IMF also called for stricter antitrust regulations and put them into practice. Due to these changes, Korea has an economic system that is more open to competition both domestically and internationally (Aghion, Antonin and Bunel, 2022).

The post-1950s political background can be divided into two phases. Following a succession of post-war military and authoritarian governments, in 1987 political democracy was achieved. In the mid-2010s, there was a crisis in political democracy due to the movement to regress to an authoritarian government, but the peaceful Candlelight Revolution by citizens in 2017, which is hard to find in the world, put the brakes on such a backward movement. In short, Korea has become a country that has successfully realized industrialization and democratization in a short period of about 60 years, and Korea's status was officially changed by the United Nations Conference on Trade and Development (UNCTAD) from a developing country to a developed country group on July 2, 2021.

Meanwhile, in 2016, there was a special event that made Korean society realize that a wave of great change is coming. In March, Sedol Lee, the world's top-ranked Go player, and AlphaGo, an artificial intelligence, played a series of Go matches in Korea, and the level of development of artificial intelligence shown as a result shocked people around the world. Coincidentally, the main theme of the World Economic Forum held in Davos in January 2016 was the Fourth Industrial Revolution. The perception that the rapid development of digital technology that had progressed until then has crossed the threshold of opening a new era of the industrial revolution quickly spread in Korean society.

DEVELOPMENT OF PMSs

PMSs in Korean firms have been developed within this context. HRM in Korean firms was traditionally characterized as paternalistic and collectivistic with a seniority basis of lifetime employment and tenure-based pay (Rowley and Bae, 2001, 2003). Within that tradition, appraisals designed to differentiate between individual employees based on performance and competencies were not a critical component of HRM. Employees were paid and promoted based on their seniority. In seniority-based schemes, a pay template reflecting job tenure within the firm was used without individual differences being considered in determining pay. Starting pay slots allocated in the pay template were determined by educational background and job experience in the external labour market. Once starting pay had been determined, pay moved up a pay ladder as job tenure increased. Individuals in the same slot in the pay template were collectively paid the same regardless of differences in job performance and roles.

Indeed, it was feared that differentiation among employees would actually damage teamwork and the communal nature of organizations. Records on employee performance-relevant characteristics were only kept for the purpose of justifying management's decisions and protection against litigation or internal grievances. The measurement of those characteristics may not have been accurate because they were rarely challenged.

Those characteristics were typically judged and recorded by HR staff, and the data were typically kept in HR departments. They were not fed back to employees. In short, performance assessment (PA) did not carry much real meaning and was predominantly under the control of HR departments, not line managers.

The triggers that made the existing PMSs less workable can be classified into two groups. First, due to the internal constraints inherent in seniority-based systems, such systems could be maintained while companies rapidly grew, and the average tenure of the workforce was relatively short. However, if growth and expansion slowed and tenure and seniority increased, the burden of labour costs under seniority-based systems rose steeply and inexorably (Kim, 2005). Paradoxically, a common corporate reaction of halting recruitment makes little difference as these are actually lower paid staff. In addition, it was argued that systems lacked the motivational effects and flexibility required under a fast-changing business environment with heightened uncertainties.

Second, external factors – the 1987 Proclamation of Democratization and the 1997 Asian financial crisis – gave further momentum (Rowley and Bae, 2004). Authoritarian governments had suppressed workers in favour of management (Yoo and Rowley, 2007). The 1987 Proclamation of Democratization removed major restrictions on individual freedoms and rights to organize unions, bargain collectively and take collective action were granted. Labour disputes and strikes, new trade unions and wage increases all increased (see Table 14.1). Workers' collective voices, combined with labour market tightness, were big challenges to management.

However, the 1997 Asian financial crisis bankrupted the economy and many companies and led to much debate as to its causes and implications. The International Monetary Fund's bailout required some policy changes, and companies were forced to cut costs, reform and become more adaptable to environmental turbulence. The crisis made companies realize how vulnerable they were to environmental uncertainties, as well as threats of heightened global market competition, and they reshuffled their organizational structures as well as their overarching management views (Rowley and Bae, 2004).

Table 14.1 GDP Growth Rates, Unions and Strikes

Year	Growth rates of real GDP (%)[a]	Number of unions[b]	Number of strikes[b]
1985	6.8	2,534	265
1986	10.6	2,658	276
1987	11.1	4,086	3,749
1988	10.6	6,142	1,873
1989	6.7	7,861	1,616
1990	9.2	7,698	322
1991	9.4	7,656	234
1992	5.9	7,527	235
1993	6.1	7,147	144
1994	8.5	7,025	121
1995	9.2	6,605	88

[a] Bank of Korea, *http://ecos.bok.or.kr*
[b] Stat-Korea, http://www.stat.go.kr/statcms

As a result of these factors, Korean companies began to shift their management orientation towards being more individualistic, contract-based and more meritocratic, emphasizing performance and competencies. Some managers tried to orient employees' mindsets away from seniority by establishing new PA systems with performance central to their criteria and linking pay to performance. Pay-for-performance systems (*Yunbongje* or 'annual gross pay system') were adopted, especially by large companies. These were regarded as pivotal for changing organizational culture as well as managing HR in a new fashion. Accordingly, PA became an important underpinning element for a newly oriented HRM system. Data on the performance of employees obtained from PA began to replace data on personal characteristics (e.g., seniority, educational and social backgrounds) in making decisions about important HRM issues such as pay, promotion, training and so forth.

Meanwhile, the advent of the era of the Fourth Industrial Revolution and the resulting increase in uncertainty have made Korean companies aware of the limitations of fast catch-up strategies based on imitation and the importance of securing competitiveness based on continuous innovation in the mid-2010s. This means that PMSs, which have focused on maximizing individual performance and organizational efficiency based on individual meritocracy since the 1997 Asian financial crisis, are faced with a new challenge.

FACTORS ASSOCIATED WITH THE PA PROCESS
Distal Factors

There are two categories of legal constraints on employment practices. The first concerns employee discharge, and the second concerns employment discrimination. First, the Labor Standard Act (1953 and its amendments) restricted management's discretion to discharge employees. This contrasts with 'employment at will' in countries such as the United States. With Clause 23, employers should not discharge employees, suspend them from office, transfer them to another job, cut their pay or discipline them without just cause. Due to this legal constraint, management needed to keep employees' (particularly low performers') performance records for their probable legal defence.

Second, discrimination in employment is prohibited mainly by the Equal Employment Act (1987 and its amendments) and the National Human Rights Commission Act (2001). These laws do not have a substantial binding power yet because the penalties are not large enough. Therefore, discrimination issues have not been of much interest among employers (or the public) until recently. However, as these legal restrictions gain more binding power, discrimination issues are expected to gradually influence the way management conducts and utilizes PA.

As for the cultural environment, traditional Korean culture could be characterized by several features: an emphasis on relationships with others, collectivism, respect for seniority, attaching importance to just cause and face-saving and so forth (see also Rowley and Bae, 2003; Yang, Chang and Song, 2005), although some Westernized culture is spreading among the younger generations. Korean culture attached importance to affective rather than calculative relationships. Koreans' emphasis on affective relationships was often extended to contract-based relationships, such as employment relationships. Although the nature of the employment relationship is transactional and contract-based, Koreans were reluctant to explicitly define the relationship as such. Combined with paternalism, this emphasis on an affective relationship in the context of employment relationships was expressed as employees showing loyalty to employers with little concern about how much they were paid, while employers took care of employees in return.

Korean culture has also been viewed as more collectivistic than individualistic (Hofstede, 1980). To Koreans collectivism tended to be expressed in the form of carrying out one's obligations and responsibilities toward the group they belonged to, exerting one's efforts to keep harmony with group members, trying to minimize differences and maximize common interests among group members and regressing themselves to the mean rather than distinguishing themselves in the group. Associated with a hierarchical order within collectivism, Korean society placed much importance on seniority. Older people had authority over younger people.

In addition, face-saving and just causes were very important to older Koreans. Sometimes they sacrificed their real interests in a just cause, which was thought to save their face. Those who attached importance to just causes and face-saving tended to be concerned about how they were seen by others. These cultural factors made PA implementation in the Korean context different from that in other countries.

However, the traditional culture has changed significantly over the generations. Today millennials and Gen Z are increasingly resistant to seniority and collectivist culture and tend to directly express their thoughts about their own interests and demand their rights without being bound by face-saving culture. In Korea, the MZ generation, born between 1980 and 2004, occupies an increasingly large proportion of the economically active population, which consists of 15 to 64-year-olds. In 2015, that share was about 30%, and in 2019, it increased to 47.2%.

Meanwhile, the Korean economy and companies faced many challenges since the 1990s. Markets have been globalized, increasing market competition. Information and communication technology (ICT) proliferated rapidly, changing ways of running businesses. Newly developing countries with abundant cheap labour, such as China and South Asian countries, forced Korean companies to change their competition strategies from those based on cheap labour to those based on technologies or skills. Korean companies needed to switch from low- to high-value-added sectors. Many companies reported that they changed their business strategies from growth-seeking to profitability-seeking post-1997. According to one survey of 686 members, the ratio of

Hyuckseung Yang and Chris Rowley

companies with profit-maximizing strategies to those with sales volume-maximizing strategies changed from 40%: 60% before the Crisis to 77.1%: 22.9% after the Crisis and 42.1% changed their strategies from the latter to the former over the Crisis (Korea Chamber of Commerce & Industry, 2001 in Kim, 2005). These environmental changes have driven Korean companies to think differently about their ways of managing HR.

The 2008 global financial crisis reminded Koreans and Korean companies once again of the 1997 foreign exchange crisis. Real estate prices fell sharply as the bubble burst, and conglomerates such as Kumho and Woongjin, which increased their affiliates through borrowing money, suffered a great deal. The unemployment rate rose sharply. However, Koreans who had experienced the 1997 foreign exchange crisis did not accept the global financial crisis as a panic, because they had a relatively successful experience of overcoming the previous crisis. They thought that if the past successful experiences were kept well, the global financial crisis could be overcome without serious difficulty. After the global financial crisis, however, a new competitive landscape has developed in terms of the surrounding environment and technology development. Chinese companies have rapidly emerged in the global market to compete with Korean companies, the employment inducement effect of economic growth has fallen sharply, and unemployment has become a social problem. Above all, the unemployment rate of young people was deteriorating. In addition, the development of technology called the Fourth Industrial Revolution has led to the emergence of new competition rules, and the existing fast catch-up strategy has begun to lose its effect.

Proximal Factors

Changes in the business environment and business strategies forced companies to transform their HRM, especially pay systems, which, as mentioned earlier, was the most direct factor that encouraged PMSs in Korea. *Yunbongje*, a significant shift from the traditional system, has been more rapidly adopted, with the 1997 crisis being a critical moment, as shown in Table 14.2 (Ministry of Labor, 2003).

Key features of *Yunbongje* include differences in individual contributions to organizational success being reflected in pay,

Table 14.2 Adoption Rates of *Yunbongje* around the 1997 Crisis

Year	'96.11	'97.10	'99. 1	'00. 1	'01. 1	'02. 1	'03. 1	'04. 6	'05. 6
Adoption rate	1.6%	3.6%	15.1%	23.0%	27.1%	32.3%	37.5%	41.9%	48.4%

Source: Ministry of Labor (2003).

many complex components (i.e. base pay, various allowances and fixed bonuses) being merged and performance, rather than seniority or job tenure, being more emphasized in determining pay. It was found that about 80% of companies employing 100 or more people adopted *Yunbongje* as of 2017 (Korean Research Institute for Vocational Education and Training [KRIVET], 2017). *Yunbongje* has been adopted in the form of a merit pay system in which a merit increase is added to the following year's base pay or a merit bonus system in which a merit bonus is not added to the following year's base pay. Some 15.7% and 13.8% of the companies which adopted *Yunbongje* utilized it in the form of a merit pay system and merit bonus system respectively, while 46.4% utilized it in a combined fashion of merit pay and merit bonus, while 21.3% used just a simple gross pay system without any merit pay or bonus (Choi, 2004).

Another critical aspect of *Yunbongje* is that it strengthens both the flexibility of pay by increasing the proportion of performance-linked variable pay and competition among employees by differentiating their pay and reduces labour cost pressure from increasing seniority. This is consistent with a neo-liberal perspective advocating market mechanisms in which contract-based employment relations, merit-based competition among individuals, flexibility and economic incentives as motivators are emphasized. Furthermore, the adoption of *Yunbongje* has been supported and legitimized by the argument that such systems are a global standard in competitive markets. Of course, we can question this assertion both theoretically and empirically (Rowley, 1998; Rowley and Benson, 2002; Rowley, 2003; Rowley et al., 2004a).

Nevertheless, these changes in pay systems helped move PMS from the periphery of HRM decision-making to the centre in Korean firms by forming links between performance ratings and valued outcomes (i.e. pay). Critically, linking pay to performance

Hyuckseung Yang and Chris Rowley

heightens the importance of giving and receiving high or low performance ratings, which in turn have several effects on PA (Murphy and Cleveland, 1995: 340–344; Rowley, 2003).

As far as the purposes of PA systems implemented in Korean firms are concerned, an administrative purpose has been dominant, although they have been gradually extended to feedback and developmental purposes. Traditionally, PA had been implemented for the purpose of justification for management's decisions about personnel such as promotion or dismissal. However, PA began to be newly looked at from the motivational point of view as *Yunbongje* spread. Now individual performance needed evaluating and differentiating in a substantive way. This indicates that merit-based PA systems were adopted first to serve the pay-for-performance system. The fact that the administrative and motivational purpose is dominant implies that people tend to be very sensitive to PA outcomes.

Intervening Factors

PA is typically conducted on an annual or biannual basis. Most organizations which conduct PA for an administrative purpose tend to evaluate their employees' performance on an annual basis, while organizations implementing management by objectives (MBO) tend to do so on a biannual basis, one for intermediate review of progress and the other for final evaluation. Among companies implementing MBO, 51.2% set individual employees' annual objectives based on an agreement between individual employees and their superiors. In another 24.0%, individual employees' objectives were set by superiors after a discussion session with each individual, while in another 18.0% they were set solely by superiors. However, in another 5.4%, individual employees were allowed to set their own objectives after having a discussion session with their superiors, while the remaining 1.1% were allowed to do this by themselves (KRIVET, 2019).

The main source of PA information had been a superior's observation and judgment. PA only done by superiors had been the dominant form in Korea. Meanwhile, some organizations have utilized multi-source performance evaluations. For example, about 32.9% of organizations with 100 or more employees adopted multi-source PA systems (KRIVET, 2019), and the outcomes

of multi-source PAs are reported to be taken into account for promotions and pay raises as well as individual development.

Judgement Factors

In most organizations, raters' motivations underlying their rating
behaviours have not been paid attention to seriously, although the
fact that a 'leniency tendency' was prevalent has been recognized
among HRM professionals. Typically, raters are not well motivated
to evaluate their subordinates' performance accurately. PA had
been regarded as a 'dirty' job that superiors were obliged to do
but with high costs in the form of time and energy involved in
collecting performance information or harming relationships with
subordinates.

Raters' abilities to evaluate accurately and fairly have not been
paid attention to, either. It has been assumed the abilities to
appraise performance accurately are somehow 'inherent', which
is a common myth (Rowley, 2003). Few companies have provided
raters with training on how to evaluate. According to one survey
of the top 300 companies in Korea the lack of raters' abilities to
evaluate appropriately was a problem to be most urgently handled
for improving PA systems (SERI, 2002). Of course, equipping raters
with such abilities does not guarantee accurate and fair ratings
since PA is a goal-directed, not a neutral, behaviour (Murphy and
Cleveland, 1995). However, raters' abilities to appraise accurately
are a necessary, if not sufficient, condition for accurate and fair PA.

Distortion Factors

To understand raters' behaviours fully it should be acknowledged
that rating behaviours are goal-oriented (Murphy and Cleveland,
1995). It should not be assumed that raters would appraise ratees'
performance as accurately as possible. Raters are inclined to
maximize their interests and minimize the costs they incurred. PA
conducted in the Korean context is anticipated to incur high costs
with low benefits to raters. As mentioned earlier, lots of time and
energy would have to be invested on the part of raters to collect
accurate information on ratees' performance, and affective relationships with their ratees (typically subordinates) and teamwork
are at risk as a consequence of PA. Also, reward systems for
raters are not designed to compensate for the costs they have to

bear. Although supervisors' ratings are reviewed by superiors in a higher position, those in the higher position tend to have limited opportunities to observe ratees' performance. In sum, devices to prevent raters from distorting their ratings in their interests are rarely found in real settings. The only device to try to do this found in organizations is a forced distribution system, which will be discussed later.

MAIN FEATURES OF PA

Traditionally, PA was not taken seriously and attitudes towards companies and managers, rather than performance, were the main focus. This was understandable because loyalty mattered in paternalistic, seniority-based management. However, performance and competencies have dramatically gained importance as criteria since the late 1990s. According to one survey of a representative sample of companies with 100 or more employees, performance and competency were included as criteria in 48.6% and 31.3% of companies, respectively, while attitude was included in only 13.9%. This emphasis reflects some shift in HRM orientation from paternalism towards meritocracy.

Meanwhile, in most organizations which intended to utilize PA in a substantial manner, objective performance measures have been eagerly sought. With little credit for raters' abilities and willingness to evaluate performance accurately and inherited favouritism, subjective performance measures were common. Complaints about PA due to its subjective nature occurred. HRM staff in those organizations trying to find objective performance measures as an alternative hope they would contribute to clearing up the fairness issues associated with PA. Thus, some organizations have adopted MBO which aims for objective measures rather than subjective measures. For instance, among companies with 100 or more employees, those which adopted MBO increased from 51.5% in 2005 to 59.6% in 2019 (KRIVET, 2005, 2019). However, it is not enough to say that fairness issues have been overcome in relation to PA in Korea.

As far as how to allocate ratings is concerned, forced distribution systems that represent relative evaluation systems were common among companies which began to utilize PA along with *Yunbongje*. Here fixed percentages of ratees for each grading mark are predetermined (e.g., S for the top 5%, A for the next 20%, B for the following 50%, C for the next 20%, D for the next 5%), and raters are forced to place ratees along them (Rowley, 2003). Along with a fixed budget for merit pay increases, this system was supposed to encourage the differentiation of individuals' performances. A forced distribution system has been seen as a method to avoid problems such as inflated ratings and has also been preferred by management since it was expected to stimulate and reinforce zero-sum competition among employees for the predetermined percentages of high marks. For example, among companies with 100 or more employees, those that used an absolute evaluation system solely were only 14.8% of those reporting that they implemented PA, while those which used a relative evaluation system solely or in a combination with an absolute evaluation system were 82.3% (Ministry of Labor, 2003). A relative evaluation system combined with an absolute evaluation is nothing but a relative evaluation system since in the system ratees are usually assigned to a slot of a forced distribution scale based on their performance scores on an absolute evaluation scale.

As for feedback, PA results were provided to individual workers in 51.2% of companies with 100 or more employees (KRIVET, 2019). Regarding the way feedback is provided, a majority (49.8%) of companies which reported that they were implementing a PA system provided PA results to individual workers through feedback sessions with superiors, and 10.1% provided the results only to those who wanted to get them. Another 10.1% of them provided PA results through e-mail, and the remaining 26.7% utilized an e-HR system through which individual workers could see the results (KRIVET, 2007). Korean superiors tend to feel uncomfortable articulating what their subordinates have done on their jobs against performance criteria face-to-face. Superiors may feel that teamwork and relationships with subordinates might be damaged if they articulate their performance and differentiate them based on their performance. Although they have to rate their subordinates for their business purposes, they would prefer to not talk with them about their performance directly face-to-face.

Another important feature of PA implementation in Korea is that the state-of-the-art forms of PA systems have been struggling in the local culture. The original intent of PA tended to be outwitted by raters who still felt uncomfortable with meritocracy and its individualism. They have lived in a culture emphasizing seniority and collectivistic solidarity among group members. Therefore, PA has been an arena where these two different perspectives – seniority and meritocracy – clashed. Meritocracy forced by new PA combined with pay-for-performance was strange to those accustomed to a collectivistic, seniority-based culture. Often compromises were made that the high grades required for promotion were assigned to those who would have been promoted if seniority had applied. In those settings, there is an implicit mutual understanding with management that employees would be promoted in order of seniority. Thus, even though top management was eager for meritocracy to take root in their companies and expected raters to differentiate individuals solely based on merit, middle managers or raters tried to maintain positive climates in their work groups by keeping a culture that members felt comfortable with.

In addition, combined with a traditional seniority-based ranking system, a face-saving culture encouraged people to care about their titles which showed whether they had been promoted in a timely manner in accordance with seniority. Even though senior employees accepted the changing reality that they could be outpaced by junior employees in terms of pay and promotion, they wanted their face to be saved among their family members and acquaintances. This was why some companies trying to replace seniority with merit-based systems kept traditional titles which became detached from employees' roles and pay. Companies tried to prevent morale from declining with new merit-based systems by letting employees use their traditional titles corresponding to their tenure.

KEY CHALLENGES FACING PA

Companies face a big challenge with cultural fit. In most companies which adopted new PA systems, they have been used as a key to transform traditional culture into meritocracy. However, challenging and transforming existing culture deeply rooted in ways of thinking and ways of life is very difficult since there is very strong inertia. One risk for PA is being defeated by cultural inertia. For example, it has been mentioned that raters and ratees collaborate to outwit management's desire to bed down meritocracy by giving high marks to those who are in the order of promotion in terms of seniority.

However, such practices are increasingly challenged by the MZ generations. On one hand, the MZ generations perceive their employment relationship with the company as a shorter-term relationship than the previous generations, and on the other hand, the values of the MZ generations, who are sensitive to fairness under restricted opportunities, conflict with such practices.

Korean companies which adopted PA without taking into account cultural influences need to examine what should be the relationship between PA and the existing culture rooted in their employees. Some features of PA might need to be adjusted to cultural features which could be functional in building up organizational competitiveness, with others designed to overcome existing cultural inertia. For example, management needs to think about whether collectivism should be overcome or utilized as an anchor for building competitiveness. Some features of PA in Korean companies, such as individual-based PA, forced distribution and merit-based pay, seem to have been designed to overcome collectivism. Yet, some scholars, such as Deming and Pfeffer advocate team-based work organization as desirable (Deming, 1982, 1994; Pfeffer, 1998).

Fairness issues tend to be mentioned along with the subjective nature of PA and rater favouritism in Korea. PA based on subjective judgements are prone to bias and unfairness. Combined with prevalent favouritism in Korean society, subjective PA has been assumed to be highly vulnerable to rater arbitrariness or intentional distortions in rating performance. One reason why companies have tried to adopt objective measures for performance lies here. For some people, objective performance measures are themselves just or fair, while subjective measures are unjust or unfair. However, fairness is not guaranteed with objective performance measures themselves. If construct validity of, and controllability toward, an objectively measured performance is not secured, fairness issues would not be ameliorated.

Rating inflation is another major concern in Korea. Management worries that raters engaging in lenient rating can defeat the desire to root meritocracy in organizations. Raters have a strong tendency to give ratings leniently since low ratings

Hyuckseung Yang and Chris Rowley

can lead to resentment and perceptions of inequity while lenient ratings are helpful in maintaining or improving a positive climate in the work group (Murphy and Cleveland, 1995). This phenomenon is understandable if we take into account that raters' goals are not necessarily consistent with the organization's goals. For raters it makes sense to maximize their own goals and minimize the costs that follow when conducting PA, although top management expects them to evaluate accurately for the organization's interests. For raters, the ability to maintain positive interpersonal relationships with subordinates might be viewed as much more important than turning in accurate PA (Murphy and Cleveland, 1995: 248).

As mentioned earlier, companies in Korea have tried to tackle rater leniency problems by forced distribution schemes which assume employee performances within a rater's span of control follow a certain kind of probability distribution. However, forced distribution can bring side effects (Rowley, 2003; Yang, 2022). First, it can damage teamwork while reinforcing zero-sum competition. Co-workers are seen not as team members but as competitors from an appraisee's point of view. Second, it can deprive raters of motivation to upgrade subordinates' skills and performances across the board since they remain forced to differentiate afterwards and thus end up facing resentment from those placed in lower grading marks. Third, it can distract attention away from more important causes of inaccurate and lenient rating behaviours. As Murphy and Cleveland (1995: 215) pointed out, PA is "a goal-directed communication process in which the rater attempts to use performance appraisal to advance his or her interests." Thus, inaccurate and lenient ratings need to "be understood in terms of the rater's rational pursuit of sensible goals rather than being understood in terms of errors and mistakes" (Murphy and Cleveland, 1995: 242). From the rater's perspective, there are many reasons to provide inaccurate (typically inflated) ratings and, more important, surprisingly few good reasons to give accurate ratings (Murphy and Cleveland, 1995). This perspective implies that inaccurate ratings need to be corrected mainly by aligning raters' goals with the goals intended by the PA system. In this sense, a forced distribution system can be an easy, not a proper, solution for the rating inflation problem.

More fundamentally, the administrative evaluation and reward system for the motivational purpose based on individual meritocracy is being challenged to change to a performance support system for the developmental purpose based on constant feedback (Yang, 2022). Among global leading companies, there was a movement to abolish the conventional employee appraisal system based on individual meritocracy. Microsoft, Deloitte, Gap, Adobe, and General Electric have already eliminated the forced ranking system. Human resources research firm Bersin by Deloitte also reports that about 70% of companies surveyed reconsider their performance management practices (Rock and Jones, 2015). This trend gave Korean companies an opportunity to rethink the existing performance evaluation systems.

CONCLUSION

We have overviewed the main features and issues of PMS in Korea and some factors which affected its changing nature and were driven by events, particularly democratization, the Asian financial crisis and the Fourth Industrial Revolution (Rowley and Bae, 2004). According to one survey, 60.6% of the companies which adopted *Yunbongje* pinpointed the lack of trust in PA outcomes as the most conspicuous problem in relation to its implementation. PA, which is supposed to be an important hinge around which other HRM functions, including pay, operate, have not received full credit in measuring reliable and valid performance outcomes in Korea.

The 'fertility' of the ground for PA in terms of culture and raters' motivation and competencies needs to be considered. Merit-based PA needs to be reconciled with existing culture in an appropriate manner. PA can operate in an unintended fashion, being outwitted by line managers who are supposed to play a critical role as raters. In this respect, several questions regarding the relationship between PA and cultural contexts need to be answered. These include the following. What should the relationship between PA and existing culture in Korea look like? What facets of existing culture need to be changed by PA and to what facets should PA be tuned? Which orientation of PA might be desirable taking into account the cultural context in Korea? More specifically, is PA that stems from individualistic contract-based traditions desirable in Korea, or are there other possibilities in the existing culture? These are not easy-to-answer questions. It is also important that middle managers who are supposed to play a key role as raters be trained and motivated to evaluate accurately and fairly. If some managers are not ready for PA, a meritocracy cannot be rooted in organizations.

Finally, the impact of PMSs, which has been strengthening the efficiency of organizational operation, on promoting the continuous innovation required by the Fourth Industrial Revolution era needs examining. In other words, beyond discussing the detailed characteristics of the traditional PMS and the problems at hand, it is necessary to review the characteristics of an alternative PMS that can support continuous innovation in the new era. In that sense, PMSs in Korea would be said to still be in flux.

REFERENCES

Aghion, P., Antonin, C. and Bunel, S. (2022). *The Power of Creative Destruction* (in Korean). Seoul: Eco-Livres.

Choi, J. T. (2004). Transformation of Korean HRM based on Confucian values. *Seoul Journal of Business*, 10, 1: 1–26.

Deming, W.E. (1982). *Out of the Crisis*. Boston, MA: The MIT Press.

Deming, W.E. (1994). *The New Economics for Industry, Government, Education*, (2nd ed.). Boston, MA: The MIT CAES.

Hofstede, G. (1980). Motivation, Leadership and Organization: Do American Theories Apply Abroad? *Organizational Dynamics*, 9, 42–63.

Kim, D. (2005). Human Resource Management in Korean Firms after the Foreign Currency Crisis. In G. Park et al. (eds.) *HRM in Korean Firms* (in Korean). Seoul: Pakyoungsa.

Korea Research Institute for Vocational Education and Training (2005, 2007, 2009, 2019). *Human Capital Corporate Panel Survey (HCCP)*.

Korea Research Institute for Vocational Education and Training. (2017). *Korea Research Institute for Vocational Education and Training, KRIVET*, https://www.voced.edu.au/content/ngv:78664

Ministry of Labor (2003, 2004, 2005). *Results of Survey on Yunbongje and Profit Sharing* (In Korean). Executive Summary Report. Available at http://www.molab.go.kr/

Murphy, K.R. & Cleveland, J.N. (1995). *Understanding Performance Appraisal: Social, Organizational, and Goal-Based Perspectives*. Thousand Oaks, CA: Sage Publications.

Pfeffer, J. (1998). *The Human Equation: Building Profits by Putting People First*. Boston: Harvard Business School Press.

Rock, D. and Jones, B. (2015). *Why More and More Companies are Ditching Performance Ratings*. Harvard Business Review, September.

Rowley, C. (ed.) (1998). *HRM in the Asia Pacific Region: Convergence Questioned*. London: Frank Cass.

Rowley, C. (2002). South Korea Management in Transition. In M. Warner (ed.) *Culture and Management in Asia*. London: Routledge.

Rowley, C. (2003). *The Management of People: HRM in Context*. London: Spiro Business Press.

Rowley, C. and Bae, J. (eds) (1998). *Korean Business: Internal and External Industrialization*. London: Frank Cass.

Rowley, C. and Bae, J. (2001). The Impact of Globalization on HRM: The Case of South Korea. *Journal of World Business*, 36, 4: 402–428.

Rowley, C. and Bae, J. (2003). Culture and Management in South Korea. In M. Warner (ed.) *Culture and Management in Asia*. London: Routledge.

Rowley, C. and Bae, J. (2004). HRM in South Korea after the Asian Financial Crisis: Emerging Patterns from the Labyrinth. *International Studies of Management & Organization*, 34, 1: 52–82.

Rowley, C. and Benson, J. (eds) (2002). *The Management of HR in the Asia Pacific Region: Convergence Reconsidered*. London: Frank Cass.

Rowley, C., Benson, J. and Warner, M. (2004a). Towards an Asian Model: A Comparative analysis of China, Japan and Korea. *International Journal of HRM*, 15, 4/5: 917–933.

Rowley, C. and Fitzgerald, R. (eds) (1996). *Greater China: Political Economy, Inward Investment and Business Culture*. London: Frank Cass.

Rowley, C., Sohn, T.W. and Bae, J. (eds) (2002). *Managing Korean Business: Organization, Culture, Human Resources in Change*. London: Frank Cass.

Rowley, C., Yoo, K.S. and Kim, D.H. (2004b). Unemployment and labour markets in South Korea: Globalisation, social impacts and policy responses. In J. Benson and Y. Zhu (eds.) *Unemployment in Asia*. London: Routledge.

Samsung Economic Research Institute (2002). *Analysis of HR Competencies and Trend in Korean Firms* (In Korean). Executive Summary Report.

Yang, H. (2022). *People Management in the Era of Great Transformation: In the Era of Innovation, Going beyond the Conventional Wisdom of People Management*. Seoul: Cloud Nine.

Yang, H., Chang, E. and Song, B. (2005). *Exploring Korean HRM Systems That Fit in with Positive-Sum Paradigm* (in Korean). Seoul: New Paradigm Center.

WEBSITES

Korea Chamber of Commerce & Industry: http://www.korcham.net/ (in Korean) or http://english.korcham.net/ (in English)

Korea Labour Institute: http://www.kli.re.kr/ (in Korean or English)

Korea National Statistical Office: http://www.nso.go.kr/

Ministry of Labor: http://www.molab.go.kr/ (in Korean) http://english.molab.go.kr/ (in English)

Samsung Economic Research Institute: http://www.seri.org/ (in Korean)

Performance Management in Japan

Akihisa Kagami, Tomoki Sekiguchi and Azusa Ebisuya

Chapter 15

This chapter introduces the Japanese performance management system (PMS)[1] models and their evolution and identifies various factors that have influenced the transformation of the Japanese PMS models with changes in employment practices and the business environment surrounding Japanese companies. Traditionally, Japanese companies have been characterized as learning organizations, and they place significant emphasis on employee learning and skill development throughout employees' careers (Sekiguchi, 2006). Therefore, based on the premise of long-term employment, Japanese human resource management (HRM) systems have organically combined and functioned with multiple subsystems in the PMS, including an internal training system centered on on-the-job training (OJT), an employee evaluation system, an employee grading system based on ability, and multiskilling through job rotation. This traditional Japanese PMS model is called the "learning-centered" PMS (Morishima, 2008). The learning-centered PMS has served to encourage employees to acquire skills and knowledge through long-term employment and has contributed to the accumulation of proprietary technology and practical know-how within the company. It is argued that this has also contributed to

DOI: 10.4324/9781003306849-15

the formation of Japan's strengths in the field of manufacturing (Koike, 1991; Morishima, 1996 and 2006).

When the bubble economy collapsed in the early 1990s, Japan entered a period of low growth, revealing an imbalance between output and salaries due to the seniority-based compensation factor inherent in PMS based on ability. Therefore, they began to use the short-term performance of employees as one of the main factors in determining compensation, resulting in large salary disparities and fluctuations among employees (Morishima, 2002). This new practice is often called *seikashugi* or "performance-ism" (Morishima, 2008).

Performance-based management has generated a variety of reverse functions and has sparked a great deal of debate among both researchers and practitioners about the pros and cons of the system. For example, while criticisms have been made that performance-based management leads to lower employee morale (Yanagishita, 2003; Jo, 2004; Takahashi, 2004), other perspectives have offered suggestions: that the introduction of performance-based management has not had as negative an impact on organizational climate as has been suggested (Japan Management Association, 2005) and employees' morale increases when employees recognize the introduction of performance-based management (Tatemichi, 2009). So far, the debate has become more confused. In this chapter, we discuss the pros and cons of performance-based management and show how to optimize a PMS for globalizing Japanese companies to apply.

TRADITIONAL "LEARNING-CENTERED" PMS MODEL IN JAPAN

In Japanese companies, human resource development has been considered a vital function of HRM (Koike, 1988; Dore, 1989). Therefore, until the early 1990s, when the Japanese economy was on an expansionary trend, Japanese-style HRM was characterized by extensive in-house training, a compensation system that rewards both performance and skill development, a broad job structure, and HRM practices with employee participation (labor-management consultation system, quality control [QC] circles, employee stock ownership system, etc.; Koike, 1992; Nonaka and Takeuchi, 1995; Morishima, 1996). These Japanese-style HRM practices strongly encourage employees to learn and acquire skills and knowledge and are called "learning-centered" PMS (Koike, 1991: Morishima, 1996, 2006). The learning-centered PMS has greatly contributed to the formation of strengths such as the maintenance and assurance of high productivity and high quality through the training and retention of skilled workers and the advancement and high added value of products, mainly in the large-scale manufacturing industry (Morishima, 2008).

Human Resource Development and Long-Term Employment

In Japanese companies, "regular employees" (*sei-shain*) enjoy strong job security. Morishima (2008) points to the following factors as background factors leading to the strong security of regular employees: (1) the existence of the Labor Standards Law, which makes it virtually impossible for employers to fire workers; (2) Japanese government policies focused on long-term employment and job security; and (3) the labor movement of trade unions, which has made job security a pillar of its labor policy. Under such long-term employment practices backed by strong job security, there is little risk of an exodus of trained employees. Therefore, employers are more willing to invest in employee skill development and have been able to introduce and implement a learning PMS smoothly.

Many Japanese companies have focused on developing employees' problem-solving and decision-making skills for work problems, especially nonroutine problems, by systematically training workers through OJT (Koike, 1988, 1992; Koike & Inoki, 1991). This is done so that Japanese companies can develop their employees' knowledge and skills to solve nonroutine problems, thereby cultivating their ability to deal with both planned adjustments (changes in work plans) and unanticipated problems. Long-term employment practices allow employees to learn incrementally on the job. In this learning process, Koike (1994) argues that, ultimately, employees can be expected to develop the ability to identify "problems," "diagnose," and "find solutions," or what Koike calls "intellectual skills."

Although these discussions on human resource development have been mainly directed at so-called blue-collar workers, the arguments apply to the development of white-collar workers in large Japanese companies. What blue- and white-collar workers have in common is that they gradually expand the scope of work they can handle through their job duties and cultivate their ability to respond to sudden challenges. Nevertheless, unlike blue-collar workers, the development of white-collar workers in Japanese companies is often conducted for training candidates for management positions and is a long-term process lasting more than 10 years (Koike, 1991, 1993). This process involves "horizontal transfers," in which employees experience several jobs or workplaces before the "vertical transfer" of promotion. Japanese companies use such horizontal transfers to upgrade the skills of employees and to determine the promotion of the relevant employees by observing their adaptation to various jobs and workplaces (Koike, 1999). Horizontal transfers may be used as an opportunity to improve the fit when there is a misfit between people and jobs or people and groups (Sekiguchi, 2006). In other words, it can be said that, in Japanese companies, the human resource development process and the selection process are positioned as an integral part of one another, and white-collar workers have been characteristically trained from a long-term perspective.

The emphasis in "horizontal transfers" is on job rotation throughout one's career, which is used to develop the organizational skills needed to coordinate work across departments and among workers (Morishima, 2006). Job rotation is utilized to develop the organizational skills to coordinate work across departments and among workers. In Japanese companies, where broad job classifications and decentralization have made "horizontal" coordination among individual employees essential (Aoki, 1988), communication and coordination skills are considered important regarding task execution (Kagono, Nonaka, Sakakibara, & Okumura, 1985).

Although long-term human resource development through job rotation has been appreciated as one of the sources of competitiveness in the Japanese economy (Koike, 1999), several shortcomings have also been pointed out. For example, employees have become increasingly dependent on employing firms for their career development (Watanabe, 2001), there has been a delay in the development of highly specialized human resources (Takeishi, 2000), and there has been a lack of formation of management skills (Mishina, 2004). Such human resource development systems, especially job rotations involving geographic location transfers, have been designed and operated on the assumption that employees are implicitly male and thus become a barrier when utilizing female employees (Komagawa, 2013 and 2017). With the globalization of the economy, there is an increasing need to train specialists who can be accepted at the global level, and the human resource development system that trains generalists within companies based on the assumption of long-term employment practices is becoming dysfunctional.

Ability-Based Evaluation and Compensation

To implement a learning-centered PMS, it is necessary to explicitly encourage employees to acquire knowledge and skills and to link this to compensation and promotion. The "ability-grading system" (*shokuno-shikaku-seido*) has been installed as the core system for this purpose. The ability-grading system is one in which employees are graded according to the level of their ability to perform their jobs, and their treatment is determined based on their grades. The ability-grading system is based on "job ability" and is distinct from the Western job-based pay system, which is based on "job duties." Because it is a human resource system that focuses on ability rather than job duties, salaries remain basically the same even if an employee's affiliation or responsibilities are changed. Therefore, it has been pointed out that the ability-grading system has the following advantages: (1) it facilitates human resource transfers and helps maintain organizational flexibility; (2) it enhances a sense of organizational unity; and (3) it functions as an incentive for skill development (Kambayashi, Zushi, and Morita, 2010). Most Japanese companies in the 1990s introduced the ability-grading system. According to a survey conducted by the former Ministry of Labor (now Ministry of Health, Labor, and Welfare) in 1990, 79.6% of approximately 6,000 companies with 30 or more employees and almost 100% of large companies with 1,000 or more employees had introduced the ability-grading system at that time and used it as one of the criteria for determining salaries. Most of the surveyed companies also used the ability-grading system to determine salaries for blue- and white-collar workers. This suggests that Japanese companies have encouraged white-collar workers to improve their ability through long-term service and to learn rather than per fiscal year.

In the ability-grading system, employees are evaluated according to detailed criteria regarding their ability to perform their jobs, not only based on their actual demonstrated ability but also on their job attitude and potential as future possibilities to perform their jobs (Koike, 1991, Sekiguchi, 2006). Because job performance is considered to be formed through cumulative OJT and in-house training, an employee's job performance is strongly related to tenure. Therefore, the ability-grading system encourages employees to develop their skills and build their careers over a long period.

In a learning environment centered on OJT, it is difficult for employees to gain experience in various types of work in a short period, and the rate at which knowledge and skills are acquired is slow. As a result, there is no difference in ability among employees with relatively short tenure, keeping the salary gap small (Sekiguchi, 2006). This contributes to harmony among employees and may have positive effects on teamwork and productivity (Levine, 1991). However, as employees stay with the company longer, the cumulative difference in the speed of advancement among employees may widen, resulting in a more significant salary gap (Mitani, 1992). In other words, the salary gap between workers is small only during the short period of service and experience, and in the long run, differences in ability among workers will undoubtedly be reflected in the salary gap.

The ability-grading system has the advantage of providing incentives such as ability grades (progress) and promotion to higher levels of positions of authority, in addition to annual salary increases. However, in promoting employees to higher positions, Japanese companies tend to take a very long time to identify the employees to be selected and promoted (Wakabayashi and Graen, 1989; Koike, 1993). For example, the first screening of candidates for white-collar managerial positions who joined the company at the same time is made 7 to 10 years after they joined the company (Wakabayashi and Graen, 1989). Even if they are promoted as a result, the newly granted authority is not much different from those who were not promoted. In the case of blue-collar workers, this period is shorter, lasting only 3 to 5 years.

A prominent feature of promotion practices in Japanese companies has been called "slow progress" (Wakabayashi and Graen,

1989) or "late promotion" (Koike, 1993). This "slow selection" allows Japanese companies to maintain employee motivation as long as possible, improve employee skills through intense competition, and flexibly staff higher positions for multiskilled employees (Yashiro, 1995). At the same time, this explains why Japanese companies have rarely promoted outside human resources to higher-level positions. In other words, Japanese companies were able to maintain a learning-centered PMS by placing employees who had "learned" through previous incremental promotions in higher positions, thereby creating incentives for long-term learning for employees (Morishima, 2008).

Problems With the Ability-Based System and the Transition to a Performance-Based System

The learning-centered PMS can be described as an "ability-based" PMS because it has ability-based HRM at its core. The ability-based PMS has been effective in performance management for blue-collar workers in the manufacturing production systems that drove the Japanese economy until the early 1990s (MacDuffie, 1995). This is because it was easy to measure both output and ability on the production floor, and the standard setting was clear. However, the 4-year college enrollment rate, which was 24.6% in 1990, rose nearly 15 percentage points to 38.2% in 1999 (Ministry of Education, Culture, Sports, Science, and Technology, n.d.), and the rapid increase in white-collar workers caused the ability-based PMS to become institutionally incompatible. This is because the output produced by white-collar workers is often intangible, and the relationship between input (ability) and output (achievement) is not clear, making it difficult to set standards for measuring the relevant factors. Because white-collar output depends on various factors, such as the motivation of the individual concerned, skills, and cooperation among team members, it is not always possible to identify highly productive and excellent employees by focusing only on ability (Morishima, 2008). Therefore, around the late 1990s, cases began to emerge in which the ability-based PMS did not fit well with the performance management of the increasing number of white-collar workers.

During the long period of low growth in the Japanese economy that had lasted since the mid-1990s, structural flaws in the ability-based PMS became even more apparent, namely, (1) because of the difficulty of evaluating intangible ability, the PMS becomes a seniority-based operation using years of experience as a proxy variable for ability, (2) as the price of seniority-based operations, employees may lose motivation to acquire diverse skills, and (3) the lack of a direct correlation between employee effort and compensation may eliminate the incentive for employees to perform their daily work diligently (Miyamoto & Kubo, 2002).

The ability-based PMS is essentially a system in which salary costs rise yearly, regardless of the post held or the employee's output, because it contains many elements of seniority. In the Japanese economy, which has entered a period of low growth, companies are unable to expand their scale and hire more low-salary young workers, whereas the employment of high-salary middle-aged and older workers is protected and cannot be easily reduced. Thus, the imbalance between salaries paid by companies to their employees and their output became more severe in Japanese companies. As a breakthrough, a new approach was steered toward performance-based PMS with MBO (management by objectives) at its core, and it was adopted and rapidly spread in the late 1990s. However, the rapid spread of performance-based HRM among Japanese companies in a short period, regardless of industry or business category, cannot be explained solely from the SHRM (strategic human resource management) perspective that performance-based HRM contributes to improved corporate performance. It can be pointed out that in a country with a relatively collectivist culture such as Japan, the trend (management fashion) and institutional pressures among managers may have been heavily influenced by the imitative and normative isomorphisms that occur concerning business and management practices (Sekiguchi, 2013).

The Reverse Function of "Performance-Based" Management

The definition of performance-based HRM varies considerably among researchers and practitioners, and no unified and established definition of performance-based HRM can be found (Sekiguchi, 2013). In this chapter, we use Okunishi's (2001) definition of performance-based pay, which has become widely used in Japanese performance-based salary research because it operationalizes the concept of performance-based pay with three simple elements. Okunishi (2001) added the element of the "widening salary gap" to the definition of performance-based pay that was widely spread in Japan by the Japan Federation of Employers' Associations (Nikkeiren[2]) through labor-management discussions and defined performance-based pay in terms of three elements: (1) outcome orientation of salary-determining factors, (2) short-term orientation of salary-determining factors, and (3) widening salary gap. Okunishi's (2001) inclusion of the element of the widening salary gap in his definition of performance-based pay further clarified the characteristics of performance-based pay, which spread rapidly in Japan in the 2000s.

The rapid introduction of a performance-based PMS with a "short-term perspective," a "results orientation," and a "widening salary gap" has had the reverse function on Japanese companies, which until then had promoted employee skill development based on a "long-term perspective," "small salary gaps," and "slow selection" under an ability-based PMS. The reverse functionality that emerged became problematic and a social issue in the mid-2000s, giving rise to a debate involving industry and academia. This is reflected in the publication of books exposing the inner workings of Japanese companies that introduced performance-based management (e.g., Jo, 2004) and books criticizing performance-based management (e.g., Takahashi, 2004), which became best sellers. Some of the points discussed as reverse function include the following: individuals are so driven by the pursuit of short-term results that they do not challenge higher goals for fear of failure, thus neglecting the acquisition of individual skills and the improvement of intrinsic productivity in the workplace; employee dissatisfaction increases because individual efforts and work processes are not valued; and solidarity with peers is weakened, leading to neglect of subordinates and junior staff development (Kusuda et al., 2002).

While the spread of performance-based management has been rapid, stirring up controversy, it has been pointed out that seniority salaries are still persistently applied to core workers in many Japanese companies (Endo et al., 2015; Ono, 2018) and that seniority still plays an important role in HRM (Lehmberg, 2014).

Even if many Japanese companies superficially adopt a performance-based system, the reality is that such PMS does not cover all employees (Sekiguchi, 2012; Yanadori, 2018).

EFFORTS TO OPTIMIZE PMS

In the late 2000s, Japanese companies began to show interest in ways to control the reverse function of performance-based PMS and at the same time take advantage of other HRM practices that work in tandem. Since then, Japanese companies have been trying to optimize their PMSs based on performance standards through a process of trial and error.

Japanese Hybrid PMS

One of the attempts to optimize the PMS is to create a hybrid PMS that combines the traditional ability- and performance-based systems. On one hand, on the ability-based side, the traditional ability-grading system will be continued with some modifications to maintain the idea of employee learning and development. On the other hand, on the performance-based side, to manage employees' output more clearly, the number of bonuses and salary increases will be differentiated according to the degree of achievement of individual employees through MBO and other means. The introduction of this hybrid system aims to increase the number of salary resources allocated to performance while determining the base portion of salaries based on ability, thereby making salary costs more flexible. In other words, it is an attempt to establish a PMS that combines the advantages of both ability- and performance-based systems.

Modifications made to the job qualification system in the process of establishing the hybrid PMS include, for example, (1) abolishing automatic annual salary increases and introducing or expanding appraisal salary increases, as well as negative salary increases; (2) reducing or abolishing age pay and pay based on tenure; (3) abolishing range pay for each grade and introducing single rate; and (4) broad-banding multiple ability grades together and reducing the number of grades to allow for earlier selection (Okubayashi, 2003). Through these changes, various innovations were incorporated to eliminate the traditional seniority and gerrymandering pay elements.

Even with the various improvements incorporated, the adoption of the ability-grading system inherently entails the treatment of seniority. Once an employee's ability is acquired, it is maintained over a long period, and because the acquisition of ability is proportional to experience, salaries will inevitably remain at a high level. In particular, it is difficult to completely correct the salary balance for middle-aged and older workers, especially those in management positions. Therefore, Japanese companies are increasingly introducing a new type of PMS that focuses on a third factor other than inputs (ability) and outputs (performance), namely, throughput (role).

In the mission grading system, a new type of PMS, employees are graded according to their role (mission), not the degree of ability they possess in performing their job duties. Because the mission grading system is a natural outgrowth of the trial-and-error process of redesigning the employee grading system, its operational methods are diverse, and there is no agreed-on standard (Hirano, 2006). Generally, the mission grading system in Japanese companies is an employee grading system in which the mission grade is determined by measuring and scoring the role required for a certain position in terms of its level of responsibility, the scope of authority, the difficulty of the job, and the expected results (Kagami, 2018). In addition, it differs from job-based pay in that compensation is linked not only to job duties but also to the achievement of goals (results) in which the employee has specifically developed their role (Kagami, 2018).

Roles in the mission grading system are characterized by the fact that "unlike job value, which is strictly determined by job analysis and job evaluation, roles in the mission grading system are determined flexibly by department heads while observing changes in business conditions and corporate organization" (Tsuru, Abe, & Kubo, 2005). In addition, in determining mission grades under the mission grading system, especially in promoting and lowering grades, consideration is given not only to determine the size or change of job value but also to adjust the level of the role to be assigned after the supervisor determines the level of the subordinate's ability growth (Ishida & Higuchi, 2009). Thus, the mission grading system has the characteristics of both ability-based and job-based systems in that it incorporates capability provisions into job definitions (Hirano, 2010). Furthermore, the mission grading system is a more evolved hybrid PMS because it also has performance-based characteristics that emphasize the evaluation of goal attainment linked to roles.

Japanese companies adopted a mission grading system based on a mixture of job- and ability-based pay because it was challenging to introduce the job-based pay system, which is common in Europe and the United States in its original form. The extant job-based pay system had the following disadvantages: (1) because jobs were evaluated by subdividing them, there was a risk that salaries could not be changed each time in response to frequent changes in employees' jobs, and (2) because subdivided jobs determined salaries, flexible transfer of employees was inhibited (Imano & Sato, 2020). These disadvantages were a severe problem in Japanese companies that train employees through frequent job changes and periodic rotations. Therefore, adjustments were made to the evaluation system to make it easier to cope with job changes and transfers by broadly grouping job duties based on a mission grading system, calling each grouping a role (designed with fewer ranks for general staff), and using a simplified method for evaluating roles that do not require the creation of detailed job descriptions. Through these adjustments, the PMS was designed to reduce the weight of the "person standard," which is based on ability, and increase the weight of the "job (role) standard," which is based on job duties.

Under the person-based ability-grading system based on ability, the concept is that "a price is put on a person." Hence, salaries are not significantly different between executives of the same rank rated in the same job classification (e.g., job classification: M2, position: general manager). However, under the role-based mission grading system, which is based on roles, there is a wide disparity in salaries depending on the post one assumes because the idea is that a price is attached to the role. This is expected to be more effective in determining employee salaries based on merit, and many Japanese companies are introducing this system. According to a survey of 24,492 companies conducted in 2021 by the Research Institute for Labor Administration, the mission grading system has been introduced by 35.7% of managers and

26.5% of general employees. However, the introduction rate of the ability-grading system, which boasted an overwhelming share in the 1990s, has declined to 40.3% of managers and 52.6% of general employees, indicating that the mission grading system is gradually taking over that share.

RESPONDING TO CHANGING INDUSTRIAL STRUCTURE AND LABOR FORCE

Japanese companies are facing two significant environmental changes. These are changes in industrial structure and changes in the working population. In recent years, Japan has entered a full-fledged advanced information society and is faced with the need to procure and utilize highly specialized and scarce human resources such as artificial intelligence engineers and data scientists from around the world. A PMS that works on a global level is essential to attracting this type of talent. The industrial structure in Japan is also changing significantly: the number of workers in the tertiary industry (service industry), which was 59.4% in 1991, accounts for 74.1% in 2021, an increase of about 15 points over 30 years (Ministry of Internal Affairs and Communications, n.d.). Therefore, Japanese employment practices and learning-centered PMS, which were previously suitable for large-scale manufacturing, are likely to be less suitable for the current industrial structure.

Japan's working population is also showing remarkable changes. Due to the rapid decline in birth rates and the aging of the population, Japan has already entered an era of a declining labor force. For Japan to maintain its current economic scale, drastic measures must be taken to secure the labor force.

From Membership-Based Employment to Job-Based Employment

For many years, Japanese companies have hired employees without limiting their job descriptions in exchange for guaranteeing their employment until retirement and have forced employees to follow blindly when they are reassigned after hiring, even if it involves a change in job title or relocation. This employment practice, which emphasizes which company one becomes a member of rather than which job one becomes a specialist in, has recently become known as "membership-based employment". At the same time, there is a growing debate over the pros and cons of this type of relationship between companies and individuals as a fundamental factor in the creation of uniquely Japanese employment practices. According to Hamaguchi (2017), who coined the term "membership-based employment" for the first time, new employees enter the company under a membership-based employment on the assumption that they will follow any human resource orders from the company and that company orders determine their job duties. As job duties can change at the company's order, it is challenging to link salaries to job duties, resulting in a seniority system rather than job-based pay. In addition, because job duties are not fixed, OJT after employment becomes essential. Furthermore, since salaries are linked to position within the company rather than job duties, labor unions are organized by the company rather than by industry, as in the West. Hamaguchi (2017) thus points out that membership-based employment is a fundamental factor that has brought about various characteristics of conventional Japanese employment practices.

The counterpart to membership-based employment is "job-based employment." This type of employment is called as such because the company specifies the employee's job duties at the time of hiring and assigns the employee to a limited number of jobs. This is the same concept as the job description–based pay system common in Europe and the United States. In Japan, some companies have long introduced a job-based pay system under the "job grading system," but it has not been widely adopted because it does not fit the characteristics of Japanese companies, which frequently transfer employees and change their responsibilities.

If one considers the concept of balancing job duties and salaries, job-based employment (job grading system) would be more effective than a mission grading system. In Japan, however, the need to balance the practice of human resource development through rotations with ability-based salary makes the job grading system a difficult fit, and membership-based employment is the common practice. The mission grading system was devised to introduce a job-based element into membership-based employment practices, and it is a Japanese-style job-based PMS optimized to be right in between the ability-grading system and the job grading system (Hayashi, 2016).

The job-based employment (job grading system), which was considered unsuitable for Japanese companies, has rapidly gained attention in recent years, and discussions on its introduction are gaining momentum. In 2020, Keidanren, a Japanese management organization, proposed a review of the Japanese employment system.[3] It recommends that the so-called lump-sum hiring of new graduates, in which new graduates are hired at the same time in April without specifying the type of job, be abolished and replaced with "hiring by job category" for the entire year. Such a review of Japanese-style employment practices proposed by Keidanren would encourage a shift from traditional long-term employment and amorphous jobs to external labor market–type, highly specialized, and routine jobs (Yamazaki, 2021).

The number of companies adopting job-based employment is increasing. According to a 2018 survey conducted by the Institute of Labor Administration, the percentage of companies introducing a job grading system increased from 9.1% in 2001 to 24.1% in 2018. Some of Japan's leading cutting-edge companies have already begun to shift to job-based employment with a view to globalization and securing highly specialized human resources, focusing on global standards (e.g., Hitachi, KDDI, Fujitsu, Shiseido, Panasonic, and Mitsubishi Chemical). However, even in these companies, job-based employment targets only a small number of employees, such as managers and high-level professionals, and the fact that employees employed under the membership system also exist is extremely suggestive of the Japanese company model. Although the shift to job-based employment is expected to continue, especially among global companies, the combination of membership- and job-based employment is likely to continue for the foreseeable future because of the difficulty of terminating employees on a liquidation basis under the legal system. Thus, even multinational firms that are globalizing their operations tend to modify their HRM to optimize it for Japan rather than introducing the global standard HRM as it is. This may hurt the company's attractiveness to global human resources (Froese et al., 2018).

Huang, Yang, and Sekiguchi (2020) found that the sense of belonging and uniqueness (recognizing the individual's value and developing individual strengths) offered by companies are important in attracting talented foreign workers from around the world and that performance-based PMSs is more attractive to foreign job applicants than seniority-based PMSs. As this study shows, it is clear that HRM optimized only for Japan is no longer viable for multinational companies to acquire and utilize human resources globally.

Declining Labor Force and Work Style Reform

Another reason why job-based employment is being considered is the "work style reform" promoted by the Japanese government. In 2018, the Japanese government promulgated the "Act on Arrangement of Related Acts to Promote Work Style Reform" to enable workers to choose diverse work styles to cope with the declining working-age population due to the falling birthrate and aging population (Ministry of Health, Labor and Welfare, 2019). Furthermore, as one of the pillars of this policy, it was set to eliminate unreasonable differences in treatment between regular employees (permanent full-time workers) and nonregular employees (part-time workers, fixed-term workers, dispatched workers) within the same company (MHLW, 2019).

Traditionally, there have been considerable differences in treatment between regular employees, whose long-term employment is protected under membership-based employment, and nonregular employees, who are not, in various aspects such as bonuses, retirement benefits, and welfare packages, even when they are engaged in the same job. Such differences in treatment have been explained as differences in their ability, including employee potential, rather than differences in work, under the ability-based PMS. However, due to the severe labor shortage caused by the decline in the working population, there are an increasing number of cases in which employees who have retired are rehired to continue performing the same job duties or in which female employees who left the company due to marriage or childbirth are rehired at their former work styles. In these cases, they are often rehired as nonregular employees and paid at a lower salary level than when they were regular employees. However, their ability to perform their jobs is no different than when they were regular employees, and the ability-based PMS can no longer successfully explain this disparity in treatment.

Disparities in treatment between workers in the same job are a barrier to diversifying human resources. Disproportionate treatment between regular and nonregular employees can increase the dissatisfaction of nonregular workers and discourage potential workers, such as housewives and older adults, from entering society. In response, the government has revised the Part-Time Work Law, the Labor Contract Law, and the Worker Dispatch Law to effectively correct unreasonable differences in treatment within the same company, and it is promoting improvements in the treatment of nonregular employees. Companies can no longer efficiently utilize nonregular workers as cost adjusters, as they have done in the past, and more severe employment management is now required.

To promote equal pay for equal work, it is necessary to shift from a PMS based on "people" criteria, such as ability, to a PMS based on "job" criteria. However, even if the PMS is job-based, the mission grading system is designed on the premise of membership-based employment, so it is comprehensive and highly abstract in its understanding of roles (missions), and the mission grades are broad, making it difficult to accept apparent differences in work and reflect them in salaries. On the other hand, the job grading system is easy to use as a platform for promoting equal work and pay because it can specifically and limitedly indicate individual jobs using job descriptions. This is why the job grading system has attracted so much attention.

Another catalyst for the discussion of job-based employment was the proliferation of telework due to the post-2020 COVID-19 pandemic. Supervisors often assign work to members as needed based on their workload in membership-based employment. Some companies have had difficulty promoting telework because it is difficult to do so unless subordinates work right before them. In addition to assigning work, under a PMS that focuses on "ability" and "job behavior," it is inevitably necessary to observe the behavior of subordinates. Trying to force this in telework can lead to excessive monitoring and over-interference of employees by supervisors, which can induce the undermining effect (Deci, 1971) that reduces intrinsic motivation. For telework to work well, the scope of work and performance standards must be clarified in advance, and the way work is performed must be left to the employee's discretion. In addition, managers are expected to be dedicated to managing the achievement of results and progress at critical points. Job-based employment is appropriate for this type of work process, and membership-based employment has its limitations.

In Japan, many factors hinder introducing "new ways of working," which is essential for utilizing diverse human resources, such as inefficient business processing and the accompanying delay in responding to the digitization of work. Membership-based employment has been criticized as one of these barriers, and discussions on the introduction of job-based employment are gaining momentum. However, because some see membership-based employment as a core element that characterizes Japanese-style employment, the entire PMS needs to be reviewed and optimized if a switch to a job-based system is to be made.

CONCLUSION

From the preceding discussion, the following four vital points can be drawn. First, Japan's traditional PMS focused on promoting organizational learning among employees, especially long-term employment of core human resources. In other words, Japan's traditional PMS was a collection of internal human resource development systems (e.g., OJT, rotation, internal training) backed by HRM based on ability and long-term employment. As a result, companies were able to accumulate know-how and technology within the company and gain a competitive edge, especially in the manufacturing industry.

Second, after the Japanese economy entered a period of low growth, the traditional PMS was replaced by a performance-based system, which was devised and modified to fit in with Japanese employment practices. A unique Japanese hybrid PMS that focuses on both inputs (ability) and outputs (results) has been constructed, and a flexible salary cost structure has been sought

Akihisa Kagami et al.

by encouraging skill development through long-term service and performance allocation. In addition, trial-and-error efforts to reduce the reverse functions of the performance-based system and the deficiencies of the ability-based system have been ongoing to this day.

Third, throughput has come to be emphasized as a third element other than inputs and outputs. PMSs such as the mission grading system and the job grading system, which focus on job duties, a typical element of throughput, are being introduced. Among these, the mission grading system was used to somehow make the job-based PMS function within the very Japanese membership-based employment, and the PMS was optimized by transforming the employee grading system based on individual, specific, and limited job duties into a comprehensive and highly abstract "role (mission)"–based employee grading system; thus, the PMS has been optimized.

Fourth, the Japanese PMS, optimized through various innovations, has been exposed to environmental changes to the extent that it can no longer survive as long as it is based on Japanese-style employment practices. In addition to the global competition for human resources that is occurring as technology becomes more sophisticated, it is now necessary to utilize a diverse range of human resources from Japan in various forms of employment. In such a time of change, the relationship between employees and companies, such as membership-based employment, must be reconsidered. Because membership-style employment is a fundamental factor that has shaped Japanese employment practices and is closely related to the foundation of Japan's PMS and HRM, the impact on the surrounding systems must be carefully considered if the company is to steer the course toward job-style employment. In today's increasingly fierce global competition, Japanese companies need to use wise and quick decision-making to maintain their competitiveness.

ACKNOWLEDGMENTS

In writing the revised version of this chapter, the previous version of this chapter written by Professor Motohiro Morishima was used as a great reference. We would like to express our gratitude once again.

NOTES

1 PMS consists of various subsystems of HRM necessary to improve employee performance (Roberts, 2001; DeNisi and Smith, 2014), and at the same time, PMS is one of the subsystems that make up HRM (PMS is a subset of HRM). Therefore, in this chapter, "HRM" will be used with two semantic contents: the entire HRM system, including PMS, and HRM as a component of the PMS.
2 In 2002, it merged with Keidanren to form Nippon Keidanren (Japan Business Federation).
3 Keidanren is the counterpart of the World Business Council of Sustainable Development in Japan. For more details on Keidanren, see https://www.keidanren.or.jp/en/.

REFERENCES

Aoki, M. (1988). *Information, Incentives, and Bargaining in the Japanese Economy.* New York: Cambridge University Press.

Deci, E.L. (1971). "Effects of externally mediated rewards on intrinsic motivation." *Journal of Personality and Social Psychology,* 18, 105–115.

DeNisi, A.S., & Smith, C.E. (2014). "Performance appraisal, performance management, and firm-level performance. A review, a proposed model, and new directions for future research." *The Academy of Management Annals,* 8, 127–179.

Dore, R.P. (1989). "Where we are now: Musings of an evolutionist." *Work, Employment and Society,* 3: 425–446.

Endo, T., Delbridge, R., & Morris, J. (2015). "Does Japan still matter? Past tendencies and future opportunities in the study of Japanese firms." *International Journal of Management Reviews,* 17(1), 101–123.

Froese, F.J. Sekiguchi, T., & Maharjan, M.P. (2018). "Chapter 15: Human resource management in Japan and South Korea." In Fang Lee F. Cooke & S. Kim (Eds.), *Routledge Handbook of Human Resource Management in ASIA* (pp. 275–294). New York: Routledge.

Hamaguchi, K. (2017). "Challenges for Japan's employment system." *Planning and Administration,* 40(4), 9. (In Japanese).

Hayashi, K. (2016). "Evolving personnel systems: How to promote work standard personnel reforms." *Labor Administration,* 39. (In Japanese).

Hirano, M. (2006). *Nihongata Jinji Kanri: Shinkagata no Hassei Process to Kinousei.* [Japanese style human resource management: Evolutionary development process and functionality]. Tokyo: Chuo Keizai-sha. (In Japanese).

Hirano, M. (2010). "The transformation of the employee rating system." *Japan Institute for Labor Policy and Training. Japan Labor Research Journal,* 597, 77.

Huang, L. Yang, Y., & Sekiguchi, T. (2020). "Attractiveness of Japanese firms to international job applicants: The effects of belongingness, uniqueness, and employment patterns." *Asian Bus Manage,* 19, 118–144.

Imano, K., & Sato, H. (Eds.). (2020). *Introduction to Human Resources Management* (3rd ed.). Tokyo: Nippon Keizai Shinbun-sha. (In Japanese).

Ishida, M., & Higuchi, J. (2009). *Jinjiseido no Nichibei Hikaku. Seikashugi to America no Genjitsu* [Comparison of HR Systems in the U.S. and Japan: Performance Based System and the Reality in the U.S.]. Kyoto: Minerva Shobo. (In Japanese).

Japan Management Association. (2005). *Seika-shugi ni kansuru Chousa* [Announcement of the results of the survey on performance-based HRM]. Tokyo: Japan Management Association. Retrieved from https://www.jma.or.jp/img/pdf-teigen/teigen_2004_shiryo_2.pdf.(In Japanese).

Jo, S. (2004). *Uchigawakara mita Fujitsu: Seikashugi no Hokai* [The inside of Fujitsu: Breakdown of result-orientation]. Tokyo: Kobunsha. (In Japanese).

Kagami, A. (2018). *Jinzaisaiyo Jinjihyouka no Kyokasho* [Textbook of Recruitment and Human Resource Assessment]. Tokyo: Doyukan (In Japanese).

Kambayashi, N., Zushi, N., & Morita, M. (2010). *Human Resource Management: Learning from Our Experiences*. Tokyo: Yuhikaku Publishing (In Japanese).

Kagono, T., Nonaka, I., Sakakibara, K., & Okumura, A. (1985). *Strategic vs. Evolutionary Management: A U.S.-Japan Comparison of Strategy and Organization*. North-Holland: Sole distributors for the U.S.A. and Canada Elsevier Science Pub.

Koike, K. (1988). *Understanding Industrial Relations in Modern Japan*. London: Macmillan.

Koike, K. (Ed.). (1991). *Human Resource Development of White-Collar Employees*. Tokyo: Toyo Keizai Publishing (In Japanese).

Koike, K. (1992). "Human resource development and labor-management relations." In K. Yamamura & Y. Yasuba (Eds.), *The Political Economy of Japan, Volume 1: The Domestic Transformation* (pp. 289–330). Stanford: Stanford University Press.

Koike, K. (1993). "Human resource development among college graduates in sales and marketing." In K. Koike (Ed.), *An International Comparison of Professionals and Managers*, JIL Report No. 2 (pp. 42–64). Tokyo: Japan Institute of Labor (In Japanese).

Koike, K. (1994). "Learning and incentive systems in Japanese industry." In Aoki Masahiko and Ronald Dore (Eds.), *The Japanese Firm: Sources of Competitive Strength* (pp. 41–65). New York and Oxford: Oxford University Press.

Koike, K. (1999). *Shigoto no Keizaigaku* [Economics of Work]. Tokyo:Chuo Keizai-sha (In Japanese).

Koike, K., & T. Inoki. (1991). *Skill Formation in Japan and Southeast Asia*. Tokyo: University of Tokyo Press.

Komagawa, T. (2013). "Women office workers and careers as objects of analysis: From the arrangement of white-collar studies and women's labor studies." *Bulletin of the Graduate School of Education, Hokkaido University*, 119, 119–139 (In Japanese).

Komagawa, T. (2017). "Efforts to achieve numerical targets for female managers and organizational change." *Journal of the Ohara Institute of Social Problems*, 703 17–31, 2017-05-01, Hosei University, Ohara Institute of Social Problems (In Japanese).

Kusuda, K (Ed.). (2002). *Nihongata Seikashugi: Jinji Chingin Seido no Wakugumi* [Framework and Design of Japanese-style Performance-based HR and payroll systems]. Tokyo: Seisansei Shuppan. (In Japanese).

Lehmberg, D. (2014). "From advantage to handicap: Traditional Japanese HRM and the case for change." *Organizational Dynamics*, 43(2), 146–153.

Levine, D.I. (1991). "Cohesiveness, productivity, and wage dispersion." *Journal of Economic Behavior and Organization*, 15, 237–255.

MacDuffie, J.P. (1995). "Human resource bundles and manufacturing performance: Organizational logic and flexible production systems in the world auto industry." *Industrial and Labor Relations Review*, 48, 197–221.

Ministry of Education, Culture, Sports, Science, and Technology, (n.d.). "Basic school survey annual statistics." Retrieved from https://www.e-stat.go.jp/dbview?sid=0003147040

Ministry of Health, Labor and Welfare. (2019). "Hatarakikata Kaikaku, Ichioku Soukatsuyaku Shakai wo Mezashite." [Reform of Work Styles: Toward the Realization of a 100 million Actively Engaged Society]. Retrieved from https://www.mhlw.go.jp/content/000474499.pdf (In Japanese).

Ministry of Internal Affairs and Communications. (n.d.). "Labor Force Survey (Basic Tabulation), long-term time series data." Retrieved from https://www.jil.go.jp/kokunai/statistics/timeseries/html/g0204.html.

Ministry of Health, Labor, and Welfare. (1990). *Comprehensive Survey on Pay and Working Hours*. Tokyo: Ministry of Finance Printing Office. (In Japanese). https://www.mhlw.go.jp/english/database/

Mishina, K. (2004). *Senryaku Fuzen no Ronri* [The Logic of Dysfunction of Strategy in Japanese Firm]. Tokyo: Toyo Keizai Shimpo-sha (In Japanese).

Mitani, N. (1992). "Job- and ability-based pay structure." In T. Tachibanaki (Ed.), *Assessment, promotions and pay determination* (pp. 109–136). Tokyo: Yuhikaku Publishing (In Japanese).

Miyamoto, M., & Kubo, K. (2002). "Chapter 3–1 Two patterns of institutions." In K. Kusuda (Ed.), *Nihongata Seikashugi: Jinji Chingin Seido no Wakugumi* [Framework and Design of Japanese-style Performance-based HR and payroll systems] (pp. 106–111). Tokyo: Seisansei Shuppan (In Japanese).

Morishima, M. (1996). "Evolution of White-Collar HRM in Japan." In L. David, E.K. Bruce, & S. Donna (Eds.), *Advances in Industrial and Labor Relations* (Vol. 7, pp. 145–176). Greenwich, CT: JAI Press.

Morishima, M. (2002). "Pay practices in Japanese organizations: Changes and non-changes." *Japan Labor Bulletin*, 41(4), 8–13.

Morishima, M. (2006). "Evolution of White-Collar HRM in Japan: An update." In H. Itami, H. Fujimoto, T. Okazaki, H. Ito, & T. Numagami (Eds.), *Japanese Corporate System: Readings* (Vol. 4, pp. 269–303). Tokyo: Yuhikaku Publishing (In Japanese).

Morishima, M. (2008). "Performance management in Japan: A Global Perspective." In A. Varma, P.S. Budhwar, & A.S. DeNisi (Eds.), *Performance Management Systems: A Global Perspective* (pp. 223–238). New York: Routledge.

Nonaka, I., & Takeuchi, H. (1995). *The Knowledge-Creating Company*. Oxford and New York: Oxford University Press.

Okubayashi, K. (Ed.). (2003). *Seika to Kouhei no Houshu series-Jintekishigen wo Ikaseruka*. [Series of Achievement and Fairness Compensation System Series - Can we make the most of our human resources?]. Tokyo: Chuo Keizai-sha. (In Japanese)

Okunishi, Y. (2001). "Conditions for the introduction of 'performance-based' wages." *Organizational Science*, 34(3), 6–17.

Ono, H. (2018). "Career mobility in the embedded market: A study of the Japanese financial sector." *Asian Business & Management*, 17(5), 339–365.

Roberts, I. (2001). "Reward and performance management." In I. Beardwell & L. Holden (Eds.), *Human Resource Management: A Contemporary Approach* (pp. 506–558). Edinburgh: Pearson.

Sekiguchi, T. (2006). "How organizations promote person-environment fit: Using the case of Japanese firms to illustrate institutional and cultural influences." *Asia Pacific Journal of Management*, 23(1), 47–69.

Sekiguchi, T. (2012). "Part time work experience of university students and their career development." *Japan Labor Review*, 9(3), 5–29.

Sekiguchi, T. (2013). "Theoretical implications from the case of performance-based human resource management practices in Japan: management fashion, institutionalization and strategic human resource management perspectives." *The International Journal of Human Resource Management*, 24(3), 471–486. DOI: 10.1080/09585192.2012.703414

Takahashi, N. (2004). *Kyomou no Seikashugi: Nihongata Nenkosei Fukkatsu no Susume* [Groundless performance-based: Recommendation for revival of the Japanese-style seniority system]. Tokyo: Chikuma Shobo(In Japanese).

Takeishi, E. (2000). "Career management of professional human resources in the financial services industry." *Special Issue of Nissay Research Institute's Journal*, 1, 42–69. Nissay Research Institute (In Japanese).

Tatemichi, S. (2009). "Seikashugi ga Morale ni Ataeru Eikyou" [The Impact of Performance-Based Policies on Morale]. *Sociological Review*, 60(2), 225–241. https://doi.org/10.4057/jsr.60.225,

Tsuru, Y. Abe, M., & Kubo, K. (2005). *Nihon Kigyo no HR Kaikaku: HR Data ni yoru Seikashugi no Kensho* [HR Reforms In Japanese Companies-Validating Performance-Based Payments with HR Data]. Tokyo: Toyo Keizai Shinposha (In Japanese).

Wakabayashi, M., & Graen, G. (1989). 'Human resource development of japanese managers: Leadership and career investment." In A. Nedd, G.R. Ferris, & K.M. Rowland (Eds.), *Research in Personnel and Human Resources Management, Suppl. 1* (pp. 235–256). Greenwich, CT: JAI Press.

Watanabe, S. (2001). *Corse-bestu Koyoukanri to Josei Roudou: Danjo Kyoudou Sankaku Shakai wo Mezashite* [Course-Based Employment Management and Women's Labor: Toward a Gender-Equal Society (Revised and Enlarged Edition)]. Tokyo: Chuo Keizai-sha (In Japanese).

Yamazaki, Ken (2021). "White Collar exemption system and job type employment." *The Journal of Commerce, Chuo University*, 62(5 & 6), 348.

Yanadori, Y. (2018). "HRM research on Japanese organizations in the twenty-first century: Review and emerging research topics." In T. Nakano (Ed.), *The Japanese Firm System in Evolution: New Directions, Breaks, and Emerging Practices* (pp. 293–311). New York: Routledge.

Yanagishita, K. (2003). *Kokogachigau Kachigumi Kigyo no Seikashugi.* [Characteristics of the Performance Pay for Winner Companies] Tokyo: Nihon Keizai Shinbun Sha.

Yashiro, A. (1995). *Careers of White-Collar Workers in Large Japanese Firms.* Tokyo: The Japan Institute of Labor (In Japanese).

Performance Management in Australia

John Shields

Chapter 16

This chapter examines continuity and change in performance management systems (PMSs) and outcomes in Australia, with an emphasis on developments since the publication in 2008 of Helen De Cieri and Cathy Sheehan's contribution to the first edition of this text (De Cieri and Sheehan, 2008). While seeking to maintain continuity with its predecessor, the revised chapter focuses on factors that have shaped and reshaped Australian PMSs since the initial edition of this text appeared in the depths of the global financial crisis (GFC).

Following the example set by De Cieri and Sheehan, the discussion draws on the model of performance management offered in this and the previous edition of the text by Murphy and DeNisi (see Chapter 6). This model identifies two sets of environmental factors that are likely to influence PMS practices and operations and outcomes: first, 'distal factors' (industry, national and cultural norms; strategy and firm performance, legal systems and technology) and, second, 'proximal factors' (PMS purpose, organisational norms and stakeholder acceptance of the PMS). The Murphy and DeNisi model also identifies a number of operational factors (including 'intervening factors', 'judgement factors' and 'distortion factors'). For the purpose of examining the determinants, nature and operation of PMSs in Australia, we have chosen to apply a

DOI: 10.4324/9781003306849-16

modified version of this model, one that addresses two overarching themes: (1) *environmental factors* (focusing on country-specific 'distal' factors) and (2) *organisational and operational factors* (including both 'proximal' factors influencing management and employee thought and action regarding performance management and PMS configuration, processes and outcomes and encompassing the 'intervening', 'judgement' and related PMS-specific factors identified by Murphy and DeNisi). Regarding organisational and operational factors, we pay particular attention to the tension and interplay between more traditional approaches to managing individual employee performance, including prominent features of 'performance appraisal' such as formal annual rating and review, and what has come to be known as the 'New Performance Management' (NPM) or 'Performance Management 2.0', with its emphasis on future-focused performance development as opposed to the evaluation of past performance.

ENVIRONMENTAL FACTORS

As Murphy and DeNisi note, 'distal' factors that operate at international, national and/or regional levels set the larger stage on which performance management is played out within organisations. While the GFC (2008–10), the COVID-19 pandemic and megatrends such as digitisation and related aspects of the 'Fourth Industrial Revolution' are worldwide in their influence, in this section, we focus on three national-level factors that have continued to have a major influence on the landscape of performance management in Australia: (1) economic structure and business strategy, (2) workforce profile and (3) employment law and regulation. Our examination of each of these environmental factors includes an assessment of the implications for the general nature, purpose and significance of performance management at the organisational level. As Cleveland also argues (2020), in understanding the dynamics of PMS developments, 'context matters'.

ECONOMIC STRUCTURE AND BUSINESS STRATEGY
The Ascendancy of the Service Sector

Until the economic reforms ushered in by the Hawke-Keating government in the 1980s, Australia's economy was heavily tariff-protected, heavily reliant on primary sector exports to Japan, the

US and the UK, and heavily dependent on foreign direct investment from the US. The dismantling of tariff barriers and the floating of the Australian dollar removed the final props supporting the ailing manufacturing sector while giving a fillip to the growth of the services sector, particularly banking, finance and tourism. Since the early 1970s, employment growth has been dominated by service-sector employment, which has culminated in almost 90 per cent of the Australian workforce being employed in various service industries, up from 75 per cent in the mid-2000s. The industries with the largest share of persons employed in 2020 were health care and social assistance (13 per cent); retail trade (9.9 per cent); professional, scientific and technical services (9.1 per cent); construction (8.6 per cent); and accommodation and food services (7.6 per cent; Australian Bureau of Statistics, 2020a).

During the 2000s, surging demand from China for Australian iron and coal saw the primary sector resume its preeminence as the engine of economic growth, with the 'mining boom' serving to insulate the economy from the effects of the GFC. Post-GFC, however, it is the services sector, including an emerging high-tech industry, that has made the running. A key consequence has been a major shift in sector contributions to national economic output. Over the past 30 years, the contribution of the manufacturing sector has fallen dramatically, while that from the services sector has soared. In 2020–21, the country's services and goods industries accounted for about 81 per cent and 19 per cent of real gross value added (GVA) respectively. Australia's mining sector generated 10.6 per cent of GVA, followed by financial services (9.3 per cent), ownership of dwellings (8.9 per cent) and healthcare and social assistance (8.2 per cent). Technology-driven sectors – including professional, scientific and technical services, education and information technology (IT) – are worth 15 per cent of total economic production (Austrade, 2021).

Internationalisation

While Australia has been primarily a trading economy for all but the initial decades of European occupation in 1788, recent decades have witnessed unprecedented growth in off-shore activity by Australian businesses, particularly in the Asia-Pacific region. As Australia is a small domestic economy heavily dependent

John Shields

on international trade, Australian companies are vulnerable to the pressures of globalisation. The movement of labour that has been concomitant with the expansion of international business has meant that global competitiveness and issues related to the management of a global workforce have become increasingly critical to Australian employers. While many large firms originating in Australia, such as BHP-Billiton, News Corporation and Qantas, are already multinational corporations that span the globe, it is increasingly the norm for many medium-sized and small organisations to be involved in international business. To be successful in the global marketplace, a major challenge for all businesses is to manage human resources (HR) in ways that will lead to effective performance across cultural and national boundaries (Bartram et al. 2015; De Cieri, 2007; Fish and Wood, 1997). With respect to the emerging focus on services, research suggests that, to maximise customer service, companies in the service sector require progressive human resource management (HRM) approaches, including an emphasis on performance management, to create a positive experience for the employee and the customer (Batt, 2002; Korczynski, 2002).

From Shareholder Value to Environment, Social and Global Responsibility

The increased exposure to international market competition, particularly from countries with low labour costs, has intensified the focus on cost containment, process efficiency and productivity improvement. In the HR field, this has required far greater attention to the tenets of 'strategic HRM' and the role of human resources in supporting the achievement of strategic objectives. During the 1990s, HR strategy focused chiefly on downsizing and delayering and improving individual and group performance while during the economic boom prior to the GFC the emphasis was on business process improvement and 'enterprise resource planning'. Post-GFC, and in the context of the dawning realisation of the challenges posed by climate change, business strategy appears to be shifting focus from shareholder primacy to the imperative of environmental, social and government responsibility and sustainability. There are some indications that, partly as a consequence of the pandemic, this strategic reorientation is beginning to influence approaches workplace performance management, although, as Kramar (2021) contends, the transition to sustainability being the paramount strategic objective is still far from complete.

The 'New Public Management'

The primacy of the shareholder value in corporate thinking in the 15 years preceding the GFC was paralleled in the public sector by a thoroughgoing transformation in line with the tenets of neo-liberalism and dictates of 'the new public management'. The latter encompassed everything from the corporatisation and privatisation of government-owned banks, public utility providers and airlines to an emphasis on individual performance pay for executives, managers and line employees alike. Related changes included tighter constraints on public expenditure on the provision of health, medical, welfare, educational and administrative services and increased contracting out of service provision in these and other areas to charities and businesses, including multinational consulting firms. During the 1990s and 2000s, the consequences for public-sector performance management were profound – and frequently profoundly dysfunctional (O'Donnell, 1998; O'Donnell, O'Brien, and Junor, 2011; Podger, 2017).

Economic and Strategic Change: Implications for Performance Management

Taken together, the structural and strategic factors noted earlier imply a greater role for PMS in improving business competitiveness and administrative efficiency and, as we explain in the following, the last three decades have witnesses a far greater emphasis on the potential contribution of individual and team performance management to organisational success, particularly in service provision. Adherence to the mantra of shareholder value and the drive to internationalise between the end of the Cold War and the onset of the GFC inclined companies and public-sector organisations alike to frame the value of their PMSs largely in terms of labor cost reduction, productivity improvement and process efficiency. Now, however, climate change, accelerating automation, global geo-political volatility and the erosion of old business and economic verities by the pandemic (not least the likely end of the era of neo-liberal policy hegemony) have radically transformed the environmental settings, and there are early indications of the emergency of a new discourse centred on social and environmental responsibility, a human-centred approach to organisational purpose and an overarching accent on the principle of sustainability. As well shall see, in the Australian context, there are now early signs of a change of approach to PMS purpose. What is surprising is the nature of the organisations that seem to be at the forefront of this change.

WORKFORCE PROFILE

Employment Patterns

Australia's paid workforce has changed dramatically in recent decades, having become more casualised, feminised, older and more urbanised than ever before. There are currently (August 2022) about 13.56 million people employed in Australia, of whom 9.47 million are employed full-time and 4.12 million part-time. Females now compose just under half of the total, while around 40 per cent are aged 45 years and over, with young jobseekers – those aged 15 to 24 – accounting for a further 16 per cent. Two thirds work in major metropolitan areas (Australian Bureau of Statistics, 2022a and 2022b).

Many employees in work in small to medium enterprises rather than in super-sized companies. In mid-2019, there were 882,255 businesses with employees, including 608,930 with 1 to 4 employees, 212,243 with 5 to 19, 56,824 with 20 to 199, and just 4,250 with over 200 (Australian Bureau of Statistics, 2022c). Small and medium-sized enterprises (SMEs; which the Australian Bureau of Statistics defines as those having fewer than 200 employees) thus comprise about 90 per cent of Australian employers. On this basis, it is sometimes claimed that SMEs are the country's main engine of employment growth. As detailed later, this skew towards SME employment carries important – and in some ways surprising – implications for both the HR function generally and for performance management in particular.

The 'Gig Economy'

Across Australian industry, there is increasing diversity in working arrangements, increasing use of information technology, more flexible working time patterns and more people working part-time hours. The contingent workforce includes temporary, part-time and self-employed workers. Many companies have reduced the number of full-time employees to lower the associated labour costs and give organisations the flexibility to contract for skills when needed. Companies that use contingent employees from labour hire agencies and other outsource providers are likely to experience a reduction in the administrative and financial burden associated with human resource management because the agencies take care of selecting, training and compensating the workers. Contingent work can be attractive from the worker's perspective. Some employees have chosen to work on a contingent basis as a result of interests, values and needs. Another emerging trend in Australian work patterns – one accelerated by both digitisation and the pandemic – is that more work is being done outside the traditional office or worksite (i.e., remote/distributed work), and it includes work done at home, while travelling, or anywhere a person can connect to the office or colleagues using IT (Lindorff, 2000). The trend away from permanent employment and towards insecure work has gone further in what is now referred to as the 'gig economy'. Here the combination of online ordering platforms, AI and commercial contracting arrangements have fundamentally transformed service industries such as car hire and fast-food delivery and opened the way for heated public debate about the diminution of employment rights (Shields, Rooney, Brown, and Kaine, 2020: 427–434).

A Multicultural Workforce

While immigration has been a major driver of increased labour supply and economic growth since the gold rushes of the 1850s, due to successive waves of European and non-European immigration since the 1940s, Australia now has one of the world's most multicultural societies and workforces. The social, economic and political implications of this multiculturalism are significant for organisations and Australian society in general. The workforce diversity is particularly interesting when taking into account the relatively small size of the Australian resident population, which now stands at just over 25 million (Australian Bureau of Statistics, 2022b).

Prior to the 1960s, the majority of migrants to Australia came from Europe, particularly the United Kingdom. Historically,

John Shields

multiculturalism in Australia was regarded as a governmental social policy problem and attempts were made to reduce cultural heterogeneity by restricting immigration to white Europeans (Jupp, 2001; Wilkinson and Cheung, 1999). There has, however, been increasing national awareness of the importance of Australia's Asian geographic positioning vis-à-vis European cultural heritage, with significant demographic change within Australia. Australia now has a rich mix of cultural backgrounds and heritage, with the proportion of Australian residents that were born overseas (first generation) or who have a parent born overseas (second generation) now standing at 51.5 per cent. While English remains the dominant language used in the public sphere, the languages used at home reflect growing cultural and linguistic diversity, with the most commonly used languages other than English being Mandarin, Arabic, Vietnamese, Cantonese and Punjabi (Australian Bureau of Statistics, 2022b). However, to date, culturally and linguistically diverse communities remain under-represented in senior managerial and executive roles (Groutsis, Cooper, and Whitwell, 2018).

Workforce Ageing and Generational Change

Australia's total population is projected to reach 38.8 million in 2060–61. This is lower than previous projections due to the lower level of migration resulting from the COVID-19 pandemic and a lower fertility rate. Australia is currently in the middle of a significant demographic transition, as people in the baby boomer generation retire. This has already driven a rapid fall in the ratio of working-age people to those over 65 through the past decade, which will continue for the next decade. Migrants are expected to continue to be the largest source of population growth. The population will continue to age, largely as a result of improved life expectancies and low fertility. In 2060–61, 23 per cent of the population is projected to be over 65, up from 16 per cent in 2020–21. The 'dependency ratio' is also expected to rise substantially, with the ratio of working-age people to those over 65 projected to fall from 4.0 to 2.7 over the next 40 years. (Treasury, 2021). Younger workers will thus have to shoulder a greater burden of support for eldercare, they will also have to accommodate to working beside a greater proportion of older workers, which is also a looming challenge for HRM professionals. The weight

of evidence also suggests that the newest workforce entrants –
Gen Z – place substantially more value on in-house opportunities for personal growth and development than was the case for
previous generations (Aggarwal et al., 2020; Shields et al., 2020:
434–441).

Greater Workforce Participation by Women

Between 1978 and 2021, labour force participation by women
rose from 43 per cent to over 60 per cent, with growth being most
pronounced amongst those aged 45 and older (Treasury, 2021).
Women still dominate the part-time and contingent workforce
as well as that of the 'caring' professions. However, there has
been some positive change in women's representation in senior full-time roles over the past decade. Over the past 15 years,
the introduction of more stringent corporate governance best
practice provisions has seen the proportion of the largest listed
company board positions held by women rise from around 10
per cent to 33 per cent. Women now also occupy 19.4 per cent of
CEO positions and 18 per cent of board chair roles. Furthermore,
the application of EEO reporting requirements in larger organisations has contributed to a growth in the proportion of managerial
positions held by women, with the figure currently being 32.5 per
cent (Workplace Gender Equality Agency, 2021a). Nevertheless,
the overall pace of change here has been modest. The gender
pay gap also remains stubbornly high, although it has been falling since 2014 and is currently (2021) 13.4 per cent (Workplace
Gender Equality Agency, 2021b).

Declining Union Density

Australia was once a bastion of trade unionism, but this is no
longer so. Between 1986 and 2016, union membership fell from
46 per cent of the workforce to just 14.6 per cent, with the sharpest fall being among males in the private-sector 'blue-collar' workforce. Over the same period, membership amongst professional
workers actually rose from 34 per cent to 46 per cent, with female
and male public-sector workers being at the forefront of this
trend. Since 2014, women have outnumbered men in union ranks,
with particularly high rates of membership in female-dominated
occupations such as nursing, teaching and childcare (Australian
Bureau of Statistics, 2020b; Bowden, 2017).

John Shields

Workforce Change: Implications for Performance Management

The accelerated pace of change to Australia's workforce profile is resetting the possibilities and prospects for PMS purpose and configuration. Clearly, more than ever before, PMSs need to be designed and managed for a workforce that is service sector–based, increasingly non-permanent, culturally diverse and multi-generational – a workforce for which future skill needs will be of a higher (i.e. less narrowly technical) order than those of the past.

Changing workforce demography poses several challenges for PMSs. In particular, systems need to be designed and administered so as to eliminate cultural, gender and age bias in performance criteria and assessment – and there is now a large body of evidence that traditional systems based on annual rating and review by solo assessors is prone to unconscious bias as well as conscious manipulation (Shields et al., 2020: 133–46). It also appears that women, particularly those in non-permanent jobs, are more likely than men to be subjected to traditional appraisal methods. Brown and Heywood (2005) found that performance appraisal is more likely in Australian establishments with more women workers and without large proportions of permanent workers. The same study indicates that the underlying purpose in such cases is more likely to be evaluative rather than developmental. For these groups of workers, then, the purpose of an appraisal is simply to monitor performance and provide appropriate rewards. PMS outcomes should provide adequate developmental opportunities for women, minorities and contingent workers, along with reward outcomes that are free of social bias. Despite Australia being notionally an 'equal pay' country, the persistence of a substantial gender pay gap is attributable at least partly to gender bias in the determination of performance-pay levels.

The combination of high immigration and a growth of jobs in the service sector has created a further challenge – that of recurrent shortages of key skills. New entrants to the labour force often arrive without the skills needed for success and therefore require training. However, Australian employers have a long-standing aversion to investing in in-house training and development programs (van Onselen, 2022). In the context of an increasingly multicultural and feminised workforce, service-sector employers who are willing to invest in this way, and to move to a developmentally focused PMS, may well reap a competitive advantage.

Likewise, the increasing use of information technology and non-permanent work creates additional challenges. On one hand, businesses might be tempted to abandon the employment relationship and formal performance management completely in favour of gig economy practices. On the other hand, not only are these practices now under serious legal challenge in Australia, but they are also incapable of leveraging the potential benefits of a developmentally focused PMS, including improved worker commitment, loyalty, motivation and well-being.

EMPLOYMENT LAW AND REGULATION

In Australia, two main areas of employment law have had a major influence on performance management. These are, first, anti-discrimination and equal employment opportunity (EEO) legislation, and, secondly, the unfair dismission provisions in the federal Fair Work Act 2009 (Cth) (Act).

Anti-Discrimination and EEO Legislation

From the later 1970s on, federal and state antidiscrimination and EEO legislation has reduced significantly the scope for employment-related decisions to be made on the basis of factors that bear no relation to valid job requirements, including performance specifications. Building on earlier federal and state legislation, the Fair Work Act prohibits 'adverse action' (i.e. discrimination) against a current or prospective employee on a number of specific grounds. It is unlawful to make decisions for or against an individual on the basis of the following 'protected attributes': race, colour, sex, sexual orientation, age, physical or mental disability, marital status, family or carer's responsibilities, pregnancy, religion (with exemptions for religious bodies), political opinion, national origin/extraction or social origin. Therefore, any decisions based on a performance assessment that was judged to be discriminatory would be unlawful. This discrimination does not have to be conscious or intentional, and it may result from a manager's attitudes or beliefs (Australian Human Right Commission, n.d.). Even so, discriminatory and unequal decision-making persists, not least in performance and reward management and in access to senior management positions.

John Shields

Unfair Dismissal

The unfair dismissal provisions in section 387 of the Fair Work Act 2009 identify a number of procedural fairness requirements that the relevant judicial body, the Fair Work Commission, must consider in determining whether any dismissal decision, including for unsatisfactory performance, is defensible or 'harsh, unjust or unreasonable'. These factors include whether there was a valid reason for the decision, whether the person was notified of that reason, whether they were given an opportunity to respond, whether they were allowed a support person, whether they were warned about unsatisfactory performance prior to the dismissal, whether the procedures followed were appropriate in terms of the size of the employer's enterprise and the degree to which the presence of dedicated HR expertise in the enterprise would be likely to impact on the procedures followed. The employee's prior work performance is also a salient factor, with a long and unblemished record weighing in the employee's favour in determinations made by the commission. Since they are enshrined in law, these requirements establish clear guidelines for procedural justice in the management of performance by employees covered by awards and enterprise agreements under the national employment relations system and earning less than the specified high-income threshold (approximately 2.2 times the average full-time equivalent weekly earnings). A special 'Fair Dismissal Code' applies to employers with fewer than 15 employees, with these employers protected from unfair dismissal claims by employees who have been with them for less than 12 months. However, any dismissal on the grounds of redundancy must be for genuine business reasons (Australian Government, n.d.). Overall, these Fair Work Act provisions offer a clear incentive to employers wishing to avoid potentially costly litigation for unfair dismissal to develop and maintain a formal PMS (Fair Work Commission, n.d.). In line with these legislative provisions, the commission and the Fair Work Ombudsman have formulated the following five-step checklist for managing underperformance in a solution – focused and legally defensible manner: (1) Identify the problem, (2) assess and analyse the problem, (3) meet with the employee, (4) jointly devise a solution and (5) monitor performance (Fair Work Ombudsman, n.d.).

Legal/Regulatory Change: Implications for Performance Management

The employment law context poses challenges and obligations for both employers and employees with respect to performance management. For employers, there is an obligation to adhere to procedural justice principles and practices, in particular, communication of performance standards ahead of any assessment, judgement against these standards using valid and reliable evidence, adequate warning of any areas of under-performance, opportunity and resourcing for performance to improve and remedial action (including possible disciplinary action or dismissal) only after documented failure to improve. Building, as they do, on prior statutory and judicial precedents, these prescriptions for procedural fairness strongly favour a formal system of performance rating, review and improvement along traditional lines. As discussed in the following, at least for larger organisations, such an approach may well serve to limit the scope for the adoption of the less formalistic methods associated with the so-called New Performance Management (NPM), including abandoning formal rating practices. Indeed, the absence of formal rating and review processes may well constrain the organisation's ability to manage repeated under-performance in a legally defensible way. Abandoning rating-based reviews may attenuate the negative feelings workers have about having their contribution judged. However, removing performance reviews entirely may add to management bias and lead to subjective employee ratings. Other consequences might include an inability to properly manage both high and lower performers and a consequent worsening of business outcomes (Bryant et al., 2020; Grogan, Geard, and Stephens, 2015).

ORGANISATIONAL AND OPERATIONAL FACTORS

In this section, we first review the major proximal factors shaping the PMS presence in Australian organisations, including trends regarding the general acceptance of PMSs, the purposes associated with their use and stakeholder perceptions of PMS effectiveness. We then examine current PMS practices and plans for the post-COVID-19 era, with a particular focus on the relative importance of 'old' and 'new' approaches to PMS purpose and configuration.

PMS TRENDS, OBJECTIVES AND PERCEPTIONS IN HISTORICAL PERSPECTIVE

Growing Acceptance of Formal Performance Management as a Mainstream HRM Function

Past approaches continue to weigh heavily on current performance management practices. To fully appreciate this point, it is necessary to reprise the development of performance management in Australia. Formal performance measurement emerged in the US and in Britain during the First World War, with the introduction of psychological testing and systems for monitoring work contribution (DeNisi and Murphy, 2017; Dulebohn, Ferris, and Stodd, 1995; Ling, 1965). In Australia, however, due to the relatively small size of organisations and the restricted scale of manufacturing, it was not until the production demands of World War II that many employers invested in a permanent personnel function and set about the task of systematically measuring work activity and developing bureaucratic procedures (Dunphy, 1987; Smart and Pontifex, 1993; Wright, 1995).

According to Lansbury (1995), during the 1950s, performance appraisal – as it was then termed – was dominated by a measurement approach that focused on valid rating scale development and retrospective judgement rather than interactive performance interviews. It was not until the 1970s and 1980s that performance appraisal began to focus more on employee feedback and development, and even then, the traditional emphasis on rating and rewarding (or punishing) past performance remained predominant. In the 1980s, economic pressures to become more competitive led to a refinement and sophistication of the appraisal techniques used (Lansbury, 1995). Problems identified with early and rudimentary forms of performance appraisal, such as rating scales, included concerns about the subjectivity and inconsistency in the way that supervisors were using scales, and the incidence of central tendency, with appraisers avoiding the extreme ends of the scales. A study conducted in the mid-1980s reported greater involvement of the appraisee, with almost 57 per cent of Australian organisations including some form of self-appraisal in the appraisal process (Wood, Collins, Arasu, and Entrekin, 1995). Used in conjunction with the appraisal interview, this participation allowed employees to voice their grievances and discuss development and training needs.

Pressure on Australian companies to become more competitive led to a growing awareness of the need to build a connection between performance appraisal and strategy. Dunphy and Hackman (1988) outlined the need for performance appraisal systems to contribute to organisational adaptability and flexibility. An outcome of the push for a more strategic contribution was the development of PMSs that incorporated a clearer focus on goal alignment. An example of this was the introduction of management by objectives systems to support corporate planning and budgeting targets.

A further fillip came with the move away from centralised wage determination in favour of enterprise-level bargaining in the late 1980s and early 1990s (Deery, Plowman, Walsh, and Brown, 2001; Shelton, 1995). This opened the way for a significantly greater accent on measuring and rewarding short-term individual performance, including coupling performance ratings to performance-related pay (PRP). By 1991 PRP was in evidence in a number of industries. Results from the first Australian Workplace Industrial Relations Survey (AWIRS) showed that in 1990 approximately 34 per cent of workplaces with 20 or more employees had some form of PRP in place for non-managerial employees, although this figure remained largely unchanged by the time of the second AWIRD study in 1995, when the 33 per cent of establishment reported using some form of PRP. Thereafter, however, the use of PRP increased significantly in both the private sector (driven by the pursuit of improved process efficiency and competitiveness) and the public sector (O'Donnell and Shields, 2002). As reported by Long and Shields (2005), using a survey conducted in 1999, PRP for individual performance, particularly merit raises, was used by the majority of companies in Australia, with changes in the legal employment framework accelerating the uptake. The federal Coalition government's Workplace Relations Act 1996 (Cwlth) and Amendments to the Workplace Relations Act (Workchoices) 2005, included provisions intended to create a more direct relationship between employers and employees. This legislation dismantled the remaining elements of the old centralised system and widened the scope for negotiation and agreement-making at the workplace level, including decisions relating to performance management and PRP. While tempering this trend towards individualisation of the employment relationship, the current federal legislation – Labor's Fair Work Act 2009 (Cth) – has not diminished the prevalence and acceptance of PMSs.

For these reasons, the use of formal and broadly based PMS methods increased markedly between the 1990s and 2010s. Contemporary studies showed that Australian organisations, both private and public, were making extensive use of formal performance rating and review methods for managers and, increasingly it seems, for line employees. Drawing on multiple rounds of survey data from the Cranet Network for the period from 1996 to 2009, Kramar (2012) identified four main trends in HR practice, including increased prioritisation of organisational strategic objectives, increased individualisation of the employment relationship, and increased use of performance appraisal and performance-based pay. The use of performance appraisal for managerial and professional positions was consistently above 90 per cent over this period, while its application to clerical roles rose from 78 per cent to 91 per cent, and for manual roles, from 55 per cent to 68 per cent. Supervisor input to appraisal also remained above 90 per cent, while input from the employees themselves also remained above 80 per cent, with slight increases in the use of subordinate input (from 14 per cent to 19 per cent), peers (from 14 per cent to 21 per cent) and customers (from 14 per cent to 16 per cent). The same data also indicated an increased use of appraisal to inform decisions on pay (58 per cent to 79 per cent), training and development (85 per cent to 92 per cent), career planning (79 per cent to 84 per cent) and workforce planning (58 per cent to 67 per cent; Kramar, 2012: 139). In a further study using Cranet data to compare formal performance appraisal use in Australia with other Asia-Pacific countries, Kramar and Parry (2014) found usage in Australian organisations to be relatively high across all job categories (Kramar and Parry, 2014: 411). According to Kramar and Parry (2014), the contextual drivers of this trend included the decline of union density, the growing individualisation of the employment relationship and the widespread adoption of the precepts and prescriptions of the 'strategic HRM' model across the private and public sectors. Included here were policies designed to align employee performance more closely with organisational objectives and capability requirements, including individual performance ratings and reviews and individual performance pay. While limited in scope, the findings of the Australian Workplace Relations Study – the successor of the AWIRS studies of the 1990s – confirmed that, at the time the survey data were gathered (2014), 'performance assessments' were in widespread use for determining pay increases. While enterprises with more than 200 employees had the highest incidence (85.5 per cent), small and medium-sized organisations also made considerable use: 91.3 per cent in enterprises with 20–199 employees and 75.6 per cent in those with 5–19 employees. This study also found that 77 per cent of enterprises used performance development planning and review for individual employees, with 59 per cent of enterprises making it available to all employees (Fair Work Commission, 2015).

PMS Purpose

As noted earlier, performance management emerged with the overriding purpose of evaluating past performance and the evidence shows that this has remained the dominant purpose in Australia until relatively recently. Kramar's (2000) national survey established that organisations typically used the information from the performance appraisal component of a PMS for short-term evaluative and administrative purposes, rather than for longer-term developmental and strategic purposes. The primary purpose of information from performance appraisals was to make decisions about improving employee performance in their current job, rather than for making decisions about organisational training needs or future career and organisational training needs (Kramar, 2000; Milliman et al., 2002; Nankervis and Leece, 1997). A review of performance systems in a sample of large Australian organisations in 2015 by PwC reported that performance management was regarded as a compliance requirement, rather than a development, Run-on (Grogan et al., 2015).

Nevertheless, there are indications that the talent shortages that characterised the years prior to the GFC may have prompted the beginnings of a shift in perceived PMS purpose, a shift from retrospective judgement and reward/punishment towards a more forward-looking approach emphasising strategically aligned contribution and employee development. Nankervis and Compton's (2006) review of the status of performance systems established that the main purpose of performance management was almost equally distributed across training and development needs (89.2 per cent) and the appraisal of past performance (88.9 per cent) and to a lesser extent alignment of objectives (75.5 per cent). The same study also sought to explore in more detail the strategic element of the PMS, by examining the uptake of the balanced scorecard (BSC) amongst Australian organisations. These researchers argued that the BSC makes explicit links between performance measures and organisational objectives and strategies and as such is worthy of particular investigation. A total of 25.5 per cent of total respondents reported using the BSC and 95 per cent of this group felt that their performance measures are consistent with their organisations' missions, visions and long-term goal strategies. Most of the respondents using a BSC approach felt therefore that their performance measures were generally consistent with organisational goals and strategies. A more recent study, by Askarany and Yazdifar (2018), found that while 28.6 per cent of organisations in their Australian sample reported having adopted BSC, there were major shortcomings in how it was put into practice, particularly regarding processes for establishing and maintaining strategic alignment and stakeholder acceptance. Taken at face value, this suggests that if the BSC is the exemplar of strategically aligned performance management, then Australian practices have continued to fall short of the intended purpose.

PMS Effectiveness

One of the most consistent findings in prior international research is that objective outcomes from traditional PMS operations are either negligible or negative (Pulakos, Mueller-Hanson, and Arad, 2018: 250). Furthermore, studies of stakeholder perceptions of traditional PMS, including those undertaken in Australia, are, at best, lukewarm and, in the case of employees, largely negative (e.g. Brown, Hyatt, and Benson, 2008; Brown, Kraimer, and Bratton, 2020). A 2015 PWC study (Grogan et al., 2015) of PMS in a sample of 27 Australian firms reported that 28 per cent of employees felt that their organisation did not have an effective PMS. The most comprehensive Australian study in this vein, that by Nankervis, Stanton, and Foley (2012), based on a sample size of 304 respondents, reported that, across six specific criteria, managers and executives were less than effusive regarding PMS effectiveness. While line managers were most likely to see their organisation's PMS being disconnected from other organisational practices, HR professionals were less sanguine about the system's alignment with organisational vision, values and goals. Line managers were also more likely to view the PMS as being 'bureaucratic and time-consuming'. They also seemed less willing to accept 'ownership' of the PMS. Not surprisingly, executives/senior managers and HR professionals (in that order) were generally more positive about the effectiveness of their systems than either middle or line managers, perhaps because executives at least are more inclined to view their PMS more from a strategic than an operational perspective (Nankervis, Stanton, and Foley, 2012: 52).

A recent survey of Australian HR practitioners (Kim, Shields, and Chhetri, 2021) asked respondents to rate the effectiveness of their overall PMS against the nine specific criteria. The results are presented in Figure 16.1. Whilst a majority of the respondents

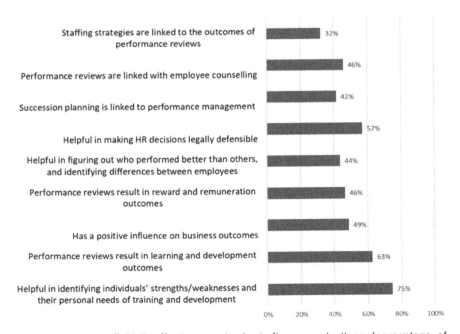

Figure 16.1 Overall PMS effectiveness in Australian organisations (percentage of organisations with 'agree' and 'strongly agree')

Source: Kim, Shields, and Chhetri (2021).

agreed that their PMS was helpful in identifying individuals' strengths, weaknesses and development needs (75 per cent agreed or strongly agreed), and in supporting learning and development (63 per cent agreed or strongly agreed), only a minority agreed that it contributed to business outcomes, influenced reward systems, identified good and poor performers, and aided succession planning, performance counselling and staffing plans. From these findings, it appears that Australian HR professionals still have serious doubts about the contributions of their PMS to desirable strategic business outcomes. These findings are largely in accord with those reported by Nankervis, Stanton and Foley (2012) from their Australian study conducted a decade ago. They found that 62 per cent of their sample considered their PMS relatively effective, as compared to 64 per cent reported in the study by Kim, Shields, and Chhetri (2021).

Murphy and De Nisi recognise in their model that 'intervening factors', such as rater skills and motivation, and rater–ratee relationships, may influence performance management processes and deficiencies in these factors do stand to compromise both perceived and actual PMS effectiveness. For example, while the quality of performance feedback and the traditional review meeting is in large part driven by the interpersonal skills possessed by the manager, there has been a long-standing concern about the lack of 'soft'/interpersonal and communication skills of Australian managers (*Enterprising Nation*, 1995). A study by Connell and Nolan (2004) proposed that Australian managers lacked proficiency in providing meaningful feedback to employees. As reported in the following, it is still the case that only around one-third of organisations currently provide rater training, a shortcoming that is arguably a persistent and major shortcoming in Australian PMS practice.

The NPM

In recent years, traditional performance management practices have been subjected to unprecedented criticism and disruption on a global scale. Critics of traditional practices have argued that the annual performance review is often an empty ritual with little connection to other human resource functions or business objectives and outcomes (Adler et al., 2016). Furthermore, the top-down and bureaucratic nature of traditional systems is said to be incompatible with today's organisational and social context (Baker, 2017; Colquitt, 2017: Kramar, 2021; Shields et al., 2020). The emergence of new technologies such as AI and rapid shifts in employee expectations also challenge the strategic relevance of traditional PMSs (Kramar, 2021; O'Leary and Lentz, 2020; Shields et al., 2020). Furthermore, the traditional accent on judging/punishing/rewarding past performance may be misaligned with the emerging reality of lifelong learning and the expectations of younger, tertiary-educated employees for future-focused developmental opportunities and support (Deloitte Global, 2022). Some commentators have argued for a shift of focus from past performance ('feedback') to future performance ('feedforward'; Buckingham and Goodall, 2015). Some proposed a greater emphasis on obtaining performance feedback from multiple sources (Campion et al., 2019), while yet others suggested engaging in ongoing performance conversations (Aguinis, 2019; Pulakos, Mueller-Hanson, and Arad, 2019; Pulakos, Mueller-Hanson, Arad, and Moye, 2015). In a 2016 US study, Ledford, Benson and Lawler (2016) identified three practices associated with what they termed 'cutting edge' performance management: (1) ongoing feedback, (2) rating-less reviews and (3) crowd-sourced feedback. Midway through the 2010s, a number of prominent multinational firms announced that they had decided to abandon annual performance reviews altogether. IT firms Adobe, Dell, Microsoft and IBM led the way and were joined by professional services firms such as Deloitte, PwC and Accenture (Cappelli and Tavis, 2016; Pulakos, Mueller-Hanson, and Arad, 2019; Rock and Jones, 2015). On one reading, these developments signal the advent for has been referred to variously as the NPM or 'Performance Management 2.0'. The apparent impetus away from traditional PMS methods can be seen as one element of the transformation of HRM concepts and practices in the wake of the GFC. It is also salient to explore whether/how the most recent worldwide crisis – that caused by COVID-19 – may have inhibited or accelerated the adoption of NPM methods.

CURRENT PMS PRACTICES AND PLANS

In the first broadly-based study of Australian performance management in more than a decade, Kim, Shields and Chhetri (2021) draw on data from 165 HR professionals on existing and planned performance management practices, to examine the relative incidence and workforce coverage of 17 specific PMS practices in Australian organisations as well as practice usage by organisational size and sector. While not revealed to respondents, the study classified 10 practices as 'old'/'traditional' and 7 as being associated with NPM. Respondents were also asked to indicate whether they planned to adopt any of these practices over the next 2 years. Furthermore, since data were gathered at the midpoint of the COVID-19 pandemic, the study also examined the reported effects of pandemic-related disruptions on current and planned practices. In this section, we draw on the findings reported in this study to map the main PMS contours as they currently stand in Australia.

'Old' and 'New' Practice Incidence

As reported in Figure 16.2, the majority of respondents reported that their organisations use such 'traditional' performance management methods as performance planning sessions (84 per cent), self-assessments (75.5 per cent) and rating scales (63.8 per cent), with a minority employing such techniques as cascaded goals (46 per cent) and 360-degree feedback (40.5 per cent). Other 'traditional' methods such as rater training (29.4 per cent), deep competency assessment (28 per cent), peer feedback (27.6 per cent) and team or business unit assessments were used considerably less frequently. However, a relatively large number of respondents suggested that their organisations are planning to introduce some of these practices in the near future, especially rater training (30.7 per cent), deep competency assessment (27.6 per cent), team assessment (27 per cent), cascaded goals (24.5 per cent) and peer feedback (22.6 per cent). It seems that such changes in Australian organisations are likely to be cautious and staged, with traditional practices continuing to be embraced by many organisations.

Nonetheless, there are indications (see Figure 16.2) that more significant innovations may be on their way, especially in respect of some non-traditional performance management techniques. The most prominent examples here are ongoing or continuous feedback (74.2 per cent currently using and a further 19 per cent planning to do so) and development coaching (72.4 per cent using and 17.8 per cent planning to adopt).

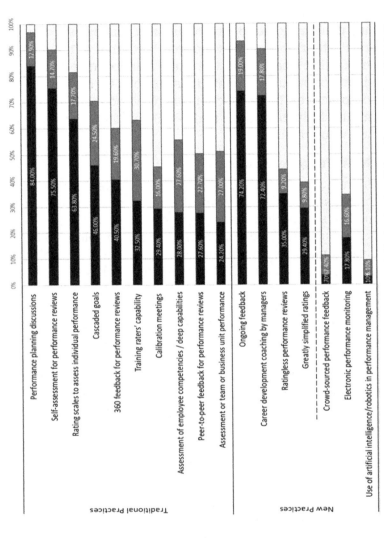

Figure 16.2 Practice Incidence and Planned Introduction, All Respondents

Source: Kim, Shields, and Chhetri (2021).

John Shields

However, non-traditional practices such as rating-less reviews (35 per cent), simplified employee ratings (29.4 per cent) and crowd-sourced feedback (3 per cent) received less support. Applying the Ledford, Benson and Lawler (2016) criteria for 'cutting edge' and 'established' practices to compare Australian and US usage of NPM methods, adoption in Australia as of 2021 still lagged significantly behind the level of take-up in the US 6 years earlier. Furthermore, Australian organisations have so far been extremely cautious in the adoption of technology-based performance management practices, with only 3 per cent reporting that their organisations used AI in their systems currently, and only a further 6 per cent intended to do so in the near future. Almost 18 per cent currently use electronic performance monitoring, with an equal number planning to use it in the future, possibly encouraged by the pandemic and associated remote/hybrid work trends.

In sum, Kim, Shields and Chhetri (2021) find that while traditional practices remain prevalent, they no longer have exclusive dominance. Innovation is underway, albeit very selectively, with signs that NPM is becoming more prominent in both current practice and plans for system change.

Practice Coverage

Respondents to this study were also asked to indicate the percentages of their workforce included in each practice, and we then calculated overall coverage means. Of the 10 traditional performance management practices specified, nine covered, on average, at least half of the workforce. The exception was 360-degree feedback, with a small minority only included. Other traditional practices such as rating scales, self-assessment, performance planning discussions, deep competency assessment, cascaded goals and calibration meetings were reported to be applied to between 60 per cent and 80 per cent of the workforce.

By the same token, workplaces using NPM techniques also tend to involve a large proportion of their workforce, suggesting that these practice innovators have embraced their potential for more holistic PMSs with enthusiasm. Where they are in use, NPM practices such as ongoing feedback, rating-less reviews, greatly simplified ratings and developmental coaching were applied to a significant majority of the workforce. Yet, not all NPM practices had wide coverage. In the few organisations where crowd-sourced feedback was implemented, only half of the workforce was involved, and electronic monitoring was only used for a small minority of the employees. Finally, with respect to new practices, embedded AI technologies were applied only to around 20 per cent of the workforce.

Incidence by Organisational Size

Prior studies indicate that the greatest adopters of formal performance appraisal have tended to be relatively large organisations with both the need and the resources to develop and maintain performance measurement and management systems covering most of their workforce. Using survey data obtained in 2011 from a sample of 527 multinationals operating in Australia, Bartram et al. (2015) found that larger firms used a wide range of performance management and reward practices, with those having an HR shared-services model and global HR integration also making greater use of formal performance measurement and reward practices for both managers and their largest occupational group. Not only were large multinationals more likely to use formal appraisal; those originating in Australia were found to make somewhat greater use of formal performance appraisal for the largest group in their workforce than did those originating in the US – 87.5 per cent usage compared to 81.5 per cent – although those from the US made significantly greater use of other traditional though more recent practices such as forced distribution and 360-degree feedback (Bartram et al., 2015).

Kim, Shields and Chhetri (2021) compared the mean incidence of performance management practices in small to medium-sized organisations with 100 employees or less with very large organisations (1,000 plus), focusing on both traditional and new practices. The results (see Figure 16.3) indicate that very large organisations employ more traditional practices (except deep competency assessment) than their smaller counterparts, while the latter are making considerable use of NPM methods. These findings are consistent with those reported in the US study by Ledford, Benson, and Lawler (2016), although it should be noted that that study uses a very different taxonomy of organisational size. Taking these findings at face value, however, it may be that

John Shields

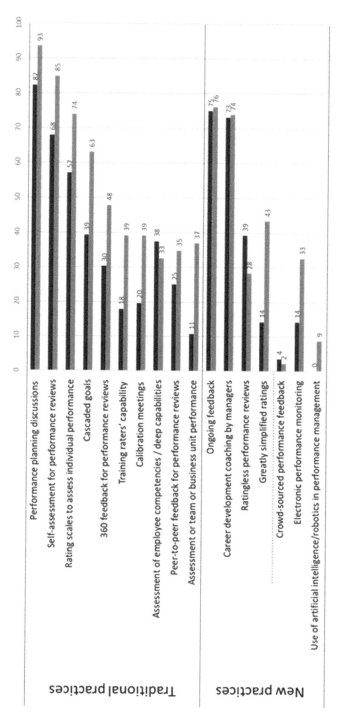

Figure 16.3   Practice Incidence by Organisational Size

* Numbers – percentage of the companies that currently use the practice (e.g. 82% of small organisations are using 'performance planning discussion' while 93% of large organisations are using it).
Source: Kim, Shields, and Chhetri (2021).

small organisations lack the resources to sustain practice complexity and, in any case, have less need for it. A cognate reason might be that, compared to small organisations, very large organisations are generally older, more path dependent and have less agility to transition away from traditional to newer practices.

Incidence by Sector

Here, too, the findings reported by Kim, Shields and Chhetri (2021) and summarised in Figure 16.4, hold some real surprises. Given the imperative to deliver value to shareholders, it is reasonable to suppose that managers of publicly listed for-profit companies will be far more inclined to favour system innovation promising higher productivity and profit margins. All else equal, this may make these companies more willing than NFP and public-sector organisations to embrace the promise of NPM methods than either privately owned companies or public-sector organisations. Kim, Shields and Chhetri (2021) report that publicly traded firms are the highest users of a blend of traditional and NPM practices, followed by privately owned firms, although the latter tend not to employ cascaded goals or 360-degree feedback to the same degree as the publicly traded firms. Public-sector organisations, however, also use both kinds of techniques but with less prevalence of new practices such as peer feedback, rating-less reviews, crowd-sourced feedback, electronic performance monitoring and integrated AI technologies. However, a particularly surprising finding of this study is that many not-for-profit organisations employ a range of traditional practices – for example, performance planning discussions, self-assessment and peer feedback, in tandem with some of the newer techniques – development coaching, rating-less reviews, electronic monitoring and integrated AI technologies. By the same token these NFPs do not use rating scales, rater training, calibration meetings or greatly simplified ratings and crowd-sourced feedback to a significant extent.

In summary, the different sectors appear to have chosen their performance management practices according to their relative organisational size and agility, but it seems clear that the range of techniques used – both traditional and new – is broader and more comprehensive in publicly traded firms than in privately owned organisations.

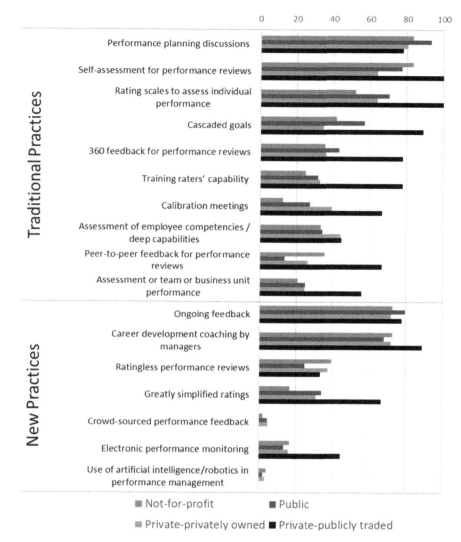

Figure 16.4   Practice Incidence by Sector

Source: Kim, Shields, and Chhetri (2021).

Pandemic Impact and Plans

Notwithstanding the disruptions caused by the pandemic – or perhaps even because of this — it is possible that COVID-19 has set the stage for the accelerated adoption of NPM ideas and methods. While the qualitative data generated by Kim, Shields and Chhetri (2021) indicate that the organisational trauma and uncertainty caused by the pandemic led many organisations to suspend PMS operations completely, in a minority of cases, the disruption caused by the pandemic actually increased workplace receptivity to PMS change. In a few cases, the crisis increased the pace of change, particularly away from systems that were ill equipped for the digital world. Some had already discontinued annual ratings and reviews, while others bought forward plans to do so. Some moved to consolidate a shift from behavioural assessment and attendance to measurable results, goal setting, and other outcomes-based methods. Likewise, some respondents reported switching to technology-based solutions – from online check-ins and multi-source feedback to cloud-based management of individual and team performance data. Still, the most profound and perhaps enduring effect of the pandemic on PMS operations appears to have been less on practices per se and more on the associated values, management–employee relationships and plans, especially in relation to trust and employee well-being, with an emphasis on conversations and joint planning aimed at performance development and enhancement. As one respondent explained, '[I]t reinforced the importance of regular performance and development discussions outside of the "formal" reviews'. This seems to offer fertile ground for experimenting with NPM practices, particularly check-ins and ongoing feedback.

CONCLUSION

As in other countries, the temporal, spatial, ideational and con-figurational dimensions of PMSs are influenced by the complex interplay or factors operating at global, national, sectoral, organi-sational, group and individual levels. As we have seen, in the case of Australia, factors operating at the national level – economic, strategic, social and legal – have prefigured PMS development and design and continue to do so. At organisational level, a PMS can serve strategic, administrative and/or developmental pur-poses. Furthermore, as global volatility and uncertainty intensify and as the pace of technological and climate change accelerates, issues related to performance management become ever more critical to organisational success and sustainability. Arguably, the net effect of these distal, proximal and operational influences is an approach to performance management that is identifiably – if not uniquely – Australian.

A notable feature of the existing literature on PMS in developed economies is its near-exclusive focus on large, for-profit organisations (e.g. Pulakos and Battista, 2020). Yet the latest Australian research suggests that these may not be the organisations at the forefront of innovation. Furthermore, the commonly assumed connection between organisational size, resource capability and innovation in HR practice should now also be questioned. Likewise, the theoretical frameworks that predominate in existing macro-level research on HR practice (e.g. institutional theory, contingency theory, configurational theory, resource dependency theory; see Cleveland, 2020) may no longer be adequate to the challenge of explaining current developments in PMS principles, practices and outcomes. In their contribution to the first edition of this text, De Cieri and Sheehan (2008) remarked that '[w]hile there have been noteworthy developments in performance management in Australia over recent decades, there remain many challenges for the development of this field of research and practice, and the opportunities for progressing this field are substantial'. This observation remains as relevant today as it did in the first year of the GFC as, indeed, do the need for evidence-based advancement of knowledge in the field.

ACKNOWLEDGEMENTS

This chapter draws liberally from the previous version, authored by Helen De Cieri and Cathy Sheehan. The author would like to thank Helen and Cathy for consenting to allow him to use their chapter as the basis for this revision.

FURTHER READING

Bartram, T., Boyle, B., Stanton, P., Sablok, G., & Burgess, J. (2015). Performance and reward practices in multinational corporations operating in Australia. *Journal of Industrial Relations*, 57(2): 210–231.

Brown, M., Hyatt, D., & Benson, J. (2010). Consequences of the performance appraisal experience. *Personnel Review*, 39(3): 375–396.

Brown, M., Kraimer, M.L., & Bratton, V.K. (2020). The influence of employee performance appraisal on intent to quit and sportsmanship. *Personnel Review*, 49(1): 1–18.

Kim, S., Shields, J. & Chhetri, A. (2021) *Performance management in Australian organisations: Current practices and future plans. A report on the state of play.* Melbourne: Australian Human Resources Institute.

Kramar, R. (2021). Workplace performance: A sustainable approach. *Asia Pacific Journal of Human Resources*, 59(4): 567–581.

Nankervis, A., Stanton, P., & Foley, P. (2012). Exploring the rhetoric and reality of performance management systems and organisational effectiveness – Evidence from Australia. *Research and Practice in Human Resource Management*, 20(1): 40–56.

REFERENCES

Adler, S., Campion, M., Colquitt, A., Grubb, A., Murphy, K., Ollander-Krane, R., & Pulakos, E.D. (2016). Getting rid of performance ratings: Genius or folly? A debate. *Industrial and Organizational Psychology*, 9(2): 219–252.

Aggarwal, A., Sadhna, P., Gupta, S., Mittal, A., & Rastogi, S. (2020). Gen Z entering the workforce: Restructuring HR policies and practices for fostering the task performance and organizational commitment. *Journal of Public Affairs*, e2535. Advance online publication. https://doi.org/10.1002/pa.2535

Aguinis, H. (2019). *Performance management for dummies*. Hoboken, NJ: John Wiley & Sons.

Askarany, D., & Yazdifar, H. (2018). The diffusion of balanced scorecard from the perspective of adopters; evidence from Australia. *Review of Economics and Finance*, 14(4): 71–82.

Austrade (2021). *Why Australia? Benchmark report*. Sydney: Australian Trade and Investment Commission. https://www.austrade.gov.au/benchmark-report/resilient-economy

Australian Bureau of Statistics (2020a). Labour account Australia, March 2020. https://www.abs.gov.au/statistics/labour/labour-accounts/labour-account-australia/latest-release

Australian Bureau of Statistics (2020b). Trade union membership. https://www.abs.gov.au/statistics/labour/earnings-and-working-conditions/trade-union-membership/latest-release

Australian Bureau of Statistics (2022a). Labour Force, Australia, June.

Australian Bureau of Statistics (2022b). Snapshot – Australia. https://www.AustralianBureauofStatistics.gov.au/statistics/people/people-and-communities/snapshot-australia/latest-release#culturally-and-linguistically-diverse-communities

Australian Bureau of Statistics (2022c). Business indicators. https://www.AustralianBureauofStatistics.gov.au/statistics/economy/business-indicators/counts-australian-businesses-including-entries-and-exits/latest-release#employment-size

Australian Government (n.d.). Small business fair dismissal code. https://www.fairwork.gov.au/sites/default/files/migration/715/Small-Business-Fair-Dismissal-Code-2011.pdf

Australian Human Rights Commission (n.d.). A quick guide to discrimination laws. https://humanrights.gov.au/our-work/employers/quick-guide-australian-discrimination-laws

Baker, T. (2017). *Performance management for agile organizations: overthrowing the eight management myths that hold businesses back*. London: Palgrave MacMillan.

Bartram, T., Boyle, B., Stanton, P., Sablok, G., & Burgess, J. (2015). Performance and reward practices in multinational corporations operating in Australia. *Journal of Industrial Relations*, 57(2): 210–231.

Batt, R. (2002). Managing customer services: Human resource practices, quit rates, and sales growth. *Academy of Management Journal*, 45: 587–598.

Bowden, B. (2017). Three charts on the changing face of Australian union members. *The Conversation*, 5 July. https://theconversation.com/three-charts-on-the-changing-face-of-australian-union-members-80141

Brown, M., & Heywood, J.S. (2005). Performance appraisal systems: Determinants and change. *British Journal of Industrial Relations*, 43(4): 659–679.

Bryant, P.C., Brown, D., Cotton, C., Hill, B., Gibbs, M., & Sturman, M.C. (2020). Five experts respond to five questions about five trends in compensation and benefits over the next 5 years. *Compensation & Benefits Review*, 52(4): 138–155.

Buckingham, M., & Goodall, A. (2015). Reinventing performance rankings. *Harvard Business Review*, 94(4): 40–50.

Campion, E.D., Campion, M.C., & Campion, M.A. (2019). Best practices when using 360 feedback for performance appraisal. In A.H. Church, D.W. Bracken, J.W. Fleenor, & D.S. Ros (Eds.), *Handbook of strategic 360 feedback*. Oxford: Oxford Scholarship online.

Cappelli, P., & Tavis, A. (2016). The performance management revolution. *Harvard Business Review*, 94(10): 58–67.

Cleveland, J.N. (2020). Context matters. Importance of cultural, economic, and legal/political values in performance appraisal/management. In E.D. Pulakos & M. Battista (Eds.), *Performance management transformation: Lessons learned and next steps* (pp. 233–263). Oxford: Oxford University Press.

Colquitt, A.L. (2017). *Next generation performance management. The triumph of science over myth and superstition*. Charlotte, NJ: Information Age Publishing.

Connell, J., & Nolan, J. (2004). Managing performance: Modern day myth or a game people play. *International Journal of Employment Studies*, 12(1): 43–63.

Deery, S., Plowman, D., Walsh, J., & M. Brown (2001). *Industrial relations: A contemporary analysis* (2nd ed.). Sydney: McGraw-Hill.

De Cieri, H. (2007). Transnational firms and cultural diversity. In P. Boxall, J. Purcell, & P. Wright (Eds.), *Handbook of human resource management*. Oxford: Oxford University Press.

De Cieri, H., & Sheehan, C. (2008). Performance management in Australia. In A. Varma, P. Budhwar, & A. DeNisi (Eds.), *Performance management systems: A global perspective*. Global HRM Series. London: Routledge, pp. 239–253.

Deloitte Global (2022). *Striving for balance, advocating for change. The Deloitte Global 2022 genZ and millennial survey*. London: Deloitte Global. Available at: https://www2.deloitte.com/global/en/pages/about-deloitte/articles/genzmillennialsurvey.html

DeNisi, A.S. & Murphy, K. (2017). Performance appraisal and performance management: 100 years of progress? *Journal of Applied Psychology*, 102(3): 421–433.

Dulebohn, J.H., Ferris, G., & Stodd, J.T. (1995). The history and evolution of human resource management. In G.R. Ferris, S.D. Rosen, & D.T. Barnum (Eds.), *Handbook of human resource management* (pp. 18–41). Oxford: Blackwell Business.

Dunphy, D. (1987). The historical development of human resource management in Australia. *Human Resource Management Australia*, 25: 40–47.

Dunphy, D.C., & Hackman, B.K. (1988). Performance appraisal as a strategic intervention. *Human Resource Management Australia*, 26(2): 23–34.

Fair Work Commission (2015). *Australian workplace relations study. First findings report*. Canberra: Pay Equity Unit, Fair Work Commission. https://www.fwc.gov.au/sites/default/files/2021-12/awrs-first-findings.pdf

Fair Work Commission (n.d.). 'Unfair dismissals benchbook'. https://www.fwc.gov.au/benchbook/unfair-dismissals-benchbook

Fair Work Ombudsman (n.d.). *Managing underperformance – formal steps checklist*. Canberra: Australian Government. https://www.fairwork.gov.au/ArticleDocuments/715/managing-underperformance-formal-steps-checklist.docx.aspx

Fish, A., & Wood, J. (1997). Cross-cultural management competence in Australian business enterprises. *Asia Pacific Journal of Human Resources*, 35(1): 37–52.

Grogan, E., Geard, D, and Stephens, E. (2015). *Performance management effectiveness in the ASX150. Performance management change is on the way but will it be enough?* Sydney, PwC Australia. Available at: https://www.pwc.com.au/people-business/assets/publications/performance-management-mar15.pdf

Groutsis, D., Cooper, R., & Whitwell, G. (2018). *Beyond the pale. Cultural diversity on ASX 100 boards*. Sydney: University of Sydney.

Jupp, J. (Ed.) (2001). *The Australian people. An encyclopaedia of the nation, its people and their origins*. 2nd edition. Cambridge: Cambridge University Press.

Kim, S., Shields, J., & Chhetri, A. (2021). *Performance management in Australian organisations: Current practices and future plans. A report on the state of play*. Melbourne: Australian Human Resources Institute.

Korczynski, M. (2002). *Human resource management in service work*. London: Palgrave.

Kramar, R. (2000). *Cranfield-PricewaterhouseCoopers survey on international strategic human resource management*. North Ryde, NSW: Macquarie University.

Kramar, R. (2012). Trends in Australian human resource management: What next? *Asia Pacific Journal of Human Resources*, 50: 133–150.

Kramar, R. (2021). Workplace performance: A sustainable approach. *Asia Pacific Journal of Human Resources*, 59(4): 567–581.

Kramar, R. & Parry, E. (2014). Strategic human resource management in the Asia Pacific region: similarities and differences? *Asia Pacific Journal of Human Resources*, 52(4): 400–419.

Lansbury, R. (1995). Performance appraisal: the elusive quest. In G. O'Neill & R. Kramar (Eds.), *Australian human resources management* (pp. 123–144). Melbourne: Pitman Publishing.

Ledford, G.E., Benson, G., & Lawler, E.E. (2016). *Cutting-edge performance management: 244 organizations report on on-going feedback, ratingless reviews and crowd-sourced feedback*. Los Angeles: World@Work and Centre for Effective Organizations.

Lindorff, M. (2000). Home-based telework and telecommuting in Australia: More myth than modern work form. *Asia Pacific Journal of Human Resources*, 38(3): 1–11.

Ling, C. (1965). *The management of personnel relations: History and origins*. Chicago: Irwin.

Long, R., & Shields, J. (2005). Performance pay in Canadian and Australian firms. *International Journal of Human Resource Management*, 16: 1783–1811.

Milliman, J., Nason, S., Zhu, C., & De Cieri, H. (2002). An exploratory assessment of the purposes of performance appraisals in North and Central America and the Pacific Rim. *Human Resource Management*, 41(1): 87–102.

Nankervis, A., & Compton, R. (2006). Performance management: Theory in practice? *Asia Pacific Journal of Human Resources*, 44(1): 83–101.

Nankervis, A., & Leece, P. (1997). Performance appraisal: Two steps forward, one step back? *Asia Pacific Journal of Human Resources*, 35(2): 80–92.

Nankervis, A., Stanton, P., & Foley, P. (2012). Exploring the rhetoric and reality of performance management systems and organisational effectiveness – evidence from Australia. *Research and Practice in Human Resource Management*, 20(1): 40–56.

O'Donnell, M. (1998). 'Creating a performance culture?' Performance-based pay in the Australian Public Service. *Australian Journal of Public Administration*, 57(3): 28–40.

O'Donnell, M., O'Brien, J., & Junor, A. (2011). New public management and employment relations in the public services of Australian and New Zealand. *The International Journal of Human Resource Management*, 22(11): 2367–2383.

O'Donnell, M., & Shields, J. (2002). The new pay: Performance-related pay in Australia. In J. Teicher, P. Holland, & R. Gough (Eds.), *Employee relations management: Australia in a global context* (pp. 406–434). Frenchs Forest, NSW: Pearson Education.

O'Leary, R., & Lentz, E. (2020). Technology's impact on the performance management transformation. In E.D. Pulakos & M. Battista (Eds.), *Performance management transformation. Lessons learned and next steps* (pp. 264–288). Oxford: Oxford University Press.

Podger, A. (2017). Enduring challenges and new developments in public human resource management: Australia as an example of International Experience. *Review of Public Personnel Administration*, 37(1): 108–128.

Pulakos, E.D., & Battista, M. (Eds.) (2020). *Performance management transformation: Lessons learned and next steps*. Oxford: Oxford University Press.

Pulakos, E.D., Mueller-Hanson, R.A., Arad, S., & Moye, N. (2015). Performance management can be fixed: an on-the-job experiential learning approach for complex behavior change. *Industrial and Organizational Psychology*, 8: 51–76.

Pulakos, E.D., Mueller-Hanson, R., & Arad, S. (2019). The evolution of performance management: Searching for value. *Annual Review of Organizational Psychology and Organizational Behavior*, 6: 249–271.

Rock, D., & Jones, B. (2015). Why more and more companies are ditching performance ratings. *Harvard Business Review*, September 8. Retrieved from: https://hbr.org/2015/09/why-more-and-more-companies-are-ditching-performance-ratings.

Shelton, D. (1995). Human resource management in Australia. In L.F. Moore & P.D. Jennings (Eds.), *Human resource management on the Pacific rim* (pp. 31–60). Berlin: Walter de Gruyter.

Shields, J., Rooney, J, Brown, M., & Kaine, S. (2020). *Managing employee performance and rewards: Systems, practices and prospects*, 3rd edition. Cambridge: Cambridge University Press.

Smart, J.P., & Pontifex, M.R. (1993). Human resource management and the Australian human resources institute: The profession and its professional body. *Asia Pacific Journal of Human Resources*, 31(1): 1–19.

Treasury (2021). *2021 Intergenerational Report*. Canberra: Australian Government. https://treasury.gov.au/publication/2021-intergenerational-report

van Onselen, L. (2022). Why won't businesses train Australian workers? *Microbusiness*, 5 January. https://www.macrobusiness.com.au/2022/01/why-wont-businesses-train-australian-workers/

Wilkinson, I., & Cheung, C. (1999). Multicultural marketing in Australia: Synergy in diversity. *Journal of International Marketing*, 7(3): 106–125.

Wood, R., Collins, R., Arasu, S., & Entrekin, L. (1995). *A national survey of performance-appraisal practices. In Australian personnel management*. North Ryde, NSW: CCH.

Workplace Gender Equality Agency (2021a). Women in leadership. https://www.wgea.gov.au/women-in-leadership

Workplace Gender Equality Agency (2021b). Australia's gender pay gap statistics. https://www.wgea.gov.au/data/fact-sheets/australias-gender-pay-gap-statistics

Wright, C. (1995). *The management of labour. A history of Australian employers*. Melbourne: Oxford University Press.

Performance Management around the Globe

Where Are We Now?

Angelo S. DeNisi, Arup Varma and Pawan S. Budhwar

Chapter 17

All modern organizations face the challenge of how to best manage performance. That is, they must determine the best ways to set goals, evaluate work and distribute rewards in such a way that performance can be improved over time. While *all* firms face similar challenges, the way a firm responds to those challenges may well depend on where the firm is located and the context within which it is operating. Differences in culture, technology, or simply tradition make it difficult to directly apply techniques that have worked in one setting, to a different setting (see, for example, Hofstede, 1993). This, of course, is what the present volume is all about. We began with some "universals" in terms of issues, challenges, and a proposed model to help guide discussion and then moved to solutions and performance management systems (PMSs) that have been used in various countries around the world.

In this chapter, we present brief synopses of the various chapters in the two parts of the book, comparing and contrasting key

DOI: 10.4324/9781003306849-17

findings, as appropriate. However, as noted at the outset, this is the second edition of this book – the first appeared in 2008. Therefore, another goal of the present chapter is to suggest where we have made progress over the past years and where we have not. One aspect of this topic that has not changed over the years is the fact that there are some things about performance management (PM) that can be applied almost universally but that there are other aspects of performance management that are incompatible with some cultures or traditions so that, when we compare systems in different countries, we find both universal and unique aspects of the PMSs in each. In the earlier edition, we used the term "crossvergence" to describe this phenomenon. This term refers to the blending of work practices around the globe, due to the level of active interface among human resource (HR) managers from different countries (see also Gopalan & Stahl, 1998). We still believe this term applies, and we endeavor to examine where the similarities exist and where the differences/uniqueness endure and try to understand how these findings can help guide multinational enterprises (MNEs) in setting up effective PMSs across the globe.

The first part of the volume focused on critical issues for performance management and serves as the framework for the second part that describes practices in different countries. The opening chapter again laid out the need for understanding PM in different settings and explained the logic of the rest of the volume – including the rationale behind choosing which countries or regions to focus on. The second chapter (Vance and Anderson) went one more step toward setting the stage. As these authors argue, much of the global commerce in this day and age is carried out by MNEs. These large, global firms dominate the world business setting because they have the capacity to do business across a wide variety of settings. This is not to suggest that there is no place for national enterprises, or even for small businesses, but the role of these smaller operations has been largely to funnel goods and services to the multinationals who then trade and do business globally.

Multinationals face unique challenges when designing PM systems. On the one hand, having consistent policies and practices across national settings is both efficient, and when these systems are based on "best practices", they are also ideal. But, at the same time, multinational corporations (MNCs) must face the reality that they are operating in different cultures, and they must therefore adapt their policies and practices to fit those cultures. This dilemma is at the heart of the Vance and Anderson chapter, as they discuss convergence and divergence across national settings. More critically, these authors note that recent criticisms of traditional PM practices have led to many firms adopting new systems that focus on things such as continuous feedback and coaching. These changes make it easier for individual countries to adapt policies consistent with their own culture, as there is much more open acceptance that the old ways of doing PM must change.

The next three chapters deal with issues in the field of PM that, arguably, affect everyone, regardless of where they are doing business. Hu and Meng focus on the basic issue of employee motivation. Why does any firm implement a PMS? There may be several reasons for any particular firm, but, in all cases, a major reason underlying all such systems is the attempt to improve performance. This means that the system must somehow motivate employees to exert effort in the directions the company desires, to help the company meet its' goals. The authors review the major models and theories of motivation, pointing out how need-based theories, process-based theories, and goal-based theories can all contribute to how organizations can motivate employees through their PMSs. Much of the chapter is devoted to explaining how combining goals, and the basic tenets of expectancy theory can lead to more successful PMSs. Specifically, the authors point to the need for clear goals, clear consequences tied to performance, and fair, transparent, systems as the key to effective PMSs.

Risner, Pichler, Petty, and Varma discuss the ways in which the relationship between a rater and a ratee can influence performance appraisals and PM. Specifically, they argue that this interpersonal process may well be as important as any other aspect of a PMS in determining the system's effectiveness. Their discussion focuses on the role of interpersonal affect and how this influences performance ratings and the overall PM process. They also discuss how leader–member exchange affects how supervisors manage the performance of their subordinates.

Angelo S. DeNisi et al.

They further argue that we need to pay more attention to the motivation of raters when they are rating performance and trying to manage that performance. They conclude by reviewing the literature, which suggests how the relationships between raters and ratees can affect ratee reactions to the appraisal process. They stress the notion that these relationships can influence perceptions of fairness concerning the process, which is critical for determining how ratees will react to the ratings and feed-back they receive. This discussion is extremely interesting in the present context because these models and constructs have been based, primarily on US-oriented research. There is evidence that these constructs have meaning in other cultures, but the exact nature of the bias and the source of the bias may well differ from country to country. Nonetheless, there is little question that, in all cultures, interpersonal relationships will continue to play a critical role in the PM process.

Gerhart, Trevor, and Scott, in their chapter, deal with another issue that is part of most PM programs – merit pay. They explain some of the basic concepts underlying any merit pay plan, as well as some of the mechanics for such a program, and they point out that merit pay plans actually have two major functions – incentives and sorting. That is, the plans should be designed to provide an incentive for higher performing employ-ees while also encouraging lower performing individuals to move on to other jobs. They also discuss the role of cultural differences, in terms of both the importance of merit pay and the extent to which there are constraints on merit pay plans. They conclude by noting that any successful incentive plan must be transparent to all those involved and impacted and must consider how performance will be measured, how large the differences should be between high- and low-performing employees, whether employees should be evaluated on the basis of results or behavior, whether incentives should be based on individual performance or aggregate performance, who does the evaluation, whether incentive pay should be in the form of pay increases or bonuses, and whether standards for evaluation should be relative or absolute. Their final note, however, is that there is still a lot we don't know about the effectiveness of merit pay plans, especially in multinational firms.

Finally, this section closes with a chapter by Murphy and DeNisi, where they lay out a model of the PM process that is used as the framework for the discussion of the specific country-based programs later on. Specifically, these authors note a number of distal factors (such as cultural norms) and proximal factors (such as company norms and the purpose for appraisal) will impact the effectiveness of a PM system. They also discuss intervening factors (such as the frequency of appraisal, and rater–ratee relationships) and distortion factors (such as the nature of reward systems for raters), which can also influence ratings and the entire PM process. Finally, they also discuss the role of judgment factors – factors that directly influence the judgments raters make about their ratees, and the authors stress the importance of reducing the gap between actual performance and judgments about performance that lead directly to performance ratings. The major points from their model were incorporated in several of the chapters regarding PM practices in different parts of the world, and these points also provide a framework for discussing these different practices. As such, these chapters provide an excellent backdrop for the remainder of the book. They address reward systems based on ratings issues that are relevant to performance management programs, wherever they might exist, and they raise issues that help to frame the discussions of specific programs in the subsequent chapters. These early chapters also introduce a level of scholarship that is not typical of this type of book. These early chapters touch on issues and questions from the scholarly side of the field, which need to be addressed when discussing practical programs. We believe that this is one of the unique aspects of the present volume.

The discussion of specific programs begins with a description of performance management systems in the United States (Pulakos, Mueller-Hanson & O'Leary). This chapter provides a comprehensive and clear picture of how US firms have struggled to deal with ways to improve the PM process. The authors provide an excellent review of how US firms moved from a focus on measuring performance to a focus on managing and improving performance. Their discussion also makes clear how practices in the United States have been driven (in part) by the culture of the United States and (in large part) by the county's legal framework, and these forces can be compared and contrasted with how cultural, and especially legal, forces play a role in the development of PM systems in places such as the United Kingdom (Ridgway, Shipton and Sparrow), France and Germany (Barzantny & Festing), and Australia (Shields). It is also interesting to note that, in each of these countries, diversity issues are growing more important. That is, even if certain practices might not be illegal, it is important, in each of these countries, for PMSs to overcome the differences found in increasingly diverse workforces (also see Vance and Paik, 2006). Finally, both sets of pressures make it more important to be concerned with issues of rater bias. That is, once there are clearly identifiable subgroups in the population, there is the potential for bias towards the "out-group," whoever that may be in a given country. This tendency, of course, reinforces the need for legal checkpoints, and leads to a need to train raters when it is possible to help them avoid bias and develop employees. Thus, it would seem, that legal concerns and potential bias are the major issues that companies must deal with when implementing performance management systems in countries such as these, which have had considerable experience with the field of PM.

It would also seem that the transfer of knowledge about PMSs across these countries would be relatively easy, given the individualistic nature of these countries (Hofstede, 1993). That is not to suggest that there are no differences across settings, since there are clearly important differences. For example, legal pressures on US firms are confined to equal employment issues, while legal pressures on firms in Europe and the UK are also concerned with wealth redistribution and the funding of social welfare programs. Furthermore, employees in those countries have much stronger rights than do US employees. Nonetheless, as we noted earlier, the relatively individualistic nature of these cultures means that it is easier to get the kind of variance in appraisals needed for merit pay and that rewards based on individual performance are more likely to be acceptable. Furthermore, hierarchical relations in these countries tend to be similar and there are lots of similarities between these cultures.

The review by Pulakos et al. and the conclusions drawn from the review make it clear that, although performance appraisal will likely always be part of the PM process, it is more important to provide regular feedback and discussion and provide clear goals to employees if we wish to improve performance. The authors provide clear guidelines on the critical components of any effective PMS and make it clear that old solutions are no longer acceptable. Given that a fair amount of research on performance appraisal and performance management has been conducted in the United States, this chapter makes it clear that any discussion of convergence across cultures will take place in an atmosphere where new ideas are being generated and tested for better ways to improve performance.

This discussion is followed by information about PMSs in Mexico (Gonzalez, Perez-Floriano, and Rodriguez). This chapter is especially interesting because the authors work to show how things have changed since the chapter dealing with Mexico in the earlier edition of this book (Davila & Elvira, 2008). The present authors note that the role of culture is still important for the design and effectiveness of Mexican PMSs and that the Mexican culture is very old and therefore very hard to change. They point out, for example, that, whereas many managers believe in a form of benevolent paternalism when dealing with their employees, there is increasing evidence that PMSs, imported from the United States and other places, can be effective in Mexico if they are adapted to fit the culture. For example, the culture of México is such that employees take negative feedback from supervisors as being personal, but yet, they cite evidence that multisource feedback and PMSs have been successfully implemented in a number of Mexican firms. These authors also note that the Mexican legal system makes it difficult to terminate employees for poor performance, which is a critical challenge for any PMS. Gonzalez et al. conclude their chapter on a more positive note than the authors of the previous chapter had. They believe that more modern PMSs are being implemented in Mexico and that the culture will slowly adapt to allow more effective PMSs.

The focus next moves to Western Europe and begins with a discussion of performance management in the United Kingdom (Ridgway, Shipton, and Sparrow). These authors begin by noting that the British legal system is an interesting combination of individual and collective agreements, implied and explicit understandings, and rights and obligations for all parties involved in relationships. This had led to the development of PMSs that are similar to those in other developed counties but still uniquely British in flavor. The authors then recount the history of the development of PMSs, noting that the UK's exit from the European Union (i.e., BREXIT) meant that the country was no longer bound by EU laws. Nonetheless, laws concerning expanded rights against discrimination and expanded social protection have remained a part of UK law, even after BREXIT.

In discussing the contemporary landscape relative to PM, Ridgeway et al. note that PMSs have become much more interested in developing and maintaining good employment relationships and that the focus of researchers and practitioners has been on ways to improve acceptability rather than trying to improve the accuracy of ratings. They also describe the world of PM being presently characterized by debates over the effectiveness and usefulness of PMSs and the importance of the details of any PMS as opposed to simply having open discussion and feedback for employees. These debates are quite similar to those described by Pulakos et al., regarding the United States, and this is probably due to the fact that the United Kingdom, similar to the United States, has a long history of PM and so has a very mature approach to dealing with PM and its challenges.

Systems in France and Germany (Barzantny and Festing) are discussed next, and much of this chapter is devoted to comparisons between systems in these countries and the United States and the United Kingdom and discussions of the uniqueness of the systems in each country. Some common elements discussed relative to the PMSs in France and Germany is a move toward international standards in terms of PMSs and the use of some version of a balanced scorecard. But the more tolerant view of labor unions – the view that unions should be seen as partners – in both countries (and especially in Germany) marks an important difference in how PMSs operate in these countries versus the United States and the United Kingdom. Furthermore, both France and Germany have fairly rigid legal systems and the influence of legal issues on PM is stronger than in the U.S. or U.K.

The discussion of PM systems in France also helps us to understand some of the factors that are uniquely French that are important for PM systems. For example, the authors discuss the higher education system in France and how this leads to a certain elitist culture that plays a role in PM. Access to higher education is generally through an exam (for the top schools), and a lot of weight is placed on where someone received their degree. Also, France has only lately moved from a measurement approach to performance appraisals to a more motivational approach to PM, and change is slow in many areas of HR. Germany also has a fairly rigid legal system that plays a role in the development of PMSs. For example, merit-based pay is difficult in Germany because pay raises must be approved by work councils before they can be implemented. In fact, the entire idea of codetermination and the role of unions in top-level decision-making in a critical element affecting how PM is conducted in Germany. The authors also note that the German approach to higher education is more egalitarian and that there is more attention paid to how a person performs rather than to where they went to school. Finally, the authors also note that long-term work relationships are valued in both countries – especially in Germany – so that tenure is seen as an important factor in evaluation. Thus, the authors conclude that PMSs in both countries are moving toward adapting international best practices but that legal and cultural factors in both countries will mean that their systems will also retain unique factors.

The next set of chapters moves the focus from Western Europe to Asia and Australia. The opening chapter in this group is by Ozcelik, Aycan, and Yavuz, and describes the state of PM in Turkey. The picture here is one of transition, and more modern PMSs are starting to become more common, especially among larger firms and multinationals, but most of this change has occurred over the past two decades. Most of the economic activity in Turkey, however, comes through small and medium-sized firms, and these firms are less willing to adopt newer HR practices. In fact, these firms are described as being generally reluctant to carry out performance appraisals or job analyses. Furthermore, many of these are family-run businesses and they are even less willing to adopt newer PM practices.

But even among the larger firms, paternalism is still important and personal relationships are critical. These facts hinder the application of many PM processes, and managers who are highest

Angelo S. DeNisi et al.

on paternalism are least likely to conduct any performance appraisals. New labor laws, however, have made performance appraisal more important, as a defense for terminations. The authors also describe new trends toward more "people-oriented" PMSs as opposed to "profit-oriented" PMSs. The recent financial crises, including the COVID-19 pandemic, have been very costly to the Turkish economy, and this is likely to further slow the introduction of new PMSs. Finally, it is worthy of note that although modern Turkey is a secular society; it is the only country represented in this volume that has come out of the tradition of Islam. These traditions have produced some friction in Turkey concerning the extent to which the country should remain strongly secular, and the resolution of this friction will probably be a strong determinant of the rate of economic growth in the country and the adoption of new PM processes.

The focus next shifts to India, where Sharma, Budhwar, Varma, and Norlander describe a setting that may well be the most unique situation of all the countries covered in this volume. Although India may technically be a collectivist society, it has also been strongly influenced by the British and their more individualistic culture. This background has been coupled with a huge explosion in foreign investment in India, a huge wave of foreign investments, a high degree of globalization by Indian companies, and the government's recent push to connect education and employment (see Varma et al., 2021), such that there is a greater emphasis on vocational training. At the same time, the Indian economy is extremely diverse – ranging from small village manufacturing operations to huge multinational firms. Accordingly, PM in India ranges from no performance appraisals to sophisticated PMSs implemented by multinational conglomerates (MNCs) on a global level. Also, while there have been substantial advances in PMSs in the private sector, many family-owned firms and government organizations tend to cling to the old ways of doing things.

Of course, the MNCs operating in India are dealing with the same issues that firms everywhere are, trying to decide the right mix of formal evaluations and informal feedback and coaching. But despite differences across firms, there is a general trend to place more emphasis on environmental factors and sustainability. Interestingly, despite these trends in the private sector,

PM in the public sector is still largely dominated by informal appraisal processes. This degree of diversity is typical of the challenges facing HR managers in India. India has a rich cultural diversity, with many different languages spoken and large differences between different parts of the country. Thus, it is extremely difficult to speak about any "typical Indian" situation. This diversity, combined with perceptions of mismanagement of PMSs, coupled with a culture that favors hierarchical structures, will continue to present challenges for India as it develops new PMSs (see also Varma, Budhwar, & Singh, 2015). Fortunately, a large number of MNCs have been using sophisticated PMSs for years and are well informed about new developments. These firms will hopefully be the model for the rest of the Indian economy as it moves forward.

PMSs in China (Cooke), South Korea (Yang & Rowley), and Japan (Morishima) share certain characteristics because all are functioning in collectivist cultures. But the differences in the levels of economic development result in few similarities in terms of what actually happens in PM. In China, Cooke suggests that Western-style PM systems have limited applicability. This is not to suggest that many large, global companies are not adopting newer and more sophisticated PMSs. But for the most part, more advanced PMSs face several significant challenges in China.

One of these is the nature of Chinese culture. Although Cooke suggests these effects are diminishing over time, there still remains a value for seniority and the hierarchy, social harmony, and egalitarian distribution of rewards. Furthermore, Chinese culture has always favored elitism (in terms of education and class), and this also is also present in modern Chinese firms. Cooke also notes that Chinese managers often do not have the HR skills needed to manage performance effectively. In part, this is due to the relatively recent concerns over PM, but it also reflects a view that PM is not a particularly effective management tool, and much of the appraisal of performance is seen as a mere formality with no real impact on anything. Finally, Cooke notes that Chinese firms still tend to favor appraisals that focus on behaviors rather than outcomes, and also systems that focus on moral and ideological beliefs. All of this seems to be changing but there are still significant barriers to the application of Western PMSs to China.

Angelo S. DeNisi et al.

The situation in Korea (Yang & Rowley) appears to be a bit more evolved than the situation in China, but Korea faces many of the same challenges as China relative to PM. Here too, traditional appraisal systems emphasized seniority and tenure, as the Korean culture, like the Chinese culture, favors paternalism, the importance of seniority, lifetime employment, and tenure-based pay. Also, Korean laws make it relatively difficult to terminate an employee, and appraisal systems were used primarily as a basis by managers to defend the decisions they made. But, even as Korean firms begin to adopt Western PM systems (especially larger firms), there are still issues of fairness and accuracy of ratings, and there is a general lack of trust in PMSs. Thus, although the Korean systems of PM are more mature than those in China, the major challenge in the future is how to integrate modern PMSs with the Korean culture and, hopefully, efforts to do so will be able to inform HR managers in other collectivist countries.

The case of Japan (Kagami, Sekiguchi, & Ebisuya) is somewhat different from what is happening in either China or Korea, largely because Japanese firms have long been considered learning organizations, and PMSs in Japan have focused on skill acquisition and lifelong learning. Nonetheless, traditional PMSs actually hurt employee morale. These systems were often supported by in-house training programs, compensation systems that rewarded both performance and skill acquisition, and HR systems that encouraged employee participation through techniques such as quality circles and practices such as employee stock-ownership plans. It is also important to note that HR practices in Japanese firms have also traditionally included lifelong employment for "regular" employees, job rotation as a training model, and compensation based on ability acquisition which is actually tested via an "ability grading" system. The authors note that many in Japan see the need to move toward PMSs based on performance rather than on learning but that these changes are slow because of the strength of the Japanese work culture.

Finally, in Australia (Shields) we find a country where the economy has shifted in recent years from one based largely on manufacturing and mining to one based largely on the service sector. Along with these changes, Australian firms have also recently become much more international in focus, but the "gig" economy is growing as is the reliance on contingent workers. Also, the workforce in Australia is becoming more diverse but older and with more participation by women. Traditional PMSs were primarily focused on rewarding past performance, with less concern about alignment with strategic goals. But, more recently all of this has changed, reflecting the other changes in the Australian economy and workforce. The author describes the "New Performance Management" as shifting focus away from formal appraisals and more towards alignment with strategic goals, as well as emphasis on lifelong learning and employee development. As a result, more recent systems have been characterized by less formal ratings (although few firms have moved to "ratingless" appraisals) and more by continuous feedback and developmental coaching. These new systems are becoming more common but, as the author notes, he was surprised to find that, in Australia, public sector and not-for-profit firms were more likely to introduce innovative systems than were larger, for-profit firms.

SO, WHAT HAVE WE LEARNED?

Reading through the various chapters describing PM developments in different parts of the world, it becomes quite clear that the dilemmas described in the chapter by Vance and Anderson are the main concern of MNCs attempting to develop effective PMSs. In chapter after chapter, we encounter the shifts from more traditional appraisal systems to more advanced PMSs. In some cases, more advanced levels of development have allowed firms to introduce innovative systems with less reliance on formal ratings and more reliance on continuous feedback and employee development, coupled with a strong linkage between the goals of the PMS and the organization's overall strategic goals. In other cases, the move toward these more innovative systems is taking more time, and there are still issues to be dealt with relating to more traditional types of systems. In several cases, strong country cultures have made it relatively more difficult to introduce any type of serious PM system, but in others, the cultural and/ or legal frameworks have made it difficult to move beyond those traditional systems to more innovative systems.

But, while there are forces operating toward convergence, a general dissatisfaction with more traditional, measurement-oriented systems has also made it possible for firms in any country to adapt PMSs to fit that country's culture and laws. There seems to be a simultaneous convergence toward systems that favor more feedback and less formal rating, with a divergence in the details of systems in different locations, which allow the systems to operate within that location's culture.

It is also clear that the trend, everywhere, is to eventually move towards systems that are more flexible, more closely tied to an organization's strategic goals, and are more concerned with providing employees with the feedback and developmental coaching they need to improve their own performance and contribute to the firm's performance as well. There is limited evidence that the idea of "rating-less" systems is growing in popularity, especially in countries where string antidiscrimination laws mean that organizations have to defend HR decisions concerning pay and possible termination with some type of formal evaluation. There is strong evidence, however, that firms all over the world are moving toward systems in which PM is ongoing and happens every day. The movement away from systems in which formal appraisals of past performance, occurring once or twice a year, with annual feedback and focus on short-term performance goals, unrelated to corporate strategic goals, is clear and compelling. Different countries will only differ in terms of when their systems move fully to these new types of systems.

WHERE DO WE GO FROM HERE?

As we compare the chapters in this volume to the chapters in the previous edition, it seems clear that the degree of convergence across countries and regions is accelerating. But, as noted earlier, at the same time, HR managers in different regions are also working to find ways to adapt PMSs to their own cultures. As general dissatisfaction with more traditional PMSs grows, there is more space for such customization. As a result, it should be easier for MNCs to implement PMSs, across locations, that follow a general framework or structure, but have unique features suitable for the specific location.

It also seems clear that there are trends (developing more slowly in some parts of the world than in others) toward PMSs that rely less on formal ratings and more on continuous feedback. These trends seem well intentioned and may well prove to be more effective, but as of now, we don't have sufficient empirical data to support their effectiveness, and that is what is needed going forward. We cannot rely solely on anecdotal data regarding effectiveness – instead, we need research on exactly how employees react to evaluations without formal ratings. Also, in countries where there is strong antidiscrimination legislation, we need to determine how defensible decisions to terminate an employee (for example) might be, if that decision is based on evaluations without formal ratings.

The other characteristic of some of the new PMSs being proposed is continuous feedback. Although it is difficult to argue that more feedback would not be preferable, it would be a mistake to assume that feedback, in any form, will always improve subsequent performance. Kluger and DeNisi (1996) conducted a meta-analysis of feedback research beginning with studies from the early 20th century. They found that feedback actually reduced subsequent performance in about one third of the cases, and this was regardless of whether the feedback was positive or negative. This doesn't mean that we should avoid providing feedback, but the Kluger and DeNisi (1996) paper suggests ways in which feedback could be more or less effective, and firms considering relying heavily on feedback should spend time ensuring that their feedback delivery systems are designed to obtain the desired results.

Finally, there is a need for more research examining exactly how effective PMSs really are. As noted by DeNisi and Murphy (2017), in their review of 100 years of appraisal research, these authors concluded that although there was evidence that effective appraisal and PMSs could help improve individual performance, there were no data directly linking improvements in individual performance with improvements in firm performance. These authors also noted, however, that there was a body of research linking certain HR practices to firm-level performance (e.g., Huselid, 1995) but that most of this research suggested that improvements in firm-level performance only came when "bundles" of HR practices were implemented. Thus, research needs to examine whether the entire notion of PM needs to be broadened to include other HR practices to support performance improvements at both the individual and firm levels of analysis.

In conclusion, the chapters in the present edition have provided a rich body of information concerning how PMSs have been developed and are used in different parts of the world. The information concerning both how these different systems are similar to each other and also how they differ from each other provides useful information for MNCs who must install PMSs in different locations. While there is still more to be learned about how to effectively manage performance, and how culture affects any such system, the present edition demonstrates that progress has been made, and we look forward to seeing how much further we can move by the time of the next edition. Hopefully, by then we can see exactly what long-term effects the COVID-19 pandemic had on PMSs and how different countries managed to deal with these.

REFERENCES

Davila, A., & Elvira, M. M. (2008). Performance management in Mexico. In A. Varma, P.S. Buhwar, & A. DeNisi (Eds.), *Performance management systems* (pp. 115–130). London: Routledge.

DeNisi, A.S., & Murphy, K.R. (2017). Performance appraisal and performance management: 100 years of progress? *Journal of Applied Psychology, 102*, 421–433.

Gopalan, S., & Stahl, A. (1998). Application of American management theories and practices to the indian business environment: Understanding the impact of national culture. *American Business Review, 16*(2), 30–41.

Hofstede, G. (1993). Cultural constraints in management theories. *Academy of Management Executive, 7*(1), 81–94.

Huselid, M.A. (1995). The impact of human resource management practices on turnover, productivity, and corporate financial performance. *Academy of Management Journal, 38*(3), 635–672.

Kluger, A.N., & DeNisi, A.S. (1996). The effects of feedback interventions on performance: Historical review, meta-analysis, a preliminary feedback intervention theory. *Psychological Bulletin, 119*, 254–284.

Vance, C.M., & Paik, Y. (2006). *Managing a global workforce*. New York: M.E. Sharpe.

Varma, A., Budhwar, P., & Singh, S. (2015). Performance management and high performance work practices in emerging markets. In F. Horwitz & P.S. Budhwar (Eds.), *Handbook of human resource management in emerging markets* (pp. 316–335). Cheltenham, UK: Edward Elgar Publishing.

Varma, A., Patel, P., Prikshat, V., Hota, D., & Pereira, V. (2021). India's New Education Policy: A case of indigenous ingenuity contributing to the global knowledge economy? *Journal of Knowledge Management, 25*(10), 2385–2395.

Index

Note: Pages in *italics* refer figures, pages in **bold** refer tables, and pages followed by n refer notes.

ability-grading system in Japan 307–310, 315
Academic Journal Guide 182
Accenture 33–34
acceptance of appraisal system 114
achievement, need for 44; *see also* McClelland's three needs theory
Act on Arrangement of Related Acts to Promote Work Style Reform, Japan 318
Adobe 233, 244, 300, 346
affective relationship 289
affiliation, need for 44; *see also* McClelland's three needs theory
affiliative orientation 152–153
Airbnb 235
Airtel 248
Alderfer's ERG model 43
AlphaGo 286
Álvarez, Ordaz 163
Amazon 51
ambivalence-amplification hypothesis 65–66
Amendments to the Workplace Relations Act 340–341
American Express 158
Andersen, T. 3, 6, 362, 372
annual confidential reports (ACR) 241
annual performance assessment reports (APAR) 241
Anonyuo, C. 68
antidiscrimination laws/legislation 336, 373, 374
Antoni, C. 91
Aon India report 245–247, *246*
Apple Turkey 235
Armstrong, M. 190
artificial intelligence (AI) 223, 244, 276, 286, 315, 332, 346, 349
Asian financial crisis of 1997 15, 285, 287, 291
Askarany, D. 343
Australia 16–17, 91, 326–355, 365, 368, 371–372; business strategy 327–331; COVID-19 333, 338, 346–354; culture(s) 332–333, 335–336; current practices and plans 346–354; economy 16–17, 327–332, 336, 339, 371–372;

effectiveness of PMS 343–345, *344*; employment law and regulation 336–338, 340–341; internationalisation 328–329; legal/regulatory change 338; NPM 327, 338, 340, 345–347, 349–350, 352–354, 372; organisational and operational factors 338–346; service sector 16, 327–328, 335–336, 371; trends, objectives and perceptions of PMS 339–346; workforce profile 331–336
Australian Workplace Industrial Relations Survey (AWIRS) 340, 342
Austria 90
automation 132–133
autonomous motivation 44–45; *see also* self-determination theory (SDT)
Aycan, Z. 12–13, 228
Aydinli, A. 227

Bai, X. 265, 271
Bailey, J. 271
balanced scorecard (BSC) 367; Australia 343; France 191, 196, 197; United States (US) 191
Balance Scorecard methodology 165
Baron, A. 190
Barry, B. 64
Bartol, K. M. 127
Bartram, T. 350
Barzantny, C. 11–12, 367–368
Basly, S. 197
Bata India 242
Battista, M. 141
Bechter, B. 181
Beck-Krala, E. 89–90, 91
behaviorally anchored rating scales (BARS) 128, 129, 134
behaviorally based measures 99
benevolent paternalism 151–152, 366
Bennington, L. 265, 271
Benson, G. S. 346, 349, 350
Bersin 300
Bescos, P.-L. 197
Bharat Petroleum 243
BHP-Billiton 329
bias(es), performance evaluation 53

Bigan, I. 227
Bindl, U.K. 185
Bititci, U.S. 179
Björkman, I. 264
blue-collar workers 305–306
Bock, L. 133
bonuses 100
Borman, W.C. 63–64
Bouamama, M. 197
Bourguignon, A. 191, 200
Bournois, F. 181
Boyatzis, R. E. 131–132
Brandl, B. 181
Brewster, C. 193–194, 211, 214
Brexit 171, 367
BRIC countries, Goldman Sachs' report
    on 2
Brown, B. B. 127
Brown, M. 91, 335
Bryson, A. 91
Budhwar, P. 13, 17, 369
Bulgaria 179

Candlelight Revolution of South
    Korea 285
career systems in France 194–195
Carlson, D.S. 65, 68–69
Casademunt, A.M.L. 91
cascading goals 125, 130, **130**
case study: merit pay 102; motivation
    55–57; rater-ratee relationships 76–77
Cauvin, E. 197
CEB research 135–136
CEMEX (cement and building materials)
    153, 159, 161
central tendency bias 53
Chartered Institute of Personnel
    Development (CIPD) 183
Chauchat, J.H. 181
Chhetri, A. 345–347, 349, 350, 352–354
China 4, 14, 90, 260–281, 328, 370;
    behaviour measurement 267;
    business nature 269; challenges to
    performance management 272–280;
    Cultural Revolution 261, 263; culture
    270–272; development of PMS 263–265;
    digital technology 276; economy 14,
    260–264, 271, 277; elitism 277–278, 370;
    employee retention 279–280; factors
    influencing PMS 265–272; foreign-
    invested enterprises 264; GDP 263;
    high-performance culture 277–278;
    human resource environment 261–263;
    interventions in appraisal process 276–
    277; lack of strategic HRM 272–273;
    managerial thinking and skill 273–274;
    market economic development
    264; mixed 253; open door policy
    262; outcome measurement 267;

performance appraisal as a formality
    274–275; state-owned enterprises
    265; state-planned economy 263–264;
    subjectivity 275–276; Western-style
    performance management system
    264–265; work-oriented social media
    278
Church, A. H. 142
Citigroup 153
Civil Rights Act of 1964 126
civil rights movement 126
Civil Servant Law of China 265
Cleveland, J.N. 71, 114, 115, 299, 327
Cloninger, P. A. 161–162, 164–165
coaching 25–26
collectivism/collectivist cultures 4, 8, 34,
    66
commitment 172
communication 24–25, 31; leader–
    member exchange 68–69; technology
    31–33
competence/competencies 131–132,
    171–172, 174, 175, 248, 254
competency-linked *vs.* competency-
    based system 175
Compton, R. 343
CompuSoluciones 159–160, 164
Confederation of Mexican Workers
    (CTM) 156
Connell, J. 345
consequences 54–55
contextualization of PMSs 184
contrast biases 53
controlled motivation 45; *see also* self-
    determination theory (SDT)
Cooke, F.L. 14, 370
cooperation 33–34
corruption 164
cost-effectiveness 171
COVID-19 pandemic 13, 21, 143, 244, 319,
    327, 375; Australia 333, 338, 346–354;
    China 265; France 197; India 240;
    remote working arrangements 31–33,
    170; Turkey 223, 232, 369; United
    Kingdom (UK) 170, 185; United States
    (US) 136–137; working from home
    (WFH) 51–52, 136–137
Cranfield Research Report (Cranet data)
    12, 179, 181, 202, 214, 224, 230–232,
    341
critical incident technique 128
Cropanzano, R. 70
crossvergence 361
crowdsourced feedback 30, 136, 349
cultural differences 4, 21, 34–35
cultural norms 34; merit pay and 91–92;
    performance appraisal (PA) 66
Cultural Revolution of China 261, 263
cultural values 92

culture(s) 4, 5, 34, 372, 373; Australia 332–333, 335–336; China 270–272, 277–278; France 199–203; Germany 206–209; India 251–254; Japan 310; Mexico 150–153; South Korea 289–290; Turkey 225–228; United Kingdom (UK) 180–181; United States (US) 4, 8, 9, 91, 108, 124, 138; see also collectivist cultures; individualistic culture
customer relationship management 177

Daewoo 285
DaimlerChrysler Corporation 213
Darbishire, O. 214
data analytics 184
Dávila, A. 148–151, 154–155, 158, 159–160
decentralization 31
De Cieri, H. 326, 355
360-degree rating process 129, 248–249, 349, 352
de La Madrid, Miguel 163
Dell 346
Deloitte 248, 300
demographic similarity and interpersonal affect 65, 66, 67
DeNisi, A.S. 3, 8–9, 11, 17, 61, 65, 66–67, 138, 150, 169, 172–174, 176, 177, 192–194, 198–200, 202, 203, 207, 209, 211–213, 326–327, 364, 374
Department of Public Enterprise (DPE) 244
Dickmann, M. 203–204, 205
digital technologies 184–185, 276
direction 25
discrimination legislation of UK 171
distal factors 107–112, 120, 193, 289–291, 326, 364; see also specific country
distortion factors 116–117, 364
distributive injustice 46, 162
Dorsey, D.W. 63–64
Dr. Reddy's Lab 243
Drucker, Peter 129–130
Drumm, G. 183
due process model of performance appraisal (PA) 70–71, 75, 76
Dulebohn, J.H. 71
Dunphy, D.C. 340
Durazo, Miguel Ángel 157
Dusterhoff, C. 70

Easterby-Smith, M. 270–271
Ebisuya, A. 3, 15–16, 371
economy 20–21, 35; Australia 16–17, 327–332, 336, 339, 371–372; China 14, 260, 261–264, 271, 277; European 11, 194; France 194; Germany 194, 205–206, 210–211; India 13, 240, 244, 249–250, 369–370; Japan 304, 306–307, 309–310, 320; Mexico 153–155; non-unionized

sectors 108; South Korea 15, 284–285, 287, 290–291; Turkey 12, 222–225, 229–230, 368, 369; United Kingdom (UK) 169–171
educational system in France 197; see also higher education
effort-to-performance link 51–52
Elicker, J.D. 70
elitism in China 277–278, 370
Elvira, M.M. 148, 149–151, 154–155, 158, 159
emerging markets 2
employee-as-consumer-to-organization relationship 177
employee retention in China 279–280
employee segmentation 177–178
employment law and regulation see legal framework/systems (laws and legislations)
employment regulations and merit pay 90–91
English language management journals 183–184
environmental factors 327
Equal Employment Act of South Korea 289
equal employment opportunity (EEO) 95, 334, 336
Equality Act 2010 (UK) 171
equity theory 45–46; see also motivation
ERG (existence, relatedness, and growth) model see Alderfer's ERG model
esteem needs 43; see also Maslow's hierarchy of needs
Europe: career systems 194–195; differences 193; economic cooperation 194; integration 194; nationalist ideologies 194; pluralism 193
European Economic Area 210–211
Eurostat 197
evaluation(s) 5, 52–54; biases 53; consequences 54–55; expatriate 5; interactional justice 54; see also performance appraisal (PA)
evaluation-to-rewards link 52, 54–55
expatriates 5, 21, 24, 26, 29, 32–33; see also multinational enterprises (MNEs)
expectancy theory 46–48, 51, 71; see also motivation

Fair Dismissal Code of Australia 337
fairness perceptions 45–46, 162, 163
Fair Work Act of Australia 336, 337, 341
Farr, J.L. 128
feedback 9, 25, 28, 51–52, 118–119; crowdsourced tools 30; cultural differences 34–35; frequent 30–31; meta-analysis 374
Feldman, J.M. 64

Ferris, G.R. 65, 68, 71
Festing, M. 11–12, 191–192, 367–368
Fischer, R. 92
Fletcher, C. 183, 215
flexibility 31
floor of rights, UK 170
Foley, P. 343, 345
Folger, R. 70
forced distribution of performance
    ratings 94–95, 99–100, 131
foreign-invested enterprises in China 264
Fortune 100 firms 70
Fourth Industrial Revolution 15, 286, 288,
    291, 300, 301, 327
Fox, Vicente 163
France 11–12, 180, 190, 365, 367–368;
    balanced scorecard 191, 196, 197;
    career systems 194–195; cultural
    environment 199–203; educational
    system 197; engineering 198; European
    context 193–195; governance 194;
    higher education 195, 368; legal
    environment 198–199; overview
    192; performance-based pay 203;
    specificities 195–198; technology/ICTs
    197; World War II 194
Freeman, R. 91
French Ministry of Industry 198
frustration-regression hypothesis 43
future orientation 225, 226, 251

Gap 300
Ge, C. M. 278
GE (General Electric) 94, 131, 158, 233,
    300
gender similarity and interpersonal
    affect 66
Gerhart, B. 8, 96, 363
Germany 11–12, 91–92, 179, 190,
    365, 367, 368; cultural environment
    206–209; European context 193–195;
    governance 194; higher education
    195, 368; legal environment 204–206;
    overview 192; specificities 203–204;
    World War II 194
Gifford, J. 183, 184
gig economy 332, 371–372
Glass, D.C. 65
global financial crisis of 2008 (GFC)
    291, 326, 327, 328, 329, 330, 342, 346,
    355
globalization 6, 90, 151, 203, 210, 255,
    307, 317, 369; vs. localization 92
GLOBE (Global Leadership and
    Organizational Behavior Effectiveness)
    Project 91, 225–226, 251
goal(s) 24–25, 232–233; cascading 125,
    130, **130**; performance management
    interventions 119; specificity 51

goal-setting theory 48–49;
    challenging/difficult goals 48;
    incentives 49; specific, measurable,
    and time-bound goals 48; see also
    motivation
goals-to-effort link 49, 51
Goldman Sachs' report on BRIC
    countries 2
Gonzalez, J.A. 3, 10–11, 366
Gooderham, P. 204, 214
Google 51, 133, 233–234, 244
Grande Ecole system 195
graphic rating scales 126, 242
Greece 90, 179
Greenberger, D.B. 68
Grodzicki, J. 91
Grove, Andrew 234
Gu, F. 271–272
Guest, D. 193
Gutek, B.A. 64

Hackman, B.K. 340
Hall, D.T. 5
Hall, R.J. 70
halo/horns bias 53
Hamaguchi, K. 316
Harrell-Cook, G. 71
Harris, K.J. 65, 68–69
Harvard model of human resources 171
HayGroup 96
Heneman, R.L. 68
HepsiBurada 235
Herzberg's motivation-hygiene theory 44
Heywood, J.S. 335
hierarchy of needs see Maslow's
    hierarchy of needs
higher education: France 195, 368;
    Germany 195, 368
high-performance culture in China
    277–278
Hill, K. D. 151
Hiltrop, J.M. 179–180
Hodgkinson, I.R. 184
Hofstede, G. 91, 92, 180, 181, 199, 206,
    207, 212, 225, 226
honor culture 152
Hooper, D.T. 68
horizontal transfers 306
Hu, B. 3, 6–7, 362
Huang, L. 318
Huawei 277–278
Hughes Software Systems 249
HUL 248
humane orientation 226, 251
human rating process 128–129
human resource (HR) systems 1
human resource information systems
    (HRISs) 132
hybrid PMS in Japan 312–315

IBM 346
ICT (information and communication technologies) 197
incentives 49, 83, 85, 86, 95, 98, 101–102; *see also* merit pay
India 13, 30, 240–256, 369–370; Aon India report 245–247, *246*; challenges 241–242, 244–256; cultural factors 251–254; diversity 13, 370; economy 13, 240, 244, 249–250, 369–370; factors influencing PA 241; GDP 240; gender egalitarianism 252; graphic rating scales 242; information technology (IT) 241, 245, 250; legal system 252; multinational corporations (MNC) 247–249, 369–370; service industry 250; start-ups 240; subjectivity 253
Indian Oil Corporation Limited 248
individualistic culture 4, 8, 9, 34, 91, 108, 124, 138, 181, 226, 288, 300, 365, 369; *see also* United States (US)
Industrial Relations Service (IRS) survey 182
information processing theories 129
information technology (IT): Australia 331–332, 336, 346; China 266, 278, 279; India 241, 245, 250; Mexico 159; *see also* technology
Infosys 243
ING Bank 234
ingratiation 71
input-based system 173
Institute of Labor Administration 317
institutional differences 21
institutional structure 34; merit pay and 91
Intel 51, 233–234, 244
intellectual skills 305
interactional justice 46, 54
International Monetary Fund (IMF) 153, 285, 287
interpersonal affect 63–67, 362; ambivalence-amplification hypothesis 65–66; cultural norms 66; deep-level perceived similarities 65, 67; defined 64; demographic similarity 65–67; gender similarity 66; ingratiation 71; past performance 65; personality similarity 67; rating errors 64; *see also* rater-ratee relationships
interpersonal variables 63–64
intervening factors 114–115, 293–294, 364; *see also* specific country
intrinsic rewards 55
Islam 369; *see also* Turkey

Jacobs, R. 64
Japan 4, 15–16, 90, 303–321, 371; ability-grading system 307–310, 315; bubble economy crisis 304; culture 310; economy 304, 306–307, 309–310, 320; horizontal transfers 306; HRM practices 304–305; human resource development 305–307; hybrid PMS 312–315; industrial structure and labor force 315–320; job-based employment 316–321; learning-centered PMS 303–312; long-term employment 305–307; membership-based employment 315–321; mission grading system 313–315; nonregular employees 318–319; optimizing PMSs 312–315; performance-based PMS 310–312; promotion practices 308–309; regular employees 305, 318–319; work style reform 318
Japan Federation of Employers' Associations 311
Jenkins, A. 196
Jensen, Brian 233
job analysis 98
job-based employment in Japan 316–321
job design 24, 26–27
job dissatisfaction 44; *see also* Herzberg's motivation-hygiene theory
job performance goals/expectations 24–25
job qualifications 24
job redesign 26
job satisfaction 44; *see also* Herzberg's motivation-hygiene theory
joint problem-solving 172, 180, 181
joint problem-solving in UK 172, 180, 181
Judge, T.A. 68
judgement factors 115–116, 138–139, 174, 294, 364; *see also* specific country
judgements *vs.* ratings 115

Kacmar, K.M. 65, 68–69
Kagami, A. 3, 15–16, 371
Kahn, S. C. 127
Katz, H. 214
Katz, I. 65
Kayas, O.G. 184–185
Kehoe, P. E. 127
Keidanren 317, 322n2–322n3
Keles, S. 228
Kim, S. 345, 346–347, 349, 350, 352–354
Klein, A. L. 132
Kluger, A.N. 375
Knappert, L. 191–192
Koc Holding 235, 237n1
Koike, K. 305
Konovsky, M.A. 70
Korean War 285
Kossek, E.E. 76
Kougiannou, N.K. 185
Kozlowski, S.W.J. 64

Kramar, R. 330, 341–342
Kumho 291

Labor Contract Law of Japan 319
Labor's Fair Work Act 341
Labor Standard Act of South Korea 289
Labour Act Law No 4857 of Turkey 229
Lam, S.S.K. 66, 67
Landy, F.J. 128
Lane, C. 201
Lansbury, R. 339
Lanzarone, M. 127
Larsen and Toubro 242–243
Latham, G.P. 48
Latin America 153, 164
law and regulation *see* legal framework/
    systems (laws and legislations)
Lawler, E. E., III 346, 349, 350
leader–member exchange (LMX)
    7–8, 67–71; affect 67; communication
    68–69; ingratiation 71; perceptions 68;
    procedural justice 74–75; self-fulfilling
    prophecy 69; theory 67–68; *see also*
    rater-ratee relationships
learning opportunities 26
Lebas, M. 212
Ledford, G. E. 346, 349, 350
Lee, Sedol 286
legal framework/systems (laws and
    legislations) 110–111, 373; Australia
    336–338, 340–341; China 265, 271,
    281n3; France 198–199; Germany
    204–206; India 252; Japan 305, 317,
    319; Mexico 155–158; South Korea
    289; Turkey 229; United Kingdom (UK)
    110, 111, 170–171; United States (US)
    126–127, **127**; *see also country-specific
    law and legislation*
Lehr, A. 181
leniency/strictness bias 53
Levy, P.E. 70
Liden, R.C. 67, 69, 71
Life Insurance Corporation 243, 244
liking bias 53
Lindholm, N. 264
LinkedIn 233–234
Locke, E.A. 48
locus of control 47
Long, R. 91, 340
long-term employment in Japan 305–307
L'Oreal Turkey 235
Lu, Y. 264
Lucifora, C. 91

Malos, S. 127
management by objectives (MBO) 200;
    South Korea 293, 295; United States
    (US) 129–130
Marchington, M. 181, 277

market economic development in
    China 264
Martin, D. C. 127
Martin, R. 68
Maslow's hierarchy of needs 42–43
Mayrhofer, W. 193, 214
McClelland, David 131; three needs
    theory 44
McCord, Patty 28
Meinecke, A.L. 76
membership-based employment in Japan
    315–321
Mendonça, P. 185
Meng, L. 3, 6–7, 362
merit awards in United States (US) 90
merit increase grid 87, **88**, 95, 97
merit pay 8, 83–102, 363; budget/
    budgeting 88–89; case study 102;
    concept 83, 84–85; cost control
    mechanism 88; cost-effectiveness 87–
    88; cultural norms 91–92; employment
    regulations 90–91; evaluations
    89–90, 101; global perspective 90–92;
    implementation challenges 93–96;
    institutional structure and 91; key
    decisions 98–101; pay strategies 83–86;
    pay transparency 92–93, 100; reasons
    96–98; skepticism 94, 96; unions and 91
Mexican Institute for Social Security
    (IMSS) 157
Mexico 10–11, 148–165, 366; legal and
    labor relations 155–158; practical
    implications of research 164–165;
    profit sharing 157–158; proximal
    (organizational) factors 158; research
    on PA 159–164; socio-economic factors
    153–155; technology 159; unionism
    156–157
Meysonnier, F. 196, 198–199
Microsoft 34, 300, 346
migrants/migration to Australia 332–333
Millman, J. 69–70
Misisazek, E. 191
mission grading system in Japan 313–315
models of performance appraisal (PA)
    105–116, 362; distal factors 107–112,
    120; distortion factors 116–117; first
    model 106, *107*, 107–117; intervening
    factors 114–115; interventions
    119; judgement factors 115–116;
    judgements *vs.* ratings 115; overview
    105–106; proximal factors 112–114,
    120; purpose of appraisal 112–113;
    recommendations for research
    120–121; second model 106–107,
    108, 117–118; strategy and firm
    performance 109–110
Mohrman, A.M. 69–70
monitoring 26–27

Montaño, Rodriguez 163
Morales, E. 91
Morley, M. 214
motivation 6–7, 41–57; Alderfer's ERG
    model 43; case study 55–57; defined
    41–42; effort-to-performance link
    51–52; equity theory 45–46; evaluation-
    to-rewards link 52, 54–55; expectancy
    theory 46–48, 71; goal-setting theory
    48–49; goals-to-effort link 49, 51;
    Herzberg's motivation-hygiene theory
    44; Maslow's hierarchy of needs 42–43;
    McClelland's three needs theory 44;
    model 50; needs-based theories 42–45;
    performance-to-rewards link 52–54;
    process-based theories 45–48; rater, in
    performance ratings 71–73; rewards-
    to-need fulfillment link 55; self-
    determination theory (SDT) 44–45
Mueller-Hanson, R. 9–10, 346
Mulder, M. 201
multicultural workforce in Australia
    332–333
multinational enterprises (MNEs) 1, 3–6,
    361–362; challenges 21; decentralized
    and flexible processes 31; increasing
    presence 20; India 247–249, 369–
    370; local PM application 34–36;
    management practices 21; remote
    work arrangements 31–33; trends in
    PM 29–34; Western-based theory and
    practice 21; see also expatriates
multisource ratings 129
Murphy, K.R. 3, 8–9, 11, 71, 114, 115,
    138, 150, 169, 172–174, 176, 177, 179,
    192–194, 198–200, 202, 203, 207, 209,
    211–213, 299, 326–327, 345, 364, 374
MZ generation of South Korea 290

Nankervis, A. 343–345
Nathan, B.R. 69–70
National Dairy Development Board
    243, 244
National Human Rights Commission Act
    of South Korea 289
National Stock Exchange 243
National Syndicate of Education Workers
    (SNTE) 156
National Thermal Power Corporation
    244, 248
NatWest 176
need as a hypothetical concept 42
needs-based theories of motivation
    42–45; Alderfer's ERG model 43;
    Herzberg's motivation-hygiene theory
    44; Maslow's hierarchy of needs 42–43;
    McClelland's three needs theory 44;
    self-determination theory (SDT) 44–45
negative appraisals 72–73

Nehru, Jawaharlal 253
NetEase 279–280
Netflix 244
neuroscience research 134
New Performance Management (NPM)
    327, 338, 340, 345–347, 349–350,
    352–354, 372
News Corporation 329
NH Kristal Mexico 158
Nikandrou, I. 193
Nolan, J 345
Nolan, J. 271–272, 345
Norlander, P. 3, 13
norms: cultural 108–109; organizational
    113–114
Nueva Ley Federal del Trabajo (NLFT)
    155–157
Nyberg, A.J. 100

OKR (objectives and key results) 51,
    234, 244
Okunishi, Y. 310–311
O'Leary, R. 9–10
ongoing feedback 22, 52, 136
on-the-job training (OJT) 303, 305,
    308, 316
open door policy of China 262
operational factors 326
organisational and operational
    factors 327
Organisation for Economic Co-operation
    and Development (OECD) 154, 156, 197
organizational capability review 174–175
organizational life cycle 110
Oriot, F. 191
output-based system 173
Özçelik, G. 3, 12–13, 228

Pareek, U. 242, 255
Parry, E. 341
Part-Time Work Law of Japan 319
paternalism: benevolent 151–152, 366;
    India 252; South Korea 285, 286,
    289, 295, 371; Turkey 225, 227, 236,
    368–369; see also culture(s)
Patterson, D. G. 126
pay basis 84
pay level 84
Paytm 244
pay transparency 92–93, 100
Pelaez, J. 91
Pelled, L. H. 151
Pellizzari, M. 91
Peper, J.R. 100
Perceptyx 143
Perez-Floriano, L. 3, 10–11, 366
performance appraisal (PA) 2, 4, 8–9,
    27–28, 60; absolute rating approaches
    31; acceptance 114; cognitive models

62; cultural norms 66; due process model 70–71, 75, 76; leader–member exchange 67–71; literature 62–63; models 105–121; negative appraisals 72–73; procedural justice 74–75; psychometric model 61, 62; purpose 61, 112–113; reactions 73–75; strengths based 73; trust *see* trust; rater-ratee relationships; *specific country*
performance-based pay 310–311; France 203; Germany 208; Japan 310–311; Turkey 232
performance goals *see* goals
Performance Management 2.0 *see* New Performance Management (NPM)
performance management (PM) 2; best-practices model 22–23, *23*; concept 19–20, 190; local application 34–36; process 21–29; trends 29–34; *see also specific country*
performance management systems (PMSs) 1–2, 362; context-specific nature 5; global perspective 3–5; purposes 3–4; trends 373–374; *see also specific country*
performance ratings 60, 364; forced distribution 94–95, 99–100, 131; human process 128–129; ingratiation 71; interpersonal variables 62; judgment *vs.* 115; lack of variance 94; problem 94; rater motivation 71–73
performance-related pay (PRP) 208, 232, 244, 264, 271, 274, 276, 340–341
performance-to-evaluation link 52
performance-to-rewards link 47, 52–54
Perkins, S. 91
Perotin, V. 91
personality similarity and interpersonal affect 67
Petty, R. 7–8, 362–363
physiological needs 43; *see also* Maslow's hierarchy of needs
Pichler, S. 7–8, 66, 74, 253, 362–363
PNT (Plataforma Nacional de Transparencia) 163–164
power, need for 44; *see also* McClelland's three needs theory
power distance culture: France 199, 201; United Kingdom (UK) 180
Presidency of the Republic of Turkey Human Resource Office 236
PRI (Institutional Revolutionary Party) 156
procedural justice 46, 74–75, 162; *see also* performance appraisal (PA)
process-based theories of motivation 45–48; equity theory 45–46; expectancy theory 46–48

Proclamation of Democratization (1987) 287
professional development opportunities 26
profit sharing in Mexico 157–158
promotion practices in Japan 308–309
promotions (of employees) 97
Provisional Regulations for State Civil Servants, China 265
proximal factors 112–114, 120, 158, 291–293, 326, 364; *see also specific country*
Pudelko, M. 204, 211, 214
Pulakos, E. 9–10, 141, 142, 365–366

Qantas 329
quality of rater-ratee relationships 61, 73–75; affect 67; appraisal process variables 70; due process 75; fairness perceptions 70–71; procedural justice 74–75; reactions to appraisal 73–75; shared reality perceptions and agreement 74; trust 74

Ranbaxy Laboratories 245
Randstadt Employer Brand Research Global Report 235
Rao, T.V. 242, 255
rater motivation 71–73; empirical research 71, 72; relationship-based reasons 72–73; self-interest-based reasons 73; theoretical work 71–72
rater-ratee relationships 7–8, 60–77, 113, 176, 362–363; case study 76–77; ingratiation 71; interpersonal affect 63–67; leader–member exchange 67–71; model *63*; negative appraisals 72–73; quality 61, 73–75; rater motivation 71–73; strengths-based appraisals 73; United Kingdom (UK) 181; *see also* performance appraisal (PA)
rater–ratee relationships 60–77
rating format 127–128
rating-less systems 373
rating scales in United States (US) 125–126, 139–140
Raychaudhuri, Sarthak 32
reactions to performance appraisal (PA) 73–75
recency bias 53
regular *vs.* nonregular employees in Japan 318–319
Reliance 248
remote working arrangements 31–33, 185; *see also* work from home (WFH)
Ren Zhengfei 279
Repsold, B. 93
Research Institute for Labor Administration 314–315

results-oriented measures 99
rewards management models 178
rewards-to-evaluation link 52, 54–55
rewards-to-need fulfillment link 55
rewards-to-performance link 47, 52–54
Ridgway, M. 3, 11, 367
Risner, A. 3, 7–8, 362–363
Robbins, T.L. 65, 66–67
Rodriguez, R.A. 3, 10–11, 366
Ronen, S. 2
Rowley, C. 15, 370, 371
Ruiz, C. E. 152
Rule of 72, 88
Rynes, S.L. 96

safety needs 43; see also Maslow's
    hierarchy of needs
savings retirement system (SAR) 157–158
Scanlon Plans 109
Schaubroek, J. 66, 67
scientific management movement 126
Scott, D. 3, 8, 89–91, 93, 363
Scott, Walter 126
Sekiguchi, T. 3, 15–16, 318, 371
self-actualization, need for 43; see also
    Maslow's hierarchy of needs
self-appraisal 247, 269, 276–277, 339
self-determination theory (SDT) 44–45, 54
self-efficacy 47, 49, 51, 52
self-fulfilling prophecy 69
Selvarajan, T.T. 74–75, 161–163, 164–165
service sector 14; Australia 16, 327–328,
    335–336, 371; China 263; India 241,
    250, 253; Japan 315
Services for State Workers 157
Sharma, T. 13, 369
Sheehan, C. 326, 355
Shenkar, O. 2
Shields, J. 3, 16–17, 91, 340, 345–347, 349,
    350, 352–354, 371–372
Shih, H.A. 5
Shipton, H. 3, 11, 366–367
Singh, V. 247
Six Sigma 158
Sixth Central Pay Commission in
    India 244
Smale, A. 193, 214
SME (small and medium-sized
    enterprises) 196, 198–199, 210–211
Smith, M. 179
Smith, P. 92
Smith, P. B. 179
social needs 43; see also Maslow's
    hierarchy of needs
Society for Industrial and Organization
    Psychology 127
socio-economic conditions/factors:
    Mexico 153–155; South Korea 284–285;
    Turkey 222; see also economy

Somersan, R. 93
sorting effects 86, 92, 97–98, 101–102; see
    also merit pay
South Korea 15, 284–301, 371; Asian
    financial crisis of 1997 285, 287, 291;
    challenges in PA 297–301; collectivism
    290; culture 289–290; as a developed
    country 286; development of PMSs
    286–288; distal factors 289–291;
    distortion factors 294–295; economy
    15, 284–285, 287, 290–291; global
    financial crisis of 2008 291; intervening
    factors 293–294; Japanese occupation
    285; judgement factors 294; legal
    framework 289; management by
    objectives (MBO) 293, 295; political
    background 285–286; Proclamation of
    Democratization (1987) 287; proximal
    factors 291–293; socio-economic
    background 284–285; Yunbongje
    (pay-for-performance systems) 288,
    291–293, **292**, 295, 300
Spain 91
Sparrow, P. 11, 179–180, 366–367
Srinivas, E.S. 66, 253
staffing decision 27
stakeholder-based system 173–174
Stanton, P. 344, 345
state-planned economy in China
    263–264
Stillwell, D. 67, 69
strategic role of HR functions 181–182
streamlining 172
Streeck, W. 214
strengths-based appraisals 73
Stroh, L.K. 66
supervisor-focus impression
    management 71; see also ingratiation
supervisor–subordinate relationship see
    rater-ratee relationships
Sweden 90

talent management 177, 183
task/process-based system 174
Tata Iron and Steel Company 242, 243,
    245
technology 31–33, 111–112; digital 184–
    185, 276; Mexico 159; Turkey 232–234;
    virtual communication 32–33; see also
    information technology (IT)
technology-based solutions 354
telecommunications 31–33
telework in Japan 319–320
Tencent 277–278
termination 27
Tesco 178
Titan 243
Trevor, C.O. 8, 100, 363
Trompenaars, F. 252

trust 33–34; rater-ratee relationships quality 74
Tsui, A.S. 64
Turkcell 235
Turkey 12–13, 222–237; collectivism 225, 226; COVID-19 pandemic 223, 232, 369; Cranfield survey findings 230–232; cultural context 225–228; customer experience 235; economy 12, 222–225, 229–230; employee experience 235–236; HRM and PMSs 223–225; institutional context 229–230; legal framework 229; LSEs 223, 224, 227, 234, 235; OKR (objectives and key results) 234; participative PM practices 228; personal relationships 227–228; political background 222–223; population 222; power distance 226–227; SMEs 224; socio-economic background 222; technological development 232–234; termination of employment contract 229; Western-style PMSs 236
Twitter 233–234
two-factor theory *see* Herzberg's motivation-hygiene theory
two-way communication 24–25, 31

UGESP 127
uncertainty avoidance 150, 180, 226
unconscious bias 335
unemployment in United Kingdom (UK) 170
unfair dismissal in Australia 337
Union Carbide 242
unions/unionism 35, 367, 368; Australia 334; France 195, 203, 204; Germany 205; India 253; institutional structure and regulation 91; Japan 305, 316; merit pay and 91; Mexico 156–157; South Korea 287, **288**
United Breweries 245
United Kingdom (UK) 11, 90, 169–186, 365–367; adages characterizing PMS 174; critical challenges 182–185; culture 180–181; employment 169–170; EU membership 170–171; factors impacting PMSs 179–182; floor of rights 170; importance of PMS 172–173; joint problem-solving 172, 180, 181; legal framework 110, 111, 170–171; occupation group 170; strategic role of HR functions 181–182; unemployment 170
United Nations Conference on Trade and Development (UNCTAD) 286
United States–Mexico–Canada Agreement (USMCA) 154

United States (US) 4, 9–10, 123–143, 364–366; administrative burden 137–138; automation 132–133; balanced scorecard 191; cascading goals 125, 130, **130**; challenges characterizing PMSs 137–139; competency 131–132; COVID-19 pandemic 136–137; culture 4, 8, 9, 91, 108, 124, 138; evolution of PM 125–137; forced distribution ratings and rankings 131; history 123–124; human judgment factors 138–139; human rating process 128–129; legal context 126–127, **127**; management by objectives (MBO) 129–130; merit awards 90; multisource ratings 129; performance conversations 140; rating format 127–128; rating scales 125–126, 139–140; reform in PM 134–135; SMART goals 130; trends 125; working from home (WFH) 136–137
U.S. Federal Civil Service 126

values 175, 176; strategy execution and 176
Vance, C.M. 3, 6, 362, 372
van der Klink, M. 201
van der Wijk, G. 196
Varma, A. 7–8, 13, 17, 66, 253, 362–363, 369
virtual communication technology 32–33
Voltas 242, 243
voluntarism 170
VUCA (volatility, uncertainty, complexity, and ambiguity) 31

Wang, M. 266
Wayne, S.J. 65, 67, 69, 71
Web of Science 182–184
Welch, Jack 94, 131
Western-based theory and practice 21
Western-style PMS: China 264–265; Turkey 236
White, L.A. 63–64
white-collar workers 305–306
Williams, R.E. 114
women, workforce participation 334, 372
Woongjin 291
Worker Dispatch Law of Japan 319
workforce profile in Australia 331–336; ageing and generational change 333–334; changes 335–336; employment patterns 331; gig economy 332; multicultural workforce 332–333; unionism 334; women participation 334; working arrangements 331–332
work from home (WFH) 51–52, 136–137; *see also* remote working arrangements
work-oriented social media in China 278
workplace cooperation *see* cooperation

Workplace Relations Act 340–341
work style reform in Japan 318
World Economic Forum 286
World War I 126
World War II 194, 210, 339

Xerox (India) 243
Xi Jinping 267

Yan, A. 5
Yang, H. 15, 370, 371

Yang, Y. 318
Yavuz, S. 12–13
Yazdifar, H. 343
Yunbongje (pay-for-
    performance systems) 288, 291–293,
    292, 295, 300

Zhang, L. H. 273
Zhu, G. 5
Zian, H. 197
Zivnuska, S. 65, 68–69

Printed in the United States
by Baker & Taylor Publisher Services